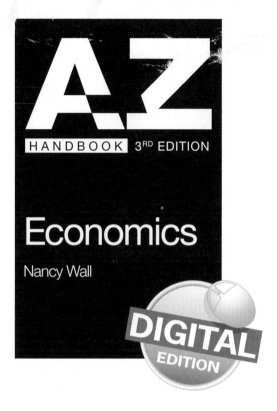

AZ

HANDBOOK 3RD EDITION

Economics

Nancy Wall

DIGITAL
EDITION

PHILIP ALLAN
UPDATES

Philip Allan Updates, an imprint of Hodder Education, an Hachette UK company, Market Place, Deddington, Oxfordshire OX15 0SE

Orders

Bookpoint Ltd, 130 Milton Park, Abingdon, Oxfordshire OX14 4SB
tel: 01235 827720
fax: 01235 400454
e-mail: uk.orders@bookpoint.co.uk

Lines are open 9.00 a.m.–5.00 p.m., Monday to Saturday, with a 24-hour message answering service. You can also order through the Philip Allan Updates website: www.philipallan.co.uk

ISBN 978-0-340-99101-5

First published 2001
Second edition 2003
Third edition 2009

Impression number   5   4   3   2
Year   2014   2013   2012   2011   2010

Typeset by Macmillan, India.

Printed by Antony Rowe, Chippenham, Wiltshire.

Environmental information

Hachette UK's policy is to use papers that are natural, renewable and recyclable products and made from wood grown in sustainable forests. The logging and manufacturing processes are expected to conform to the environmental regulations of the country of origin.

Contents

How to use this book

The *A–Z Economics Handbook* is an alphabetical textbook designed for ease of use. Each entry begins with a one-sentence definition. This helps the user to add precision to the completion of reports or case studies.

Entries are developed in line with the relative importance of the concept covered. *Monopsony* is covered in a few lines, whereas a central economics issue such as *mergers* or *economic growth* receives half a page. The latter would provide sufficient material to enrich an essay. Numerate topics are developed through the use of worked examples. All formulae are set out explicitly.

The study of economics can be developed further by making use of the cross-referenced entries. For example, the entry for *unemployment* refers the reader to *demand deficiency* and *structural unemployment*. Cross-referenced entries are identified through the use of bold italics. Therefore essay or project writing should benefit from following the logical pathway indicated by italicised entries.

Economics students have always had difficulties with the language of the subject. This stems from several factors:
- economics has its own jargon
- the media and politicians use or invent new terms (such as 'private finance initiative'); some of these prove temporary, while others need assimilating into course content
- textbooks recommended by the awarding bodies use technical terms in different ways.

The *A–Z Economics Handbook* is a glossary providing a single solution to these problems. Where terms have more than one meaning, both are explained. In addition, the entries have enough detail to make the book a valuable reference/revision companion. This third edition provides full coverage of the GCE A-level specifications.

The content of the various specifications for A-level economics varies quite considerably. Where possible, terms that are required for one but not others are identified but it is impossible to do this all the time. The only sure way to avoid learning things you don't need is to check the specifications you are following.

To aid the revision process, carefully selected lists are provided at the back of the book. Those facing examinations can use the lists to make the best use of the handbook during their revision time. The revision recommendations are split into units, for ease of use. You can also use the website that accompanies this handbook to access revision lists specific to your exam board unit. You should find these lists valuable when you come to do your revision. The section on examiners' terms provides an explanation of the trigger words used on exam papers, such as 'analyse', 'discuss' and 'evaluate'.

A–Z Online

This new digital edition of the *A–Z Economics Handbook* includes free access to a supporting website and a free desktop widget to make searching for terms even quicker. Log on to **www.philipallan.co.uk/a-zonline** and create an account using the unique code provided on the inside front cover of this book.

Once you are logged on, you will be able to:
- search the entire database of terms in this handbook
- print revision lists specific to your exam board
- get expert advice from examiners on how to get an A* grade
- create a personal library of your favourite terms
- expand your vocabulary with our word of the week

You can also add the other *A–Z Handbooks (digital editions)* that you own to your personal library on A–Z Online.

The *A–Z Economics Handbook* will help anyone who wants to understand current events in the economy. Many terms that are used in the financial media are fully explained so that their significance will become clearer. We hope that, as well as providing an invaluable resource for A-level economics, this handbook will be used more widely by people with an interest in the general field.

Acknowledgements

In compiling this dictionary, I had help from a huge range of sources. Colin Bamford provided valuable clarification of OCR requirements, as did Andy McCann for CCEA.

I am much indebted to Ian Marcousé and to the late Tim Gregson-Williams, who created the series and gave much help.

Researching, writing and editing a book of this size requires the occasional willingness to sacrifice technical accuracy in favour of clarity. A considerable amount of time went into checking the entries, but if any mistakes have slipped through, the author apologises and accepts full responsibility.

Nancy Wall

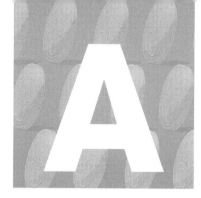

ability to pay: the principle by which people should be taxed according to the level of their incomes. People need a minimum income to cover the basic costs of food, clothing and shelter. So people on very low incomes are usually not taxed directly, i.e. by income tax. This principle is reflected in the **personal allowance**, which is not taxed. In another context, ability to pay is used as a basis for deciding whether people have access to benefits in kind, such as free school meals or certain social services.

abnormal profit: see **supernormal profit**.

absolute advantage: a country has an absolute advantage in trade in a particular good with another country if it can produce that good using fewer real resources. This means that its costs will usually be lower in money terms. For example, Jamaica has an absolute advantage over the UK in the production of bananas because its climate is suited to banana production.

absolute poverty: a standard of living which fails to provide basic necessities of life. Poverty may also be relative, in the sense that some people have very much less income than others, and may therefore be unable to buy the things which are regarded as necessary in that society. Poverty can therefore be defined in different ways in different societies: a poor person in the UK will usually have a higher standard of living than a poor person in India.

Some international organisations have defined poverty as having to live on less than $1.25 per day. Low-income countries were defined by the **World Bank** in 2007 as those with annual income of less than US$936 per head.

Selected low-income countries, including India for comparison

	Income per head, 2007, US$	% of population with less than $1.25 a day
Bangladesh	470	50
Congo D.R.	140	35
Ethiopia	220	39
India	950	42
Kenya	680	20
Nigeria	930	64
Rwanda	320	77

Source: World Bank, World Economic Indicators, 2008

The percentage living on less than $1.25 a day is calculated using **purchasing power parity (PPP)** figures; income per head uses current exchange rates. (See also **poverty line**.)

ACAS: see *Advisory, Conciliation and Arbitration Service (ACAS)*.

accelerator: the relationship between *investment* and the rate of change of output. The theory is that investment will be determined not by the level of output but by the rate at which it changes. If output grows faster than before, the rate at which new productive capacity is created will need to increase. In contrast, if output stabilises, no additional investment will be needed, other than that needed to replace worn-out machines. So investment will actually fall. In short, the accelerator relationship causes investment to fluctuate much more than output.

accelerator/multiplier model: the theory that the *accelerator* and the *multiplier* interact to bring about cyclical changes in the economy. An increase in investment during the upswing of the business cycle will have a multiplier effect, generating a larger increase in income. As the economy approaches full capacity and real growth slows, the accelerator theory predicts that investment needs will fall, leading to a downturn. The fall in injections will have a downward multiplier effect, until such time as the need for replacement investment again causes investment to grow. At that point the cycle repeats itself.

accountability refers to the way in which people may be required to explain their decisions in both the *private sector* and the *public sector*. An organisation in which responsibilities have been clearly defined will identify the people who are accountable for the various actions of that organisation. If mistakes have been made, individuals may be held responsible. In the public sector, particular organisations or people may be answerable to a higher authority such as a minister or the House of Commons. The government is accountable to Parliament and ultimately to the electorate.

accounts: a statement of any financial activity, most usually a summary in money terms of all the activities of a business. This will be produced for a certain period, most often one year, but also quarterly or half-yearly. *Public limited companies* are required by law to produce a *balance sheet*, a *profit and loss account* and a *cash flow statement*.

accumulated profit is the total of profits which have been kept in reserve from previous years and ploughed back into the company rather than being distributed to shareholders. These profits are important to the business as a source of funds for investment in new production capacity.

acid rain occurs when emissions of pollution from industrial activities are blown away but then absorbed into rain. This may fall in areas far removed from the original source of the pollution, so that acid rain becomes an international problem. Lakes have been badly affected in parts of Scandinavia because they are downwind from industrial areas in the UK and other parts of Europe.

ACP states are the African, Caribbean and Pacific states which had colonial links with member countries of the European Union. To some extent they have been able to negotiate favourable trading arrangements with the EU. India is not included despite its ex-colonial status.

acquisitions: a term used to refer to firms which have been or are being taken over. (See also *mergers*, *takeovers* and *Competition Commission*.)

activity rates: see *participation rates*.

adaptive expectations: the idea that people's expectations about the future will be affected by their observations about the present. For example, if the rate of *inflation* is increasing, then expectations about future inflation will also tend to increase over a period of time. This could apply to other variables such as *unemployment*.

added value refers to the value added to an input by a business, as it creates its final output. (See also *value added*.) It can be calculated by subtracting the cost of all the material inputs from the value of output. It reflects the value of the services of land, *labour*, capital and entrepreneurship which have been used in the process of production.

administration: when a business is unable to pay its debts, the courts may bring in an administrator who will try to restructure the company in order to enable it to carry on trading. Sometimes a part of the business may be sold or closed down. If these measures do not bring the business back to profitability, it may go into *liquidation*.

administrative costs are part of *fixed costs*.

ad valorem tax: a tax which is charged as a proportion of the price. The tax will be set as a percentage of the price charged by the retailer, and then included in the final price to the customer. A good example is *value added tax (VAT)*.

advances: banks use the term 'advances to customers' to describe their loans and over-drafts. These are usually the most profitable part of the bank's activities but they are also likely to be the most risky. The bank may require some kind of collateral as security for the loan. For example, land or buildings can be collateral for a business loan or a house for a personal loan. *Shares* can also be used in this way.

advertising involves paying for activities which will help to sell products. Many different media may be used including radio and TV, newspapers and magazines, billboards, cata-logues and websites, to name just a few. The objective is to shift the *demand curve* to the right, so that at any given price more will be sold than before the advertising campaign. The effect is to engineer a change in consumer tastes or fashions.

Though many different types of firms advertise, advertising spending is most likely to be high when there is intense *non-price competition*, as often happens under *oligopoly*.

advertising costs: the high cost of national advertising can shift the average total cost curve for the firm upwards. However, if the advertising is successful, the firm may be able to reap *economies of scale* such that the amount of average total cost is actually less. (See diagram below and on page 91.)

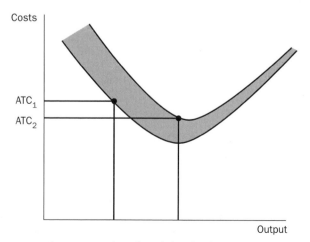

Advertising increases sales; economies of scale lead to lower average cost

Advisory, Conciliation and Arbitration Service (ACAS) was set up in 1975 to settle or help to prevent industrial disputes. Help may be sought by individuals, businesses or trade unions in both small and large cases.

after-sales service is often an important part of the product itself and can be seen as a *complement* to the item actually sold. The most obvious example occurs with a new car or machine, which will usually be guaranteed for a certain period, with spares, repairs and advice made available through a local agent. After-sales service may be an important part of the package which makes the product competitive and attractive to potential consumers.

age-earnings profile: on average, there is a process by which earnings start relatively low at the beginning of the working life, peak in middle age and then decline. In many occupations, young people start out with very little experience and become progressively more useful to their employers as they become trained and experienced. Their earnings reflect this. As they become older, the benefits of increasing experience become less marked and are usually out-weighed by the disadvantages of becoming older. So their earnings gradually fall somewhat.

ageing population occurs where people are living longer and therefore the average age of the population is rising. Japan and a number of European countries have rapidly ageing populations. The UK population is ageing more slowly. The economic implications include the necessity of providing more health care and pensions. Also, there may be problems arising as the ratio of the working population to the dependent population becomes lower. A larger transfer from the *working population* to the retired population may become necessary. The pressures created by this trend can lead to rethinking of pension policies.

ageism is discrimination in the *labour* market against people who are older. It is illegal in the UK under the Age Discrimination Act 2006. It is less likely to be a problem where labour is scarce or there are skill shortages.

aggregate demand refers to the total demand for goods and services from all sources in the economy. It includes:
- consumer spending
- *investment* by firms in plant, machinery and stocks
- government spending
- the net effect of *international trade*, i.e. exports minus imports.

An increase in aggregate demand may lead to an increase in output provided there is underutilised productive capacity in the economy. If there is no spare capacity, and the economy is producing using all available, suitable resources, rising demand is likely to lead to inflation. (See also *circular flow of national income*.)

The level of aggregate demand will to a large extent therefore determine the level of activity in the economy. A low level of aggregate demand is likely to be associated with high levels of unemployment. This situation is usually described as *cyclical unemployment* or *demand deficiency unemployment*. It is usually accompanied by a high level of business failures and sometimes also by declining real incomes. Rising levels of aggregate demand will increase profitability, encouraging firms to increase output and take on more *labour*. This will tend to have a *multiplier* effect on the economy.

Aggregate demand is affected by changes in all its constituent components:
- A fall in savings can lead to an increase in consumption and vice versa.
- Changes in interest rates affect levels of investment.

- Tax changes affect disposable incomes and therefore both consumption and investment. Government expenditure changes feed directly into the level of aggregate demand.
- Rising imports reduce demand for domestically produced goods and services. Export levels have a direct effect.

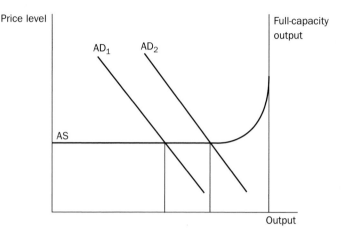

An increase in aggregate demand leads to increased output if there is underutilised productive capacity in the economy

(See also ***macro-economic equilibrium.***)

aggregate demand curve: *aggregate demand* can be graphed by plotting output on the horizontal axis and the price level on the vertical axis. It will be downward sloping because lower prices will allow higher levels of output demanded for any given income level. In combination with the ***aggregate supply curve***, it can be used to analyse macro-economic events.

aggregate demand shock: any sudden change in a component of aggregate demand which has a noticeable effect on the economy. For example, a change in interest rates may rapidly affect both consumer and investment demand, so that there is a shift in the aggregate demand curve.

aggregate supply: the total of all goods and services produced in the economy. In the short run, aggregate supply may increase in response to rising ***aggregate demand***. In the long run, it can increase only if more resources become available (e.g. oil) or if there are improvements in technology or if efficiency is increased in some other way. (See also ***full-capacity output.***)

In the long run, aggregate supply has increased in the UK by a little over 2% per year. This is the long-run trend rate of growth, made possible by investment and improved technologies. Better, more efficient management can also help. These are sometimes associated with increases in ***human capital*** – the expertise available in the economy.

Long-run aggregate supply is shown diagrammatically as a vertical line which shifts to the right as the capacity of the economy to supply goods and services increases. At any one time the total amount which can be supplied is fixed, being determined by the quantity of resources available to produce. As the stock of capital increases and people acquire more knowledge and skills, the line shifts outwards, increasing full capacity output. The result will be a process of economic growth, provided demand is increasing to absorb all the goods and services which can now be produced. The increased quantity of resources will make it easier to achieve rising standards of living and to avoid inflationary pressures.

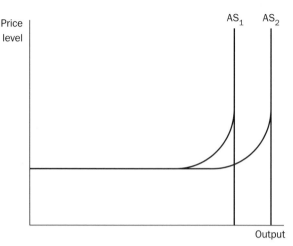

Rising aggregate supply

aggregate supply curves show aggregate supply diagrammatically. Short and long-run *aggregate supply* can be distinguished. In the short run, the aggregate supply curve slopes upwards because an increase in *aggregate demand* will raise profits and encourage producers to expand. However, unless there are ample supplies of underutilised *labour* and capital, prices will tend to rise in the process. (See diagram above.) In the long run, aggregate supply is determined by the stock of resources, land, labour and capital. So the long-run aggregate supply curve is a vertical line. This can only be shifted outwards by an increase in the stock of resources, e.g. through investment in plant, machinery, development of new technologies or education and training. These kinds of changes take time. (See also *short-run aggregate supply*.)

aggregate supply shock: a sharp change in the capacity of the economy to supply goods and services. This may occur if there is a natural disaster, a war, or a sudden change in the price of an important commodity such as oil. These kinds of events will cause the *aggregate supply curve* to shift.

AGM: see *annual general meeting (AGM)*.

agricultural stabilisation policies: many governments intervene in some way in agricultural markets. In developed countries, the objective is to raise farm incomes, usually by keeping prices above the world market price, and perhaps to keep out cheap imports. This tends to raise food prices to consumers. Within the EU, most policy decisions are embodied in the *Common Agricultural Policy*. These policies are unpopular with food exporting countries, especially those that are also developing countries. They have caused much difficulty in the context of the *Doha Round*. Some developed countries sell subsidised food to very poor countries, which is useful if there is a famine. But it is counter-productive when it reduces farm prices and thus poor local farmers' incomes and their incentive to increase output and productivity.

Developing countries sometimes intervene more directly, sometimes trying to keep prices down so that food will be cheap for urban populations. These interventions tend to distort markets and can lead to both shortages and surpluses.

aid is provided by wealthier developed countries to countries with low per capita incomes. It includes payments made by charities. However, the political aspects of foreign aid can be extremely complex. It may be given as a grant or a loan, and loans may be at market or at concessional rates of interest. Some kinds of aid are more effective in meeting poor countries' needs than others. Much depends on how the money is spent. Spending on some major construction projects such as dams has attracted criticism because it has been unsuited to the long-term needs of the country concerned. There are serious controversies surrounding much aid spending. Some of the money which is classed as aid is spent on defence.

Many developing countries have tried to negotiate larger aid donations. Their efforts have not been successful: over the years, aid payments have tended to fall as a percentage of the donor countries' GDP. Some developing country governments have instead tried to improve access to developed country markets through trade negotiations. There have been some improvements on this front but much more could be done by the developed countries.

Aid remains an important source of finance, particularly for spending which does not have an easily measured rate of return, such as education, and disaster relief. Current debates include proposals to withhold aid where governments are known to be particularly corrupt. (See also *Doha Round*, *foreign aid* and *good governance*.)

air pollution is the discharge of waste products into the air. The main sources are vehicle exhausts, power stations and industrial processes.

allocation of resources: economic decisions about the uses which should be made of land, *labour* and capital leading to an overall allocation of resources, which generally matches the pattern of consumer demand. Consumer demand creates profitable opportunities for **entrepreneurs** to organise inputs of **factors of production** so as to meet that demand. In this way the allocation of resources responds to the pattern of demand exhibited by consumers. However, the idea of the allocation of resources can be applied much more widely to a range of decisions which may be taken by individuals or by governments.
- People decide how to allocate their own resources when they choose between work and leisure or whether to save more or consume more.
- Governments make resource allocation decisions when they consider making changes to different categories of spending: they may consider whether to allocate more towards defence or education or towards health care or unemployment benefit.

It is not always the case that the allocation of resources conforms to the pattern of consumer demand. Firms and governments can sometimes control certain aspects of the allocation of resources through monopoly power or through administrative decisions. Where this happens, there is said to be a distortion of the allocation of resources so that it does not accurately reflect consumer preferences. (See also *market economy*.)

allocative efficiency describes the extent to which the *allocation of resources* matches consumer preferences. The most efficient allocation of resources will be the one which fits the genuine needs and wants of consumers most closely. An economy can move closer to allocative efficiency when ways are found to help firms to respond effectively to consumer demand. For example, in a *centrally planned economy* such as North Korea, some producers may be bound by administrative decisions and will not necessarily be able to produce the type of goods which consumers want most. The transitional economies, such as Hungary and Poland which have moved a long way towards being market economies, have become more allocatively efficient because enterprises producing items which consumers do not want have gone out of business. Government controls of any kind are liable to reduce the responsiveness of markets to consumer demand. However, they may be able to protect consumers from the market power of large firms.

When consumer demand changes, prices respond. If consumers want less of, say, CDs, demand falls and prices fall. Production becomes less profitable and will be cut back. This will remove any **excess supply** and the price will return to its previous level. Similarly, if demand increases, say for blueberries, production becomes more profitable and growers expand production. More growers will enter the market and compete with the existing ones until the price is back close to the cost of production. All this depends on the **market system** and the **profit-signalling mechanism** working well.

animal spirits is the term used by J M Keynes to describe the way in which many investment decisions are taken. Often the crucial deciding factor will be expectations about the future performance of the economy. This can be governed by careful reasoning, but can also be affected by a kind of herd instinct. When in general business expectations are optimistic, many investors take risks which they would not take if expectations were gloomy. Once they see others doing this they become more likely themselves to take risks. (See also **self-fulfilling prophecy.**)

Annual Abstract of Statistics is an annual publication containing a wide variety of useful statistics. It comes from the Office for National Statistics and includes population, social, legal, employment, production, income and price data as well as some industry-specific figures.

annual general meeting (AGM): a meeting held each year by public and sometimes also private limited companies to which all shareholders are invited. They are expected to:
- approve the year's accounts
- elect directors
- question the company chairman.

However, some AGMs can be acrimonious affairs as shareholders hold directors accountable for company policies.

annualised hours agreements are used when the firm wants to employ people on a flexible basis. They will be hired for a certain number of hours' work each year and then employed when they are needed. This can help firms which experience seasonal fluctuations as longer hours can be worked without the use of overtime payments. This type of agreement has become more common as competition in both product and **labour** markets has led to contracts which allow **flexible working**.

annual report and accounts: the report which all companies must send to their shareholders and to Companies House each year. They include: a **balance sheet**, a **profit and loss account**, a **cash flow statement**, a **directors'** report and an **auditor's** report.

anticipated inflation: expected **inflation**, which has rather different consequences from unanticipated inflation. People will build their inflation expectations into their wage demands. In this way anticipated inflation may become self-perpetuating.

anti-competitive activities: firms which have a degree of *monopoly* power in their markets may be able to take steps which give them some control over the prices they charge and the quantity sold. They may also be able to damage the chances of competing producers. For example, two dominant producers may agree to share the market, one selling in the North, say, and one in the South. In this way they avoid competing with each other. Or a firm may insist on an exclusive dealership arrangement with its distributors.

The main categories of anti-competitive activities include:
- *cartels*, where a group of businesses agree a marketing strategy which avoids strong competition
- *market-sharing agreements*, in which competing firms agree not to sell in each other's territory
- *price fixing* agreements which avoid competing on price
- pushing up prices by not supplying retailers who charge less than the recommended price
- refusing to supply retailers that stock competing products
- *predatory pricing*
- refusing to supply a competitive product unless customers also buy a less competitive complementary product.

Anti-competitive activities are usually illegal under competition legislation. However, the *Office of Fair Trading (OFT)* and the *Competition Commission* sometimes allow them if there are compelling reasons.

anti-dumping measures are designed to prevent other countries from selling their products at a price lower than their costs of production. Despite *trade liberalisation*, it is still legal under certain circumstances for governments to use import controls to exclude dumped imports. Although these will be very cheap and competitive, they may disrupt the market for domestic producers. The *WTO* has strict rules about the use of anti-dumping measures but it is still difficult to decide exactly when dumping has taken place because it is hard to isolate genuine costs of production. So some economists suspect that dumping is used by governments as an excuse to exclude cheap imports.

antitrust laws are the laws in the USA which control the growth of large businesses in order to prevent monopoly power from developing.

applied economics involves the use of economic theories to analyse real world situations.

appraisal is used as a management tool to ensure that employees are reaching the standards required of them. It provides an opportunity for discussion of the employee's situation as well as a review of targets and performance.

appreciation occurs when the value of something rises. *Capital appreciation* means a rise in the value of an asset such as a factory building or land. *Currency appreciation* means a rise in the exchange rate such that the same amount of one currency will buy more than before of another. This means that import prices will be lower and exports will lose some competitiveness.

apprenticeship: this used to be the main way to acquire craft skills and a full understanding of a particular job. Typically apprentices were based in the workplace, with day release to the local college. As employment in manufacturing dropped during the 1980s, apprenticeships became very few in number. Training became much less uniform in approach, with new technologies and *multi-skilling* affecting the outcome. Modern apprenticeships have developed and to some extent fill the gap.

appropriate technology is a term applied to the production method which has the lowest costs in the particular situation under discussion. Where capital is relatively cheap and *labour* costs are high, a *capital-intensive* technology will be the most appropriate. This would apply to agricultural activities in developed countries. Where labour is cheap, it is inappropriate to use capital-intensive methods, but small-scale equipment may still increase *productivity* and incomes. For example, a wheelbarrow may have an advantage over a basket carried on the head. (See also *intermediate technology*.)

a priori is a Latin term meaning from first principles. It will usually be used in relation to a theoretical argument which cannot be derived directly from observation of the real world but relies on logical connections.

arbitrage involves buying in one market and selling at a higher price in another. It prevents prices from diverging in different markets by more than the *transaction costs*.

For example, for many years dealers bought antiques in the UK and shipped them to the Netherlands, where prices were higher. Similarly, when a *currency* is losing value in one country as the *exchange rate* falls, dealers will buy it and sell it again in a country where the exchange rate is higher. This tends to even out exchange rates so that they are normally very similar in different countries.

arbitration: where there is a dispute which cannot easily be settled by the parties concerned, they may choose a process of arbitration in preference to legal or industrial action which would have high costs to both sides. Arbitration means that both sides accept a mediator who will listen to the arguments and make a decision. This decision can be legally binding if both sides have agreed. (See also *conciliation* and *Advisory, Conciliation and Arbitration Service (ACAS)*.)

arithmetic mean: a measure of average value. It is calculated by adding the values of all the observations in the series and dividing by the total number of observations.

$$FORMULA: \quad \frac{\text{sum of all observations}}{\text{number of observations}}$$

The mean is a useful measure provided there are few extreme observations. In this situation the *median* may be more useful. For example, average income data may be misleading if it is distorted by some very high incomes.

ARR: see *average rate of return (ARR)*.

Asian Development Bank exists to provide development finance for developing countries in Asia and the Pacific. Its affiliate, the Asian Development Fund, provides loans at concessional rates of interest to poorer countries in the region.

Asian financial crisis: in 1997, Thailand and Korea encountered serious problems with loss of confidence in their banking systems. There followed very rapid selling of their *currencies* and sharp falls on their *stock exchanges*. This quickly led to depressed trading conditions and similar problems in other countries including Japan and Indonesia. Confidence was gradually restored and by 1999 the problems were much reduced, but the crisis interrupted the usually high *economic growth* rates in the affected countries.

assembly line: manufacture of complex products may be designed as a sequence of work stations, connected by conveyor systems, which take the product along a line of employees, each having a different part to play in the production process. Originally, assembly lines took advantage of the opportunities created by a **division of labour**, so that each person on the line had a single task to accomplish. Assembly lines have been much modified in recent years to get around two problems: difficulty in achieving good quality control and the boredom associated with repetitive tasks.

asset: anything of value which can be made to yield benefits. Financial assets include cash, shares, savings, **bonds** and **derivatives**. Real assets include property and machinery.

In accounting terms, assets are balanced against liabilities in the **balance sheet**. Liabilities are all the payments that the business is liable to have to make in the future.

asset markets are the markets where various different types of **asset** are traded. The stock exchange is a physical location where shares can be traded. The foreign exchange market, on the other hand, has no physical location but is just as much a market, as is the property market. The **inter-bank market** is the wholesale money market within which banks make loans to each other.

asset prices: most assets can be bought and sold in the marketplace. Prices can vary very sharply because they are influenced by expectations about what will happen to them in the future. For example, if people expect property prices to rise, they may rush to buy, thus driving up prices. (This is known as a **self-fulfilling prophecy**.) Similarly, share prices are affected by business optimism or the lack of it and the prospect of gains and losses can cause rapid buying and selling with price fluctuations. Sharp fluctuations in asset prices were a feature of the credit crunch in 2007–09, as the markets responded to new information about likely future risks.

asset stripping occurs when the value of the individual parts of the firm are greater in total than the value of the business as a whole. It may happen after a **merger** or **takeover**, when the new owners want to rationalise production and avoid duplication of some of their facilities. It may occur if a part of the business has been run rather inefficiently and could be more profitable under different ownership. The polite term for asset stripping is corporate restructuring, which has fewer overtones of destruction.

assumptions are important in economic theory because they make it possible to simplify the basis for the economic analysis. **Economic models** are based on assumptions about behaviour. For example, the theory of the firm is to a large extent based on the assumption that the firm's objective is to maximise profits. This may be regarded as a useful approximation even though in reality business objectives are often somewhat more complex.

asymmetric information refers to the fact that decision takers usually do not all have the same information. People who are taking business decisions cannot know what other businesses are planning in the same market. Some kinds of information are private. Everyone is aware that the information they have is different from the information others have, but they cannot know what others know or do not know. This is a potential source of **market failure**.

Markets only function well if people have good information. Imperfect information can mean that you make a mistake when you choose what to buy. Where customers do not have all the information that sellers have, the latter's **market power** is increased. (See also *principal–agent problem*.)

auction is a situation in which potential buyers bid against one another openly until the highest bidder gets the sale. It is used to organise a sale when the **market clearing** price of the item concerned is uncertain. Common examples include properties with unique features, antiques and live farm animals.

audit: company law requires that accounts be checked by independent auditors who will uncover any inconsistencies or irregularities. Internal bookkeeping will be checked to ensure that all transactions have been accurately recorded. An audit should ensure that accounting conventions have been followed and that there has been no fraud. However, auditors are paid by the company and may not always be entirely independent in their view.

automatic stabilisers: *fiscal policies* which work to reduce fluctuations in income over the course of the *economic cycle* without needing adjustment at the time. For example, spending on unemployment benefits automatically rises with the level of unemployment. So during **recession**, government spending will rise as firms contract employment. The extra spending helps to compensate for the reduction in earned income. Consumption spending will fall more slowly than it otherwise would have done if the unemployed had lost all their income at once.

The other important automatic stabiliser is *income tax*. As incomes rise in the *boom* phase of the economic cycle, income tax receipts rise more than proportionately because income tax is progressive. Similarly, if incomes are falling during a recession, tax receipts will fall more than proportionately. In this way the tax system takes more spending power out of the economy in a boom than it does in a recession, so helping to counteract the fluctuations in aggregate demand and to diminish their impact.

automation means using machines to produce, rather than people. Increasingly, machinery is computer controlled although people are still needed to design, organise and monitor the production process.

average cost is the total cost divided by the number of units produced. It is also known as *unit cost*.

$$FORMULA: \quad \text{average costs} = \frac{\text{total cost}}{\text{units of output}}$$

Worked example

A firm buys materials at 50p per unit and spends £1 000 on weekly fixed costs and labour; the production rate is 4 000 per week.

$$\text{So average costs are: } \frac{(£0.5 \times 4\ 000) + £1\ 000}{4\ 000} = 75p$$

Average costs vary according to the level of output. In general they fall at first as output is increased, because the fixed costs are being spread across a larger quantity of output. This can be seen in the diagram opposite.

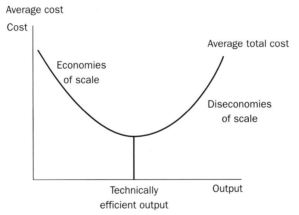

A U-shaped average cost curve

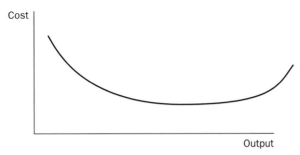

Long-run average cost curve with a range of efficient outputs

Average costs may also fall because there are **economies of scale** to be reaped. At higher levels of output it may be more efficient to use larger machines and invest in different technologies. This can cause costs to fall considerably at higher levels of output.

If levels of output continue to increase, then it is possible that there will be **diseconomies of scale**. These will cause average costs to rise with output. These may possibly be caused by the difficulties of communication and co-ordination in a large organisation. They can lead to **diminishing marginal returns**.

These two contrasting trends give the textbook average total cost curve its characteristic U-shape. However, in practice there may be a large range of possible outputs at which average costs are more or less constant. This gives the curve a long flat bottom.

The minimum average cost, lowest point on the ATC curve, is associated with **productive efficiency**. When all resources are being used as efficiently as possible, it follows that average costs will be at a minimum. At this point, price will be equal to **marginal cost** in competitive markets.

average cost pricing: setting a price so that it just covers the average cost, which allows the organisation to break-even. This may not be the most profitable price, so firms in the private sector are rather unlikely to use this strategy. However, it can make sense for non-profit making organisations or for government agencies.

average fixed costs are the costs of all inputs which cannot be changed in the short run, per unit of output. Land and capital will be important fixed costs, but they may also include

13

the cost of key employees. Fixed costs fall as output increases in the short run because the costs are spread between more units of output.

FORMULA: average fixed costs $= \dfrac{\text{total fixed costs}}{\text{units of output}}$

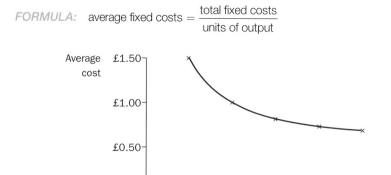

Average fixed costs falling as output rises

In the long run average fixed costs can change as machines are replaced and new technologies are adopted. They may rise if more capital intensive production methods are used. They may rise or fall under the impact of new technologies.

average propensity to consume: that proportion of income which people choose to allocate towards consumption spending.

average propensity to import: the average proportion of total income which is spent on imports. In an open economy, the average propensity to import is quite high, perhaps 30% or 40%.

average propensity to save: the average proportion of total income which is saved. This will tend to be higher in rich developed countries than it is in very poor countries.

average rate of return (ARR): a measure of profitability which can be used to assess the relative merits of alternative investment projects. It relates the average annual profit to the amount spent on the investment. This can then be compared with current interest rates.

FORMULA: $\dfrac{\text{total profit over project life} \div \text{number of years}}{\text{capital outlay on project}} \times 100$

It is not enough to be able to cover the interest rate alone. The investment decision should depend on whether the intended project is the most profitable available given the risks involved.

average revenue: total revenue derived from sales divided by the number of units sold.

average tax rates: the average percentage of total income which is paid in taxes. If the tax system is progressive, i.e. the proportion paid rises as income rises, the average rate of tax will be lower than the marginal rate of tax.

average variable costs are the costs of variable factors of production such as *labour*, raw materials and components. In the short run they may rise as output rises, because efforts to produce more without increasing the amount of capital (a fixed factor) may make production less efficient.

FORMULA: average variable costs $= \dfrac{\text{total variable costs}}{\text{units of output}}$

backward integration is the extension of the firm's activities to include production of inputs which were previously bought in from outside. If Birds Eye bought farms on which to grow peas, instead of buying the peas from independent farmers, that would be backward integration. The objective could be to ensure regular supplies of a crucial input.

backward sloping supply curve of labour: initially, increases in pay encourage people to work longer hours. However, beyond a certain level, people will not necessarily be induced to work more and may prefer to work less. Effectively, they are choosing to use their increased incomes to consume more leisure. This means that the curve showing how much *labour* they are willing to supply will bend backwards.

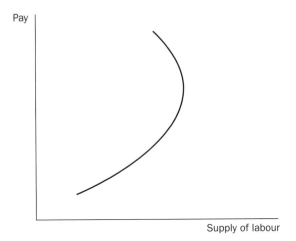

Supply of labour

This analysis works for individuals. It does not work for the firm. The supply of labour to an individual firm is unlikely to slope backwards because increases in pay will attract recruits from other firms which are paying less.

bad bank: most banks, as of 2009, were struggling with mountains of debts with a high risk of default (i.e. non-repayment), sometimes called *toxic assets*. Proposals included setting up so-called bad banks which would take over these assets and hold them until they could be sold, probably at a substantial discount. An element of government support would be needed to do this. The idea was to take the toxic assets off the banks' balance sheets so that they would cease to deter banks from lending to businesses.

bad debt: a debt which is unlikely to be paid. Banks realise that they have bad debts when customers to which they have made loans are unable to make the scheduled interest payments.

Firms encounter bad debts when businesses to which they have sold their product become insolvent or go into liquidation. In this way unsuccessful firms can drag others down with them.

balance of invisibles: the balance between invisible exports and invisible imports. Invisibles are the traded output of the service sector, as opposed to visible exports and imports which are all goods, i.e. output from the primary or secondary sector. Invisibles include tourism, financial services, shipping and consultancy services. This invisibles balance is one component of the *balance of payments*.

balance of payments: a record of all transactions associated with imports and exports, together with all international capital movements. It consists of the *current account*, the *capital account* and the financial account. The current account shows trade in goods and services, income from employment and investments abroad, and transfers which may be made by governments or individuals.

UK balance of payments, 2007, £ billion

	Credits	Debits	Balance
Current account			
Total goods	220.7	310.0	−89.3
Total services	147.6	106.0	41.6
Income			
employment abroad	2.0	1.8	−0.6
investment income	284.6	275.3	9.3
Current transfers	15.7	29.4	−13.7
Current account balance	**670.6**	**728.7**	**−52.6**
Capital account			
Totals	–	–	2.6
Financial account			
UK investment overseas less)	–	–	39.8
Overseas investment in UK)			
Net errors and omissions	–	–	10.1

Source: ONS, Pink Book 2008

Visible exports and imports consist of goods, while services are often referred to as invisibles. The balance on current account is the total of visible and invisible exports and imports. It is not always possible to identify all payments: unrecorded transactions are shown as 'errors and omissions'.

The capital account is of little significance, accounting for changes associated with immigration and emigration together with transfers of EU funds and foreign aid payments.

The financial account shows the capital outflow from the UK caused by investments overseas and the capital inflow resulting from foreign investment in the UK. These investments may consist of factories or offices built by foreign companies in the UK. Or they may be payments for shares, property or other assets, or money flowing into or out of UK bank accounts (known as *portfolio investment*).

balance of payments crisis: if imports persistently exceed exports (i.e. there is a deficit), and if holders of the currency begin to lose confidence in the capacity of the economy to pay for those imports, there is said to be a balance of payments crisis. The usual consequence would be a fall in the exchange rate which might create a problem for the government in power. The key factor in the situation will be the confidence of holders of the currency. However, a depreciating exchange rate can lead to increased exports, which in time solves the problem.

balance of payments deficit/surplus on current account: this occurs when total imports exceed total exports. If this remains fairly small and is balanced by capital inflows on the financial account, it may be of no great consequence. However, by 2007 (see table above) the deficit was significant. As the financial crisis developed in 2008, capital inflows fell as overseas investors saw London as a less safe location for their funds. The consequence was a sharply depreciating pound.

A surplus occurs when the exports exceed imports. The surplus can be used to increase *foreign exchange reserves*. Large *current account imbalances* can threaten economic stability.

balance of trade: the record of all trade in visible exports and imports, i.e. goods from the primary sector or manufactures. It is a component of the balance of payments. The UK balance of trade has for many years tended to be in deficit. This deficit is usually balanced by a surplus on the invisibles (service) account, or it may be covered partly by a capital inflow on the financial account.

balance sheet: all companies are required by law to produce a balance sheet as part of their annual report. This shows a breakdown of its *assets* and its *liabilities*. The objective is to indicate where the firm's capital has come from and how it has been used.

balanced budget: if the government exactly balances tax revenue and expenditure it is said to have a balanced budget. In fact, on an annual basis this happens rather rarely. Most often there is a budget deficit, sometimes a budget surplus, and very occasionally the budget nearly balances. Over a period of time the annual budget deficits and surpluses may balance each other out. Gordon Brown had a 'golden rule' as Chancellor of the Exchequer, that expenditure should not exceed tax revenues by more than the level of public investment. Borrowing to invest can be justified because of the expected future income which the investment will create. However, this rule has been blown away by the need for the government to borrow to recapitalise the banks and provide a stimulus to the economy in 2008.

balances with the Bank of England: the operational balances kept by the banks with the Bank, which they use to settle accounts with each other. These accounts provide an important reserve for the banks, which can be used if they need cash to meet the demand from customers who are withdrawing funds.

ballots: during industrial action, there may be a ballot in which employees or trade union members can vote for or against a particular outcome. Under the terms of the Trade Unions Act 1984 and the Employment Act 1988, ballots to decide for or against a strike are held under strict rules and must be secret.

bank: a bank is a *financial intermediary* which takes deposits from people or businesses that wish to save, and lends money to people or businesses that wish to borrow. By doing this on a large scale, and by exploiting the fact that not all of its deposits will be withdrawn at any one time, a bank can expand its lending over and above the total of deposits which it receives from savers. This process is known as *credit creation*. Normally, banks are supposed to be carefully regulated to ensure that they do not over-lend. (This safeguard broke down in the period of increased lending, 2005–07; it eventually became clear that many banks had taken big risks with sub-prime mortgages based on an expectation that house prices would rise indefinitely.)

Traditionally, banks make their money by 'borrowing long and lending short'. Borrowing long means taking deposits which are unlikely to be withdrawn and which are available at relatively low *interest rates*. Lending short, i.e. making loans for short periods, will be profitable because a higher interest rate can be charged. The margin between the two rates gives the bank its income.

Banks supply a wide range of financial services. Some also specialise. Retail banks take deposits from all kinds of small and large customers. *Investment banks* exist to meet the needs of large businesses and specialise in funding large projects and advising on finance for individuals with significant wealth. In recent years a number of building societies have become banks.

Normally governments do not get involved in banking business, but the threatened bank failures in 2007–08 led the UK government to nationalise Northern Rock and take a very large share of Lloyds TSB/HBOS and RBS. It remains to be seen how this story will end.

bank advances are the loans which banks make to individual or business customers. They may be made in the form of an *overdraft* or a fixed term loan. Overdrafts provide permission to borrow up to an agreed total level, as and when the funds are required. Interest is paid only on the amounts outstanding. They suit businesses which have difficulty in predicting their need for finance and experience variations in their income and outgoings. Fixed term loans are more appropriate where the loan is for a specific purpose, e.g. the purchase of new machinery. The *interest* payments and repayments will be fixed in advance.

bank bills: very short-term loans, usually for three months only. They can be bought and sold on the *money market*. There is no interest to pay on them but the maturity value will be larger than the loan, so giving a rate of return to the lender. This means that until maturity they are traded at a *discount*.

bank deposits: the amounts deposited by customers with their banks. They may be current accounts or deposit accounts. (In the US these are known respectively as sight deposits and time deposits.) With a current account there may be no interest payable but the depositor can withdraw the money at any time. With a deposit account interest will be paid but there may be a period of notice before withdrawals can be made.

Bank for International Settlements: an international bank which co-ordinates banking activities for many countries. It has at times been important in arranging currency swaps between central banks when countries had surpluses or deficits on the *balance of payments*. It now sets *capital adequacy ratios* for European banks and has been active in seeking ways to strengthen banking supervision. (See also *bank supervision* and *Financial Services Authority*.)

bank note: a note issued by a bank which makes a 'promise to pay on demand the bearer…'. Originally the promise was to pay in gold but this is long since discontinued, merely guaranteeing that the note is legal tender.

Bank of England: the central bank of the UK. It is responsible for the note issue and for the determination of *monetary policy* including interest rate and exchange rate policy. It is also responsible for ensuring that the *public sector net cash requirement* is funded through the sale of bills and bonds. Until 1997 the Bank of England acted as a watchdog for all banking activities in the economy. This *bank supervision* is now carried out by the *Financial Services Authority*, an independent body whose other main objectives are to ensure that financial services such as insurance, accounting, stockbroking and investment advice operate honestly and competently.

Traditionally there was always close collaboration between the **Chancellor of the Exchequer** and the Governor of the Bank of England. This changed when the **Monetary Policy Committee** was set up in 1997. This gave the Bank operational independence in setting interest rates. However, during the 2007–09 financial crisis the government had to become much more involved because the rescue of failing banks required **recapitalisation**, achieved with large amounts of government money. The stability of the system could only be underpinned by the government's ability to raise tax revenue. There was no other way to restore confidence in the banking system. It is likely that once all the banks are self-supporting again, the government will withdraw and leave the Bank of England operating independently again. It is open to question whether the then government will choose to make the Bank fully and legally independent, similar to the US Federal Reserve or the ECB.

The MPC has been a crucially important body while the banks have been in crisis. It is responsible for decisions relating to **quantitative easing** as well as **bank rate**, as policies to reduce the impact of recession.

The role of the Bank of England will change dramatically if the UK adopts the **euro** as its currency. The determination of monetary policy will shift to the **European Central Bank (ECB)**.

bank rate: this is the interest rate set by the **Monetary Policy Committee** of the **Bank of England**. This is the rate which the Bank charges when the banks need to borrow on a short-term basis to cover day-to-day customer withdrawals. It is thus a basis for determining interest rates throughout the banking world, and influences rates on loans taken out by individuals and firms. It is the main weapon in **monetary policy**, which attempts to influence the level of economic activity.

In an attempt to stop inflation from accelerating, the MPC raised interest rates during 2006–07. As signs of impending recession developed it began to reduce bank rate during 2008, slowly at first and then dramatically to an all-time low. Some people argue that it should have been reduced earlier and faster.

UK bank rate (%), August 2006 to February 2009	
August 2006	4.75
November 2006	5.00
January 2007	5.25
May 2007	5.50
July 2007	5.75
December 2007	5.50
February 2008	5.25
April 2008	5.00
October 2008	4.50
November 2008	3.00
December 2008	3.00
January 2009	1.5
February 2009	1.00

Source: Bank of England

bank supervision: the process by which the *Financial Services Authority* (FSA) aims to ensure that banks do not lend more than they ought to, also known as bank regulation. If they do they may eventually be unable to meet the demands of their customers to withdraw their cash. This is known as bank failure: it happened to Northern Rock in late 2007, when the fall in its share price panicked depositors, who then created a 'run on the bank' for the first time in the UK since 1866. The bank had increased mortgage lending by taking on customers without adequate checks on their ability to keep up with payments. When house prices began to turn down and unemployment rose, it became clear that the bank's reserves were insufficient to cover the risky loans they had made.

Supervision means making sure that the banks are holding a sufficient quantity of liquid assets, enough to balance the growth of their lending, so that they do not run out of cash even if there is a downturn in economic activity. There was widespread criticism of the FSA for allowing this to happen. It was clear that the FSA had paid insufficient attention to the risks which Northern Rock was taking by rapidly increasing lending. Reforms are expected in the future but they will need to be internationally agreed and this will take time.

bankers' balances: the accounts held by banks with the *Bank of England*, which they use to settle their accounts with each other, and which are a very liquid asset.

banking system: this includes the banks, the central bank and the bodies which regulate the banking system. In the UK this would mean the retail banks which deal with individuals and businesses, the investment banks which advise and lend to major businesses and wealthy individuals, the *Bank of England* and the *Financial Services Authority*. A well-developed banking system is essential to the smooth running of a *developed economy* because it provides a safe income for savers and channels their funds towards borrowers who can use the money to generate incomes. The effects of systemic failure of the banking system are easy to observe in the financial crisis of 2007–09 and the subsequent recession.

bankruptcy: individuals who cannot pay their debts become bankrupt, which means that their creditors are starting legal proceedings against them in order to recover their funds. Their assets will be taken over by an official receiver who will sell them to repay the creditors if possible. The term bankruptcy does not apply to limited liability companies. If they cannot pay their debts they face *insolvency* and possibly *liquidation*.

bargaining power refers to the capacity of any party to negotiate to achieve their objectives. In the marketplace, the bargaining power of any seller who is desperate to sell and raise some cash may be quite limited. The bargaining power of a *trade union*, which can by striking cause the employer serious losses, may be great.

barriers to development include lack of capital and poor infrastructure, low levels of education, high levels of debt repayment and *protectionist policies* making it hard to compete in export markets.

barriers to entry occur when it is difficult for new firms to enter an industry. This most commonly arises because there are substantial *technical economies* of scale being reaped by existing firms, and a new entrant to the industry, starting up in a small way, would have higher costs. Many manufacturing industries have barriers to entry because the production process is very *capital intensive*. Other economies of scale, financial and marketing (especially where there is extensive advertising), may be important too.

Barriers to entry may be legal arising from **patents**. When an invention is patented, only the holder of the patent is allowed to produce it for a specified number of years. This means that no other company can copy the product until the patent expires. Other barriers include exclusive dealership arrangements, any kind of collusive agreement between existing firms in the industry, **sunk costs** and **limit pricing**.

barriers to trade: see *import controls*.

barter occurs when people trade without using money by exchanging one good or service for another. It is used when people want to avoid paying expenditure taxes or sometimes when nations have **bilateral trade** deals which allow them to save on scarce **foreign exchange**.

base rate: a term used in the recent past for the interest rate at which the Bank of England lends to the banks whenever they are short of cash. This is now known as the **bank rate**.

base year: *index numbers* are calculated with a base year value of 100. It is important to select a base year which has a reasonably representative value. The purpose of index numbers is to allow easy comparisons when using **time series data**. For example, an index number of 150 will show clearly that the value has increased by 50%. The base year is often now referred to as the reference year.

basic prices are the prices used by the Office for National Statistics (ONS) to value output. They are based on the price received by the producer, less taxes, plus subsidies. They replace factor prices and reflect the actual costs of production for the firm.

basis point: literally, 1% of 1%. It is a term used in the financial markets to measure very small changes over the very short run. So if a particular interest rate rises by ten basis points, it has gone up by 0.1%.

basket of currencies: when exchange rate changes are measured, an **index number** is created which shows the extent of the change for one currency against those of its main trading partners. The currencies selected for this are known collectively as a basket of currencies. (See also **exchange rate index**.)

basket of goods and services: a representative list of products that can be used to determine weights when creating a price index. This ensures that items that figure large in people's spending pattern are given more weight in the index. (See also **Family Expenditure Survey**.)

bear market: a time when expectations are that share prices and the returns on **shares** are likely to fall. This will encourage people to sell shares in order to avoid losses. The result will be falling share prices so that bearish expectations can become a **self-fulfilling prophecy**. A **bull market** has the opposite effect. Expectations of rising prices will make the market buoyant with steadily increasing prices. The falling share prices during 2008 provide an example.

beggar my neighbour policies: measures which restrict trade with the intention of protecting domestic industries, but have the effect of reducing trade overall. The term is used to describe the events of the 1930s when many governments brought in **import controls** to protect their domestic producers from competition from cheap imports. This had the effect of reducing the exports of many countries, so reducing aggregate demand and worsening the plight of the many countries caught up in the depression. The onset of recession in 2008 brought fears that governments would again try to protect their economies in this way.

behavioural theories of the firm: theories based on business objectives other than profit maximisation. For example, small businesses may have objectives relating to an easy life, possibly *satisficing*. Managers of large businesses may seek power or *perks* rather than profit as such. Or they may seek to maximise output and turnover.

benefits: payments from the government in cash and in kind which ensure that individual incomes cannot fall below a floor level which provides a minimum standard of living. Examples include *unemployment benefit* and *income support*. Benefits may be means tested or universal. The latter avoids the unpopularity of enquiring into individual sources of income but are expensive because they are paid to all.

benefits in kind: people receive many benefits from the welfare state which are not given in the form of money. Health care, education and other services provide benefits in kind which add to people's well-being but do not increase their money income in the short run.

benefits system: a full system of benefits aims to ensure that people are provided with a minimum income whatever the reason for their inability to work. Their benefits may be in cash or in kind. They may be universal, i.e. given as of right, or means tested according to income. The objective is to protect the young and the old, the sick, the disabled and those who cannot find work.

BERR: the former name for the *Department of Business Innovation and Skills (BIS)*.

bias occurs in any investigation where the findings tend to be different from the reality. For example, if a sample for survey is for some reason not representative of the population as a whole, it will give biased results. It might have too many or too few of a particular age group. Bias can also occur when the investigator allows a personal view to influence the conclusions.

Big Mac index measures exchange rates in terms of the local price of a Big Mac. The price in one country relative to the price of a Big Mac in the USA provides an exchange rate that may suggest over- or undervaluation of the market exchange rate. Big Macs are much cheaper in China than in the USA (given the existing exchange rate). This suggests that possibly the yuan is undervalued in the foreign exchange markets. The *Economist* magazine invented this series and calls the study of it Burgernomics. It can provide useful insights.

bilateral monopoly occurs where there is a single seller and a single buyer. A *trade union* which represents all the workers in an industry and a dominant employer can create a bilateral monopoly, as in the case of the British Medical Association which negotiates doctors' pay, and the National Health Service which employs most of them.

bilateral negotiations involve two parties. Bilateral trade negotiations might involve two governments.

bilateral trade occurs when two countries swap equal quantities of exports and imports. More often trade is multilateral, characterised by surpluses and deficits between pairs of countries, so that the UK might export engineers' services to Saudi Arabia, which might in turn export oil to Japan, which in turn exports cars to the UK.

bill: see *bank bills*.

biotechnology involves applying understanding of biological processes to the development of new products and production methods. It has the potential to lead to big cuts in production costs as well as to improved products and *productivity*.

birth rate: the average number of live births occurring in a year per 1000 population. Information derived from the birth rate can be an important basis for production decisions, for the planning of the education system and for understanding a number of long-term trends. Low birth rates in developed countries are leading to *ageing populations*. High birth rates, for example in Africa, are making it difficult to increase per capita incomes. There is strong evidence that rising incomes in the long run lead to falling birth rates.

black economy is the term used to describe all those transactions which do not appear in the *national income statistics*. Some of these are legal, others are not. The black economy includes the wages of people who are on means-tested benefits while actually working more than the few hours allowed. It also includes payments, e.g. to babysitters, which do not need to be recorded for tax purposes. It is estimated that 3–5% of tax revenue is lost through illegal activities taking place on the black economy.

black market: when a market is controlled, e.g. by rationing, a black market develops, where people who have things to sell and people who want to buy them evade the controls. A black market developed during World War II in the UK and more recently countries with strict foreign exchange controls have experienced black markets in *currencies*.

Blue Book: a publication of the Office for National Statistics which contains the UK National Income Accounts.

blue chip: a company the shares of which are regarded as being a very safe investment.

blue collar union: a *trade union* that represents manual workers.

board of directors: the people who have ultimate responsibility for the affairs of a business. They represent *shareholders* and are elected by them at the *annual general meeting (AGM)*. Day-to-day and strategic decisions will usually be in the hands of executive directors who work for the firm full-time. *Non-executive directors* may be elected to provide additional expertise or to give an impression of independence.

bonds: a borrower may issue a bond, which is a promise to repay a certain sum of money at a date some time in the future (from one to 20 years or so). In return for the loan which is the price of the bond, interest will be paid, usually at a fixed rate. Bonds may be traded on the *Stock Exchange*, and the price will reflect the attractiveness of the interest rate relative to current market rates. Bonds issued by the *Bank of England* to finance government spending are known as Treasury Bonds, also as gilts, because the government will always be able to repay on maturity, since it has the right to tax. (Hence, they are said to be 'as good as gold'.) Bonds issued by companies are known as corporate bonds. Because the rate of interest and the maturity value are fixed, bonds are much less risky than shares, but are likely also to have a lower rate of return.

bonus: an amount over and above normal salary paid to employees who are considered to have done their job particularly well. They can be used to try to ensure loyalty or to act as an incentive. Sometimes they are used to pay very large amounts, the wisdom of which has been questioned by some shareholders and members of the public, especially in relation to bankers whose banks became very weak during the 2007–09 financial crisis.

boom: the phase of the *economic cycle* in which economic growth is at its most rapid. As recovery gathers pace, economic growth becomes faster until in a boom it is growing at a rate which cannot be sustained in the long run. The economy will be characterised by relatively low levels of *unemployment* and little underutilised capacity.

In the later stages of a boom, bottlenecks or **supply constraints** develop. Employers find it hard to recruit some scarce types of skilled **labour**. Firms producing **investment** goods develop long order books, so that buyers have to wait. Wages will tend to be bid up in an attempt to recruit more people. This increases costs and may lead to increasing prices so that **inflation** accelerates. In any case, the ease with which firms can sell their output in a growing market encourages them to raise prices. In these ways inflation may accelerate. This was the situation in the UK at the end of 2007; growth for the year was just under 3%, which was probably unsustainable, being somewhat above the **long-run trend rate of growth**.

If governments implement counter-inflation policies, the heat will be taken out of the economy and the downswing of the cycle will begin. Even without such policies the economy is likely to slow down because expectations that growth is likely to slow will reduce the rate of investment, which in turn reduces **aggregate demand**.

bottlenecks in the economy occur when it is impossible to increase supply to match an unexpected surge in demand. In **boom** years, for example, there have been shortages of microchips, forcing producers of a huge range of products to slow down their rate of output. There may also be shortages of skilled **labour** which make it difficult for firms to hire the kind of people they need in order to expand. Bottlenecks can lead to prices of scarce resources being bid up as buyers compete for them. This can be the start of an acceleration in **inflation** during a boom.

boycott: a movement to stop buying certain products because of consumer concern, usually about ethical issues. Over the long run, the boycott of South African products was a factor in the ending of the apartheid regime and the holding of free elections with votes for all. On a much smaller scale, the boycott of Nestlé products by consumers worried about sales of baby milk in developing countries has given the company some cause for concern.

brand: a way of differentiating the product to make it recognisably distinguishable from competing products. This may be done with logos and packaging and there may be quality factors which can give the brand a genuine edge. In the long run, some products can acquire **brand loyalty** because they are seen as a reliable choice. Rowntree brands were a great attraction for Nestlé when they launched their hostile takeover bid. This is a factor in the increasing concentration of some industries.

brand loyalty refers to the way in which certain brands become associated with particular qualities so that consumers will buy them again and again in preference to competing products. Brand loyalty can allow the producer to raise prices above those of similar products because people come to rely on them. It can give the firm some degree of **market power**.

breach of contract: contracts specify the conditions under which a transaction takes place. Breach of contract means that one or more of these conditions has not been adhered to by one of the contracting parties.

The law of contract is an essential basis for an efficient economy. Both buyers and sellers need to be sure that they can rely on the terms of an agreement in order to deal with one another. If they cannot, business becomes extremely risky. The lack of a reliable legal system is a major factor in the risks which dog firms expanding in developing countries. This applies to domestic firms as well as international ones. For example, China is an attractive market but a risky one because its legal system is slow and unpredictable, and commercial law is limited in its scope.

break-even level of output is that at which neither losses nor profits are made. In the early stages of its existence, breaking even is an important objective for a business. It will be able to survive losses for a while but in time it will need to become profitable. For non-profit making organisations, breaking even may be a long-term objective.

Bretton Woods: the name given to the post World War II economic system that sought freely convertible currencies within a worldwide *fixed exchange rate* system. Between 1945 and 1971 this was remarkably successful, helping world economic growth achieve its highest ever levels.

BRICs: Brazil, Russia, India and China. These are the four largest fast-growing economies. Using *IMF* data at *PPP*, China with *GDP* of US$8 trillion is now the third largest economy in the world, after the USA ($15tn) and the EU ($14tn). Russia, India and Brazil are trailing a little but have the capacity to become similarly large in time. This data is all about the size of the economy and tells little about per capita income.

broad money: a measure of the stock of money which attempts to capture total potential purchasing power. In the UK this is M4, which is defined as notes and coin and all bank and building society sterling deposits.

broker: a person or firm which creates a link between buyers and sellers. The broker often has more information than the buyer or the seller, so can make a living out of acting as an intermediary.

brownfield site: an urban location which has already been built upon once, which could now be redeveloped. There is pressure to build on brownfield sites rather than on greenfield sites (which have never been built on before) for environmental reasons.

bubble: a situation in which the price of an *asset*, such as a *share*, rises fast because of buyer enthusiasm which is speculative in nature. Expectations of higher prices in the future cause people to buy, driving up the price. Eventually, the market loses confidence that the price will rise further. Demand dries up, the price collapses and the bubble bursts. The financial crisis which began in 2007 was preceded by an asset price bubble.

Budget: the Budget is the occasion on which the *Chancellor of the Exchequer* sets out taxation and expenditure plans for the year. Detailed changes will be made to both *direct* and *indirect tax* rates as they affect firms and individuals. There may also be changes in certain areas of expenditure such as health and *social security*. Because it has a direct effect on almost everyone, which can be measured in money terms, the Budget attracts a great deal of attention.

Budget day is usually in March each year. Each November the Chancellor of the Exchequer sets out the government's spending plans. Both occasions provide all-embracing statements of economic policy, including detailed forecasts of expected levels of economic activity.

The Budget performs a macro-economic management function, as well as involving detailed adjustments to policies which affect the allocation of resources. An example of the latter occurs when there are changes in expenditure taxes on fuel, which have environmental objectives.

A significant part of the Budget speech will review *macro-economic policy*. Tax and expenditure changes will lead to changes in the overall budget deficit or surplus. This will have an effect in turn on the level of **aggregate demand** and the prosperity of the economy.

budget balance: a situation in which tax revenues are equal to government expenditure. A precise match is rather unlikely; more often than not there is a **public sector deficit**. From time to time there is a surplus.

budget constraint: the maximum amount of spending possible within a given sum of money, which may come from income or from accumulated wealth or borrowing. The budget constraint prevents anyone from spending above that amount. Within the budget, choices may be made and people can have more of one product so long as they have less of another.

budget deficit: the amount by which government expenditure exceeds tax revenue. The deficit can be financed by borrowing. The **Bank of England** will sell Treasury **bonds** and **bills** in sufficient quantities to raise the funds. Useful amounts may also come from **National Savings**. In general the government can borrow at low rates of interest because it can guarantee to be able to pay back the money, because of its right to tax. However, if it needs to borrow a great deal more to finance the deficit, it may be necessary to raise **interest rates**. This may have the effect of discouraging investment and therefore future economic activity.

Normally the budget deficit varies over the course of the **economic cycle**. During a boom, tax revenues rise, usually even faster than incomes. Unemployment is fairly low and benefits will cost less. There may be a surplus. During the downturn, increased unemployment leads to increased spending on benefits and tax revenues may be static or falling. There will be a public sector deficit. This will help to stimulate the economy into growing again. In recent years governments have generally aimed to balance the budget over the course of the economic cycle, but not in the short run.

Borrowing for **investment** makes sense when the income generated by the investment is likely to be sufficient to pay the interest on the debt. The annual budget deficit is known as the **public sector net cash requirement**. The combined deficits from the past are called the **National Debt**. (See also **fiscal rules**.)

budget surplus: the amount by which tax revenue exceeds government expenditure. (See also **Budget** and **budget deficit**.) The surplus in any one year is called the **public sector debt repayment**.

buffer stock: stocks of **commodities**, such as wheat, which are held in many countries and can be used in the event of shortages at some time in the future. Some are held by government bodies and some in the private sector. For many commodities, both demand and supply can vary. The demand for oil is affected by the level of economic activity, worldwide; the supply can be affected by wars. So prices do fluctuate from time to time. Releasing buffer stocks onto the market – or buying up a glut – helps to keep prices stable. The supply of agricultural products varies because of weather and other problems. So keeping a buffer stock can help to prevent very low prices during a glut or very high prices at times of shortage.

Buffett, Warren (1930–): an outstandingly successful investment manager, sometimes known as the Sage of Omaha (where his business is located). He is usually named as second richest man in the world (after Bill Gates). Most of his wealth is being given to the Bill and Melinda Gates Foundation, to be spent on good causes such as health care in Africa. His pay is modest and he never tries to avoid tax. Some of his investment decisions during 2008 have been less successful than hitherto.

building society: a *financial intermediary* which specialises in lending for house purchase, i.e. very long-term loans. In recent years building societies have diversified into offering retail banking services to customers and several have changed their status to become banks.

built-in stabilisers: during different phases of the *economic cycle*, the government will automatically be changing the level of spending on benefits and will receive varying levels of tax revenue. These changes offset the changes in *aggregate demand* in the economy as a whole. As more people become unemployed, their benefit entitlement rises and they are able to continue spending, albeit on a lower level, even though they are no longer earning. Similarly they will pay little or no tax. The reverse happens as the economy recovers. So as demand falls in *recession*, it is offset by a rise in government expenditure and a fall in taxation, which reduces leakages from the circular flow of money. This reduces the severity of the slump. The opposite happens as the economy recovers and so the boom is slowed.

bulk–value ratio: the relationship between bulk or weight and the value of the product. When the ratio is very high, transport costs will be high in relation to the final price and this may affect the location of production. Firms located close to the market may have a cost advantage.

bull market: one in which there is long term rise in prices generally. At the height of a bull market, expectations of price rises may generate a rush to buy immediately. On the *Stock Exchange*, a bull market may last for some time as prices rise and confidence becomes infectious. If the higher prices are justified by reasonable expectations of profit there may be no problem. But if there is *irrational exuberance* and a *bubble* develop, then the bull market may turn into a *bear market*, as happened in 2008. Similarly in the *Wall Street Crash* of 1929, a bull market was followed by loss of confidence and collapsing prices.

business confidence is an important element in the formation of *expectations*. These in turn affect firms' decisions, particularly in relation to investment. The CBI Industrial Trends Survey monitors business optimism, export optimism and perceptions of limiting factors, i.e. the availability of skilled *labour* and the cost of finance. These are all known to be important indicators of willingness to invest in the immediate or near future.

business cycle: the sequence of *slump*, *recovery*, *boom* and *recession* which has been a feature of economic life for many years. Go to *economic cycle* for full coverage.

Business Link: a government-funded body set up under the auspices of *Department for Business Innovation and Skills (BIS)* to facilitate business start-ups and provide support for existing businesses.

business objectives: the range of targets which a firm may have. For some these will be related to profit. In economics it is often assumed that firms will in fact seek to maximise profits. However, there are other possible objectives. These include achieving a significant *market share*, such that the firm has some control over prices, having a reputation for excellence in design or quality, taking ethically responsible decisions or sometimes just breaking even over the long run. (See also *satisficing* and *behavioural theories of the firm*.)

business rate: the payments to local authorities which are levied on businesses and determined on the basis of the value of the premises. For some firms these are an important cost.

business responsibility: the idea that businesses should take their decisions in a way which considers the needs and interests of all their *stakeholders*. As well as *shareholders* and employees, these include customers, suppliers, creditors and the community. Some managers see business responsibility as being part of effective management and believe that it can be achieved without reducing profits because it is in the long-term interests of all. Most firms say that they abide by the laws of the countries in which they are operating but some go beyond that and actively try to improve employment conditions or look for production methods which minimise environmental impact.

business taxation includes *corporation tax* and *business rates*.

buyers' market: if there are large numbers of sellers trying to sell to a relatively small number of buyers, then the buyers will be able to force a drop in price. This is sometimes used to describe the housing market when the number of houses for sale exceeds the number of potential buyers at current prices.

buyout: see *management buyout (MBO)*.

bygones: there is an old saying in economics, bygones are bygones. These are events which happened in the past and should have no impact on current decision taking. For example, after the Millennium Dome was built, it became clear that it was unlikely ever to make enough money from entrance fees to cover its costs. The correct decision at this point would have been to close it down and dispose of it in the most economical manner, since it could never be profitable. However, people sometimes have great difficulty with the concept of bygones, believing that if much money has been poured into a venture, it should therefore be kept open. What do you think?

by-product: when a production process leads to the production of other goods which are not the main objective for the producer, these are known as by-products. The term is often used in relation to the chemical industry. Straw, however, is a by-product of wheat.

A–Z Online

Log on to A–Z Online to search the database of terms, print revision lists and much more. Go to **www.philipallan.co.uk/a-zonline** to get started.

CAP: see *Common Agricultural Policy (CAP)*.

capacity: the maximum amount which can be produced with given amounts of fixed capital. For example, a chemical plant may have a maximum output which is technically possible with the equipment it has. Capacity can be increased by investing in a new plant or by extending the existing one. However, it is sometimes possible to increase capacity by improving the efficiency with which resources are used.

capacity utilisation means the extent to which existing capital equipment is in use. An individual business might be operating at 50% of capacity if it normally operates two shifts a day but there is actually only one shift a day or if a single shift is normal and half the machines are idle.

$$FORMULA: \quad \frac{\text{actual output per period}}{\text{full capacity output per period}} \times 100$$

Underutilised capital raises costs because the fixed costs are spread over fewer units of output. It can be a serious problem during *recession* because cuts in output inevitably lead to underutilised capacity. Eventually, if demand for the product does not recover, the capital equipment will be taken out of use permanently in order to cut losses.

Capacity utilisation for the economy as a whole is an important indicator. It shows how close the economy is to *full-capacity output* and will help to show when the pressure of *aggregate demand* is likely to lead to accelerating *inflation*, because the amount of unused resources in the economy is diminishing.

Capacity utilisation fell sharply in late 2007 as the financial crisis led to aggregate demand growing first more slowly and then actually declining.

capital has several different meanings but all of them imply that capital can be used to generate an income stream over a period of time.
- Capital is a *factor of production* consisting of buildings, plant and machinery which can be used in the production process. With the other factors of production, land and *labour*, it can be combined to produce goods or services which can be sold.
- Capital can also mean *financial assets*. The funds available to a firm include shareholders' capital and loan capital. This can be used to invest in property, capital equipment, plant and machinery. Alternatively it provides *working capital* which finances the production process until sales revenue comes in.
- *Human capital* means the skills and experience which individuals accumulate and which are a valuable asset which can be used to make the production process more efficient.

The return to capital may be *interest*, *profits* or *rent*. These provide compensation to the owner of the capital for not having the use of it at the present time for consumption purposes.

capital account: that part of the *balance of payments* accounts which records capital movements. It is shown as a series of changes to the level of assets and liabilities held outside the UK, and by overseas residents inside the UK.

capital accumulation: the process by which investment adds to the stock of capital and the capacity of the economy to produce. Much investment in capital equipment simply replaces worn-out plant and machinery. However, when there is *net investment*, i.e. spending on capital which is greater than the amount needed to replace worn-out equipment, the stock of capital increases. This is one element in the process of economic growth (the others being *population growth* and *technical change*).

capital adequacy ratio defines the amount of capital needed by banks to ensure that they do not run out of funds when customers ask to withdraw their deposits. The amount is fixed in relation to the amount and types of loans which the bank is providing to customers.

capital appreciation: an increase in the value of assets. This could be an increase in the market value of a house or other property, of land or buildings owned by a firm or of the prices of a particular share. If the capital assets are going to be used for the same purposes as before the appreciation, then the increase is in the book value of the assets. However, if they are to be sold, the owner will make a *capital gain*.

capital consumption measures the amount of capital needed to replace equipment which has worn out during the course of one year. The term is used in the national accounts to show how much of total (gross) investment can be attributed to normal wear and tear or depreciation and how much reflects a net addition to the nation's stock of capital or productive capacity.

capital deepening occurs when more capital equipment is provided for each person employed. It will normally lead to an increase in *productivity* or output per person employed.

capital deficiency: many developing countries experience slow growth, or sometimes no growth at all, because there is a low level of investment in capital equipment and infrastructure. This is particularly prevalent in sub-Saharan Africa where the capital stock has in most countries remained small in relation to the population.

capital expenditure is spending on investments which will yield an income in the future. This may apply in the public or the private sector. In the public sector it might apply to new motorways or hospitals.

capital flight: when there is a serious loss of confidence in the performance of a particular economy, many owners of capital assets may try to sell them very quickly. For example, they will try to sell the currency, exchanging it for another currency which they believe is safer. They may also try to sell shares. Usually a capital flight will lead to a sharp drop in asset prices. A recent example occurred in 2008 when confidence in the Icelandic banks fell away, so that most depositors tried to withdraw their money. This led to loss of confidence in the Icelandic economy; the Icelandic currency was sold on a vast scale and fell to a fraction of its previous value over a few months.

capital gain: the increase in the value of an asset between its purchase and a subsequent sale or revaluation. The term applies mostly to shares or to homes and other property.

capital gains tax (CGT): a tax on gains made when an asset which has appreciated in value is sold. This is a way of taxing the gains made by *shareholders* or property owners when they sell at a much higher price than they originally paid. Only the increase in value which exceeds the increase in the *retail price index (RPI)* is taxed. No tax is payable on a person's main residence.

capital gearing shows the extent to which a firm uses loan finance rather than equity (share) finance to pay for its capital investments. Capital gearing is, as a percentage:

$$FORMULA: \quad \frac{\text{total loans}}{\text{total capital employed}} \times 100$$

High gearing means that the business is heavily reliant on loans. This may matter if the business finds itself in difficult trading conditions. It will still have to pay interest on its loans. If it had relied more on equity finance (an issue of shares), dividends could have been reduced during that year to reduce the overall financial pressures. This is one of the risks that *shareholders* expect to have to carry. A gearing level above 50% is seen as being high, for this reason. High gearing can be risky for the lender.

capital goods means equipment of any kind which can be used as an input to the production process. Some capital goods can only be used as such; for example, a power station or a railway line. Others can be used as consumer items or as capital goods; for example, a car or a sewing machine.

capital inflows are the movements of large amounts of money into the country from abroad. These can be bank balances which are coming in search of high interest rates or they can represent investment in productive capacity – plant and machinery. For example, many US and Japanese companies have invested in factories in the UK, such as Ford and Toyota. These inflows will be recorded in the *capital account* of the *balance of payments*.

capital-intensive production uses a high proportion of capital equipment and a relatively low proportion of *labour*. Most manufacturing is now capital-intensive in the UK. The introduction of computerised production systems and robots makes processes more capital-intensive.

The decision as to how capital-intensive production should be, will be determined by the relative prices of capital and *labour*. In countries with relatively low wage rates, *labour-intensive* production will be more appropriate. As wage rates rise during the process of economic development, firms increasingly substitute capital for labour. This raises productivity and often also wage rates, leading to further investment in labour-saving capital.

capitalism: the system in which the price mechanism is used to determine how resources are allocated. Land and capital are owned by individuals who will decide how they are used on the basis of the profit that can be obtained. Similarly, they will pay employees according to the amount needed to attract them to undertake the required work.

The extreme alternative to capitalism is a *centrally planned economy*. Most economies, however, fall between those extremes, being mixed economies, with market systems and some government involvement in economic activity. The advantage of capitalism is that the allocation of resources is determined primarily by the demand for final products.

capital-labour ratio: the proportion of capital used in production relative to the proportion of *labour*. Where wages are relatively high, the capital-labour ratio will tend to be high also and production will be *capital-intensive*. The ratio may vary over the course of the economic cycle: during recession, redundancies may reduce the labour input. The capital used will be a fixed factor of production in the short run.

capital markets are the markets in which borrowers can obtain funds and lenders can find suitable borrowers who will pay a rate of interest. For example, in the short-term money market, banks and other businesses with a surplus of funds for a few days can lend to banks and other businesses who need extra funds for a similar period, sometimes just overnight. Also part of the capital market is the *Stock Exchange*, which brings together buyers and sellers of shares and *bonds*. In between these two there are markets for a range of different kinds of assets.

Efficient capital markets make it easy for lenders to make a return on their assets and for borrowers to obtain funds to finance production. They therefore have an important role in the process of income and wealth creation. Developing countries often experience difficulty in financing entrepreneurs because they do not have well-organised capital markets.

capital mobility: the extent to which capital can be switched to alternative uses. Generally speaking, capital invested in plant and machinery is not very mobile in the short run because it has a particular use, e.g. a car assembly line. The capital is only mobile insofar as it need not be replaced in the long run if there is no longer sufficient demand for the product. The capital invested then becomes available for use in producing a more profitable product.

Capital mobility can be important in international terms. The EU provides for the free movement of capital between member countries. Owners of capital can invest it in the EU location considered most likely to be profitable.

capital movements are flows of capital from one currency to another. The location of the money may or may not change: it could be moved from a dollar account in New York to a sterling account in London, but it might equally be moved from a dollar account in London to a sterling account in London. Money which is 'footloose' in this way and moves from one currency to another in search of the best rate of interest is sometimes called *hot money*.

capital outflow: a movement of large sums of money to destinations abroad. This could be for any of three reasons:
- a *capital flight*
- the money may be being moved into a currency with higher interest rates
- the capital may be being invested in factories and other productive capacities in other countries.

Globalisation has brought rising flows of capital from one country to another as the world economy becomes more integrated.

capital output ratio measures the amount of capital employed in producing a given amount of output. A high capital:output ratio will indicate *capital-intensive production* because wage rates are relatively high and some labour-saving investment has taken place.

capital stock: the amount of capital currently available for use in the economy. Changes in the capital stock provide a guide as to the productive potential of the economy.

capital widening occurs if employment is increasing and there is investment in new plant and machinery to give them the capacity to produce. This contrasts with **capital deepening**, which enlarges the amount of capital available to a given number of people.

carbon emissions trading: see *emissions trading schemes*.

carbon offsetting: firms and governments can buy carbon offsets to reduce the impact of activities that result in greenhouse gas emissions. These can be used to comply with regulatory caps on their total emissions. Individuals can also buy carbon offsets to counter the effects of emissions resulting from personal air travel.

carbon tax: see *green taxes*.

cartel: a group of firms which agree to limit output in order to keep prices higher than they would be if there were free competition. The best-known cartel is OPEC (the **Organization of Petroleum Exporting Countries (OPEC)**) which at times in the past has restricted output so that world oil prices would rise. This is different from the standard cartel in that governments are involved.

Firms which collaborate in this way may have market sharing agreements in which they each have a geographical area where they can operate without fear of competition. Or they may agree a minimum price or limit their range of products or non-price competition.

Cartels are now relatively infrequent for two reasons:
- In most developed countries, **competition policy** makes cartels illegal. By restricting competition, they lead to lower levels of output and higher prices for consumers.
- Cartels are quite hard to create and maintain, because the high prices act as an incentive for other firms to enter the market. Also, participating firms may try to cheat by offering secret discounts or not sticking to their output quotas. The parties to the agreement have to have a large share of the market in order to achieve the desired effect.

The process by which cartels achieve their objectives is called **collusion**. Evidence of this will encourage the Office of Fair Trading and the **Competition Commission** to investigate. In 2008 the Competition Commission investigated the way that supermarkets show price comparisons with other chains, usually showing all the same prices. They concluded that this was a sign of a 'de facto cartel'.

cash means literally notes and coin. However, it is usually used now to mean very liquid assets, as in 'cash in the bank', i.e. money held in instant access accounts.

cash flow statement: a component of a firm's **annual report and accounts**. It records all the revenues and payments made by the business. A cash flow forecast indicates possible times when money may not be available to cover necessary payments. Firms in this situation can run into difficulties even though they are likely to be profitable over the long run. Having adequate liquidity available to deal with cash flow problems can be important to the survival of the firm.

CBI: see *Confederation of British Industry (CBI)*.

CDO: see *collateralised debt obligation (CDO)*.

ceiling price: a maximum price which may be set by a government or a regulatory body. If this is below the **equilibrium price**, there will be excess demand and shortages, unless the government holds **buffer stocks** which can be sold. Ceiling prices set by regulators, e.g. **OFGEM**, usually affect the producers' profits rather than the supply of the product.

cell production: a way of splitting up an assembly line process into separate areas where teams can be responsible for a particular part of the overall process. It has been used as a way of increasing *productivity*. Its advantages are:
- the team can be jointly responsible for quality
- in time, members of the team become expert at solving production problems without having to call in outside help
- motivation may improve as the work may be less repetitive and more challenging
- the team may be able to improve the working arrangements in ways that cut costs.

census: the government's enquiry into population trends which takes place every 10 years. Information covers age, sex, family status and occupation. Other information can be collected at the same time, e.g. on housing or ethnic groups.

central bank: the bank which is responsible for overseeing the banking system as a whole and operating *monetary policy*. In the UK it is the Bank of England and in the US the Federal Reserve Bank (the Fed). The central bank acts as banker to the other banks and to the government, issues notes and coin and acts as lender of last resort; this means it ensures that the banking system is kept as stable as possible by lending to banks which find themselves temporarily short of cash to meet their depositors' needs. Within the *euro* zone, the central bank function has been taken over by the *European Central Bank (ECB)*, the ECB. Whether central banks should be independent or controlled by the central government is an open question. In normal circumstances, the Bank of England has operational independence, although it is not been made legally independent of the UK government. However, all central banks have had to collaborate with their governments to find ways to deal with the financial crisis that began in 2007.

central bank independence: in recent years there has been a trend towards making the central bank independent of the government. Where governments control monetary policies, they may be tempted to allow monetary expansion at a time of slow growth or high unemployment. This may in the long run lead to accelerating inflation. Where the central bank is independent, monetary policy can be decided on the basis of the need to maintain stability and control inflation. Short-term political considerations will not be a major factor in decisions. The *Federal Reserve System* in the US has always been independent. Other central banks have moved in this direction in order to strengthen the commitment to control of inflation, as in the UK.

central bank intervention most often describes the process by which central banks buy the domestic currency in order to keep up its value. This would happen if the central bank wanted to maintain the existing *exchange rate* at a time when market forces were causing a *depreciation*. The bank can use its foreign exchange reserves to buy currency so that the increased demand counteracts the market forces which are pushing it down.

central government refers to the highest level of government which controls the affairs of the nation as a whole. In contrast, *local government* deals with the provision of local services such as housing and environmental services. The situation is complicated in the UK by the process of devolution. Wales, Scotland and Northern Ireland have their own representative bodies and areas of particular responsibility. Even so, the scope of central government in the UK is greater than in federal systems such as the US and Germany, where state governments have wider responsibilities.

centrally planned economies are those in which the allocation of resources is determined by the planning process rather than by market forces. Many previously centrally planned economies (such as Russia and Poland) began the process of becoming market economies in 1989. China and Vietnam remain partly centrally planned, although market forces are operating in some sectors of their economies. Some economies have retained a measure of central planning within what is mainly a market economy. India falls into this category. Most developed countries have privatised most of their state enterprises, thus reducing the amount of central planning within individual economies.

ceteris paribus: a Latin term meaning 'other things being equal'. When using economic theory, it helps to be able to isolate a single change and think of all other conditions as being unchanged, so as to simplify the analysis. For example, we can say that ceteris paribus, an increase in the price will act as an incentive for firms to produce more. In practice, things are often not equal: an increase in costs might reduce the price incentive to nothing. Nevertheless, the *assumption* of ceteris paribus allows us to analyse one change at a time.

CGT: see *capital gains tax (CGT)*.

chained volume measures provide real values for *GDP* data without the distortions involved when inflation affects current prices. They are based on a reference year; the ONS related the data to prices for that year.

Chancellor of the Exchequer: the chief finance minister in the UK, who determines fiscal policy, i.e. the levels of taxation and expenditure across the whole economy. Plans are set out in the Budget each year, usually in March. The Chancellor, with the Treasury, must decide important aspects of stabilisation policy which can have a considerable impact on individuals and on business. The Chancellor's decisions may also have a substantial effect on income distribution. Until 1997 the Chancellor would decide monetary policy in consultation with the Bank of England but that role was then passed to the Bank's *Monetary Policy Committee*.

In addition to the *Budget*, the Chancellor reviews all aspects of taxation and spending in November each year. This creates an opportunity to prepare for the Budget, which then defines the precise changes required.

change requires that decision takers constantly review their policies. Constant change in the economy requires a flexible response. For example, rapid shifts in the pattern of demand mean that production has to be changed to match. This is much easier if the workforce is flexible enough to adapt fairly quickly. *Retraining* may be necessary and *multi-skilling* helps. Both can promote occupational *mobility*. Governments can help this process through their education and training policies. Firms have responded by requiring employees to have more flexible *employment contracts*.

Chicago School: a group of economists who have either worked at or been associated with the University of Chicago, who have promoted the importance of market forces in creating efficient, growing economies. They have tended to criticise government interventions in the economy as being likely not to produce the desired effect. Their work on the consumption function, on regulation and on monetary theory has been important. In particular, *Milton Friedman*'s thinking underpinned much of the Conservative government's monetary policy in the early 1980s.

Chinese walls: within financial firms, employees are forbidden to pass on information about events which may lead to big changes in share prices. For example, a department of an investment bank which is advising a business on a possible takeover bid must not allow the information about it to reach the bank's stockbroking department. If they had the information early enough, dealers could make big profits by buying shares which will rise in value once the information is made public. They may then be guilty of *insider dealing*, which is illegal.

choice: underlying much basic economic analysis is the idea that resources are scarce and therefore everyone has to make choices. The three fundamental areas of choice are:

- *what* goods and services will be produced. There are not enough resources to produce everything people want. So choices must be made which will reflect personal preferences.
- *how* goods and services should be produced. There will usually be several different ways of production. The choice of production method will depend on the relative prices of the inputs and the technologies available. Firms will decide which strategy is likely to be the most cost effective.
- *for whom* goods and services will be produced. In other words, how income will be distributed. Incomes depend partly on the level of wages needed to attract particular types of *labour* and partly on how much wealth individuals have accumulated through saving, inheritance or luck. However, the distribution of income which results from market forces can be altered by *fiscal policy* and the benefits system.

circular flow of national income: the way in which income flows around the economy, from firms to households and back to firms in a continuous process. Payments to employees are income, as are profits and rent. Income from all these sources is spent on goods and services. This spending becomes the revenue received by firms. Hence, the flow of money is circular. The model can be extended to take in savings and investment, taxes and government expenditure and imports and exports. These *withdrawals* and *injections* respectively reduce or increase the circular flow.

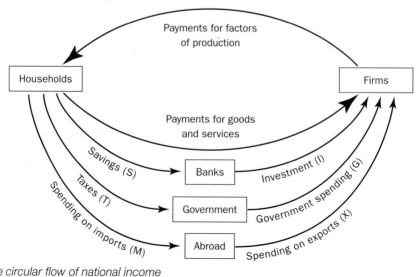

The circular flow of national income

The City: the network of organisations based in the City of London which includes the banking system, the money markets, insurance companies, commodity exchanges, the *Stock Exchange* and other firms concerned with financial affairs.

civil law: legislation which allows individuals to take their disputes with one another to the courts. (See also *commercial law*.)

claimant: a person who is claiming benefits, e.g. unemployment benefit.

claimant count: the number of people who are claiming unemployment benefit. This is a rather rough and ready way of measuring unemployment which is still used but is recognised as unsatisfactory. The problem is that it does not count people who want to work and do not have a job but are not eligible for unemployment benefit. *Labour Force Survey* data includes this group and therefore gives a fuller picture.

classical economics was developed by, among others, Adam Smith, David Ricardo and J S Mill, between 1776 when Adam Smith's *Wealth of Nations* was published, and 1848 when J S Mill's *Principles of Political Economy* was published. These economists laid down the general principles of the market economy, perfect competition and the theory of comparative advantage. They were concerned mainly with the principles of micro-economics and the assumption of *perfect competition* was crucial to their analysis. They held that government intervention was mainly unhelpful and that the operation of self-interest would bring about efficient production in the long run. The classical economists continue to influence thinking right up to the present day, being the forerunners of what is now known as *neoclassical economics*.

clearing banks are the main high street banks. The name comes from the fact that these banks belong to the London Clearing House. This body organises the payments between banks which result from the massive number of cheques exchanged each day.

clearing price: the price at which the market is cleared, with neither excess demand nor excess supply. The quantity that buyers wish to buy is the same as the quantity that sellers wish to sell. This is also the *equilibrium price*.

climate change: the warming trend that has been observed along with the change in composition of the earth's atmosphere. Although there have been many observations relating to a warming trend overall, scientists expect climate change to lead to less predictable weather and different effects in different places. This will have striking economic effects in the years to come, leading to increased migration, changes in output for many products and changes in prices. Some of these may be affected by policy decisions. The *Stern Review* (2006) set out proposals for UK policy.

climate change levy: a tax on the use of fossil fuels by businesses and public sector organisations. The objective is to reduce emissions of greenhouse gases that are thought to be causing global warming. Organisations are being given an incentive to economise in their use of electricity, gas, petrol and coal. This is in line with international commitments. There is a discount scheme which can save organisations up to 80% of the levy if they have met energy or carbon saving targets.

closed economy: one which does not trade with the rest of the world. The idea of a closed economy is used in economic theory simply so that the effects of certain changes on the macro-economy can be studied in isolation. In contrast, an *open economy* is one in which trade is important. However, some economies are more open than others. Larger countries such as the US tend to be less open because they can be relatively self-sufficient.

closed shop: the requirement that all employees in a particular workplace belong to a specific trade union. Enforcing this is illegal under the Employment Act of 1988, which reduced union bargaining power considerably. Where it does occur, which must be with the consent of both employer and workforce, it gives the union some monopoly bargaining power. See *Employment Acts*.

clusters: groups of competing producers who locate in the same area. For example, there are several prestigious restaurants in the small Shropshire town of Ludlow. They attract large numbers of customers from outside the surrounding area because of their reputation. High technology clusters also develop in specific locations such as Cambridge. Sometimes but not always, clusters develop where there are *external economies of scale*.

coalition: a group of individuals, firms, pressure groups or political parties which each have their own objectives but co-operate in order to achieve shared goals. Coalitions can be unstable; individual coalition members may over time perceive advantages in seeking new allies or simply returning to solo operation.

cobweb theorem: a theory which analyses the changes which occur in markets over time when there are time lags between the decision to produce and the arrival of the output in the marketplace. For example, farmers may decide to produce less lamb because the price is currently low (point A on the diagram). If they all make the same decision, there will in time be much less lamb on the market (B) and this will cause the price to rise sharply (C). This in turn will make farmers want to expand their flocks (D). The situation is thus inherently unstable, although it may eventually settle down (E).

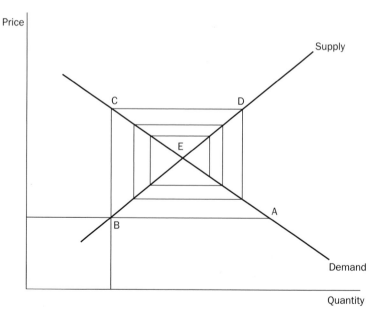

Cobweb theorem

Whether or not the resulting diagram makes a nice-looking spidery cobweb like the one above depends upon what is assumed about the price elasticity of the supply and demand curves. It is possible to show that the situation may be unstable and characterised by wide fluctuations in price over time. Sugar is one commodity with a tendency towards regular periods of unstable prices on world markets.

coefficient: the numbers in an equation which provide the structure. For example, in the equation $y = 2x + 3$, 2 is the coefficient of x and 3 is the constant term. Coefficients represent some of the assumptions about the relationships depicted in the equations which underlie an economic model.

collateral: when taking out a bank loan, it is usually necessary to provide some kind of security, known as collateral. For new businesses, this will often be the owner's own home. The bank will get the property in the event of the business failing and it being impossible to pay back the loan in any other way.

collateralised debt obligation (CDO): a type of structured *finance* consisting of a *bond* backed by a package of mortgages or other loans with variable rates of risk. Many of the *toxic assets* which became troublesome during the 2007–09 financial crisis were of this type. Buyers (i.e. lenders) did not have a clear view of the risks involved and these increased as house prices fell and mortgage defaults rose.

collective bargaining involves direct negotiations between the trade union representing the employees and the employers or the employers' organisation. Some employers welcome collective bargaining as it allows them to make a single agreement covering all employees. Others prefer to negotiate directly with individuals who may have less bargaining power than the union. It is hard to say how much difference trade union membership makes to rates of pay. Research studies have shown that pay could be about 5% higher in the private sector, where union membership is the norm. It could be rather higher than that in the public sector.

collusion occurs when firms act together in an informal way to avoid strong competition with each other. They may agree on a minimum price or share the market on a geographical basis. Firms will take great care to conceal their agreements from the *Competition Commission*, which has the power to investigate them. Collusion is most likely to occur where there is an *oligopoly*, with relatively few producers and *barriers to entry*. Because of the law, there may be *tacit collusion* which involves no overt discussion between competing firms.

collusive oligopoly: where producers in an oligopoly situation collude, they can collectively behave like a monopolist. By operating jointly, they can maximise profit in the same way that a *monopoly* would. This means that output will be reduced and prices will be higher than they would be in a competitive market. Collusive behaviour includes creating a *cartel* and *tacit collusion*.

colonialism: the process by which European countries took possession of large parts of the rest of the world during the 17th to the 19th centuries. Although few colonies remain as possessions of other countries, the aftermath of the colonial period has entailed a large number of very uneven trading relationships. Some developed countries still try to exclude imports from competitive producers in developing countries, just as they did in the colonial period. Although the EU has concessional trading arrangements with its ex-colonies, these are not nearly as generous as they could be.

command economy: an economic system in which decisions about how resources are to be allocated are made by the government or its agencies. The underlying philosophy was contained in the works of **Karl Marx**, as interpreted by the Communist parties of the countries concerned. The East European countries, Russia and the other component countries of the old USSR all abandoned communism in 1989 when it became apparent that the USSR government was no longer prepared to maintain the system by armed force. China, Cuba, Vietnam and North Korea still have parts of their economies operating under a command system, although all are moving closer to a market system.

The major problem for command economies is that decisions are administrative in nature and not linked to levels of demand for the final product. All the command economies tended to concentrate on heavy industry at the expense of consumer goods production. Many products were of poor quality because producers had no incentive to improve them. So in the end the system failed to provide the rising standard of living experienced in the West. See also **centrally planned economy**.

commercial law means the system of laws with which all businesses must comply. The law requires them to pay their debts and honour contracts. This is important because it creates a level playing field for all business activity and removes some of the risks associated with buying, selling, borrowing and lending.

commercial policy means the set of measures which determine how trade takes place both within the country and internationally. It includes policies on import controls and export promotion.

Commission for Racial Equality: the government organisation which aims to reduce racial discrimination in the **labour** market. Unemployment statistics and earnings data show quite clearly that discrimination is still going on, even after differences in qualifications are allowed for. Members of ethnic minorities are paid less than their market rate or are simply passed over during the recruitment process.

commodity: literally, any good which can be bought and sold. However, the term is usually taken to mean raw material or semi-manufactured goods which are traded in bulk. Examples include tea, sugar, iron ore, wheat, wool and so on. These are widely traded on world markets. In London there are specific commodity markets which deal in these goods, sometimes in a speculative fashion by effectively betting on their future prices. The term commodity is usually used when the good in question is a **homogeneous product**, so that no one producer's output is distinguishable from another's. For example, one load of iron ore is much the same as another of the same grade, irrespective of which firm mined it.

Commodity markets have some particular features:

- Commodity prices can be very volatile. Most of them can be stored and demand and supply are not always in equilibrium. Demand for metal ores varies with the **economic cycle** and the supply of agricultural products depends on weather conditions. Markets may be slow to respond to changes. Time lags can delay producers' responses to changes in demand and make prices even more volatile.
- Many commodities have rather inelastic supply. Relatively small changes in demand and supply can lead to large changes in price. For example, when the demand for metal ores rises during a boom, little can be done in the short run to increase supply and the price may rise sharply, rationing existing supplies amongst the buyers prepared to pay the highest prices. Developing countries that are heavily reliant on one or a few commodity exports are vulnerable to the very unstable prices that they experience.

Copper prices fell 60% in late 2008 as recession took hold, creating a very difficult situation for Zambia and the Democratic Republic of Congo.

Rising demand leads to a sharp rise in price if supply is inelastic

commodity agreement: for some commodities which have experienced fluctuating prices, the exporting countries have in the past agreed on measures which might stabilise the world price. This may involve producers agreeing to restrict output, or to limit exports. Or a *buffer stock* may be created; this can be added to when prices are low, helping to prevent them from falling further. Stocks can be sold when the price rises, limiting the increase. The idea was to stabilise producer incomes. The most important example was the International Coffee Agreement. It is very hard to make commodity agreements work because it is so difficult to control the market effectively. Currently none are in operation.

commodity markets: the means by which commodities are bought and sold. In the past, commodity markets would be in a specific location, such as the London Metal Exchange. This is no longer necessary to the existence of a market, which consists of buyers and sellers who keep in touch with one another electronically. Provided the commodity is classified and graded in a way which minimises disputes over quality, the market may consist simply of a network of dealers.

Common Agricultural Policy (CAP) embodies all of the agricultural policies of the EU. The original objectives were to support and stabilise farm incomes and to provide food at a reasonable price. It was set up at a time when agriculture was declining in economic importance and many European farmers were operating on a small scale and rather inefficiently. Consequently farm incomes were low and were growing more slowly than average incomes.

Shortly before entry to the EU in 1973, the UK adopted similar policies to the CAP. The basic framework involves:
- guaranteed prices for farm products and an arrangement by which farmers can sell their output at that price
- a variable levy on imported foods, which brings their prices up to the EU level
- export subsidies for surpluses
- grants to encourage efficient operation
- a set-aside scheme designed to prevent overproduction, by which farmers are paid to leave a part of their land fallow.

41

EU prices have mostly been above the level of world prices. Keeping the prices high, and not allowing competition from imports, gave farmers an incentive to increase output. The increase has made the EU including the UK largely self-sufficient in food but it has also led to the accumulation of surpluses. Subsidies were used to enable the CAP authorities to sell the surpluses on world markets. These cheap food exports have caused some disruption on world markets and are very unpopular with major food exporters such as the US and Australia. They have at times depressed world prices for some products. They may also have depressed food prices in Africa and so reduced local production. The diagram below shows how high prices lead to excess supply.

Since 1992 the CAP has been much reformed and the guaranteed prices are now considerably lower than they were. This policy was aimed partly at reducing the huge cost of the CAP. At various times the CAP has absorbed between one half and two thirds of the EU budget. There are increased grants available to farmers to help compensate for the lower guaranteed prices. Many of these address environmental objectives.

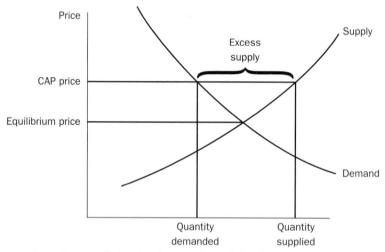

If prices are above the equilibrium level, a surplus will develop

The EU has come under heavy pressure to reduce **protection** of agriculture in **WTO** negotiations (especially the **Doha Round**). Meantime, EU farmers have become very much more efficient. New technologies have had a big impact on farming methods and levels of output.

Recent fluctuations in food prices suggest that there may be some tendency for world food prices to rise as incomes rise. Shortages may develop when real incomes are rising steadily. This will have some impact on farm incomes.

common external tariff: the import duties which are set by the European Union to cover certain imported goods for all member countries. The common external tariff favours producers within the EU and discriminates against producers outside the EU. In recent years the **tariffs** on many manufactured products have been reduced as a result of international trade negotiations under the auspices of the World Trade Organization. The common external tariff remains an important element in EU trade policy.

common market: a commonly used term meaning an area within which there is free trade and free movement of people and capital.

commons: resources which can be used freely by anyone. No one has property rights over these resources. The simplest examples are common grazing land and sea fishing. The resources have no price so everyone has an incentive to make as much use of the commons as is profitable for them. If the resources are abundant this causes no problems but if they become scarce, e.g. through overfishing, the resources are destroyed. Some way has to be found to assign property rights, e.g. through quotas or charges. 'The tragedy of the commons' refers to the dangers of overuse.

communism: the political system which underpins *centrally planned economies*. Until 1989 communist governments maintained power across Eastern Europe, Russia and the Central Asian republics. China, Vietnam, North Korea and Cuba remain communist inspired though with varying degrees of liberalisation in their economic organisation. Communist countries are characterised by the repression of political opposition, limitations on human rights and a considerable degree of economic control on the part of the government, even where some decisions are market determined.

Communist ideology was inspired by the work of *Karl Marx*. It was originally intended to improve the standard of living of ordinary people by restricting the power of private sector businesses.

company: the basic organisational structure for a firm. The company is legally separate from the people who own or run it and can own assets and enter into contracts. The formation of companies is controlled by law. An important objective of company law is to encourage entrepreneurs to take risks in ways which are likely to be productive. The important element in this process is *limited liability (Ltd)*, which means that the owners of the business (i.e. the *shareholders*) cannot lose more than the money put into the business. Personal possessions cannot be seized in order to pay the firm's debts. This encourages a flow of finance for investment in productive capacity.

company taxation: the taxes levied on firms' profits. The main tax is *corporation tax*. However, companies may be liable for other taxes such as *capital gains tax (CGT)*.

comparability: a yardstick for determining wage levels in negotiations between employers and trade unions. Unions may use wage rates in other comparable occupations as part of their argument for a pay increase. There is economic logic in this as a comparable wage could be seen as the *opportunity cost* of continuing to work for the current employer.

comparative advantage: the economic theory which holds that countries can produce more if they trade with one another. This theory has been immensely influential. Although the theory is very much a simplification, the impact which international trade has had on economic growth in a number of countries is very striking. The theory does help to explain the connection.

The theory of comparative advantage was first set out by David Ricardo in his book *The Principles of Political Economy*, published in 1817. He argued that all countries would be able to increase output if they specialised and traded with each other. This would hold even if one country was more efficient at producing everything than the other, i.e. it had an *absolute advantage*. Specialisation works to increase output whenever the *opportunity costs* of particular products are different between countries. If one country is not the best at producing anything, it can still gain by specialising in the product it is least bad at producing.

It works like this. The theory assumes that there are two countries and two products. Think of a country like the US, producing computers and wine. It is highly efficient at producing both. Still, it trades with Chile, which also produces computers and wine, but is less efficient at producing both. It will still pay to specialise because Chile's comparative disadvantage is less in wine.

Think of each country having 1000 workers. Before trade, half produce computers and half produce wine. The table shows how much each can produce.

	Output of computers	Output of wine (cases)
US	100	250
Chile	20	200
Total output	120	450

For Chile it takes 25 people to produce a computer. These 25 people could produce 10 cases of wine. So the opportunity cost of a computer is 10 cases of wine. Similarly, it takes 2.5 people to produce a case of wine and these people (i.e. this amount of *labour*) could produce one tenth of a computer, so this is the opportunity cost of the wine.

By contrast, in the US, it takes five people to produce a computer. Those five people could produce 2.5 cases of wine. The opportunity costs are shown in full in the table.

	Opportunity cost of computer	Opportunity cost of a case of wine
US	2.5 cases of wine	2/5 of a computer
Chile	10 cases of wine	1/10 of a computer

Now it is possible to see that the opportunity cost of wine in Chile is lower than it is in the US. It will pay Chile to specialise in the production of wine and give up producing computers. If each country concentrates on the product with the lowest opportunity cost, total output will increase. If the US moves people into computer production so that there are 800 altogether, it will be able to produce 160 computers, while still producing 100 cases of wine. Chile, specialising entirely in wine, will produce 400 cases of wine. The table shows the totals.

	Output of computers	Output of wine
US	160	100
Chile	0	400
Total output after specialisation	160	500

It is not possible to say which country will benefit most from the increase in output. In the real world, trade is greatly affected by all kinds of import restrictions and also by exchange rates. The theory of comparative advantage explains why trade and growth are linked and draws attention to the damage caused by trade restrictions. It does not make precise predictions possible.

compensation principle shows that society gains from a certain change if the gainers gain more than the losers lose. In other words, the gainers could compensate the losers and still be better off. It is actually rather difficult to use the compensation principle in practical situations, because it is often hard to quantify gains and losses in money terms.

competition: the process by which businesses strive against one another to capture a larger market. In price competition they may try undercutting each other's prices. This is known as competitive pricing. The impact of competition on prices is plain to see. For example, since BT's monopoly of telephone calls came to an end, the cost of phone calls has fallen sharply. This is partly because of new technologies but also because of competition.

Competition is immensely important in ensuring that consumers get the products they want at the lowest possible cost. Only through competition do firms have the incentive to minimise their costs and produce as efficiently as possible. So productive efficiency is sometimes improved through the action of competition.

Perfect competition defines a theoretical scenario in which it is impossible for any producer to gain any kind of control over the market. It has the following features:
- there are many sellers
- all firms make homogeneous products, which means that it is impossible to distinguish one firm's product from that of a competing firm
- firms can enter and exit the market freely – there are no *barriers to entry*
- everyone has full information about the market
- all producers use the same technology.

Imperfect competition may still be very strong competition but involves fewer sellers. Through non-price competition they may seek to improve product quality or increase demand through advertising and other marketing strategies. Three types of imperfect competition can be identified:
- *monopolistic competition* refers to a market with easy entry and many sellers, each of whom has a slightly differentiated product
- *oligopoly* refers to a market with a few large producers who compete but devise complex strategies for gaining ground in the marketplace
- *duopoly*, in which there are just two big producers.

With both oligopoly and duopoly there may be long periods when there is little sign of price competition, but plenty of evidence of non-price competition.

Competition Commission: the organisation responsible for investigating markets in the UK to ensure that they are kept in line with *competition policy*. It has two main functions:
- to investigate planned mergers and to determine whether they will lead to excessive monopoly power
- to act as a court of appeal for firms which have been found to be engaging in *anti-competitive activities* such as a *cartel*.

An early forerunner of the commission was set up in 1948 by the then Labour government. Successive acts of Parliament gradually increased its powers and strengthened its way of working. Increasingly, UK merger policy is influenced by EU directives.

The *Office of Fair Trading (OFT)* can refer a particular market situation or possible merger to the Competition Commission. Any merger which is likely to lead to a 25% or greater share of the market will be investigated by the Commission.

The Commission itself cannot take legal action; it can only advise the **Office of Fair Trading (OFT)** that action is necessary. As the OFT has got stricter with the companies it investigates, it seems likely that the Competition Commission will deal with more appeals from aggrieved businesses which are finding that the legislation has a serious effect on their activities. In general, any abuse of a dominant position in the market will come under scrutiny.

competition policy: monopolies are generally considered to be against the interests of consumers and the public and governments legislate to restrict them. In the UK, the **Office of Fair Trading (OFT)** has the job of policing monopolies, supported by the **Competition Commission**. Any merger which creates a market share of 25% or more is likely to be referred by the OFT to the Competition Commission, which will investigate whether the merger is thought to be in the public interest. The introduction of prison sentences for infringements of competition law (in the Enterprise Act of 2002) has greatly increased the impact of the Competition Commission and the OFT.

Increasingly the power of the EU has come into play in this area. EU treaties govern many aspects of competition policy, including:
- the development of monopolies
- restrictive practices, including market sharing agreements and any other restriction on supply.

Monopoly theory shows that a firm with market power may restrict output and raise prices. This can be shown to reduce consumers' real incomes. Firms which use their market power may require an unnecessarily large quantity of real resources to produce their output, which is quite simply wasteful and inefficient. Hence the perceived need to control market power in the interests of the consumer.

It took the EU competition authorities many years to nail Microsoft on the grounds that it had withheld the information needed by competing networking software to interact fully with Windows desktops and servers. This was seen as a restrictive practice. In 2004, the courts finally compelled Microsoft to release the necessary information and fined it a record £381 million. Microsoft paid the fine quickly but accused the EU of infringing intellectual property rights and acting in a way that would deter future innovation.

competitive advantage describes the quality needed by a business which can flourish when there are many other businesses with competing products. It may be that the business has lower costs and prices, better quality or design skills or it may enjoy superior marketing skills. Investment in new technologies may sometimes yield a competitive advantage. In general, competitive advantage usually rests on the extent to which the business emphasises innovation, the way it exploits relationships with other businesses and its reputation with customers.

competitive behaviour involves striving to sell the product without collaboration of any kind with other firms. It may include price competition or non-price competition, which means competing on quality, design, special promotions or after-sales service.

competitive devaluation involves governments trying to devalue their currencies so as to achieve a price advantage for their exports. It was seen in the 1930s when many countries tried to devalue to counter the effects of depression. If all trading partners do the same, the only effect is to destabilise all their economies. It is much less likely to occur if freely *floating exchange rates* are the norm. However, governments may well try to manipulate their exchange rates during a recession. In early 2009, the US Secretary of the Treasury accused the Chinese government of manipulating its exchange rate in order to retain a competitive advantage. The Chinese expressed outrage but they and many other countries may well feel great temptation to do this when export markets shrink worldwide. This is an example of *beggar my neighbour policies*.

competitive markets are those markets where a number of firms compete strongly with one another. In these markets prices are likely to be kept close to the minimum *average cost*; they will therefore tend to be productively efficient. Alternatively, there may be little variation in prices but strong *non-price competition*.

competitiveness: the degree to which a firm succeeds in selling its product when there is competition in the marketplace. Its competitiveness may rest on a price advantage, which may reflect lower costs than those of competitors, or a willingness to accept lower profits. Alternatively, competitiveness may rest on an advantage in design, quality, reliability or customer service or some other important product feature, all aspects of *non-price competition*. Either way, it is likely to be related to consumers' perceived value for money.

International competitiveness is important to economies and to governments because it enables both domestic producers and exporters to expand, leading ultimately to economic growth. It is usually associated with strong *productivity* growth or a commitment to innovation. It can be measured by examining *unit costs* in comparison with those of other economies. Without competitiveness, both domestic producers and exporters face strong competition from foreign producers. Imports will rise and exports fall, leading generally to falling aggregate demand and depressed trading conditions.

competitive tendering occurs when several firms bid for the opportunity to provide a particular service. It has been used by local authorities in the UK in order to increase efficiency through competition. It provides an incentive to the competing firms and can mean that the quality of the service improves. It can also mean that wage rates and employment conditions deteriorate if there is *labour* available at a low wage.

complementary goods are consumed together so that a change in demand for one will lead to a change in demand for the other (see diagram overleaf). A rise in petrol prices could lead to a fall in demand for cars, particularly large ones. *Cross-price elasticity* is used to measure the closeness of the relationship between complementary goods.

In practice, price and quantity changes for complementary goods may sometimes be quite small. However, economic theory allows us to decide the direction of change, even when the overall effect is rather small.

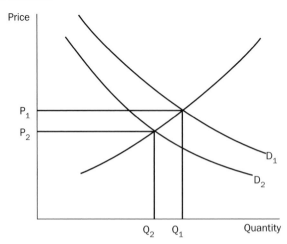

Complementary goods

complex monopoly means a situation in which a small number of oligopoly producers are not really competing effectively although there is no **collusion** or **cartel**. Often, they will all be charging very similar prices. This could be a result of **tacit collusion**. Early in 2001, the **Competition Commission** announced its findings that the big four banks, HSBC, Lloyds TSB, Barclays and the Royal Bank of Scotland, were operating a complex monopoly in services to small businesses. Between them they had 89% of all small business current accounts. It had been suggested that the banks were making 'excess profits' out of this side of their business by abusing their dominant position. All of them were thought to be charging more than they needed to cover all of their costs.

compliance costs are costs associated with legal requirements. Products which are subject to tight regulations, such as electrical goods, will have compliance costs. Some compliance costs apply to all firms, e.g. health and safety regulations.

components are inputs to the production process which have already undergone a manufacturing process. They can be made in the same factory but more often nowadays they will be bought from a specialist supplier. Car batteries and computer chips are components – on their own they have little value, but combined with other components they become a valuable final product.

Many manufacturers support large numbers of component suppliers, which depend on them for their markets.

composite demand applies to products which are used for more than one purpose. An increase in demand for quarried stone for building purposes could increase the price and have an impact on the availability of stone for road building. Maize can be a food or a biofuel crop. Increasing plantings for biofuel have led to an increase in the price of animal feeds based on maize and has contributed to rising food prices.

compound interest: over time, if interest is paid on the sum outstanding plus previously paid interest which has been reinvested, the value of the original sum can be greatly enhanced. This is important for contributors to pension funds, who will not normally take out the interest they earn until they retire.

computer-aided design (CAD) involves programs which allow the designer to visualise the design in many different ways. It thus speeds up the design process and can reduce costs or improve the product.

computer-aided manufacture (CAM) means that manufacturing processes are computer controlled. This can reduce costs of production, through improved stock control, or save *labour*, e.g. with the use of robots.

computerised trading: the use of computers in the marketplace, for example to track share prices. Computers can be programmed to sell shares automatically if their price falls by a certain amount.

concentration means the extent to which a particular market is dominated by a few firms. A high degree of concentration implies that there are relatively few firms in the market and conditions are similar to *oligopoly*. A low level of concentration implies that there are many sellers, with a market system such as monopolistic competition or near-perfect competition.

concentration ratio expresses the percentage of the market accounted for by a given number of firms, for example, by five firms. Concentration ratios are much higher in some industries than others.

Concentration ratios in selected industries, 2004

Industry	% of total output from 5 largest firms
Agricultural machinery	55
Confectionery	80
Dairy products	36
Pharmaceuticals	55
Sugar	100

Source: ONS

conciliation occurs when a person or a body intervenes to try to get both parties in a dispute to agree to an appropriate compromise. Conciliation can be important in the resolution of industrial disputes between unions and management. ACAS, the Advisory, Conciliation and Arbitration Service, exists to provide conciliation services for such situations.

conditionality refers to the practice of the IMF of offering loans on condition that the government complies with various requirements as to its economic policies.

conduct refers to the behaviour of firms in relation to their competitors. A study of the conduct of some bus companies during the period immediately following deregulation would have revealed some 'dirty tricks' such as running a very frequent, cheap service for just long enough to drive a competitor out of business. More often, conduct will be anti-competitive in a much more subtle way.

Confederation of British Industry (CBI): the UK's foremost employers' association, which acts as a mouthpiece for businesses generally. It represents their interests to the government when necessary. It is also a useful source of data.

conflicting objectives: governments often face a situation in which they can only achieve one of their policy objectives at the expense of another. The most obvious example is the short-term *trade-off* between inflation and unemployment. There were many occasions during the 1970s, 1980s and early 1990s when it would have been possible to reduce unemployment by increasing **aggregate demand** in the economy, but the consequence would have been increasing inflation due to **excess demand** in the economy. This looked like becoming a problem again in 2007, until the **credit crunch** happened.

congestion charges involve the payment of a fee on bringing a vehicle into the area where they apply. It acts as an incentive to avoid unnecessary journeys, so reducing traffic congestion. The London congestion charge, introduced in 2003, is generally regarded as having successfully reduced congestion. However, the extension to west London is being rescinded by the new mayor of London, Boris Johnson. The people of Manchester voted against a scheme that would have involved charges for using city centre roads during peak periods. It appears that many people would rather sit in traffic jams than pay for a faster journey.

conglomerate: a firm which includes many unrelated businesses. It used to be thought that a firm which had strong management skills could apply these to any type of business. So taking over a wide variety of potentially successful firms and improving their management made some sense. However, conglomerates have been less successful in recent years and some have been broken up by selling off components.

conservation concerns the way in which depletable resources are used. When production involves the use of real resources which cannot be replaced, there will be a case for conserving those resources in such a way that they do not become excessively scarce too quickly. In this way conservation measures may apply to petrol, on which taxes have been raised so as to discourage consumption. Alternatively conservation may apply to a resource which is damaged by consumption; when new roads are built, countryside which could have been conserved will be destroyed.

consortium: a group of organisations which undertake to carry out a project in collaboration. For example, large construction projects such as the Channel Tunnel have been built by consortia.

conspicuous consumption: the process of buying goods and services not for their actual usefulness but in order to impress other people. Normally economists assume that people make independent choices about the products they buy, basing their decisions on their own personal preferences. With conspicuous consumption the decision will be based on what products are most likely to impress others.

constant prices are used when it is important to be able to measure a certain variable in a way that avoids distortion by inflation. For example, real income is measured in constant prices. This term is less used now; the ONS, which publishes much of the data on national accounts, uses **chained volume measures**, based on prices in a specific reference year.

constant returns to scale: when output can be increased in such a way that exactly the same quantities of inputs are required for each unit of output, there are said to be constant returns to scale. This situation contrasts with increasing returns to scale, which means that output increases with proportionately fewer inputs. This would correspond roughly to reaping economies of scale. Similarly, decreasing returns to scale might be associated with diseconomies of scale.

constraint refers to the way in which a firm or the economy may be prevented from expanding. An obvious constraint which may affect either is a shortage of skilled **labour**. Legal constraints, in the shape of various employment laws, may affect firms. Governments are usually constrained by a wide range of factors, including the need to retain some popularity. *Supply* constraints are those which hinder the growth of output and can reflect any kind of shortage of resources.

consumer: a buyer of goods and services for their own use or for others. In economics, consumers are sometimes perceived as individuals or they may be seen as households, in which many purchasing decisions are collective. Most of us do consume more than just the products we buy for ourselves.

The consumer is an important player in the market because a decision to buy creates a potentially profitable situation for the supplier. There is then an incentive to ensure that the products desired are made available at a price which generates some profit. Equally, decisions not to buy may end in a producer going out of business or cutting back production. This is the basis of *consumer sovereignty*.

consumer confidence: decisions to buy may be curtailed if consumers are expecting hard times ahead and prefer to save for the time being. Expectations of rising unemployment or an imminent fall in income will usually depress consumer confidence, as in 2008. Similarly, a high level of consumer confidence will usually lead to buoyant sales and a high level of consumption spending. This may be financed by rising consumer credit, i.e. borrowing, as in 2007.

consumer durables are goods which provide a continuous flow of services over an extended period of time. For example, a washing machine, a car or a TV can be used over a period of 10 years or more. This means that the demand for them is more variable than it is for, say, food items. If incomes are stagnant or falling, the purchase of new durable goods can be postponed. The existing ones can be repaired or made to last longer. Demand for durables can fluctuate with the *economic cycle*. During the optimistic period of a boom people may take advantage of their rising incomes and replace their durable goods and vice versa. Demand for durables may also be affected by changes in interest rates because such purchases are often financed by borrowing.

consumer expenditure is the sum total of all spending by consumers in the whole economy over a period of time. It is a component of *aggregate demand*. The level of consumer expenditure and its likely future growth are sometimes important variables for a business which is considering whether to expand.

consumer goods are the tangible products bought by consumers for imminent use. They contrast with investment or intermediate goods which are bought by firms as inputs for the production process.

consumer preferences: the pattern of personal likes and dislikes that determine decisions to buy. Consumer preferences change over time, creating a changing market to which firms must respond. Of course, firms may try to influence consumer preferences by advertising and other means of promotion.

consumer price index (CPI) measures changes in the prices of consumer goods and services and is used for macro-economic policy purposes. It is used as the basis for the *inflation target*. It is the appropriate measure to use for international comparisons because it is standardised for that purpose. However, the retail price index is still the official measure of the UK cost of living and is used as the basis for adjusting pensions and other benefits and index-linked government bonds. Because of differences in the way the two indices are constructed, they are often not the same.

consumer protection: a set of laws designed to prevent firms from doing things which are not in the best interests of consumers. Health and safety standards and labelling requirements are obvious consumer protection measures, as are many of the requirements of **competition policy**. Some aspects of consumer protection are resented by some firms because they raise costs.

consumer sovereignty is the name for the process by which consumer demand determines the **allocation of resources**. An increase in demand will tend to make it more profitable to produce the item in question. This encourages firms to produce more. Similarly, if demand falls, losses may be made and these create an incentive for producers to move resources into some other line of production. In this way the **profit-signalling mechanism** transmits the information given by consumer demand to producers so that the allocation of resources is kept in line with the pattern of demand. This theory underlies the competitive market model upon which much of micro-economics is based.

In practice, **market imperfections** can greatly reduce consumer sovereignty. Market power and advertising can push consumers into choices that for them are less than optimal. (See also **supernormal profit** and **invisible hand**.)

consumer surplus: a consumer good will be valued more highly by some consumers than by others, yet they will all pay the same price for it. Some consumers would be willing to pay a price higher than the actual market price. The term consumer surplus refers to the value of the extra satisfaction which these consumers get from the item, over and above what they have had to pay for it. The consumer surplus is shown on a supply and demand diagram by the triangle enclosed by the demand curve and the price line. The demand curve shows how consumers value the product and all those who are prepared to pay a higher price get some extra satisfaction.

Put another way, consumers demand a quantity of the product such that the **marginal social benefit** they get from it is at least equal to the price. If it is worth less than the price, then clearly they won't buy it. But for the many consumers who would still buy the product at a higher price, the marginal social benefit of the product is actually greater than the price, by the amount of the consumer surplus. Many consumers are getting the product for less than they would be prepared to pay.

Consumer surplus is maximised at the equilibrium price. If either the supply or the demand curve shift in either direction, consumer surplus will change too.

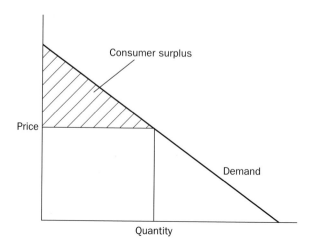

consumption means the level of all spending on consumer goods and services in the economy as a whole. It is an important component of **aggregate demand**. (See also **consumer expenditure**.) Consumption levels are related to incomes and to expectations.

consumption bundle: a collection of consumer goods which a consumer might choose to purchase.

consumption function: the relationship between income and consumption is known as the consumption function. The proportion of income consumed can be measured in two ways, using the **average propensity to consume** or the **marginal propensity to consume (MPC)**.

contestability: the extent to which the market is contestable. This means whether it is easy or not for a competing firm to enter the market and operate successfully. Contestable markets are likely to be more competitive.

contestable markets: it may be comparatively easy for newcomers to the industry to break into a contestable market. This means that existing businesses, already in the field, face a constant threat of increasing competition. We might expect that prices will be generally lower in contestable markets, merely because of the possibility of competition. If they announce very large profits, firms already in the industry may be advertising the possibility of large profits for others and this may encourage **new entrants**.

So even if there are a very few firms in the market, the threat of competition from new entrants may keep prices low. No-frills airlines provide an example of a contestable market. In the reverse case, where there are **barriers to entry**, existing businesses are protected from competition. Where economies of scale are a substantial barrier to entry, only very large firms may be able to produce efficiently. Entry costs will be high, the risks for a new competitor may be great and the market will hardly be contestable at all.

Very few markets are perfectly contestable because there are almost always some **sunk costs** which give an existing producer at least a small advantage. These sometimes relate to advertising and brand familiarity. Or they may be fixed costs associated with plant and machinery that has little or no alternative use. This means that the cost of exit will be high. An incumbent firm faced with competition from a new entrant, which has to cover all the costs of new investments in plant and machinery, could cut prices in order to delay the loss of its market share.

contract: a legal agreement between two parties which defines the relationship in terms of what is expected on both sides. It will detail the actions to be taken and the payments to be made. An employment contract is between the employer and the employee and states the work to be done, the payment to be made and the conditions of employment which the employer must provide.

Contracts are of great importance for the efficient working of a market economy. They:
- allow firms to be reasonably confident that they will be paid for work completed or orders fulfilled
- give individuals some assurance that they will not be cheated
- encourage lending and borrowing which provides finance for investment.

The absence of a system of commercial law which governs the enforcement of contracts makes business transactions risky and therefore raises the cost of doing any kind of business. This can severely hamper the process of economic development in poorer developing countries and in countries in transition from central planning to a market system.

contracting out means buying in inputs from an independent supplier rather than sourcing all inputs from inside the organisation. It may apply in the private or the public sector. In the private sector it may involve buying **components** or services from another firm. This might include canteen, cleaning or accounting services, for example. This is now often known as **outsourcing**.

In the public sector, local authorities have contracted out services such as refuse collection or street cleaning. The objectives of this are:
- to promote greater efficiency by getting access to new management strategies
- to save money by encouraging competition between potential suppliers.

Sometimes contracting out has been very unpopular because it can mean that the people who actually do the work may be paid less if the **labour** is available at the lower wage.

contraction: the process by which the economy actually becomes smaller when output falls. It starts with a fall in **aggregate demand**. Sales fall and firms find they have rising stocks. They cut back their output and quite soon make some employees redundant. This leads to a reduction in real incomes which may lead to a further fall in aggregate demand. It is associated with **recession** or depression.

contractionary policy is used when the economy appears to be growing unsustainably fast or when **inflation** is becoming a problem. The policies are of two kinds:
- **monetary policy**, which would require high interest rates, is decided by the **Bank of England**
- **fiscal policy**, in the form of either tax increases or government expenditure cuts, or both, is decided by the Treasury.

In both cases, the objective is to reduce the rate of growth of aggregate demand so that inflationary pressures are reduced. Reducing demand will slow down firms' attempts to recruit more **labour**, thus reducing the demand for scarce skills and making it harder for people to negotiate higher pay.

convergence: refers to the process of bringing the **European Union (EU)**'s economies and currencies into line with each other. This was an essential prerequisite for **Economic and Monetary Union (EMU)** and the single currency. Unless all the member countries have similar levels of economic activity, rates of inflation and interest rates, the euro could cause major economic upheavals. The main focus for convergence is upon public sector borrowing and inflation rates. (See also **convergence criteria**.)

convergence criteria: the specific conditions for entry into the EMU and adoption of the euro which must be met by all participants. These are:
- consumer price inflation not higher than 1.5% above that of the three best performing countries in the Union
- interest rates on long-term government bonds not more that 2% higher than those in the same three member states
- the government deficit to be at or below 3% of GDP

- total government debt to be at or below 60% of GDP
- the exchange rate to have been fairly stable for the past two years.

These criteria have been fudged somewhat for some countries but progress has been made towards them.

convertible currency: a currency which can be freely converted into other currencies. The advantage of a convertible currency is that it encourages *foreign direct investment (FDI)* and leads to the integration of capital markets. The disadvantage of convertibility is that it can mean that there are sudden runs on the currency which lead to instability and a sharp drop in its value. This happened to Malaysia during the *Asian financial crisis* in 1998. The government responded by suspending convertibility. In the same situation most other countries did not.

co-operative: a business owned by its employees or its customers. Retail co-operatives, like the Co-op, are owned by the customers. Some co-operatives are owned by their employees, all of whom will have some say in major decisions. Sometimes co-operative selling organisations are set up by farmers to distribute their products.

Copenhagen criteria: in 1993 the EU set out three conditions for countries wishing to join. These are:
- stability and democracy, with protection for the rights of minorities
- a market economy capable of competing within the EU
- the capability to meet all the requirements of membership including a functioning competition policy, compliance with harmonisation regulations and, eventually, joining the EMU.

copyright protects the work of authors, composers and artists and includes film and television. It is illegal to copy work which is copyright without the permission of the originator or the owner of the copyright. Copyrights confer *intellectual property* rights. Without these, there would be little incentive to produce original work.

There are some open issues relating to music which is downloaded over the Internet and also to so-called pirate copies of CDs and DVDs. Making a copy of any commercially produced musical recording, without the permission of the copyright owner, is illegal and can be regarded as stealing intellectual property rights.

core inflation: a measure of inflation that excludes items that are likely to distort the data for the underlying rate of inflation. *Consumer price index (CPI)* is the preferred measure in the UK.

corporate bonds are loans to companies which carry a fixed rate of interest and have a fixed maturity value. They may be held by individuals, by banks or other financial intermediaries. They may be traded on the *Stock Exchange*, should the holder require *liquidity*. The price at which they are traded will vary according to interest rates and the comparative profitability of other investments.

corporate governance refers to the way in which decisions are taken within a *public limited company*. It has become an issue because there has been some evidence of company directors acting in their own best interests rather than the interests of *shareholders* or of the wider community. In theory, shareholders can vote to remove directors at the *annual general meeting (AGM)* but in practice this almost never happens. Shareholder power may be limited to the influence of the big institutional shareholders such as the pension funds but they do not always act in the public interest if the share price and dividends are not at risk.

corporate objectives: see *business objectives*.

corporate responsibility reflects the extent to which a firm accepts obligations to any group of people other than the *shareholders* or owners of the business. A firm which takes corporate responsibility seriously will recognise the rights of employees, customers, suppliers and the community at large. This will mean taking into account the environmental and ethical impact of the firm's activities. Some businesses now produce an environmental report in addition to the conventional *annual report and accounts*; for example, Sainsbury's does this. Others have explicit ethical policies which change the nature of their *business objectives*.

corporate saving occurs when firms retain some of their profits, keeping them in reserve for the future. Often they will use their savings to replace capital equipment, or expand the business, in the future.

corporation: a limited company. Most often the term is used for a *public limited company*.

corporation tax is the tax paid on profits. Every business is assessed and required to pay a percentage of its profit after all costs have been deducted. The rate is set each year in the Budget; the level is currently 28%. Smaller firms pay 21%, rising to 22% in 2010. These rates are subject to change in the *Budget*.

correlation measures the extent to which two variables move together. It might be found that changes in spending on luxury cruises are closely related to changes in income, while changes in interest rates are related, but less closely, to the level of consumer spending generally.

corruption: using bribes to influence politicians or officials to secure a favourable decision. Corruption has a very bad effect on the *allocation of resources* because decisions are made on the basis of the bribe rather than the well-being of the community concerned or the market forces which reflect consumer preferences. It undermines the effectiveness of democratic systems which are designed to reflect the wishes of the electorate. It greatly reduces the efficiency with which market economies work.

Corruption probably takes place in all economies, although the US government has very strict laws against it. The problems it causes loom largest in developing economies and those making the transition from a centrally planned to a market economy. It is almost certainly a major causal factor in the unequal distribution of incomes which often persist in these countries. Powerful businesses and individuals use it to ensure that they are not too exposed to the rigours of competition. This often means that they can go on charging high prices which bring great benefit to themselves.

cost: the value of all the inputs to the production process. These will include the factors of production, land, *labour* and capital, raw material inputs, energy, transport and component inputs. (See also *average cost*, *marginal cost*, *total cost*, *fixed cost* and *variable cost*.) Costs of production are an important element in any *supply schedule*.

cost–benefit analysis examines all the costs of a particular project or decision, be they *external costs* or *internal costs*. The internal costs are private costs which are experienced by the producer, sometimes called the financial costs. For example, the chemical plant will count the financial cost to itself of all the inputs to the production process. In addition to these costs, there will be external costs which are paid by a third party who is not a producer or a consumer. These usually reflect the pollution created in the neighbourhood of the plant, which affects the people who live there. These are social costs and may be hard to quantify.

Including both private and social costs can give a better idea of the true cost to society of some projects. The Victoria Line in the London Underground, the Channel Tunnel and numerous motorway projects were subjected to cost–benefit analysis. The difficulty is that although some social costs and benefits can be quantified, others cannot. The benefits of faster moving traffic can be estimated for the people who will spend less time in traffic jams during working hours. The benefits of improved health through reduced pollution are more difficult to define, although treatment costs are quantifiable. This means that cost–benefit analysis has to be based partly on value judgements about the relative importance of different factors in the decision. However, looking at all costs and benefits does mean that decisions are not made solely on financial evidence.

Wherever private and social costs and benefits diverge, and social costs and benefits are hard to quantify, there must be careful consideration of the social priorities that might influence decisions relating to costly investment projects. Given the cost overruns that plagued the building of the Channel Tunnel, it is hard to imagine that decision takers would have decided in favour if they had known the true cost of the project in advance. But in South East England it is quite hard now to imagine life without it. Maybe the external benefits of increased economic development made it economically viable, despite the high cost.

cost curves relate the cost of the product to the quantity produced. (See also *average cost* and *marginal cost*.)

cost effectiveness means achieving a given objective in the cheapest possible way. This usually means that the cheapest solution must be checked to see that it is not causing unexpected disadvantages which are themselves costly.

cost of living: the cost of a selection of goods and services considered necessary to a normal life. This is measured by the *retail price index (RPI)*, which is based on price data for a wide range of products and retail outlets. The term 'cost of living' tends to be used rather vaguely because it is itself a very imprecise idea. The problem is that it varies from one household to another and specific price changes have a different impact in different types of household.

cost of production: see *cost*.

cost structure: the way in which costs of production are spread between different inputs. Some products will have high capital costs (e.g. electricity) while others will have high *labour* costs (e.g. medical care).

cost plus pricing means that the seller simply calculates costs and adds a mark-up for profit. This will work quite well for the seller, provided other firms are not able to compete with lower prices. It may or may not be the price which maximises profits.

The seller will have no incentive to control costs. However, even with a large contract, e.g. for military equipment using new technologies, it may be the best option for the buyer because costs will be very uncertain. Any fixed price would include a large allowance in case costs turned out to be higher than expected.

cost-push inflation is a general rise in prices caused by rising costs of production. It can occur if **commodity** prices are rising because these will be important inputs for a number of manufactured goods. Rising wages can contribute, as can rising property values. Another cause is a fall in the exchange rate, because this will make imports more expensive. Many products have imported inputs and the cost of these will rise. Cost inflation is just one element in the overall inflation process and demand factors are likely also to be present in an inflationary situation. **Expectations** of future price increases may affect cost inflation because they feed into employees' efforts to secure pay increases.

costs of growth: the negative aspects of the growth process, such as pollution and congestion and the depletion of resources generally. As negative **externalities** increase in number the benefits of **economic growth** are reduced.

council housing: housing for rent provided by local authorities on the basis of need. Rents are usually slightly below the market level and there are often waiting lists indicating **excess demand**. Priority is given to families which are homeless or living in overcrowded conditions. Those who cannot pay the rent may be given housing benefit. Once they have a council house, tenants are allowed to stay there indefinitely but will not usually be able to move to a council house in another local authority area. This may mean that they become **geographically immobile** and have difficulty in finding work close to their homes.

Council of Ministers: the group which takes the biggest decisions in the EU. There will be one Minister from each member state, chosen according to the type of decision to be made. For economic decisions the UK minister will usually be the Chancellor of the Exchequer or the Secretary of State for Business, Enterprise and Regulatory Reform.

council tax is a tax raised on the value of houses by local authorities. If it is assumed that larger houses are owned by people who are better off, it is broadly related to ability to pay. People on benefits are generally exempt. Council tax funds a part of local expenditure, the rest coming from central government.

counter-cyclical policy is used to try to reduce the severity of fluctuations in economic activity associated with the **economic cycle**. **Fiscal policy** and **monetary policy** can be used either to reduce or to increase **aggregate demand**. A good deal of careful judgement is required to ensure that the actions taken are timely and appropriate to the precise situation in the economy.

- Fiscal policy may be automatic or discretionary. **Automatic stabilisers** work without further decisions, by reducing tax payments during recession and increasing benefits paid to unemployed people. In addition, the Chancellor may choose to alter tax rates at the time of the Budget. A tax cut during a recession or an increase in government spending, financed by borrowing, may be appropriate. If the economy is booming and approaching an acceleration in inflation, tax increases and expenditure cuts might be sensible but may be difficult politically.
- Monetary policy can be implemented without political difficulty because it is in the hands of the **Monetary Policy Committee** of the Bank of England. If inflation is rising due to unsustainably fast growth and excess demand, the committee will raise interest rates at its monthly meeting. This will make spending financed by borrowing dearer. It is

likely to discourage investment and spending on consumer durables. However, it will work with rather a long time lag, perhaps up to two years. Similarly, low interest rates in a time of recession will make sense as they may encourage firms to invest and help to prevent losses leading to widespread business failures. Again, timing is critical because action too late may not help to stabilise the economy.

counter-inflation policy: if inflation is accelerating, the Bank of England may adopt contractionary monetary policies, by raising interest rates. This will have the effect of reducing *aggregate demand* and pressure on resources. (See also *monetary policy*.)

CPI: see *consumer price index (CPI)*.

credit enables firms and individuals to buy products immediately and pay for them later. In the case of firms, the credit is often provided by the supplier and is known as *trade credit*. This can be important for some firms because it enables them to pay for the goods when they have received some sales revenue. Alternatively, firms and individuals may borrow, using an overdraft or a loan to finance their purchases. This will involve a rate of interest which increases the amount which has to be paid.

credit creation: the process by which banks expand their lending by a multiple of any new deposits they receive. Not all their customers will want to withdraw their deposits at any one time. This allows the banks to keep just a percentage of their assets in the form of liquid *reserve assets* and to use the rest to make loans. As borrowers spend the money, it is deposited once more in the bank, allowing a further expansion of credit. This is the process that went too far, too fast in the period 2005–07 as banks made excessively generous loans for house purchase. This led to the *credit crunch* and the process of credit creation stalled as banks sought to avoid making any more risky loans.

credit crunch is the name given to the financial crisis that began in 2007. The main precipitating cause was the way in which banks in many countries were lending for house purchases on the basis of an expectation that house prices would rise steadily. Interest rates were low and people were borrowing more and more but the banks were not always checking their ability to repay. Unsustainably rapid increases in house prices resulted, especially in the USA and the UK, but also in many other countries, creating a *bubble*. As economic growth began to slow, first in the US and later worldwide, unemployment began to rise and the bubble burst, leading to rapid loss of confidence. It became clear that many of the assets (effectively, inter-bank loans) that had provided the underpinning finance for mortgages were much riskier than previously supposed. These were helpfully labelled *toxic assets*; they figure large in many banks' balance sheets. Governments responded by trying to help by lending to the banks but it was very difficult to make progress in restoring confidence. Banks became very reluctant to lend to firms or individuals and governments stepped in to provide more money for the banks and fiscal policies that might increase *aggregate demand* and reduce the impact of *recession*. (See also *counter-cyclical policy, credit rating, Financial Services Authority, monetary policy, recapitalisation of banks* and *recession*.)

The above is a much oversimplified story. Your course specifications call for you to be acquainted with events over the past 10–20 years so you do have to achieve some understanding of it. Advice: make a page of definitions that help you to analyse these events as they happen and build up a timeline which identifies important turning points. Try hard to understand but remember that the economy never stands still – this is what makes economics such an interesting subject.

credit rating means an assessment of the credit worthiness of a person, a business, a government bond or a bank asset (*security* or *derivative*). Its purpose is to inform lenders about the risks they are running, in terms of the likelihood of the borrower being unable to repay the loan. Credit ratings are based on:

- The promptness with which individuals have paid their debts in the past.
- A careful perusal of the accounts of the business concerned. In general, a good credit rating is likely to mean that interest rates charged will be lower.
- An assessment of the risk of a government's solvency: those with rather weak and fragile economies are likely to have to offer higher interest rates in order to make the bonds attractive to potential buyers.
- In the case of banks, an assessment from the *rating agencies* for each different type of loan. These loans may be described as bonds, securities or derivatives, depending on the nature of the contract involved.

Poorly researched credit ratings were a major factor in the development of the financial crisis in 2007–08.

creditors are those to whom the organisation owes money, perhaps through having purchased goods or services on credit so that payment is still outstanding.

cross-price elasticity of demand measures the responsiveness of demand for one good to a change in the price of another. The demand for a particular product will be affected by a change in the price of a substitute or a complement. For example, a significant increase in the price of petrol will lead to a decrease in demand for cars.

Cross-price elasticity is measured using the formula:

$$FORMULA: \quad \frac{\text{percentage change in quantity demanded of good X}}{\text{percentage change in price of good Y}}$$

Cross-price elasticity is significant when the relationship between the two products is a close one. Where two close *substitutes* are involved, an increase in the price of one will lead to a significant rise in the demand for the other. Competing *brands* may be in this position or competing foodstuffs, e.g. cauliflowers and leeks. Notice that the elasticity will be positive – both the numerator and denominator will rise.

With complements, cross-price elasticity will generally be negative. The cross-price elasticity of demand for cars with respect to the price of petrol involves an inverse relationship. If the price of petrol increases, demand for cars decreases. Of course, you can consider the different effects of petrol prices on larger and smaller cars, in which case you will get a more complex result.

cross-section data allow comparisons across different groups. For example, a cross-section of a number of countries could be compared by examining investment and growth rates in a single year. This compares with time series data, which might, for example, examine trends over a period of years in a single country.

cross-subsidy: if there is an unprofitable activity taking place within an organisation, the losses can be offset by a profitable activity elsewhere in the same organisation. This is called a cross-subsidy. When publishers bring out unsuccessful books the losses will be covered by the enormous profits made from bestsellers.

crowding out: the idea that an increase in government investment leads to a decrease in private investment. If the government borrows to finance investment, it is likely that it will have to pay higher interest rates than before. The increased demand for funds will mean higher interest rates generally and this may deter private borrowers. It makes any planned investment in the private sector somewhat less profitable than before.

culture: the general ethos of a particular business, which determines the ways in which people work together. Corporate culture can be important in influencing competitiveness and profitability because it affects managers' and employees' willingness to adopt new strategies when the market is changing.

currency: the notes and coins which are used as a medium of exchange in the country concerned.

currency appreciation occurs when the exchange rate rises and the purchasing power of the currency increases. This might reflect an increase in demand for the country's export products or a capital inflow. Either of these would increase demand for the currency and drive up the exchange rate. (See also *appreciation* and *capital movements*.)

currency crisis: if dealers on the foreign exchange market expect the value of a currency to fall, they may start selling large quantities of it. This may make it impossible for the central bank to buy enough of the currency to keep up its value, because its foreign exchange reserves are limited. This would be termed a currency crisis. (See also *fixed exchange rate*.)

currency stabilisation is attempted when there is a sense that fluctuating exchange rates are making life more difficult than it need be for people who have to take economic decisions. If the value of the currency fluctuates less, the future profitability of exports becomes more predictable. This can help potential exporters to make production decisions with more confidence. The *euro* is in part a response to the desire of some European businesses for a more stable exchange rate regime.

current account: see *balance of payments deficit/surplus on current account*. The term also refers to bank accounts kept mainly for the purpose of making transactions.

current account imbalances are deficits and surpluses resulting from significant differences between level of exports and level of imports. If they become very large they can destabilise the economy. The USA had very large deficits during the Bush presidency. These were covered in large part by loans from China, which has a very high savings rate and a policy of investing abroad by buying US government bonds (which helped to finance the US budget deficit). This eventually led to loss of confidence in the dollar and depreciation of the currency. These imbalances remained significant in the run-up to the financial crisis in 2007 and after. (See also *global imbalances*.)

current prices: a term used in relation to data which is expressed in the prices of the year concerned, i.e. not corrected for inflation. In contrast, *constant price* data gives values in real terms, using the prices of a base year. It is very important to know whether data are given in current or constant prices. In the presence of inflation, current price data, on GDP for example, could be very misleading.

customer service is often an element in the product, involving as it does the direct contact between producer and consumer. It could involve sales advice, *after-sales service* or simply a pleasant service. For some firms, it is an important aspect of competitiveness or of product differentiation.

customs duties: the taxes levied on imports as they are brought into the country, also known as *tariffs*.

customs union: a group of countries which agrees to trade freely within their borders and imposes a ***common external tariff*** on imports from outside the area. The European Union is a customs union. This may lead to ***trade creation*** and ***trade diversion***. Overall it will usually promote the growth of trade and specialisation, thus allowing member countries to become better off.

cyclical deficit: government deficits vary over the course of the economic cycle. In a ***boom***, tax receipts will rise with incomes and benefit payments will fall because relatively few people are unemployed. The reverse will happen in a recession.

cyclical instability: the fluctuations in GDP associated with the ***economic cycle***. A boom may be followed quite quickly by recession, during which expectations about the future become very gloomy. This instability is usually very detrimental to the long-term growth process. It reduces investment and incomes. ***Macro-economic policy*** is usually directed towards reducing cyclical instability by limiting unsustainable growth and stimulating recovery during recession.

cyclical unemployment occurs when ***aggregate demand*** in the economy is slowing and is not enough to buy the output which can be produced when all resources are fully employed (***full-capacity output***). In these circumstances, cyclical unemployment could be reduced if ***aggregate demand*** increased.

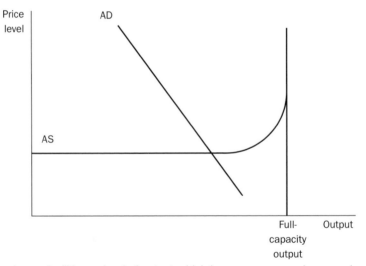

Aggregate demand will buy a level of output which leaves many people unemployed

Cyclical unemployment is sometimes lagged to the ***economic cycle***, perhaps by as much as a year. As demand falls, employers may postpone making people redundant as long as possible. Similarly, during the upturn, employers will wait to be sure that the increased demand is permanent before recruiting more staff.

Government policies to reduce cyclical unemployment could:
- reduce taxation and increase government expenditure
- try to reduce ***labour*** costs, for example by reducing the employer's National Insurance charges.

Governments have often in the past been unwilling to use counter-cyclical measures because of the perceived risk of higher aggregate demand causing excess demand and accelerating inflation. So cyclical unemployment persisted for a number of years, e.g. during much of the 1980s and during and after the recession of 1990–1992.

cyclically adjusted budget deficit: what the *budget deficit* would be if the economy were neither booming nor in recession. Normally, a budget deficit will increase during recession, because unemployment benefit payments rise and tax revenues fall. This process is automatic and occurs as employees are laid off. Similarly, in a boom, tax revenues rise and unemployment benefit payments fall, reducing the government's deficit or taking it into surplus. A modest cyclically adjusted deficit may be used to justify a much larger actual deficit during recession.

Do you need revision help and advice?

Go to pages 326–46 for a range of revision appendices that include plenty of exam advice and tips.

data: information with some basis in fact. Data can be used to support conclusions; the source must *always* be given. The information can be verbal or numerical. Great care must be taken in evaluating and selecting data. For example, is it the most suitable data for the purpose in hand? Was it collected in a reliable and impartial way?

database: a set of data which has been collected for a particular purpose. For example, Companies House keeps data on all businesses which have *limited liability (Ltd)*.

dawn raid: an unexpected sudden attempt to buy enough shares in a particular company to eventually obtain a controlling interest. The buyer has a chance to get hold of some of the shares cheaply before news of the raid pushes their price up. The term can also mean an unexpected visit from the tax authorities or others with a legal interest to examine the company's accounts or records.

DCF: see *discounted cash flow (DCF)*.

deadweight loss: the welfare loss to the consumer which occurs when an industry becomes a *monopoly*. The market power of the firms in the industry is such that they can push up prices and reduce the quantity supplied. This effectively reduces consumers' real incomes by diminishing the *consumer surplus* which they might have had. An example of deadweight loss would be where a drug company limits the supply of a new and effective drug for which it holds the patent. High prices could be charged but that would mean that some sufferers who could benefit from the drug will not be able to afford it (as with AIDS drugs in developing countries). Against this, there is always the possibility that a monopoly can rationalise production and achieve cost savings which will be at least partially passed on to consumers.

dear money: if interest rates are high, borrowing will be costly and the money borrowed may be said to be dear.

death duties: see *inheritance tax*.

death rate: the number of people dying per thousand of population. This is an important component of the rate of population increase, particularly in developing countries where life expectancy has increased dramatically.

debt: money owed by one individual or organisation to another. Debts are usually created with an agreement as to the interest payable and date of repayment. There may be a contract which can be enforced through the courts.

debt crisis: in general this could apply to any borrower unable to make interest payments or debt repayments on the due date. The term 'debt crisis' refers to the difficulties which some *developing economies* have had in servicing their debts to foreign banks, governments and international organisations. (See also *Debt Problem*.)

debt finance means using loans to pay for investments, rather than share capital. Most firms rely on a combination of debt and *equity* (share) finance. If there is heavy reliance on loan or debt finance and the business takes time to become profitable, interest payments may become a problem. This happened with the Channel Tunnel. Initially, finance came from share issues but as time went by there were cost overruns which were financed by borrowing from the banks. Eventually the company was unable to cover its interest payments out of current income and had to restructure its debts, giving the banks shares in exchange for their loans. This reduced the interest payable.

debt forgiveness means writing off all or part of an outstanding debt in recognition of the fact that the borrower will not actually be able make repayment in full. It is relevant to those *developing economies* which have become overburdened with debt.

debt management is needed when a firm or a government has borrowed from a range of sources and needs to make sure that there will always be funds available for interest and repayments. There must be forecasts of when more borrowing is needed; the cost of borrowing must be kept down and *maturity dates* on existing debt must be phased so that they are spread over an appropriate period.

Debt Problem: during the 1970s, many *developing economy* governments borrowed large sums from banks in the developed countries. When interest rates rose in the early 1980s, the borrower countries became unable to service the debt (i.e. pay the interest). The amounts of foreign currency they could generate by exporting were insufficient to cover their commitments, even after they had cut back their imports substantially. In time they were also unable to repay their debts. This became known as the Debt Problem.

Many countries had to negotiate *debt rescheduling* with the help of the IMF. Some banks wrote off part of the debt. Those most seriously affected included many countries in Africa south of the Sahara, as well as Mexico, Brazil and some other Latin American countries.

The movement Jubilee 2000, which became Jubilee Plus, a coalition of charities and aid agencies, pressed hard for the debt to be written off at the time of the millennium. They made a convincing case to developed country governments and progress was made. However, debt remains a problem for the heavily indebted poor countries (HIPCs). Targets have been written into the Millennium Development Goals, which are being worked on by the *United Nations*, the *World Bank* and the *IMF*. Thirty-four countries have been helped under these schemes and more are eligible for help.

debt ratio: the amount of a country's debt in relation to the level of its exports.

debt relief involves agreement by a lender to accept delayed interest payments or capital repayments. This will happen if the lender thinks that the borrower will eventually be able to pay but will have difficulties with agreed payments in the short run. Delayed payments may be considered preferable to *default*.

debt rescheduling may occur when a borrower (an individual, a firm or a government) with large loans cannot meet the repayments. The lenders can extend the term of the loans and postpone the repayment dates. They can also give an interest holiday, so that interest payments can be temporarily suspended to give time for the borrower to recover. On the international level, debt rescheduling means lengthening the periods over which governments can repay their debts, in order to reduce the problem. Rescheduling is often preferable to *default*.

debt service: the payment of interest on loans.

debt service ratio: the relationship between total interest payments and total export earnings. The ratio gives an indication as to whether a government can realistically cover interest payments out of export revenue, i.e. whether it has enough foreign exchange flowing in to cover the interest outflow.

debtors owe money whereas *creditors* are owed money. There is an age-related cycle of debt: young people are usually in debt for some time before they eventually pay off mortgages and other loans and become net creditors as a result of saving.

decentralised wage bargaining occurs when negotiations are between individual employers and their employees, rather than between an *employers' association* and a *trade union*, operating at a national level. Decentralised bargaining allows local variations in *labour* market conditions to be reflected in local wage rates. It may help to generate jobs in areas of high unemployment if locally agreed wage rates are lower than national rates.

decile: the boundary line between one tenth of a population and the next tenth. If the population is ranked according to income, the lowest decile marks the income level at which 10% of the population are poorer while 90% of the population are better off.

declining industry: an industry for the products of which demand is falling. There are several causes:

- a shift in *comparative advantage*, such that competing imports are becoming available at prices below those which the domestic industry can achieve (as happens with textile products in developed countries)
- *technical change* leading to the development of new products which are superior to the old one (as when air travel reduced demand for ocean liners).

The major declining industries in the UK have been coal, iron and steel, shipbuilding, textiles and footwear and, to some extent, vehicles. Unfortunately all of these have been localised industries so the effects of decline have been particularly hard on some communities.

decreasing cost industry: an industry in which expansion leads to a fall in average costs of production. This would occur if there were *economies of scale* to be reaped as output rose. The situation is sometimes described as increasing returns to scale.

default occurs when a borrower is unable to make interest payments or repay the loan itself. The lender may take steps to get the money through the courts. Alternatively, if court action may end in *liquidation*, the borrower may negotiate easier terms, allowing the borrower more time to pay.

deficit: occurs when expenditure is greater than income.

- A *budget deficit* means that the government is spending more than it receives in tax revenue and will need to borrow to cover the difference.
- A *balance of payments* deficit means that import costs are greater than export revenue on the current account. This is likely to be covered by a capital inflow or a change in the level of foreign exchange reserves held by the central bank.
- A deficit in the accounts of a charity or non-profit making organisation means that it has made a loss over the year: payments are greater than receipts.

deficit spending occurs if a government spends more than it receives in tax revenue. It will then have to borrow to make up the difference.

deflation is a term which is used in two different ways. It can be:

- A fall in the general price level. This is different from a fall in prices in a particular sector of industry (e.g. telecommunications) or a fall in the rate of *inflation* (which means that prices are rising more slowly than before). Up to and including the 1930s, prices generally fell from time to time and were as likely to fall as to rise.
- A period of reduced economic activity, when *aggregate demand* is falling, output and employment are cut and incomes fall. These, the conditions of a *slump*, can be accompanied by falling prices.

Deflation threatened a number of economies in 2009 as output and employment fell.

deflationary gap: this term is now used infrequently. See *output gap*.

deflationary policies or *contractionary policies* are those which are designed to reduce demand by the use of *fiscal* or *monetary policies*. This might occur when inflation is a problem.

deindustrialisation refers to the way in which the UK economy has tended to shift resources out of the manufacturing sector and into the service sector. The causes of deindustrialisation have been identified as:

- Loss of competitiveness in manufacturing. This can be due to relatively high wage costs or to failure to improve productivity or quality
- A shift in the pattern of consumer demand. As incomes rise, spending on manufactures may grow more slowly if people prefer to spend the extra money on services, e.g. leisure and tourism.

All mature economies (i.e. those which have had a substantial manufacturing sector for a long time) experience a tendency for resources to shift out of manufacturing and into the service sector. This is most marked in the USA and the UK. It is not necessarily a bad thing, although many commentators have regretted the process. The crucial question is whether the economy remains competitive enough in the sectors where it has a *comparative advantage* to export successfully and generate income to pay for imported manufactures.

demand means the quantity of a good or a service that people want to buy at a range of different prices. Market demand refers to the level of demand which comes from everyone in a particular market. *Effective demand* means demand backed by the ability to pay for the product. *Aggregate demand* means demand for all goods and services available in the economy as a whole.

The level of demand for individual products may be influenced by:

- incomes
- tastes or fashions
- changes in the prices of other goods, be they *substitutes* or *complementary goods*.

Individual demand will be particularly influenced by incomes and family circumstances. (See also *demand curve*.)

demand curve: a line graph which relates the quantity demanded to a range of possible prices. The curve almost always slopes downwards to the right because, as prices fall, people tend to buy a larger quantity. This is known as a movement along the demand curve and leads to a change in the quantity demanded.

A shift in the demand curve will occur if tastes or incomes change or if there is a change in the price of a related good, either a **substitute** or a **complement**. This is often loosely referred to as a change in demand (as opposed to a movement along the demand curve). It is better to be clear and use the word 'shift'.

As telephone calls have become cheaper, people are using the telephone more often. Similarly, the falling price of mobile phones has increased the quantity demanded. These are movements along the demand curve.

Equally, rising incomes could mean that more people want to own mobile phones at all price levels. This means that the demand curve for mobile phones will shift to the right. It is often important to use the **ceteris paribus** assumption when analysing market changes. It allows us to deal with one change at a time and analyse its effect in isolation.

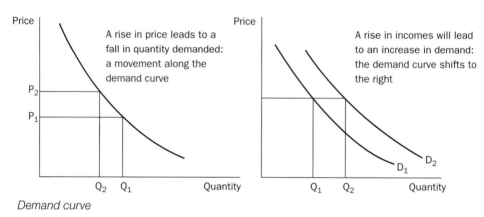

Demand curve

demand deficiency unemployment occurs when people are unemployed because the level of **aggregate demand** is well below that required to purchase potential or **full-capacity output**. This is unemployment which could be reduced if the level of expenditure in the economy were to be increased. This might be achieved by means of **expansionary policies**. Unemployment of this kind may also be described as **cyclical unemployment** because it is likely to increase during the recession phase of the **economic cycle**. Sharp increases in unemployment of this kind occurred in 1980–81, 1990–92 and 2008–09, when the UK economy experienced falling demand for many products. (See also **depression**.)

demand for labour: the number of employees required by firms at a range of different wage rates. This will be a **derived demand**, based on the demand for the final product. The number of employees required by each individual firm will depend on the **marginal revenue product (MRP)** of **labour**, i.e. how much each employee is able to produce and the price at which the output can be sold. (See also **wage determination**.)

demand for money means the amount of money which people will want to hold. This will be determined by the purposes for which they want to hold the money. Active balances are kept to finance current spending. Idle balances are kept as a way of having savings available for emergencies or as part of an investment strategy. An increase in the demand for money, other things being equal, will increase interest rates as people compete to obtain the funds available.

demand function: an equation which expresses the relationship between price and quantity demanded. It will show how quantity demanded depends on incomes, tastes and the prices of other goods (complements or substitutes).

demand management refers to government policies which aim to control the level of *aggregate demand* in such a way that there is neither excessive inflation nor high unemployment. *Fiscal* and *monetary policies* can be used in such a way as to control demand and prevent it either from growing faster than the capacity of the economy to produce or from slowing to well below that level. Demand management policies have been associated with the work of *J M Keynes*, and are sometimes called Keynesian policies. They were highly fashionable in the 1960s and 1970s; unfortunately they proved less easy to operate than many politicians suggested, mainly because they found it difficult to predict exactly how much of a change in demand would be needed to secure their objectives. Although demand management is seldom referred to by politicians nowadays, it is still used all the time. Interest rates (monetary policy) are adjusted by the *Monetary Policy Committee* of the Bank of England in order to influence both investment and consumer spending. Governments use fiscal policy in this way too but rather less frequently.

demand schedule gives the quantities sold of a product at a set of different prices. It gives the data from which a *demand curve* may be drawn.

demand-pull inflation occurs when *aggregate demand* is greater than the capacity of the economy to meet it with an equal supply of goods and services. This excess demand occurs when aggregate demand is growing fast and almost all the real resources in the economy are fully employed. Shortages, i.e. *supply constraints*, will appear, typically of skilled *labour*, and this will make it easy for people to negotiate pay rises. This in turn raises firms' costs and they will be quick to raise their prices to cover the increase. As the economy approaches its *full-capacity output*, it is impossible to increase output to meet the growing demand and any further increase in aggregate demand will quickly push up prices. Inflation will then tend to accelerate. In the diagram, aggregate demand grows from AD_1 to AD_2 to AD_3, but with the economy close to full capacity, the resources to increase output are scarce and their prices are bid up by the rising demand.

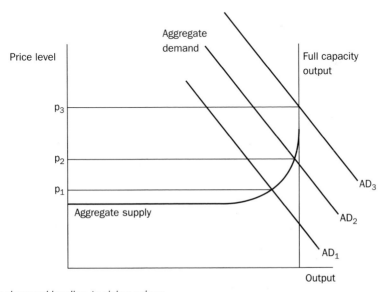

Excess demand leading to rising prices

Demand-pull inflation appeared to be threatening the UK in 2007–08 as food and oil prices rose but rapidly subsided as the financial crisis caused aggregate demand to fall.

demerger means dividing up a firm into separate companies. Usually the objective is to assign to each business the core activities in which it has the most expertise. In this way, it is thought, both businesses will be run more efficiently. Alternatively, the parent company may be selling off the less profitable parts of the business.

Demergers are sometimes referred to as *divestment*.

demerit good: a good which has been found through the political process to be socially undesirable. Illegal drugs provide the simplest example. They may be subject to *over-consumption*.

demographic projections: estimates of likely population changes. These can forecast changes in the size and age structure of the population which may have an impact on the resource needs of the economy.

demographic transition: as developing economies grow, their populations are at first likely to rise rapidly as *life expectancy* rises and *death rates* fall. Population growth slows later as birth rates fall. This has happened in all parts of the world where incomes are rising rapidly. Falling infant mortality and better welfare provision gradually persuade people of the wisdom of having smaller families.

denationalisation means returning to the private sector a business that was previously operated by the public sector. (See also *privatisation*.)

Department for Business Innovation and Skills (BIS) is responsible for the implementation of business, *consumer protection* and *employment protection* law, competition and trade policy, energy and regional issues and support for enterprise and businesses. *Business Link* is the agency that advises businesses.

Department for International Development (DfID): the government department which handles UK relations with developing countries. It provides *aid* and technical assistance where needed.

dependency culture: the set of attitudes which may lead to unemployed people giving up the search for employment and depending permanently on benefits. To combat this, everyone who can work is required to be available, and sometimes to attend for training and help in making applications.

dependency ratio: the percentage of people who are either in education or are too young or too old to take paid employment or who are unable to work because of disabilities. This group will be dependent on the working population to provide them with adequate real incomes.

dependent variable: a variable which is determined by changes elsewhere in the system and therefore depends on another variable. For example, we usually view the level of tax revenue as depending on the level of income, for a given set of tax rates. Income is thus the independent variable and tax revenue is the dependent variable.

depletable resources are things which are fixed in quantity and, once consumed, cannot be replaced. The term is used particularly in relation to energy: gas and oil are fossil fuels and once used, cannot be replaced, although it is possible to search for new sources. Similarly, tropical hardwoods are depletable in that they cannot be replaced at the rate at which they are currently being used.

deposit insurance: a system whereby bank deposits can be insured against the possibility of the bank becoming *insolvent* and running out of funds so that the depositors cannot withdraw their money. This reduces the risks for depositors but also makes it easier for banks to take risks in their lending. This became extremely important in preserving a degree of confidence in the banking system during the *credit crunch*.

deposits: amounts of money which are held in bank accounts. Deposits intended to finance current spending are held in current accounts while savings deposits are held in deposit accounts. (In the US, these are referred to respectively as sight deposits and time deposits.)

depreciation has two different meanings:

- Capital equipment depreciates over time, as wear and tear take their toll and new technologies make the equipment less useful. Its value diminishes. Prudent owners of capital equipment set aside depreciation allowances which can be used to replace the capital at the end of its useful life.
- An exchange rate, the value of which is falling on the foreign exchange markets, is said to be depreciating. It is losing value and purchasing power. It is also making exports cheaper and therefore easier to sell. (See also *exchange rate depreciation*.)

depressed area: a geographical area which is growing more slowly than the rest of the economy or not growing at all. As a result, incomes, output and employment will be lower. There are likely to be a number of declining industries which face diminishing demand in the marketplace. These may be localised heavy industries such as iron and steel and shipbuilding which have both declined through competition from imports. The workforce may have problems with *occupational immobility*.

depression: the phase of the *economic cycle* when economic growth is low or negative, when *recession* becomes prolonged and business confidence is very low. This phase will be characterised by:

- falling *aggregate demand* and output
- redundancies and high unemployment
- falling incomes and consumer spending
- very low levels of *investment*; as output falls productive capacity is reduced
- falling rates of inflation.

Depression may be countered by expansionary policies. Reduced interest rates (*monetary policy*) may induce both consumers and firms to borrow and spend. Investment may increase in some sectors. Tax cuts and increases in government expenditure will help to increase aggregate demand further. *Automatic stabilisers* such as the rise in unemployment benefits will help to protect incomes and contribute to more spending in the economy.

The unemployment which occurs will be *demand deficiency unemployment* (alternatively known as *cyclical unemployment*), caused by insufficient levels of aggregate demand. In the diagram overleaf, the level of aggregate demand is well below that needed to buy all the output which could be produced if the economy was working at *full-capacity output*.

The worst depression was that of the 1930s, when output fell by 30% and unemployment and loss of income was a serious problem all over the world. At the time of writing it is impossible to say how serious the 2008–09 recession will turn out to be.

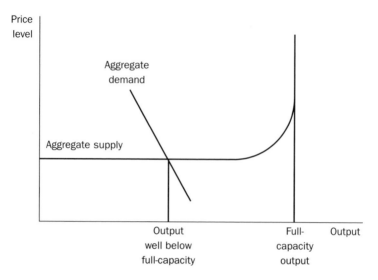

deregulation: the removal of legal restrictions on businesses. Usually the objective is to increase competition. Deregulation has proceeded alongside **privatisation**. Both were designed to reduce the role of the government in the economy. Deregulation has applied to different industries in different ways.

- In the 1960s and 1970s, banks were deregulated. Competition was greatly encouraged and probably did lead to lower prices and more varied financial products which benefited consumers.
- In the late 1980s buses were deregulated. Independent bus companies were allowed to compete with local authority-run bus companies. Competition has certainly increased but the effects on bus travellers are rather hard to determine.
- Airline deregulation over a long period has undoubtedly reduced air fares considerably, especially on some routes, e.g. the North Atlantic. Further deregulation may occur in time.

Meanwhile, increasing concern about the environmental, employment and health and safety issues is tending to increase rather than reduce regulation. UK businesses tend to think of themselves as being highly regulated but in fact international comparisons show that there is less regulation in the UK than in most other developed economies.

derivatives involve a contract, the value of which is based on the value of another asset or on an index which measures changes in values. Derivatives are used as a way of reducing risks. They may be based on interest rates, currencies, **equities** or **commodities**. They include **futures** and **options**. Futures involve an agreement to buy an amount of a commodity, or a financial asset, on a date in the future, at an agreed price. They are a way of protecting the buyer from the uncertain nature of commodity prices. If you know that you will need a certain quantity of iron ore in three months time, it may make sense to buy futures at an agreed price now, thus reducing the risk. **Financial futures** are another important derivative.

derived demand: employers' demand for *labour* is said to be derived demand, because they do not want labour for its own sake but for what it may be able to produce. The demand is thus derived from the demand for the final product.

deskilling: some jobs which were highly skilled in the past are now mechanised and only semi-skilled. People who stay in the same line of production may find that their skills are no longer valued and their pay may fall. Job satisfaction may be reduced.

destocking: at the start of a *recession*, some firms find they have unused stocks of inputs because demand for their product is falling. Stocks are costly to hold so they may reduce orders for inputs to well below the replacement level in order to get stocks back to a level which reflects the new lower level of demand and production. This will cut demand for the suppliers' products and deepen the recession. Destocking may be intensified if interest rates rise because stocks are often financed by borrowing.

devaluation: where the government has fixed the exchange rate in relation to that of other countries, it may decide to reduce the value of the currency and fix it at a new lower level. This may be because it has a persistent *balance of payments* deficit, indicating that the currency is overvalued. There may also have been a loss of international confidence in the currency. This would lead to heavy selling on the foreign exchange markets and downward pressure on prices coming from market forces. So the devaluation would really be a simple recognition that the rate could not be held at its old high value. Few economies now have fixed exchange rates although some peg their exchange rates to the currency of another country.

developed economies: the countries with high per capita incomes and high levels of investment which have become prosperous during the 20th century. This group used to consist of Western Europe, USA, Canada, Japan, Australia and New Zealand. Recently, Hong Kong, Singapore and South Korea have raised their incomes to the point where they are generally regarded as developed countries. A number of others are not far behind them.

developing economies are characterised by low incomes, low levels of *investment* and *infrastructure* and some difficulty in achieving improvements in standards of living. They are often heavily dependent on *primary products* for their export earnings and suffer if *commodity* prices fall. They tend to have small manufacturing sectors, though this is changing fast in Asia. Access to training is often a problem.

In the past many developing countries shared their distinguishing features. They are now a very diverse group. Some developing countries have moved on altogether, such as Singapore and the other so-called 'Asian tigers', Taiwan, Korea and Hong Kong. Incomes are at or approaching European levels. Many other Asian countries such as China and Thailand are developing fast. Meanwhile many African countries remain desperately poor. Some of the countries which are growing fast still have sectors of the economy where many people remain very poor. (See also *aid*, *Debt Problem*.)

development areas: geographical regions which have tended not to share the growing prosperity of the country as a whole. They include isolated areas and areas which have a legacy of localised heavy industries which have for some time been experiencing declining demand. These areas qualify for varying levels of support for firms which locate in the area. The EU determines how some regional policies will operate and some areas can obtain funding from its regeneration budget. The *Regional Development Agencies (RDAs)* have become an important vehicle for regional support.

development indicators include GDP per capita, car ownership, access to health and education and the *Human Development Index (HDI)*.

differentials are the differences in pay between employees who have different skills and responsibilities. A differential can act as an *incentive* to acquire additional skills or accept responsibility. When differentials are reduced, some people may become less occupationally mobile because they have less incentive to change jobs.

differentiated products are usually substitutes for one another, but are nevertheless subtly different. Though they may perform the same function, their design features distinguish them from each other. They contrast with *homogeneous products*; with these it is impossible for the buyer to distinguish one supplier's product from another's. Differentiated products are a feature of *imperfect competition*. By differentiating their product a particular firm may be able to exert some degree of control over the market. Some firms may use branding or qualitative differences which make their product distinctive. (See also *product differentiation*.)

diminishing marginal returns occur when, as a producer adds more of one factor of production to a fixed quantity of other factors of production, the output increases but less than proportionately. For example, if 10 people have 10 spades and are digging a trench, the addition of one extra person digging and allowing each person to take a break will allow the team to dig a longer trench in a given time. But if more people are added to the team, each extra one will add less and less to the distance dug, because the rest of the team will gain little benefit from further breaks.

Big businesses may encounter diseconomies of scale when they try to increase output. Increasing quantities of inputs may lead to progressively smaller increases in output.

direct controls: a way for the government to affect firms' decisions through regulation. Most governments say they will reduce government intervention in the economy. Generally, markets are regarded as being effective in promoting economic activity and direct controls are found to introduce *distortions*. In practice, employee and consumer protection law creates large numbers of direct controls, many of which have been effective in improving standards.

direct investment: see *foreign direct investment (FDI)*.

direct relationship: where two variables move together, they are said to have a direct relationship. For example, output and employment tend to rise and fall together, though with a time lag.

direct taxes are levied on the incomes of individuals and firms. They include income tax, corporation tax and council tax. They also include taxes on wealth, principally *inheritance tax*. Direct taxes are usually *proportional* or *progressive*. They also include *National Insurance charges (NICs)*. In contrast, *indirect taxes* are levied on expenditure and collected from the sellers of goods and services (e.g. VAT). (See also *taxation*.)

director: all *limited companies* have a *board of directors* who are responsible for major decisions. In a large company, directors will be elected by shareholders and are supposed to represent their interests. Executive directors are employees of the company. *Non-executive directors* are part-time, usually experienced managers from other companies, who are expected to give independent advice.

disclosure of information requires firms to give detailed information about the way they operate so that the various stakeholders can form a judgement on the outcome. Many firms do not want to do this, preferring to treat as confidential information on the nature of their profits, their accident rates and environmental issues. However, this is becoming more difficult as the need for business responsibility is promoted. Some firms, e.g. Sainsbury's, have taken a lead and produce an annual corporate responsibility report. One possibility would be to compel firms by law to disclose more information in their *annual report and accounts*.

discount: a price reduction designed to bring about a sale. It may be an incentive to pay quickly. In the financial markets, *bank bills* (short-term loans) may be sold at a discount which reflects the current interest rate. The discount compensates the lender for doing without the money for a short time, in the same way as an interest payment would.

discounted cash flow (DCF): a way of investigating a planned investment to see whether it will be worthwhile. It compares the expected future income stream from the investment with the opportunity cost of the funds involved. Estimated future income is discounted at a rate which reflects the interest lost while the funds are tied up. The discounted income stream is compared with the costs of the project to see if it is worthwhile.

discounting: a process by which a discount rate is used to assess the present value of a future income stream. Money now is always worth more than money later. This approach allows firms and governments to decide just how much the output from an investment project is worth right now. The discount rate might be similar to the interest rate, or higher to allow for risks.

discouraged workers: people who have been unemployed for some time, despite making an effort to find work, sometimes give up the search for a job. Effectively, they drop out of the *labour* market in the sense that they are no longer making themselves available for work.

discretionary policy refers to deliberate changes in tax rates or government expenditure which will affect the level of *aggregate demand*. In contrast, some changes in the level of taxation and spending are referred to as *automatic stabilisers*, because they will increase or reduce aggregate demand automatically as incomes and unemployment change over the course of the business cycle. (See also *fiscal policy*.)

discrimination: the practice of preferring an applicant for a job because of the person's race, gender or religion. Although discrimination is illegal there is a good deal of evidence of its continuation. Preferred groups generally are able to earn higher rates of pay and may have lower unemployment rates. Becker's Theory shows that some employers may be prepared to accept lower profits in order to avoid hiring groups they do not want to employ.

In the UK, women still earn 18% less than men on average. Some of this difference can be put down to the fact that many poorly paid jobs are done by women. But in most occupations, women's hourly rate of pay is less than men's. This applies to doctors, economists and company directors, as well as to assembly line workers and sales assistants. Possible explanations include career breaks, lack of geographical mobility, part-time work, and low levels of union membership. Clearly cultural factors and prejudice continue to play a part in both pay differentials and willingness to promote women, even though some firms could make more profit by always selecting the best person for the job.

discriminatory pricing: see *price discrimination*.

diseconomies of scale: as firms grow, they may encounter certain cost increases which make the larger scale of production less efficient.

- Communication costs: with more layers of management, communication may become harder.
- Loss of flexibility: larger organisations sometimes find it harder to react effectively to changing market conditions. In markets where nimble reactions are important, smaller firms may be able to take advantage of opportunities.

Diseconomies of scale seldom appear to trouble manufacturers. They can be more of a problem when certain kinds of customer service are an important part of the product.

Some firms which expand very quickly encounter congestion costs but these can usually be put right with time.

disequilibrium occurs when there is *excess supply* or *excess demand*, either in a particular market or in the economy as a whole. For example, if there are large stocks of unsold butter, we can say that the market is in disequilibrium. The likely explanation will be that the price is too high for *market clearing* to take place. The diagram shows how a high price may cause excess supply. Reducing the price will bring the market back into equilibrium.

Equally excess supply can result from a fall in demand that leaves producers with stocks of unsold goods. If prices are flexible the disequilibrium will not last long but if not, adjustment may take time. In the service sector excess supply might consist of underutilised capacity, e.g. empty hotel rooms.

On the macro-economic level, high levels of **aggregate demand**, in excess of the economy's capacity to supply goods and services, would indicate disequilibrium. The likely outcome would be accelerating inflation and the government might want to use *fiscal* and *monetary policies* to reduce the level of demand.

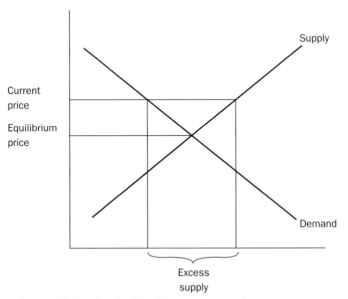

A price above the equilibrium level will lead to excess supply

disequilibrium unemployment occurs in three situations:
- when wage rates are too high for the market to clear. The supply of labour will be larger than the number of people employers want to take on at that wage rate. This could

happen in sectors where trade unions have succeeded in pushing up rates of pay or where groups of people have found some other way of developing market power. This is called real-wage unemployment

- when aggregate is so low that firms cannot sell enough to employ everyone who wants to work, i.e. *demand deficiency unemployment*
- when the supply of labour is increasing and wages are 'sticky' downwards.

disguised unemployment occurs when people who would like to work do not register, usually because they are not entitled to unemployment benefit, and therefore have no incentive to do so. The *claimant count* measure of unemployment fails to count these people. The Labour Force Survey usually produces a higher figure for unemployment because it can take account of people who do not register.

disposable income is the income left over after tax and *National Insurance charges (NICs)* have been deducted. Benefits such as income support and child benefits will increase disposable income, enabling people to spend more than they can earn. Because of taxes and benefits, disposable income is more equitably distributed than gross income.

dissaving: in the macro-economic model of the circular flow of money, dissaving occurs when consumption exceeds income and is financed by drawing on past savings. During a recession, dissaving can help to increase spending, but that is when people are apt to be nervous and want to keep their savings intact.

distortions: when prices are distorted, they fail to reflect the true costs of production. This means that either more or less will be consumed than would be if prices covered all the costs. For example, the apparent cost of motoring is less than the true cost because the road system is free to users. If road users paid the full cost of the roads they travelled (i.e. if roads were priced) they would probably choose to make fewer journeys. People who do not own cars would probably have to pay less tax for road building as the costs would be covered by road users. To the extent that road users were deterred by the pricing system from making journeys, there would be less congestion.

distribution: the system by which goods and services are actually sold in the places where consumers can conveniently buy them.

distribution of income refers to the way in which total income is shared among the different groups in society. A very equitable distribution of income might involve the richest tenth of the population having no more than three times the income of the poorest tenth. In the UK, the distribution of income became considerably less equitable after 1977. There have been some attempts to reverse this process but the UK distribution of income remains one of the least equitable in Europe.

Income distribution by quintile group

Year	bottom	2nd	3rd	4th	top	Ave real income per household, £ p.a., 2006–07 prices
1977	8.3	13.4	19.5	24.1	34.7	14,631
1986	8.1	11.3	17.9	24.2	38.6	17,814
1996–97	7.3	11.3	17.1	23.9	40.4	21,125
2006–07	7.4	11.7	16.6	23.3	41.0	27,370

Source: ONS, Economic and Labour Market Review

The intention of taxation and social security benefits is usually to redistribute income from the richer towards the poorer members of society. The more **progressive** the tax system, the more effective this process will be.

A relatively unequal distribution of income may increase incentives to work but may also increase tensions between employers and employees. Some **developing economies** have a much more unequal distribution of income than developed economies.

distribution of wealth refers to the ownership of assets and how it is spread amongst different groups of people. Wealth can consist of bank balances, shares, property, businesses and anything else which provides a continuing income or can be sold. Wealth is a **stock**, in contrast to income, which is a **flow**. Income is paid continuously whereas wealth is held over a long period. A relatively equal distribution of wealth would imply that most people had some and few had either none or a great deal. The distribution of wealth may be affected by **inheritance taxes** and by changes in property prices or ownership.

diversification means moving into the production or sale of different products. These could have similarities with the original product or be completely different. The objectives of doing this are:
- to spread risks. If the original product comes up against a sharp fall in demand, the new products may still be selling well and will reduce the risk of business failure
- to exploit additional profit-making opportunities.

Diversification is easily visible in the **conglomerate** companies like Unilever, which produces numerous cleaning and food products as well as cosmetics. At the other end of the scale, many farmers have found additional activities to supplement income when the prices of farm products fell. Yoghurt and cheese making, bed and breakfast, golf courses and farms turned into visitor attractions are all easy to find. Sometimes the management skills developed with one product turn out to be useful in producing the diversified product.

Some firms have diversified too far. They have found that they did not have the expertise needed to produce in the new field or did not fully understand the market. Sometimes they have found that combining completely different lines of production in one company was not cost effective and encountered diseconomies of scale. In some cases the solution to this is **demerger** or **divestment**, when the firm splits up into separate businesses for each product or product range.

divestment means disposing of part of the business by setting it up on an independent basis or selling it to another firm. The assumption is usually that the new management will be better able to run it profitably. This allows the original parent company to concentrate on the core products in which it has proven expertise.

Sometimes, firms which are developing some market power are required by the competition authorities to sell part of the business in order to ensure that they do not get too large a market share.

dividend policy: profitable firms can choose to pay large dividends to shareholders. Alternatively they may want to keep some of their profit for future investment projects. This is particularly likely if profitable opportunities are apparent, be they new markets or improvements in technologies which will cut costs. Higher **retained profits** in the short run may make it possible to pay bigger dividends in the future. Shareholders can express their views on this at the annual general meeting. It is sometimes said that UK firms have tended to retain too little profit; there have been suggestions of **short-termism**. There is concern at the power of big institutional shareholders such as pension funds and insurance companies in this area.

division of labour means the way in which people specialise in particular types of job. There are two elements in the division of *labour*:

- A manufacturing process is usually split into a sequence of individual tasks. This is easily seen in an assembly line. Each person has a small task which is repeated for each product which comes past. This is usually faster and cheaper than having one person or a team assembling the entire product on their own. Costs are cut and prices can come down, bringing the product within the reach of a mass market. This was the type of process observed in the pin factory by **Adam Smith** and described in his book, *The Wealth of Nations,* published in 1776.
- All jobs are specialised in a modern economy and people move into the type of occupation in which they have a **comparative advantage**. This allows them to exploit their natural advantages and also to acquire specialist skills which will increase their productivity. Experience adds further to their advantages as they learn to avoid mistakes.

The breaking down of manufacturing processes into individual component tasks has made it possible over the past 200 years to mechanise most areas of production. This has led to huge increases in productivity, and similarly large price cuts, but it has also *deskilled* many people. This means that many manufacturing processes have become very dull and it can be hard to motivate employees to maintain quality. In recent years ways have been found to reduce this problem through teamwork and *multi-skilling*, so that the division of labour has actually diminished in some workplaces.

divorce of ownership and control refers to the way in which public companies are owned by shareholders but controlled by managers. These two groups are likely to have rather different objectives and managers may not act in shareholders' best interests. In theory, shareholders can control overall policy by being active at the *annual general meeting (AGM)* but in practice this is not likely if there are large numbers of small shareholders.

Doha Round: the *WTO* trade negotiations that began in 2001 and stalled in 2008. Earlier rounds of trade negotiations had been very successful in reducing barriers to trade in manufactures; with Doha it was hoped to reduce trade barriers for agriculture and services. Some progress was made, e.g. in patent protection of pharmaceuticals. But on the big issues relating to agricultural tariffs and subsidies, the developed countries and the third world countries were deadlocked. The principal protagonists were Brazil, India, China and South Africa. The USA and the EU were generally unhappy about making concessions. It seems quite likely that negotiations will restart but probably only after there has been some recovery in the world economy. In the meantime the threat of growing *protectionism* is very real.

dollar ($): the currency of the United States of America. Other countries such as Canada, Australia, Hong Kong and Singapore also refer to their currencies as dollars but they are separate currencies with their own exchange rates. Many products are priced in US dollars because this avoids complications arising from exchange rate changes. Oil is the most obvious example. The euro appears to be becoming a similarly important world currency.

dollarisation: the process by which a currency gradually goes out of use as people in the country concerned lose confidence in the local currency and switch to using dollars whenever they can. This may or may not be part of government policy. For a few Latin American countries it has provided a means of achieving greater financial stability. Montenegro has followed suit and, at the time of writing, the dollar is the preferred currency in Zimbabwe, where the local currency has been rendered useless by **hyperinflation**.

dominant firm: one which has a position of **market leadership** within the industry. The firm would have to have a significant market share and would be able to influence prices considerably. Microsoft is the obvious example. However, dominant firms can lose some of their power through the application of competition policy or competition from smaller rivals. For many years, Boeing was the world's biggest aircraft manufacturer and very definitely dominant. It is no longer: Airbus Industrie, its European competitor, has been delivering more planes since 2003. Boeing caught up with more orders in 2007–08 but, as of 2009, both companies are taking cancellations rather than orders. No other aircraft manufacturers are in the same league.

Where a dominant firm has 40% of the market, it may be described as a dominant monopoly.

dominant price leader: a firm which is first to raise prices and is then followed by the rest of the industry. Ford has sometimes been considered to be a dominant price leader in the UK car market. This type of situation may be accompanied by **tacit collusion**. No actual agreement is made – this would be illegal – but the industry simply follows the lead of the dominant firm and avoids competing on price.

dot.com crash: starting in 1995, a number of IT-based companies saw rapidly rising share prices. Venture capitalists moved fast to fund a wide range of new businesses in the field, including some with risky business plans. Shares were much sought after and prices rose fast. Fortunes were made. But many of the dot.com companies aimed to build market share rather than profits and, after a while, it became clear that not all of the companies were going to succeed in the longer run. The market peaked in March 2000. After that, investors realised that many companies were overvalued and hastened to sell, leading to a **bear market**. By late 2002, technology shares were back down to prices last seen six years earlier. Many of the dot.coms had to close down once their venture capital was used up. The whole episode influenced share prices generally and had a big impact at the time.

Dow Jones Industrial Average is the main measure of changing share prices used on the New York Stock Exchange. It is a price index of the 30 most widely traded stocks.

downsizing: contracting the size of the firm to meet a lower level of demand. The term is sometimes used when redundancies are going to be needed.

downward multiplier: when **injections** fall or **withdrawals** rise, the level of spending in the **circular flow of national income** falls. Some firms find that demand for their products has fallen. They cut back output and eventually employment. Incomes fall and **aggregate demand** falls again. Because of the cumulative nature of the decline in demand, the eventual fall in income will be larger than the fall in spending which brought it about.

dual economy: an economy in which there is a highly developed sector coexisting alongside a traditional sector with very little capital and few benefits from advanced technology. All economies have some sectors which use more high technology production methods than others. However, in some developing countries there is a huge gap between those areas where there are modern manufacturing operations and the largely traditional agricultural sector. China is a case in point: there has been much foreign investment in the manufacturing capacity along the eastern coast but the interior is dominated by agriculture, much of which uses very traditional methods.

dumping means selling exports at less than their cost of production. Dumping occurs when:

- The producing country is very short of foreign exchange and will sell its exports at a loss in order to pay for necessary imports. This was the underlying reason why up to 1989 centrally planned economies dumped some manufactured goods.
- The industry is in decline and has spare capacity. This has been a particular problem in the steel industry. EU producers have in the past tried to delay closure of some plants by dumping surplus production.

The *World Trade Organization (WTO)* holds dumping to be illegal and has mechanisms for resolving disputes about it. Competing producers who are damaged by cheap imports have been known to use the accusation of dumping to protect themselves even when prices equate to production costs. Many governments accuse China of dumping and the Chinese government often protests. Because about half of China's manufacturers remain state-run enterprises, it can be tricky to decide what a fair price might be.

duopoly: a market with two sellers. There may be strong rivalry as each firm watches the other and devises strategies which look ahead to the likely reaction from the other. *Game theory* offers a range of predicted outcomes based on different assumptions about likely reactions.

Non-price competition is very likely as a price war might damage profitability for both firms. Advertising and various means of promotion may be strong features of a duopoly. There may be some *tacit collusion* or even *collusion* but this must fall short of exciting the interest of the competition authorities. Unilever and Procter and Gamble are a virtual duopoly in the production of washing products. Non-price competition is very visible in this market.

durable: see *consumer durable*.

dynamic efficiency: over time, resources are reallocated in a way that increases output relative to the quantities of inputs used. Firms may find more efficient ways of producing through changing technologies. They may be helped in this if they are in relatively open economies where there is growing demand for exports. There may be economies of scale; technology transfer may be easier, or increased exposure to competition may spur them on to find cost-cutting strategies.

earned income comes from wages, salaries and freelance or self-employed earnings. It contrasts with unearned income, which comes from interest, dividends, rent or profit from a business. At times in the past unearned income has been more heavily taxed than earned income.

earnings means total pay and includes overtime and bonuses. In examining the *labour* market, changes in earnings give a rather different picture from changes in wage rates, which may grow more slowly than earnings.

easy fiscal policy means tax and government expenditure policies which increase *injections* into the economy. This may be an objective when the economy is growing slowly or not at all during a *recession*. Tax cuts will lead to rising consumption expenditure which will add to *aggregate demand*. Similarly, increased government expenditure will add directly to spending. These are *expansionary policies* which should help to increase output and, after a time lag, employment. For example, a temporary reduction in VAT was introduced in late 2008 to help avert recession . This entailed some increase in government borrowing (the *public sector net cash requirement*) but this could be expected to diminish again as the economy recovered.

easy money means low interest rates which encourage individuals and firms to borrow. Investment will rise provided firms are confident about the future. Consumers will be able to borrow more cheaply and will usually increase spending on consumer durables such as cars. This is an *expansionary policy* which will be useful during *recession*.

EBRD: see *European Bank for Reconstruction and Development (EBRD)*.

ECB: see *European Central Bank (ECB)*.

e-commerce means electronic commerce and has two components.
- Consumers may shop online rather than in shopping centres. This may have the potential to cut prices in some instances. Or it may simply increase convenience. There is some evidence that online sellers are finding their costs higher than anticipated and their profits correspondingly disappointing. By the time you read this the situation may be clearer.
- Firms may buy from other firms online. This is known as the B2B market, business to business. This is now a large market.

There can be substantial cost savings for businesses which source their inputs online. E-commerce makes it easier to identify the cheapest supplier. Stiffer competition may cut costs for businesses as well as prices for consumers. This has had painful consequences for some firms including many traditional shops.

econometrics means, literally, the measurement of economic relationships. It involves generating hypotheses from economic models and testing them against the data, to determine what statistical support there is for the existence of particular relationships.

economic activity means any effort made in producing or distributing something which is scarce and can therefore be sold for some kind of reward. The NHS surgeon sells his or her services. So does the security guard. Other people actually produce tangible goods or transport them to where they will be sold. These activities create a *circular flow of national income*. The money paid for the goods and services sold goes to producers who spend it on *factors of production*. The owners of the factors of production in turn spend it on another round of goods and services.

Economic agents are people who have specialist knowledge and are employed by others to act in their interest. Chief executives and subsidiary managers are employed to act on behalf of shareholders in managing the company. Ordinary employees are the agents of the managers. Many firms employ consultants as agents. The owners of businesses are known in this context as principals. For the principals, it is vitally important that the agents act in their interests, rather than their own. (See also *principal–agent problem*.)

economic analysis: the use of economic theory to achieve an active understanding of real world events and relationships. The analysis seeks to break down complex phenomena into simpler sequences of cause and effect. When related to the *empirical evidence*, the analysis clarifies relationships and allows us to predict what may happen next.

Economic and Monetary Union (EMU): the group of EU members that adopted the single currency, the *euro*. The process began in January 1999 and completed in mid-2002. By then all the members' own currencies were out of use and the euro was used for all transactions. (See also *euro* and *European Central Bank (ECB)*.)

economic convergence is the situation when countries adopt similar economic policies and so have similar rates of inflation and public sector deficits. It is an important prerequisite for *Economic and Monetary Union (EMU)*. Without it, some countries would, within a monetary union, become increasingly uncompetitive and therefore economically depressed relative to other member countries.

The *convergence criteria* for membership set out the precise levels of the economic indicators that should be met. Although some of the EMU member countries had not achieved the convergence criteria at the time of joining, they were deemed to be close enough for membership to be realistic. It remains to be seen how EU members will be affected by the financial crisis that started in 2007, and how this will affect the process of convergence.

economic cost: an *opportunity cost* resulting from the production process. Economic costs are not the same as commercial costs. The latter include only those which the producer actually has to pay. Economic costs can include those *external costs* which can be quantified in economic terms. These increase the cost to society of the activity concerned. For example, when new factories are built, their transport needs may lead to nearby roads becoming more congested. This increases the transport costs of other local firms. Some local authorities require investors to finance road improvements as a condition of their receiving planning permission.

economic cycle: the fluctuations in output and employment which take the economy through a sequence of **boom**, **recession**, **slump** and **recovery**. (This is often also referred to as the business cycle or the trade cycle.)

The cycle varies in length and severity and must be looked at alongside the process of **economic growth**. This provides the background: a **long-run trend rate of growth**, around 2.2% in the UK, about which output growth fluctuates. The phases of the economic cycle do not form a neat, predictable pattern, but interact with other events to form a complex sequence.

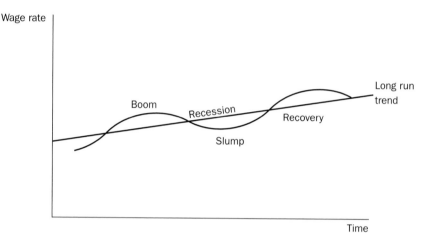

The phases of the economic cycle

- The **boom** phase occurs when there is unsustainably fast growth, which causes **supply constraints** and accelerating inflation. Between 1993 and 2006 the UK economy grew steadily but without causing accelerating inflation, enabling Gordon Brown to say that the cycle of boom and bust was over. However, by 2006 inflation had begun to accelerate and there were signs of tightness in the labour market as well as very rapidly rising house prices. Above-average growth rates were unlikely to last.
- Booms may give way to **recession**. Businesses may realise that boom-time rates of growth are not going to be sustainable and cut back their investment plans. Confidence in the economy may evaporate. Or governments may implement counter-cyclical policies that take some of the heat out of the economy and reduce the level of activity. Often this means raising the **bank rate**, as happened in late 2006 and early 2007. The economy reaches a turning point and the downturn begins. The definition of recession is two consecutive quarters in which output falls, as in the second half of 2008. The effect of falling aggregate demand may be cumulative because of a downward **multiplier**.
- If income and output fall for more than two quarters, the recession is turning into a **depression** or slump. Unemployment increases rapidly, though with a time lag. It may peak 12 months or more after output reaches its lowest level. This type of

unemployment is termed *cyclical* or *demand deficiency unemployment*. Levels of investment will be very low.

- *Recovery* may be a response to government policies to stimulate the economy. Or it may start when firms realise that they need to replace worn-out plant and machinery just to keep going. This will actually lead to an increase in investment, which will be cumulative as the multiplier takes effect. If growth rates rise too fast, the recovery may turn into a boom.

The data for *economic growth* (see page 87) shows the phases of the economic cycle described here quite clearly. In the past, the economic cycle was usually thought of as lasting roughly 10 years but there is no clear pattern for the past two decades and any trend can be affected by *shocks* in the world economy. Globalisation has changed the way the cycle works in ways that are not yet thoroughly understood. (See also *recession*.)

economic development is the process by which a country may experience economic growth and a reallocation of resources away from primary production and towards manufacturing. The term is usually used to describe what is happening in relatively poor countries which are referred to as *developing economies*. Rapid economic development is usually associated with high levels of investment and improvements in education and training opportunities and sometimes with a policy of allowing relatively *free trade* and an increasingly *open economy*. Rural development programmes that help to increase agricultural productivity also help, though in practice these are often not a high priority.

economic efficiency implies that output is being produced at the lowest possible cost in terms of resources and in the types and quantities which most closely reflect patterns of consumer demand. Minimising costs in turn implies that there is *productive efficiency* (sometimes known as technical efficiency). This means that the production process uses the best available technology and is organised so as to eliminate wasted resources. When the structure of production reflects consumers' wants there is *allocative efficiency*, arising from *consumer sovereignty*. Another frequently used way of describing economic efficiency is to say that no one can be made better off without making someone else worse off. This is sometimes referred to as *Pareto efficiency*.

economic expectations reflect the level of confidence in the economy. People will base their expectations on their experience of past events. So if they have experienced *inflation* in the past, they will tend to expect prices to rise in the future. However, the level of confidence can change quite quickly and have a big impact on investment and spending plans generally. A sense of optimism will be likely to make many managers go ahead with investment plans. The resulting increase in *aggregate demand* will itself increase expectations of future prosperity. The converse is also true, that pessimism about future levels of demand may cause many firms to abandon investment plans. Consumer spending plans tend to fluctuate rather less.

economic forecasting: the process by which economists use *economic models* to predict future trends in the main economic variables. The accuracy of forecasts depends on the extent to which the assumptions on which they are based actually correspond to reality. Forecasting is made difficult by the fact that shocks may occur which are quite unexpected and have far-reaching effects which are by their nature unpredictable.

economic goods are all those items which have a cost in terms of real resources and are therefore scarce in nature. A price must be paid in order to obtain them. The opposite of an economic good is a *free good* and it is actually difficult to identify examples of these. Sometimes wild blackberries are said to be a free good.

economic growth means an increase in output and real incomes. It is usually measured using *gross domestic product (GDP)*. In seeking to increase GDP, much depends on the quantity and quality of the factors of production in use. Some growth takes place just by increasing the quantity of factors of production, e.g. through immigration.

The important elements in the growth process are:

- *Investment*, which increases the amount of capital per person employed and increases productivity. This may be generated domestically or may come from abroad.
- Education and training which enhance *human capital*, again making people more productive.
- *Technological change* which leads to the availability of bigger and better machines, and also helps to create better ways of managing people. It can increase the *quality* of the investment that takes place.
- Exports to new markets which increase demand for the country's products.

These factors in combination have a big impact on growth rates. However, GDP figures must be interpreted with caution. A developing country may have strong growth in GDP and also a high birth rate. This means that per capita income growth is less than the growth of GDP. Also, increases in GDP do not always improve welfare because some of the external effects of growth are not always positive. Pollution, deforestation and climate change can all reduce the positive effects of growth and this will not show in the GDP figures. There is a trade-off between rapid growth and environmental protection and sustainable growth will require more investment in clean technologies. In some countries the opportunity cost of rapid growth is a deteriorating environment.

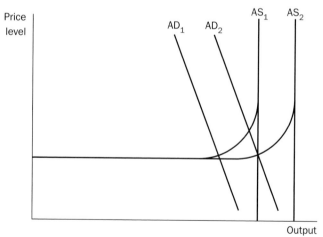

Rising capacity in the economy, as aggregate supply increases, means that output can grow without inflation accelerating

In practice, economic growth fluctuates with changes in aggregate demand and the *economic cycle*. It is often possible to follow policies that allow rapid growth in the short run. But if that rate of growth cannot be sustained in the long run then recession or worse may follow. (See also **long-run trend rate of growth**.)

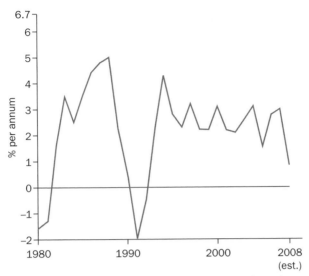

Economic growth rates fluctuate over the course of the economic cycle.
(Source: OECD Economic Outlook.)

economic incentives are price differences which encourage people to change their course of action. For example, if the price of apples rises, people have an incentive to buy bananas instead (provided their price has stayed the same). Similarly, rising prices may indicate that the product is likely to be more profitable and may provide firms with an incentive to increase supply. A wage **differential** may provide an incentive to acquire more skills.

Tax changes are often made to create incentives. Higher tobacco taxes create an incentive to give up smoking. Fuel taxes are varied to create incentives to use cleaner fuels.

economic indicators are data series that help to show what is happening to economic performance. **Leading indicators** can be particularly useful as they help to forecast the immediate future. For example, difficulty in recruiting people with scarce skills can indicate future **labour** market tightness and the likelihood of inflation tending to accelerate. The UK was in this position in 2006. However, where the data is very recent, it is subject to error and great caution is required.

economic integration refers to the increasing interdependence of modern economies. Integration grows through increased international trade and increases further within economic unions such as the EU. **Harmonisation** of regulations makes it easier to produce for all markets within the EU, because there is no need to design a slightly different product for each market. Good transport facilities enlarge markets for many producers. For energetic producers, integration creates many opportunities to sell to a larger market. **Globalisation** has increased interdependence worldwide.

economic man is a term which reflects the assumptions of neoclassical economics that people act in their own self-interest. **Adam Smith** argued that if everyone acts in their own interest, society as a whole is made better off. Self-interest leads people to choose the product they most want. This means that the price of those products will tend to rise. Self-interest also leads firms to identify products with rising prices as profitable. So resources are allocated in accordance with consumer preferences. This is the so-called *invisible hand*. (See also *allocative efficiency*.)

economic models are constructed from the relationships between different variables which enable economists to examine the connections between changes. A model may use only those variables which are most important within the situation being studied and thus can reduce the level of complication which must be considered. In this way, models may enable us to gain important insights into the way the economy works.

A model may be constructed in terms of a number of simultaneous equations or the relationships may be represented graphically or verbally. Models can be judged by their effectiveness in predicting what will happen under particular circumstances. They will not give accurate predictions if they are based on unrealistic assumptions. A model may be very simple, as in the basic supply and demand diagram, or very complex, as for example in the Treasury model of the whole economy which has over 500 equations and variables.

economic performance can be examined using a number of different criteria:
- The rate of **economic growth** is measured using GDP data, suitably deflated to remove the effects of inflation and provide a measure of the real increase in income.
- *Inflation* and *unemployment* rates provide information on the scale of economic problems.
- *Productivity* data indicates whether progress is being made in terms of increasing output per person employed. This can be achieved by investing more in both physical and human capital and by increasing technical progress through research and development.
- *Competitiveness* can be measured using data on unit costs of production in different countries.
- The level of spending on investment and research and development indicates whether efforts are being made to produce in more efficient ways.

This list could be extended indefinitely but the above would give a great deal of information about economic performance in comparison with either past experience or other economies.

economic policy encompasses a large range of different types of policy which have some impact on the economy. These are the broad categories of policy:
- Macro-economic policy involves taxation, government expenditure and interest rates, all of which can be used to influence the level of *aggregate demand* and output in the economy.
- Micro-economic policies are used to foster competition, encourage particular types of industrial development and influence the *allocation of resources*.
- Trade policies can be used to adjust import controls and sometimes to influence the level of exports.
- Exchange rate policies determine the extent to which the exchange rate floats or is managed.

Governments may be more or less interventionist in their economic policies. In the past governments used to think they could 'pick winners', i.e. decide which were likely to be the most successful industries and intervene to provide assistance. Very little of this happens nowadays, because these policies were found to be ineffective and poor value for money. EU rules forbid most direct aid to businesses.

economic principles are the fundamental ideas of the subject. They are based on hypotheses that have been extensively tested and found to correspond to real world observations. Once a hypothesis has been tested in this way, it becomes a theory which has value in helping to explain events. Theories can be used to predict possible future developments. They can also help us to understand important economic relationships. Some theories seem rather unrealistic, e.g. perfect competition, but are useful for their explanatory power as teaching tools.

economic problem: the *scarcity* of resources and the gap between what most people want and what they actually have together capture the nature of the economic problem. Real resources are in fixed supply at any one time and are always less than the sum total of human needs and wants. So *choices* must be made. Each individual decides what to buy, given their personal preferences. This creates a pattern of demand which makes some products more profitable than others. Firms will try to produce profitable products, thus channelling resources into the production of items which consumers want to buy more of. Firms will also try to minimise the resource cost of production so as to get as much output as possible from a given quantity of resources.

economic profit is the difference between total revenue from the sale of the product and the opportunity costs of all the resources used in production. It is a reward for the taking of unquantifiable risks by the entrepreneur. Profit in excess of the full opportunity cost of the resources encourages entrepreneurs to divert more resources to production because it shows that there is a high level of demand for the product. (This is the *profit-signalling mechanism*.)

economic rent is the amount which someone can earn which is in excess of their *transfer earnings*, i.e. what they could earn elsewhere. It is a demand-determined reward to *labour* and will be earned when labour is to some degree in *inelastic supply*. People with scarce technical skills can sometimes negotiate higher salaries than most could earn in other ways. Celebrities often earn economic rent because of their unique personal qualities – their supply is fixed, although they may find themselves competing with each other. Land for a specific purpose is often in inelastic supply especially in city centres, where economic rent will be high.

economic resources are all the goods which are already available, together with all the *factors of production* which can be used to create finished products, either goods or services. They include everything which can be used to satisfy demand.

economic sanctions prohibit or discourage trade in certain items with a particular country, usually with a political motive. Sanctions against South Africa were partly responsible for the government of the country eventually abandoning its policy of racial discrimination.

economic stability requires *sustainable growth* rates, low *inflation*, low unemployment and avoidance of significant trade *imbalances*, in the long term. This requires policy objectives that relate to the long term rather than the short term. Policies that help political parties to win elections can be very inimical to stability (if they keep their promises). Giving responsibility for *monetary policy* to the Monetary Policy Committee and making the Bank of England operationally independent is more likely to lead to stability than leaving it in the hands of the government of the day.

economic system refers to the way in which resources are allocated in the economy concerned. *Centrally planned economies* allocate resources according to the bureaucratic decisions of a government department. *Market economies* allocate resources using the *profit-signalling mechanism* which creates incentives for producers to meet consumer demand.

economic union involves the creation of an area composed of several different economies which all agree to use the same economic policies and regulations. Successful economies almost all have large markets, in which there are major opportunities for competent producers. This may be because the economy itself is large (as in the case of the US) or it may be because they are very *open economies* (as with Singapore) and trade extensively with the outside world. One way to create a large market is to form an economic union. As of 2009, the *European Union (EU)* has roughly 497 million people. All 27 member countries operate according to harmonised economic rules laid down by the European Commission, so producers can design their products according to the same requirements wherever they sell within the EU.

economic welfare refers to the extent to which people have the resources needed in order to lead a satisfying life. The welfare state aims to ensure that everyone has the minimum requirements for living in reasonable comfort, without providing any real luxuries. In practice it does not always provide all the basic necessities. The study of economic welfare involves deciding how particular changes affect people's sense of physical well-being. Some of the judgements required depend on how well-being is defined.

economically active/inactive: that part of the population that is economically active is either working (employed or self-employed) or available for work if a job can be found. Those who are economically inactive include the very young and the retired, students, carers and people with long-term disabilities. There is a grey area consisting of disabled people who could do some kinds of work and discouraged workers, all of whom might become active if they were able to find appropriate jobs with adequate incentives. (See also *poverty trap*.)

economics is a social science that studies how society allocates its scarce resources in order to satisfy its unlimited human needs and wants, in the most efficient way possible. Thomas Carlyle, the 19th century writer, described it as 'the dismal science' because at that time some economic theories appeared very pessimistic. Because of technological change, economic theories have become rather more optimistic.

The interesting feature of economic theory is that it is constantly catching up with events; the conventional wisdom seldom stays the same for long. This makes it much more exciting to study than a subject full of established truths. In fact, economics is not so much a set of theories as a way of thinking about economic relationships.

economies of scale: as some firms grow, they are able to produce at a lower *average cost* than before. These economies of larger-scale production can cut costs to the point where prices can be cut and larger markets can be reached. The car industry in the early to mid 20th century demonstrates the sequence of events. At first, cars were hand-built in very small numbers and were very expensive. Gradually the production process was mechanised and in the late 1920s Henry Ford pioneered the first assembly line in Detroit. Costs of production fell dramatically, so that far more people could afford a car and further economies of scale were reaped. From the 1950s onwards to the present time, the car industry has been the scene of numerous mergers, as car companies combine to reap further economies of scale in design and development, in the production of standardised components and in marketing campaigns.

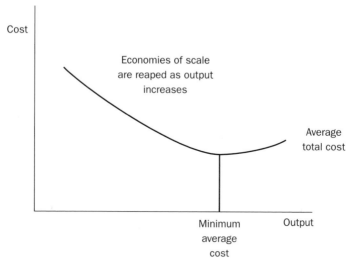

Economies of scale and average costs

The diagram above shows how costs fall as output increases. There can come a point where the level of output has increased so much that **diseconomies of scale** occur. If this happens average costs will start to rise again.

(See also **internal economies of scale**, **external economies of scale** and **diseconomies of scale**, for more detail.)

economy: as a whole, the people who make consumption decisions, the firms which make production decisions and the government bodies which oversee the process within a particular area. Normally we refer to the economy of a particular state, but we can refer to the local economy or the world economy. The term encompasses all the people who have a hand in making decisions which affect the **allocation of resources**.

effective demand: in order to actually buy a product, consumers must not just want it but also be able to afford to pay for it. If they cannot, then they are really just dreaming; we say they are not in the market. Effective demand means demand backed by the ability to pay.

effective exchange rate: the exchange rate as measured by the **exchange rate index**, which values the currency as a weighted average of the currencies of the nation's major trading partners. The weights are proportional to the amount of trade involved.

efficiency generally means using resources in the most economical way possible. This means that **average costs** will be at a minimum. Output from a given quantity of resources will be maximised. The jargon term for this is **productive efficiency**. It can be measured by examining **productivity** in one of its forms:
- *labour* productivity means output per person employed
- capital productivity means output per unit of capital invested.

The higher the level of productivity, the more efficiently the resources are being used. Waste is kept to a minimum.

The term efficiency can also mean **allocative efficiency**, which refers to the extent to which the allocation of resources tallies with the real preferences of consumers. An economy is said to be allocatively efficient when the goods and services produced are on sale at prices which reflect true costs of production and in quantities that accurately reflect levels of consumer demand.

Allocative efficiency is sometimes also known as **economic efficiency**.

efficiency/equity trade-off: see *equity/efficiency trade-off*.

EFTA: see *European Free Trade Association (EFTA)*.

elasticities measure responsiveness to change. *Price elasticity of demand* measures the responsiveness of quantity demanded to a change in price. Other important elasticities include *income elasticity of demand*, *cross-price elasticity of demand* and *supply elasticity*. All of these refer to product prices. Elasticity of demand is also important in the analysis of the *labour* market.

elasticity of demand for labour: the responsiveness of demand for *labour* to a change in the wage rate. In some occupations, this is very low. A new, higher wage rate may be negotiated and there will be little effect on the number of people hired by employers. The important determining factors are:
- whether there is a substitute for the type of labour in question. An increase in teachers' pay is unlikely to lead to a fall in the quantity of teaching services demanded, because substitutes are not very realistic
- whether labour is a significant part of total costs. In a power station the bulk of the cost comes from the capital invested and the cost of fuel; labour is a very small part of the total, so a pay increase will make little difference to the demand for labour
- whether the demand for the product is price elastic. If demand is inelastic, the increase in wage costs can be passed on to the customer with little change in the quantity sold, so there will be little change in the quantity of labour demanded.

elasticity of supply of labour means the responsiveness of the supply of *labour* to a change in price. An inelastic supply of labour means that an increase in the going wage will produce only a limited increase in the number of people available to do that particular job. This can happen when particular skills are scarce. During a boom, the wages of skilled construction workers typically rise sharply. The extreme case occurs when the supply of a particular type of labour is more or less fixed, i.e. there is perfectly inelastic supply. In this case, **economic rent** will be earned. The supply of labour is always more elastic in the long run than in the short run, because over time, more people can be trained in the required skills.

electronic mail (e-mail): sending written messages to and from computers, makes communications within a firm very much cheaper and quicker. It also creates opportunities in retailing direct to the customers from websites. (See also *e-commerce*.)

embargo: complete prohibition of trade with a particular country or prohibition applying to particular products (e.g. anything useful for military purposes). An embargo can be agreed amongst trading partners as a way to discourage terrorist activity or aggression. In the case of South Africa, the embargo was designed to stop the government from ignoring the human rights of the majority of the population.

The term can also be applied where information is being given out but is not to be published until after a certain time or date.

emerging markets: countries which in recent years have increased manufacturing output very rapidly, while also adopting a more market-oriented pattern of production. They include China, Hong Kong, India and a number of other Asian countries; Eastern European countries such as Poland and Hungary and some Latin American countries such as Mexico and Brazil. The term is used very loosely. Sometimes it refers to the ex-communist countries, Russia and Eastern Europe; at other times it includes countries which were until recently relatively poor and now have flourishing manufacturing sectors.

emissions are substances which pollute air or water, coming from the activities of individuals or firms. Liquids and solids may be discharged into rivers or the sea. Solid particles and gases may be discharged into the atmosphere.

emissions trading schemes provide for companies to be given the right to allow a certain quantity of polluting gases to escape into the atmosphere. They can sell all or a portion of their rights if they do not need them. This ensures that those companies which create air pollution above a certain level actually pay for the right to do so. Companies which do not do so will have to control emissions of polluting gases. The price of the right to pollute creates an incentive to pollute less. In the EU, the industries involved are energy, iron and steel, glass and cement. An alternative name for emissions trading schemes is carbon trading schemes.

The EU scheme has been in place since 2005 but the permitted emissions levels have been set quite high. They will only have a significant effect on the level of pollution if they are reduced. This may have been a good strategy to start with, to get firms used to paying for the right to increase pollution levels. At present the permits can be bought quite cheaply and lower permitted levels of emission overall will be needed to reduce pollution significantly. This may require some political will. In the USA, an emissions trading scheme is likely to be set up.

empirical evidence means data or information collected from the real world and reflecting the factual basis of the issue being investigated.

empirical testing is the use of data to test economic theories or the predictions of *economic models*.

employee involvement: the extent to which employees are made a part of the decision-making process. At one end of the spectrum, managers might have a suggestion box, into which employees may put their ideas for improving production methods. At the other end of the spectrum, employees may have opportunities to participate directly in the management process, through consultation and representation on the Board of Directors. In between there may be various methods of communication which ensure that employees are regularly consulted.

employee stock ownership: the process by which employees acquire shares in the company as part of their reward package.

employer: someone or some body which pays people to work for them.

employers' association: a body which represents all the employers in a particular industry or product group. Those that wish will join by paying a subscription. In return they may get:

- collective representation at government level or with local authorities, through which they may be able to increase their influence on policy
- collective bargaining with trade unions, which may make it easier for them to resist large wage demands
- joint advertising designed to increase the total market (e.g. by the Meat and Livestock Commission, which encourages people to buy more meat)
- joint market research efforts.

Where an employers' association negotiates directly with a single industry-wide trade union, there is said to be **bilateral monopoly** in the **labour** market.

employment: the process by which people provide their **labour** in a production process for which they are rewarded with a wage or salary.

Employment Acts: between 1980 and 1990, in a series of Acts of Parliament, employment legislation was overhauled by the Conservative government of Margaret Thatcher. The overall effect of the legislation was to weaken the power of trade unions to take action against employers. The important features of the legislation were:

- industrial action could be taken only in relation to the individual's own employer
- before a strike could take place, there had to be a secret ballot of members
- individuals could be dismissed for taking part in an unofficial strike (i.e. one not approved by the relevant trade union)
- trade unions were made liable for damage caused by industrial action taken by their members.

The legislation was generally credited with making the UK **labour market** much more flexible. However, it probably also increased the opportunities for employers to employ some people on very low wages.

The Employment Relations Act 1999 strengthened employee rights in certain respects. It meant that employees could claim unfair dismissal after one instead of two years and increased provision for parental leave.

employment contract: a legal document that defines the employee's responsibilities as well as the rate of pay and conditions of employment. In recent years, employment contracts have become much more flexible, so that employers can vary the number of hours worked and their timing much more easily. This has made the **labour market** in the UK much more flexible but has also removed some of the employee's security.

employment protection: the laws which protect the position of the employee at work. Employees are protected from unfair dismissal and are entitled to statutory redundancy payments, according to the length of time they have been with the employer. There is some concern that there is a **trade-off** between protecting the employee and encouraging employers to create more jobs. Employment protection is stronger in some EU countries than in the UK and this may help to explain why these countries have higher unemployment rates.

employment rate: the proportion of the population of working age who have work. A high employment rate means a relatively low **dependency ratio**.

EMU: see **Economic and Monetary Union (EMU)**.

endangered species: normal economic activity can lead to certain species being hunted or suffering the destruction of their environment or the encroachment of alien species. When total numbers fall so that successful breeding becomes difficult, there may be economic consequences. Measures to reduce the threat may also have economic consequences.

endogenous variable: one which is determined by changes within an *economic model*. For example, the level of consumption is determined largely by income. It is said that consumption is dependent on income. In contrast, exogenous variables are determined outside the model, i.e. they have causes which are independent of what happens within the model. Investment, for example, is determined largely by expectations of future profit and these cannot be given a specific value.

energy tax: a tax on energy purchases which would be designed to discourage consumption of *depletable resources*. Differences in energy taxes create difficulties for international road haulage businesses which have to compete with foreign businesses which pay less tax on their fuel. The international agreement which could remove this problem is currently elusive because high energy taxes are politically unpopular with a wide range of people.

enterprise is a term which is used in two ways:
- an enterprise is a business which takes risks and sells a product
- enterprise is the quality which involves initiative and willingness to take risks in order to create and sell a product.

enterprise culture: the state of mind commonly found in a market economy, where decisions are made on the basis of future profit and people are generally willing to work hard and to take risks in ways which will generate income and wealth.

enterprise policies are all those measures which are designed to help encourage businesses to set up and expand.

entrepreneur: an individual who is willing to take risks and who makes the decision to go into production. The entrepreneur develops a product and decides how it will be produced using *factors of production*. He or she carries the risks associated with bringing the product to the marketplace. Sometimes the entrepreneur is described as the fourth factor of production.

entry refers to the process by which a firm may set up in business and become part of the industry. Easy entry implies that the industry will be at least fairly competitive because profits will attract additional producers who will then compete with each other. An individual or an existing business can start off a new line of production and find ways to sell the product at a profit. Exit is the reverse process. Entry and exit are an important part of the process of *structural change*. *Barriers to entry* make it difficult for new businesses to get started.

environment: the surroundings in which people live and firms operate. The natural environment includes all the natural resources which affect and are affected by a particular activity. The built environment includes all the man-made resources which surround the activity.

environmental accounts attempt to put a value on the impact of a business on the surroundings which it affects. These may or may not be part of an annual report.

environmental audit: an attempt to measure pollution levels, recycling activities and any other activity which is likely to affect the environment of a firm. Some businesses which make *business responsibility* a high priority voluntarily carry out an audit as a way of monitoring progress towards environmental objectives. For example, Sainsbury's undertakes an annual environmental audit, the outcomes of which appear in a public report.

environmental degradation: the process by which economic activity leads to the destruction of real resources. For example, overgrazing in developing countries leads to the destruction of plant life, which makes erosion of the soil more likely when there is rain. In turn, erosion makes it harder for plant life to recover and grazing lands lose their value as such. Equally, environmental degradation can occur when there are spills from a chemical plant which lead to long-term contamination of the soil around it, and from many other causes.

Environmental degradation may involve externalities but this can be avoided if ways can be found to make the producers cover the costs.

environmental economics is the study of environmental problems and lays particular emphasis on evaluating the costs and benefits of different kinds of solutions to the problems posed by pollution, congestion and the general destruction of resources. Most environmental problems are associated with some kind of *market failure* and *externalities* which enable producers to avoid paying the full resource costs of production.

Traditionally, economics regards national income figures as a fair measure of the standard of living. However, these are constructed on the basis of recorded accounts and to the extent that there are external costs and benefits arising from economic activity, these accounts may not reflect the true improvement in welfare. Environmental economics tries to measure the standard of living in ways which allow for the costs of economic growth.

environmental market failure occurs when buyers of the end product are not paying for the external costs of production. This means that the product price is less than the true costs to society as a whole of the production process. Overconsumption may result. If the external costs can be internalised by making the producers pay whatever it costs to avoid doing environmental damage, prices will rise and the market will give the correct signals to consumers.

environmental policy: the plans of the government in relation to protection of the environment. Individual firms may also have an environmental policy.

environmental pollution: contamination of air and water by production processes. Where climate and weather conditions make it possible for atmospheric pollution to travel long distances, it may materialise as *acid rain* far away from the original sources.

equality means that people do not experience large differentials in income within a society. Total equality has seldom been achieved in any society, but some countries have for long periods had a much greater degree of equality than others. Sweden has been most notable in this respect while the USA has tended to have very little equality in its *income distribution*, though rather more equality of opportunity through its education system. (See also *equity/ efficiency trade-off*.)

equal opportunities: the provision of fair consideration for all applicants, regardless of gender, ethnic group, religion or disability, so that there will be no discrimination between employees or job applicants or those seeking educational opportunities. There is ample evidence that although some progress has been made in fostering equal opportunities, much discrimination remains. For example:

- variations in unemployment rates between ethnic groups cannot be explained by variations in their qualifications
- lower rates of pay in jobs traditionally taken by women are also very persistent.

In theory discrimination deprives employers of the best candidate for the job and employers who do not discriminate will have a **competitive advantage**. In practice, many organisations seem not to recognise that hiring the best candidate for the job can cut costs.

Equality and Human Rights Commission: an organisation set up by the government to prevent **discrimination** on grounds of age, disability, gender, race, religion and sexual orientation. It also deals with human rights issues.

equation: a statement in symbols that relates one variable to another. An **economic model** is normally built up from a number of equations, each of which links two or more variables. Together the equations form a system in which each variable is identified by its connections to other variables.

equation of exchange: connects the **quantity of money** (M), the **velocity of circulation** (V), the price level (P) and the number of transactions (T).

> *FORMULA:* $MV = PT$

Sometimes known as the Fisher equation, this is an identity rather than a relationship: it is true by definition. PT is the total value of all output, which is equivalent to national income. MV is the amount of money needed to pay for it, since the velocity of circulation is simply the number of times each unit of currency circulates within a given time period. It can, however, be used to predict the rate of inflation under certain circumstances. If the velocity of circulation is constant and the number of transactions only grows slowly, then it follows that inflation will be directly related to the quantity of money in circulation.

Some economists have taken the view that velocity is constant and that the equation of exchange illustrates simply a fundamental and direct link between money and inflation. But the data on velocity in recent years rather suggests that it is not constant, at least in the short to medium term. The reality is certainly more complicated than the equation of exchange suggests.

The credit crunch revived interest in the work of Irving Fisher. It is hard to tell at the time of writing how the money supply and the velocity of circulation are behaving but these ideas may turn out to have useful applications at the present time.

equilibrium in the marketplace means that the quantity supplied is exactly the same as the quantity demanded. This means that there is an equilibrium price at which the market clears. No one is left with unwanted stocks of unsold goods and consumers get all they want at the going price. There will be neither **excess supply**, nor **excess demand**. This process of **market clearing** comes about because the price is free to change and settles at the equilibrium level.

equilibrium prices apply in **labour** and capital markets as well as the market for goods and services. A wage rate which is above the equilibrium level can lead to unemployment and an excess supply of labour, and vice versa. A very high interest rate may lead to an excess supply of funds in the capital markets, with banks willing to lend but a shortage of viable investment opportunities.

The primary importance of the concept of equilibrium is as a tool of analysis, rather than an exact description of the real world. It allows us to identify the problems in markets which plainly do not clear, such as the housing market when many potential sellers are unable to find buyers at the price they would like to get. Price theory predicts that the houses will sell if prices fall to the equilibrium level, a prediction which sellers who must sell frequently discover to be accurate, even if the exact level of the equilibrium price is not at first obvious.

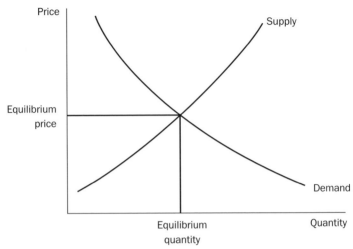

Equilibrium in the market for goods

equilibrium unemployment includes all those types of **unemployment** that can occur even when the wage rates are such that labour markets should clear, i.e. structural, frictional, technological, regional and seasonal unemployment.

equities are shares in a company. Shareholders are the owners of the company and have the right to review the directors' decisions.

equity: a term associated with the notion of fairness. Equity requires that incomes be reasonably close, without large variations between the highest and the lowest incomes. It requires also that the benefits of economic growth be reasonably equally distributed. (See also **equity/efficiency trade-off.**)

equity/efficiency trade-off: decisions which are taken in the interests of promoting efficiency may have the effect of increasing inequality. For example, incentives which encourage people to increase **productivity** may lead to an increasingly unequal distribution of income. In a different sphere, when a product is very scarce, the price will usually rise to ration the product among those most able to pay the higher price. This will hurt poorer people much more than richer people.

For governments, there may be a choice between **equity**, i.e. creating a relatively equal distribution of income, and **efficiency**, which may require some incentives. Incentives to work and take risks imply that some people receive rewards in the form of earnings or profits which make them much better off than most other people. Yet without incentives, economic growth may be slow and therefore fail to deliver the improvement in standards of living which people expect.

This area is very controversial. It is fairly clear that the limited incentives which exist in a **centrally planned economy** do not encourage people to improve productivity in the way that they usually will in a market economy. However, in the context of a market economy, it is not clear that measures to reduce inequality, such as progressive taxes and spending on social services, actually reduce economic growth and the quest for efficiency. Scandinavian countries have on the whole a fair degree of equality and acceptable or better growth rates.

equity finance means funds generated by selling shares. There is an important distinction between equity finance and *loan finance*. Shareholders expect a dividend, but in fact they may be prepared to wait some time for it if they believe that in the long run the business will be profitable. Lenders expect, and must be paid, a rate of interest which will fall due on a regular basis. Equity finance may therefore be cheaper for the company during the important early phase of a new project.

ERM: see *Exchange Rate Mechanism (ERM)*.

ethical investment is the use of finance for capital investment in projects which avoid certain kinds of unethical activity. It applies mainly to investment funds such as *unit trusts*. Businesses which might be excluded from funding could be those producing defence equipment or tobacco products or those which have a weak record on pollution control. Others might be excluded because they deal with governments which have a poor record for respecting human rights.

ethical policy: some firms have now developed an ethical policy which sets out their objectives in relation to what they see as their *social responsibilities*. The emphasis will vary from one firm to another. Likely areas for the policy coverage would include environmental targets, community programmes and the integrity of the business in its dealings with its *stakeholders* such as consumers and suppliers.

ethical pricing is an attempt by some organisations to pay higher prices to poor producers in developing countries in order to give them a fairer return for their *labour*. Cafédirect is perhaps the best known example. The Fairtrade Foundation exists to give approval to businesses which satisfy their criteria for ethical pricing.

ethical responsibility: see *business responsibility* and *corporate responsibility*.

ethics are the moral principles which may or may not be used as a basis for decision taking. Some firms are genuinely ethical in their intent, giving a high priority to the value they can provide for the customer and treating employees and other businesses fairly at all times. Others may take decisions primarily on the basis of the profit to be made. Sometimes, firms will take into account the impact of their decisions on public opinion and make an ethical decision for purely practical reasons.

EU: see *European Union (EU)*.

EU competition policy: the European Commission has the power to investigate any instance of monopoly. Mostly it works on mergers and cartels that affect more than one member country. However, all members are required to bring their competition policies into line with EU Treaty obligations. This is part of the level playing field that is a key element in the way the EU operates. The EU was a key player in the case against Microsoft, which sought to prevent competitors from getting the information they needed to make their products compatible.

EU enlargement: in 2004, Poland, the Czech Republic, Hungary, the Slovak Republic, Slovenia, Latvia, Lithuania, Estonia, Cyprus and Malta joined the EU. Bulgaria and Romania joined in 2007. Turkey wants to be given a date too; however, there are still some doubts about its government's record on human rights, despite recent improvements.

The Treaty of Lisbon, signed in late 2007, was designed to make the decision-making process less cumbersome for the 27 member states. It was based on the draft European Constitution that was rejected by voters in France and the Netherlands in 2005. Having more members inevitably involves more majority voting. Opponents of the Treaty say that it interferes with national sovereignty. Irish voters rejected the treaty in mid-2008 and are due to vote again late in 2009.

Applicants have to be able to adopt the economic policies of the EU. They must have effective competition policies and must be capable of protecting the rights of minority peoples; this means that negotiations can be very protracted. Nevertheless, a number of countries, e.g. Croatia and Serbia, want to join. Applicants also have to demonstrate that corruption is under control but recently statements of intent have been acceptable.

euro: the single European currency which has been used for all transactions in the *euro zone* since June 2002. The euro was introduced at the start of 1999 by 11 member countries: Austria, Belgium, Finland, France, Germany, Luxembourg, Ireland, Italy, the Netherlands, Portugal and Spain. Greece joined in early 2001. The UK, Denmark and Sweden are outside the euro zone. Since EU enlargement, Cyprus, Malta, Slovenia and Slovakia have joined. Several others may be ready to join soon. It is possible that the euro zone will be enlarged rapidly to cushion the East European countries against the difficulties of the 2007–09 financial crisis.

Member countries have to satisfy the ***convergence criteria***. These help to ensure that all member economies are able to achieve ***economic stability*** such that they can cope with a one-size-fits-all monetary policy. (See also ***European Central Bank (ECB)***.)

Initially, the euro depreciated against the US dollar but later it came to be seen as a potential reserve currency and attracted substantial capital inflows. It appreciated in 2008 when other currencies were under pressure from the markets.

The setting up of the euro as a single currency has had a number of far-reaching implications for member countries.

- Firms in the euro zone find it very easy to trade with one another. There are none of the uncertainties arising from having different exchange rates. Transactions costs are reduced.
- Prices across the euro zone are much more transparent. It is easy for buyers to see who is charging the least and to buy from them. This has probably led to increased competition and lower prices for consumers.
- Within the euro zone, there is a single ***monetary policy***, determined by the ECB. There can be difficulties if the ECB ***interest rate*** which is appropriate for the euro zone as a whole is too high or too low for an individual country. Adjusting the level of economic activity in that economy so that it is similar to that of the rest of the euro zone could be difficult.

euro zone along with 'euroland' and 'euro area' is a term used to describe the group of countries linked by their single currency, the euro.

European Bank for Reconstruction and Development (EBRD) was set up to provide development finance for the countries of Eastern Europe in 1990. It is based in London.

European Central Bank (ECB): the central bank of the *euro zone*. The bank itself is based in Frankfurt. Decisions are taken by a committee composed of representatives from all member countries. Each month the committee decides on the appropriate monetary policy and sets the interest rate for the whole euro zone. The Bank is charged with keeping inflation within the 2.2% limit.

When the switch to the euro took place in 1992, the ECB had some difficulty in gaining the confidence of the financial markets. The euro depreciated against the US dollar for the first two years but since then the ECB has gained widespread respect for its policies. However, there are some doubts about the speed with which it responded to the credit crunch and this may mean that member countries will have a deeper recession than expected.

European Commission: the central body which administers the affairs of the *European Union (EU)*. Very importantly, it also initiates policy by establishing policy guidelines and giving opinions. Proposals are discussed with member country governments and with employers' organisations and trade unions.

The President of the Commission has an important position as leader. There are 27 other commissioners, one from each member country. The commissioners, once appointed, act independently of the national interest and defend the EU as a whole. They work closely with the Directorates-General, the departments that act as the EU's civil service.

There is a procedure for initiating legislation within the EU:
- the Commission's proposals are sent to the European Parliament, which may amend them
- the proposals then go to the Council of Ministers for further discussion
- there will be a continuing dialogue between the Commission and the Council of Ministers. The latter provides for national interests to be considered while the former pursues the interest of the EU as a whole.

European Court of Justice in Luxembourg is the highest court of the European Union. Where the interpretation of European law and of the EU treaties is in dispute, it can decide the outcome. It can fine firms and challenge national laws.

European Development Fund: a fund created by the EU to provide finance for investment in less developed countries.

European Economic Area was created by the agreement signed in 1991 between the members of the European Union and the *European Free Trade Association*. It allows for free trade between EU countries and Norway, Iceland and Liechtenstein.

European economic integration: the process by which EU member economies are becoming more and more like a single economy. The *single European market*, with its harmonised regulations and elimination of border controls, has contributed to this.

European Free Trade Association (EFTA): was originally set up in 1960 by the European countries outside the European Union. Now, Norway, Switzerland, Iceland and Liechtenstein are the only members. It allows free trade between members, but is not a *customs union* as the EU is.

European Monetary System (EMS) was set up in 1979 to bring EU member currencies more closely into line with one another. It made sure that member currencies were kept close to each other through **central bank intervention**. Each currency was given an exchange rate band within which it might fluctuate to a limited extent. It was an important staging post on the way to the creation of the **euro**. The UK joined in 1990 but left again when the value of the pound collapsed in 1992.

European Parliament is democratically elected and exists to debate and amend the proposals which are made by the European Commission. At the time of the first direct elections in 1979, it had few powers but these have gradually been extended. In 1999 it used its power to sack all of the EU commissioners on grounds of corruption. This has made its relationship with the Commission rather delicate. Despite this and the fact that the last elections proceeded with a very low turnout, its influence is gradually increasing.

European Regional Development Fund was set up by the European Union in recognition of the fact that increased trade would cause adjustment problems in some regions. Southern Italy, parts of northeast France and Merseyside received some support in the past but, since enlargement, the main focus is on the newer member countries.

European single market: see *single European market*.

European Social Fund was set up by the European Union to improve employment opportunities for people in parts of the EU which have suffered from **structural unemployment**. It provides funds for training schemes and job creation.

European Union (EU): formerly the European Community (EC) and before that the European Economic Community (EEC). It is a **customs union**. However, many influential people have always seen it as much more, with the possibility of integration proceeding to the point where it becomes, essentially, like a single economy.

The EEC was set up with the Treaty of Rome in 1957. At that time the members were Belgium, France, Germany, Italy, the Netherlands and Luxembourg. They were joined by:

- the UK, Denmark and Ireland in 1973
- Greece in 1981
- Portugal and Spain in 1986
- Austria, Finland and Sweden in 1995
- The major **EU enlargement** in 2004
- Romania and Bulgaria in 2007.

The Single European Act in 1987 moved the EU towards much closer harmonisation of regulations and reduced the costs associated with border controls. Effectively, most businesses can rely on being able to sell the same product throughout the EU. This has helped to cut costs and increase competition.

With **free trade** between EU members and a **common external tariff**, the EU provides a market of nearly half a billion people. There is immense scope for reaping **economies of scale** in such a market. Some foreign direct investment within the EU has been attracted by this large market; locating within the EU reduces the impact of the common external tariff. There have been further benefits from the euro in that prices are very easy to compare and competition has strengthened.

The **European Commission** in Brussels initiates all new legislation. Its proposals are sent to the **European Parliament** and then to the **Council of Ministers**. The **European Court of Justice** will determine how the treaties and regulations should be implemented, whenever disputes arise. This sequence is shown in the diagram. Despite the creation of this structure, national governments retain strong influence, visible in the crucial role played by the Council of Ministers.

Although the EU has had many positive effects on member countries, its impact on the rest of the world has brought some problems. Subsidised exports of farm surpluses have upset major exporters of agricultural products such as the US and Australia. They may also have depressed food prices in parts of Africa and diminished the incentives for African farmers to increase production. The bargaining power of the EU within the **World Trade Organization (WTO)** is strong. Concessions which might enable developing countries to export more easily have been very modest.

The EU still lacks the democratic controls which are desirable as its scope increases. The **European Parliament** is hampered by the fact that the political parties are still national in scope rather than international. (See also **Common Agricultural Policy**, **EU enlargement**, **euro**.) To date, the failure of all members to agree to the EU Constitution and the Treaty of Lisbon made the decision-making processes of the EU excessively cumbersome since enlargement took place.

ex ante is a Latin term, used in economic theory, meaning before the event. It is used mainly to refer to what we might know in advance. It contrasts with **ex post**, after the event, when hindsight adds an extra dimension to what we know and understand.

excess aggregate demand means that the quantity of goods and services demanded in the economy as a whole is greater than the amount which can be produced, given the available resources (**full-capacity output**). The consequence is likely to be accelerating **inflation**. It will be possible to raise prices and still sell the product. Firms will bid up the price of **labour** as they compete for the few available employees, especially if they have scarce skills. This will raise costs and prices will rise further. Expectations of inflation may set in and influence pay negotiations. The diagram below shows that if the economy is producing at or near full-capacity output, rising aggregate demand will lead to excess demand and a rising price level. The solution will be to reduce aggregate demand using *fiscal* and *monetary policies*.

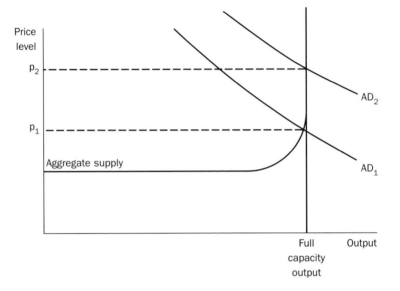

Excess aggregate demand will usually be associated with the boom phase of the *economic cycle*. Prospects of economic growth will make firms optimistic about investing and consumers will have increasing incomes, leading to higher consumption. *Aggregate demand* will grow faster than the capacity of the economy to produce. This situation is unsustainable because it will lead to inflation and probably to *contractionary policies*.

excess capacity: a situation in which resources are being underutilised. There is likely to be unemployment and many firms may contract or close down because of low levels of aggregate demand. The economy is therefore producing less than it could and some resources are being wasted.

The idea of *capacity utilisation* can be applied to the whole economy or it can be used in relation to an individual firm. Any firm which has enough capital equipment to produce more than it is doing is said to have excess capacity. Reasons for this could include falling demand for the product, lack of appropriately skilled *labour* or investment in anticipation of growing demand later.

excess demand occurs when the quantity demanded outstrips the quantity supplied, as in the diagram on page 105. This shows disequilibrium in the market, which fails to clear. Excess demand can be seen when there are large numbers of people wishing to buy an item which has just become fashionable and shops have difficulty in obtaining adequate stocks. This situation will not usually last long as either prices will rise or supplies will increase.

One market in which excess demand can persist for quite a while is the housing market. If incomes are rising, demand for housing will rise in many areas. However, in the short run the supply of housing is fixed (i.e. perfectly inelastic). It will take time to acquire land with planning permissions and add to the stock of housing by building more. In this situation, houses will sell very quickly, reflecting their scarcity on the market. Prices will usually rise, perhaps very sharply.

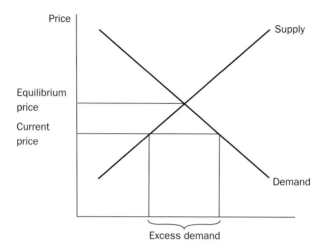

excess supply occurs when the quantity supplied is greater than the quantity demanded. On the micro-economic level, it means that the price is higher than its equilibrium level and gives producers an incentive to supply more of the product. At the same time the high price discourages buyers and the result is seen in stocks of unsold goods. (For diagram of excess supply, see *disequilibrium*.)

Excess supply will usually come to an end if sellers cut prices. However, in some markets this may take quite a while. You can see excess supply in the housing market if there are a great many 'for sale' signs, relatively few buyers looking around and people making offers well below the advertised price.

On the macro-economic level, excess supply would imply that firms were producing more than consumers wanted to buy, there would be stocks of unsold goods and in time firms would adjust production downwards. This could happen at the onset of a *recession* when there would be falling aggregate demand.

exchange is the process by which people trade with each other, offering goods and services they have produced for goods and services they need or want. Exchange is crucial to economic life, making it possible for people to specialise in the type of production in which they have an advantage. This *specialisation* allows people to produce much more than they can if they have to be self-sufficient. In a primitive system, exchange takes place through *barter* but the use of money makes the process of exchange much more efficient. Instead of having to find someone who has the products required, one's own products can be exchanged for money which is used to buy other products.

exchange rate: the rate at which one currency can be exchanged for another. Effectively, it is a price for the currency, expressed in terms of other currencies. If it is said that the pound fell against the US dollar, it means that the pound is now worth fewer dollars.

The exchange rate influences the prices of imports and exports and the ease with which producers in different countries can compete with each other. A rise in the exchange rate (*appreciation*) means that export prices will be higher and import prices will be lower. All producers who compete with overseas producers will lose competitiveness. (See also *exchange rate depreciation*.)

exchange rate depreciation: occurs if market forces cause the exchange rate to fall, so that exports become cheaper and imports dearer in terms of the domestic currency. This may happen because the demand for exports has fallen over a period of time or because *capital inflows* have diminished. Either way, demand for the currency will fall and with it the equilibrium exchange rate, as shown in the diagram below.

The same outcome will occur if there has been an increase in demand for imports or a *capital outflow*. There will be an increase in the supply of the currency (see the diagram on page 107) by people who want to buy foreign currency on the foreign exchange markets, leading to a fall in the exchange rate.

Appreciation leads to the reverse situation in which the exchange rate rises, imports become cheaper and exports become dearer.

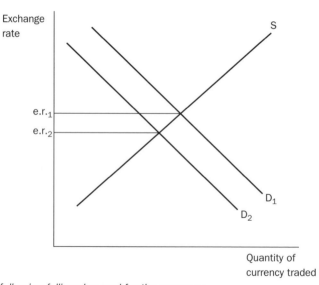

Depreciation following falling demand for the currency

Exchange rate depreciation can have a very favourable effect on the level of economic activity. It makes potential exporters more competitive. Equally it helps firms that compete with imports on the domestic market. Both are likely to find their products bringing in more profit. The potential benefits of depreciation are an important advantage of a *floating exchange rate*. The UK has probably benefited from this flexibility while outside the euro zone.

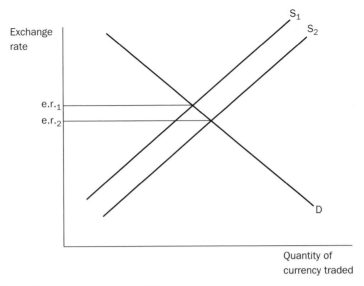

Depreciation following rising supply of the currency

exchange rate determination: normally, exchange rates will be determined by market forces. With a ***floating exchange rate***, there is no central bank intervention in the foreign exchange markets and the rate will be entirely market determined. With a ***fixed exchange rate***, there will be a very narrow exchange rate band and central bank intervention will keep the exchange rate very close to its ***parity***. This system was abandoned by the UK in 1972, since then there has been a ***managed exchange rate***, determined largely by market forces except in exceptional circumstances.

exchange rate fluctuations: when an exchange rate is floating freely, its value in terms of other countries' currencies may fluctuate markedly. This can be destabilising. Firms find it hard to predict what revenue they will get from export sales. Importers do not know what they will have to pay. Planning is made more difficult and the prices of traded goods may rise to cover the extra risk. Day-to-day changes in exchange rates are usually ironed out by central bank intervention. (The process works in just the same way as intervention to maintain a ***fixed exchange rate***.) However, fluctuations which reflect changing levels of international confidence in the currency may be hard to prevent and generally speaking central banks will usually not try to defend the exchange rate against market forces.

exchange rate index: a measure of change in the exchange rate which takes a weighted average of the changes across a number of currencies. Currencies are selected according to their importance in the trade pattern of the country concerned. For the UK, these will be first the euro, then the US dollar and the yen. These will be given the largest weights, with other currencies having smaller weightings. The resulting index number is sometimes called the ***effective exchange rate***. It provides a useful measure of changes in competitiveness due to exchange rate variations. See the table on the following page.

UK effective exchange rate, January 2005 = 100

2000	101.2
2001	99.5
2002	99.5
2003	95.8
2004	102.4
2005	101.1
2006	101.6
2007	104.1
2008	92.9

Source: Bank of England

Exchange Rate Mechanism (ERM): a forerunner of the *Economic and Monetary Union (EMU)* which linked EU currencies within the *European Monetary System (EMS)*. Member currencies were kept within fairly narrow exchange rate bands so that their exchange rates with each other could vary only to a small extent. The ERM was set up in 1979 and included most of the EU countries. The UK entered in 1990 but left again in 1992.

exchange rate policy: a government may allow its exchange rate to float freely or, in consultation with its trading partners, may seek to fix the rate or it may seek to manage the exchange rate so that fluctuations are reduced. Since 1972, most currencies have floated most of the time, with central banks intervening to eliminate day-to-day fluctuations. The drawback to a *floating exchange rate* is that it may be unstable. EMU removes this instability within the *euro zone* but the euro fluctuates against all other floating currencies.

exchange rate target: governments may choose to maintain a target for the exchange rate, as a means of controlling inflation. Then, in the event that prices rise, domestic producers become less competitive and demand for their products will fall on both export and domestic markets. This will discourage them from raising prices and reduce aggregate demand generally, reducing inflationary pressures. The UK government adopted this policy for a time in the late 1980s.

excise duty is an *expenditure tax* levied by HM Revenue and Customs. Unlike VAT which generally applies to most products, excise taxes apply to specific products and the rate varies depending on the product. The main products concerned are alcohol, tobacco, petrol and diesel. An important objective in all three cases is to reduce consumption, but these taxes are also significant revenue raisers.

excludability relates to *private goods* (as opposed to *public goods*). An important distinguishing factor of private goods is that people who do not pay for them can be excluded from using them. It is easy to see that you will not be able to consume something which has not been paid for. In contrast, no one can be excluded from consuming public goods such as street lighting in a public place or using the services of the police. If people cannot be excluded from benefiting from a particular good or service, then it cannot be sold. It is a public good and must be paid for by government. (See also *rivalry*.)

exhaustible resources are being consumed at a rate faster than that at which they can be replaced. For example, some forest products are being consumed at a rate beyond that at which new trees can be planted and grow to maturity.

exit: the way in which businesses may leave the market, or close down altogether, if the product in question has begun to make losses or just become less profitable than alternative uses of the resources. Easy exit is very important in ensuring efficiency, because without it the allocation of resources cannot adjust to changes in the pattern of consumer demand. Exit can be difficult in state-owned enterprises and may be affected by employment protection legislation. The absence of easy exit was one of the reasons why *centrally planned economies* failed to adapt to changing patterns of demand and led to rather slow growth in standards of living.

expansion: the process by which the economy grows through increasing *aggregate demand*.

expansionary policies may be used by governments which wish to reduce *unemployment* and achieve higher rates of *economic growth*. *Fiscal policies*, e.g. tax cuts and increases in expenditure, and a *monetary policy* of reduced interest rates will all tend to increase aggregate demand and encourage firms to take on more *labour* and expand output. Care must be taken not to overdo expansionary policies, lest growth leads to pressure on resources and accelerating inflation. Expansionary policies will not help in the long run to reduce *structural unemployment*.

expectations: a term which refers to what people expect to happen. Expectations are based on past experience. They have an important influence on what actually happens because expectations of change will in turn change people's behaviour.

Expectations can be very important in a macro-economic context. Investment plans are often based on expectations about future demand. Optimistic expectations may provide the business world with a self-fulfilling prophecy as the increase in investment does actually stimulate the economy. Inflationary expectations will tend to make people want to negotiate pay increases to cover whatever they expect inflation to be. So control of inflation requires that inflation expectations be reduced.

expectations-augmented Phillips curve: see *long-run Phillips curve*.

expenditure simply means spending. Consumer expenditure and government expenditure are commonly used terms.

expenditure method refers to one of the ways in which *national income* may be counted. The three methods are the expenditure method, the income method and the output method. In certain respects the expenditure method is the most reliable because sales revenue is hard to hide.

expenditure-reducing policies entail reducing the level of *aggregate demand* using *fiscal* and *monetary policies*. The term is used in relation to policies that deal with a trade deficit.

expenditure-switching policies reduce expenditure on foreign produced goods and services and increase it on domestic products. They include *import controls* and exchange rate *depreciation*.

expenditure taxes tax spending rather than income. They include VAT and the *excise duties*, but the term may also refer to a system by which people are assessed according to their expenditure rather than their income. This might give people an incentive to save more.

Expenditure taxes are important as sources of government revenue but are sometimes considered *regressive* in their effect, i.e. they have more impact on poorer people than on richer people.

exploitation means paying people less than the value of what they produce. Employers who pay less than the amount of extra revenue generated by an employee are exploiting that person. To the extent that the employer has some monopoly power in either the *labour* market or the product market, prices may be kept up and costs kept down so that some of the extra revenue becomes profit.

export credit: because of time lags in reaching the market, many exports are sold on *credit*. This is particularly important for capital equipment because it will be a long time before it generates income.

export incentives include all kinds of inducements which are designed to encourage exporters:

- subsidies (as with surplus agricultural products in the EU)
- tax incentives which require less tax to be paid on exports than on domestic sales
- low-cost loans.

Differences in the incentive structures of competing economies can lead to some unfair competition in international markets. Within the EU, this type of incentive is controlled to a degree.

export-led growth occurs when there is rapid growth of exports which then has a *multiplier* effect on the rest of the economy. China experienced this type of rapid growth up to 2008, leading to improvements in the standard of living there. An *undervalued exchange rate* may be helpful in achieving this.

export marketing means making an effort to sell in overseas markets. Some of this activity may be similar to marketing in the domestic setting. However, there are some important decisions to be made when considering new markets.

- Will a standardised product be appropriate for this market or would it be better to tailor the product precisely to the requirements of the market concerned?
- How will the product be distributed effectively?

Both questions have an important impact on costs and therefore on potential competitiveness.

export promotion means any kind of activity which can lead to an increase in exports. Governments often promote exports by trying to increase the flow of information about available products to people in countries which offer a promising market. Embassies have a role in this.

export subsidy: a payment by the government to an exporter made so that the price of the exported product can be reduced. These subsidies are illegal under the terms of the World Trade Organization, but many governments find ways around this. They may refund import duties paid on imported inputs or provide cheap loans. Subsidies can end in exports which are really *dumping*. The EU still subsidises exports of surplus agricultural products, though less than it used to due to fierce opposition from major agricultural exporters such as the US and Australia.

exports: goods and services sold for foreign currency. Goods from the *primary* or the *secondary sector* are visible *exports* while services such as tourism or insurance are *invisible exports*. (See also *pattern of trade*.)

ex post refers to the view of a situation after the event. It is possible to look back and with luck the data will give an accurate message as to what happened. This is in contrast to the *ex ante* view, essentially a forecast of the expected event.

external balance: a situation in which exports and imports are roughly the same in value. If they are not, then we might say that the external balance is in either surplus or deficit, depending on whether exports are higher or lower than imports.

external benefits accrue to third parties, not just the producer or the consumer. They may arise from production or consumption. External benefits of production occur when the production process entails something additional to the private benefits of the buyer. Firms that carry out research and development provide an external benefit to the extent that other firms have access to the new information. An external benefit of consumption occurs when the consumption process benefits third parties who are not themselves involved in buying the product. Users of public transport benefit anyone else who wants to travel and does so faster because of reduced congestion. (See also *externalities*.) With external benefits there will be *underconsumption.*

external costs occur when some of the costs of production are paid by third parties, rather than the producer or the consumer. For example, a new factory will usually create extra traffic on nearby roads. If this increases congestion, other road users will pay the costs because their journeys will be delayed. Pollution also creates a wide range of external costs. The polluting firm will not normally stop polluting without some kind of action because to do so would require extra spending, raising costs and reducing profit. These are external costs arising from production.

There are serious external costs associated with night flights into Heathrow Airport. This is an external cost of consumption. Wherever there are external costs, there will be *overconsumption* of the product. Local residents were offered major restrictions on night flights as a way of softening their opposition to the building of Heathrow's Terminal 5.

Government action can limit other external costs by direct controls, e.g. on emissions. A *cost–benefit analysis* of an investment project can be used to compare external costs and benefits as well as the internal ones, before the decision to invest is taken. Some but not all firms now set their own targets for polluting emissions from their processes because they wish to be seen to be acting responsibly. (See also *marginal social costs* and *benefits*.)

external diseconomies of scale are cost increases that affect all firms in the industry as output increases. These are likely to be local in effect and result from increased pollution and congestion or from pressure on resources generally. Expansion may drive up wage rates for specific skills.

external economies of scale: cost savings which occur as the industry grows. These will reduce costs for the whole industry and not just the individual firms. This can happen through:

- government-funded research efforts or research funded collaboratively by firms in the industry, which create new cost-reducing technologies available to all the firms in the industry
- the development of a pool of specialised skilled *labour* in the area, to which all firms have access – as with Sheffield in the 19th century when the cutlery industry developed, giving the area a general advantage in the production of special steels and in metalwork skills. This may be the result of some collaboration between firms in the industry or it may result from government training provision
- the growth of a network of suppliers with specialist skills and experience, from whom all firms can buy their inputs.

The economic development of Cambridge provides a recent example. Developments in electronics and biotechnology came from research conducted in the university. Firms set up in the area in order to have easy access to knowledge of relevance to the new technologies. The area developed a whole network of suppliers and specialists with very scarce skills, which in turn attracted more firms and further development. This is sometimes known as the Cambridge Phenomenon.

The diagram shows how external economies of scale shift the average total cost curve downwards for all firms in the industry.

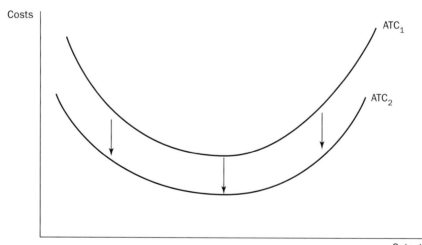

External economies of scale cut the firm's average costs as the industry grows

external financing means that the funds for investment are being obtained outside the business. In contrast, *internal finance* is generated from past *retained profits* which the firm has been able to save. External finance could come from:

- bank loans, which might be overdrafts, for day-to-day finance or fixed term loans for longer-term purposes
- share capital, which could come from a new issue or a rights issue
- very occasionally, grants may be obtainable from the government or the EU.

external growth occurs when a firm is taking over other firms or merging with them. It contrasts with internal growth, when firms develop new markets for themselves and increase output using their own resources. It provides an easy way for firms to increase their productive capacity quickly but may lead to management problems as they try to integrate different systems.

external shocks: see *shocks*.

externalities are the costs and benefits which result from a firm's operations but which are paid for by (or give benefit to) third parties. They are economic side effects. They include external costs such as pollution and congestion and external benefits such as the improvement in the general appearance of a shopping area when new shops open up in previously derelict premises.

Externalities are a sign that social efficiency is not being achieved. Social efficiency requires that the marginal social costs of each product are equal to the marginal social benefits. If they are not equal, there will be externalities, and *market failure*. Output and consumption levels will either be greater than or less than the level consistent with an optimal resource allocation, one which meets consumer needs most effectively.

- If all the external costs of a product were included in the decision to produce, total costs would be higher and so would the price. This would help to reduce the quantity demanded. The true costs of production would be included in the price. As it is, prices are less than the true cost and there is a higher level of consumption than is really efficient. It is quite likely that consumers would use electricity more economically if the price reflected the cost of cleaning up emissions. This is a situation of *overproduction*.
- Similarly, external benefits can cause *underconsumption*. If all the benefits are counted in considering the decision to produce, output might be higher. It might pay the local authority to consider subsidising new shops in areas which require regeneration, in order to get more external benefits.

One way to improve the *allocation of resources* is to ensure that the polluter pays all the costs of production. Polluters may be required to clean up their emissions; this internalises the cost of dealing with waste products. Or they may be required to pay for a pollution permit, which will give them an incentive to clean up. (See also *tradable permits*.)

factor cost describes a way of measuring national income. GDP used to be valued at the cost of the *factors of production* which contributed to production. (Alternatively the data could be expressed at market prices.) Nowadays the ONS uses *basic prices*, i.e. the price at which the firm sells the product, less taxes, plus subsidies.

factor endowment: the collection of real resources which are available within an economy. The nature of the factor endowment will depend on the *factors of production* available and will differ from one economy to another. For example, China has very abundant *labour* and much less abundant capital. Japan has relatively scarce labour but abundant capital and technical knowledge. Both countries are rather short of good flat land, useful for agriculture or manufacturing, compared to the US or Australia. Factor endowments are important in determining which products have a *comparative advantage* in each economy.

factor immobility occurs when factors of production cannot easily be moved to different uses if demand for the product declines. For example, when the demand for UK-built ships declined in the 1970s and 1980s, the shipyards (the capital) could not in general be used for other purposes. Similarly the people who had worked in the shipyards had skills which were not generally transferable to other industries, so the *labour* was immobile too.

Capital is only immobile in the short run: it need not be replaced at the end of its life. Similarly, *labour* will cease to be immobile if a move to suitable alternative employment is possible. (See also *occupational immobility* and *geographical immobility*.)

factor incomes are the returns to each *factor of production*. For *labour*, factor incomes are wages and salaries. For capital, factor incomes come from interest, profit and rent.

factor inputs are the *factors of production* needed as inputs in order to create output.

factor markets include the markets for *labour* and capital. Capital markets provide a source of finance for businesses and individuals. The price of capital is the interest rate. Labour markets are made up of the people who would like to be employed and the employers who want to hire people. The price of labour is the going wage or salary.

factor mobility: if factors of production are mobile they are able to move into alternative lines of production relatively easily. Much capital equipment is too specific for this, but sewing machines, computers and lorries are examples of exceptions. For *labour*, retraining facilities will increase mobility. Education generally increases mobility because it makes people more flexible.

factor prices: the prices of factors of production. These will be determined by the usefulness of the factor in the production process, which will generate a demand for the factor, and the supply of the factor, which will depend on availability and cost. There are markets for factors of production just as there are for goods and services. The *labour* market can be analysed using supply and demand theory, as can capital markets – the markets where funds for investment are borrowed and lent.

Differences in factor prices have a big impact on the choice of production methods. If *labour* is relatively cheap, *labour-intensive* production methods will normally be appropriate. Where capital is relatively cheap and abundant, capital will be substituted for labour as wages rise.

factors of production include *land*, *labour* and *capital*. They can be combined together in a great variety of ways which lead to the creation of output and hence of incomes and wealth. Each factor of production receives a return:

- the returns to labour are wages and salaries
- the returns to capital are interest and profit
- the returns to land are rent.

Sometimes a fourth factor of production is introduced as enterprise. The logic for this is that the entrepreneur has a special role in organising the other factors of production and taking the risks associated with the decision to produce. It is these decisions which, in a *market system*, allow profit to be made and bring about improvements in the standard of living.

factory gate prices are the prices charged by producers for output sold to wholesalers. They provide a helpful *leading indicator* of possible future consumer price changes.

fair trade means buying imported products from developing countries at prices which give a fair return to the producers. It is an attempt to avoid buying products which depend upon very cheap *labour*, implying that the producers get a very poor return for their efforts. The Fairtrade Foundation certifies firms which are engaged in fair trade so that consumers have some guarantee that producer incomes will benefit if they buy the product.

Family Expenditure Survey: carried out by the Office for National Statistics, this provides the information needed to construct the *retail price index (RPI)* and the *consumer price index (CPI)*, which measure the rate of inflation.

FAO: see *Food and Agriculture Organization (FAO)*.

Federal Reserve System (the 'Fed') is the central bank of the United States. It includes the Federal Reserve Board and 12 regional reserve banks. The governor is appointed by the President with Senate approval and presides over the Federal Open Market Committee which decides all matters of *monetary policy*. The Fed is independent of the US government.

fertility rate: the number of births per thousand women between the ages of 15 and 45. It provides a useful way of predicting population changes.

final goods: goods which are complete as a product and ready for immediate sale and use, e.g. cars. In contrast, *intermediate goods* will undergo further processing or be built into a final product, e.g. car batteries.

finance: a term covering sources of funds which may be borrowed to pay for investment or consumption.

financial assets include, cash, bank and building society balances, *bills*, *bonds*, *shares*, pension entitlements and *derivatives*.

financial conglomerates: firms which offer a wide range of financial services. For example, a bank might provide banking services to firms and individuals, mortgages, business loans, investment advice, pension plans, insurance policies, a share-dealing service

and even act as an estate agent. In the past, financial institutions were rather more specialised but a long period of takeovers and mergers has led to the formation of a number of
financial conglomerates.

financial deregulation: the removal of restrictions on *financial intermediaries*. In the
past many governments placed restrictions on the way banks operated and many of these
have now been removed. The objective was to increase efficiency and encourage competition. Regulations which have been removed included controls on the level of interest rates,
restrictions on the activities of foreign banks and restrictions on the type of business which
could be done. Banking regulation may be strengthened again in the future.

financial economies: see *internal economies of scale*.

financial futures: agreements to buy *financial assets* such as bonds at some date in
the future.

financial intermediaries include *investment* and *retail banks*, *building societies*,
pension funds and *insurance companies* and some other financial institutions. They exist
mainly to channel funds from savers who want to lend to borrowers who want to spend.
Borrowers can be consumers or firms which are investing.

financial markets fall into two categories:
- capital markets, which allow people to buy and sell bonds and shares. Governments
  and firms use them to raise the long-term finance they need. Holders of bonds and
  shares rely on them in order to be able to turn their financial assets into cash when the
  need arises.
- markets which provide opportunities to lend and borrow funds for a few months or at the
  other extreme, just overnight. They are used by firms, banks and the government which are
  constantly in need of short-term funds to finance their operations on a day-to-day basis.

financial sector reform may be needed when the financial sector is failing to deliver an
efficient system which allocates scarce capital towards those borrowers who can make the
best use of the funds. Most developed countries have a reasonably well-developed financial
sector capable of providing finance for *entrepreneurs* (except during the credit crunch).
Many developing and transition economies have people with potentially good business ideas
who cannot get the finance they need and this hinders the process of economic development. The development of an efficient banking sector can help in this respect.

Financial Services Authority: the organisation which supervises the operations of the
financial system. It was set up in 1997 to create a new, overarching system which supervises
banks as well as other financial intermediaries, such as insurance companies. It works in
close collaboration with the *Treasury* and the *Bank of England*. Supervision is important;
properly carried out it can, for instance, prevent banks from making imprudent loans and
financial advisers from misleading the public. However, during the 2007–09 financial crisis
there was widespread criticism of the FSA for allowing many banks to expand their lending in
imprudent ways, e.g. to sub-prime mortgage borrowers whose ability to repay should have
been more rigorously assessed. The FSA may be given sharper teeth in future.

fine tuning: the notion that governments can adjust *fiscal* and *monetary policy* to
create just the right amount of aggregate demand, keeping unemployment and inflation low
and encouraging growth. The idea was fashionable in the 1960s and 1970s. The results

of attempts to fine-tune the economy were disappointing because it proved very difficult to decide the exact amount of change needed. Governments tended to overshoot or act too late, partly because of weaknesses in current data and uncertainty about future events.

finite resources are resources which are fixed in supply and cannot be renewed. They are also referred to as *depletable resources*. Oil is one example, along with many other mineral products. Others include tropical timber and fish stocks which are not being exploited in a sustainable way.

firm: a collection of factors of production brought together by an entrepreneur for the purpose of producing goods or services. The term is often used when theory is being employed to analyse a particular situation, in contrast to the term business, which is used in a more practical context.

firm-specific skills are those skills which are acquired on the job and relate to that particular employer. A business will try hard not to make redundant a person with firm-specific skills because a replacement will have to be trained all over again. Their wages may be viewed as a fixed cost for this reason.

first-mover advantage can mean that one particular firm can be first into a new market or the first to develop and use a new technology. By being in the market before anyone else, the firm gets substantial market power which may last for some time if it can command some brand loyalty.

Achieving first-mover advantage can be costly and risky.

first world: the developed countries of Western Europe, the US, Canada, Japan, Australia and New Zealand. The other groups in this terminology were the second world, which was the communist bloc, and the third world, the developing countries. These terms are used much less than they used to be because increasing incomes in some parts of the third world have rendered this simple classification inappropriate. Similarly, the second world has shrunk dramatically. New categories, the transition economies and emerging economies, have been created.

fiscal drag occurs if there is *inflation* and *tax allowances* are left unchanged. The value of the allowance falls as inflation reduces its purchasing power. So the tax paid rises without any change in tax rates. Similarly, if benefits are not raised in line with inflation, their real value will fall. Fiscal drag will also occur if there is economic growth. Tax revenue will rise as the increases in income are taxed at the marginal rate.

fiscal policy includes all measures relating to taxation and other revenue-raising activities and government expenditure. It is set out each year in the Budget by the Chancellor of the Exchequer, when all new measures are announced. There is also an annual review of fiscal policy which is set out in the Pre-Budget Report which comes out each November.

Fiscal policy has certain important objectives:
- Raising revenue to pay for the provision of *public* and *merit goods* and the day-to-day operation of government. Governments have long shopping lists and even with careful consideration of priorities, all recent governments have found it difficult to reduce expenditure. There is a significant consensus amongst British voters that the National Health Service (NHS) must be preserved and improved and the *ageing population*

places heavy demands on health funding. Public spending in 2008 was roughly 43% of GDP, having risen from 39% in 2001–02.

- Influencing the **allocation of resources** by encouraging some activities and discouraging others. For example, all governments want to discourage smoking and encourage small businesses to get started. Smoking has important **external costs** in the shape of related illnesses which require health spending. So tobacco is taxed. Small businesses are an important source of new jobs so there are various measures designed to help self-employed people in the early years. **Fuel taxes** raise revenue but they are also thought to reduce demand for fuel and so reduce emissions of greenhouse gases. Every year there are changes to the tax system designed to reduce some incentives and increase others.
- Influencing the distribution of income. The tax and **benefit** system can be used to reduce **disposable income** for richer people and increase it for poorer people. The extent to which redistribution takes place is very much a political matter and there is now rather less of it than there was 25 years ago. However, the 40% higher marginal rate of income tax combined with the various benefits paid still have a significant effect.
- Stabilising the economy so that the fluctuations associated with the **economic cycle** do not become a problem. During a recession, it makes sense to increase aggregate demand by cutting taxes and raising government expenditure. This will tend to reduce the rate at which people are made redundant and encourage firms to invest. However, it will mean that there will be a **budget deficit** – perhaps quite a large one. Similarly, if the economy begins to grow unsustainably fast and there is a risk of inflation accelerating, governments can raise tax rates or introduce new taxes and cut back expenditure. There may then be a budget surplus which can be used to reduce the total debt outstanding.

Fiscal policy to stabilise the economy needs to be co-ordinated with **monetary policy**. At the time of writing, the UK government, along with most other developed country governments, is borrowing large sums to try to offset the effect of the 2007/09 financial crisis and provide loans for struggling businesses and home-owners. Monetary policy is determined by the **Monetary Policy Committee** of the Bank of England which acts independently of the Treasury, though in close consultation with it. Fiscal policy can be adapted to fit in with the monetary policy stance at the time, though there are often time lags involved.

fiscal rules: while Chancellor of the Exchequer, Gordon Brown said that the government would adhere to the golden rule. There were two elements in this:

- Over the course of the **economic cycle**, the government would balance the budget. This left some scope for counter-cyclical policy, with deficit spending in a recession to be balanced by a surplus in times of recovery.
- There would be no borrowing to finance consumption, although there would be borrowing to finance investment that had a reasonable prospect of generating funds for repayment over the long run.

In October 2008, Chancellor Alistair Darling signalled a change of policy so that the government could borrow very large amounts to provide a greater stimulus to the economy and limit the damage caused by the recession.

fiscal transfers refer to funds that are transferred from a government in one country to a government in another. Foreign **aid** is an obvious example.

Fisher Equation: see *equation of exchange*.

fixed capital formation: see *GDFCF*.

fixed costs are all those costs which stay the same regardless of the quantity produced. They include the cost of capital equipment and buildings, interest charges, management and administrative costs. Part of the wage and salary bill may be a fixed cost when the people concerned are not directly involved in the production process. Fixed costs are only fixed in the short run: in the long run, alterations can be made to the quantity of capital equipment and the way the firm is run. (See also *average fixed costs*.)

fixed exchange rates are rates which have been set at a particular level in terms of other currencies. This means that they are not determined by the forces of supply and demand. If market forces are pushing the currency outside the band within which it is allowed to fluctuate, the central bank will intervene, buying or selling the currency to keep it very close to its fixed *parity*. Even with a floating exchange rate, central banks may intervene to smooth out day-to-day variations. The main advantage of a fixed exchange rate is stability and predictability.

fixed factors of production are the resource inputs to a production process, the quantity of which cannot be altered in the short run. In other words, the quantity of the factor employed does not change with the level of output. For example, capital equipment is a fixed factor because it takes time to arrange to have more or less of it. *Labour* will be a fixed factor if there are difficulties about increasing or decreasing the quantity of it as output changes, as in the case of managers.

fixed investment is spending on capital equipment, buildings and so on, which can be expected to yield an income over a long period. In contrast, investment in stocks and work in progress will be used in the production process, or sold, very quickly.

fixed rate loan: a loan, the terms of which are agreed in advance with a specified interest rate. This can be useful to a firm which needs to be certain about what its interest rate commitments will be and works well if interest rates are tending to rise. On the other hand, it will be inflexible if interest rates fall or the circumstances of the firm change.

flexibility can be important in two ways:
- A firm which is flexible can review its decisions and make changes in its products or pricing strategies in the light of changes in the marketplace. Firms which manufacture clothing benefit from being flexible because demand can change at any time and they can keep up with the changes.
- *Flexible labour markets* can adjust to changing technologies and changing markets easily because there are people who have transferable skills and are willing to do a range of different types of work or acquire new skills.

flexible exchange rate: see also *floating exchange rate*. The way in which lost competitiveness can be regained through depreciation of a floating exchange rate has been mentioned by many people who oppose UK adoption of the euro. Competitiveness is most commonly lost through an inflation rate which is higher than those of other countries. If the UK adopts the euro and then experiences accelerating inflation, it could lose competitiveness within the euro zone.

flexible labour markets occur where employers are able to take on new employees on a full-time or a part-time basis, temporarily or permanently, at wage rates which are not set by union agreements or government controls, and are able to make employees redundant without great expense. *Labour* market flexibility can be further enhanced if employees are willing to do a range of different tasks and acquire new skills, i.e. *multi-skilling*. It is generally thought

119

that there is less unemployment in a flexible labour market. The US labour market is believed to be more flexible than the UK labour market. Within the EU, the UK and the Netherlands are thought to have more flexible labour markets than most other member countries.

flexible prices: prices which adjust so that the market clears quickly. For example, in *commodity markets*, an increase in the quantity supplied of, say, iron ore will produce a swift fall in price which will eliminate any unsold stocks. Similarly, tomatoes in a street market on Saturday afternoon will have their price reduced if they are soft. Manufactures usually have rather less flexible prices and house prices change even less readily, particularly when prices are falling. Inflexible prices usually lead to a *disequilibrium* situation.

flexible specialisation: the idea that manufacturers should be able to produce small quantities of goods aimed at particular markets, in such a way that the level of production can be varied at short notice to match changes in demand. This contrasts with the idea of mass production, where vast quantities of standardised products are produced in ways which maximise *economies of scale*. Computer-controlled processes and flexible *labour* forces are making flexible specialisation much easier than it would have been in the past.

flexible wages can change quickly to reflect *labour* market conditions and in particular, wage rates for a particular type of labour will fall if demand for those people's services decreases. In practice, wages are usually not like this because there is an agreed rate for the job and a fall in wages may cause serious disaffection in the workforce. Some economists have argued that flexible wages will reduce unemployment because there will be a wage rate for everyone at which some employer will take them on. This could be debated.

floating exchange rate: one which is determined by market forces. Changes in demand and supply are brought about by changes in imports and exports or by capital movements or by speculation. A floating exchange rate will undergo an *exchange rate depreciation* if demand for the currency falls or if supply rises and an *appreciation* if demand for the currency rises or supply falls. (See also *exchange rate*.) A floating exchange rate may be managed by the central bank so as to reduce day-to-day fluctuations.

The diagram shows how an increase in demand for exports might lead to an exchange rate appreciation. The demand for exports generates a demand for the currency needed to pay for them. The demand curve shifts to the right and the exchange rate rises.

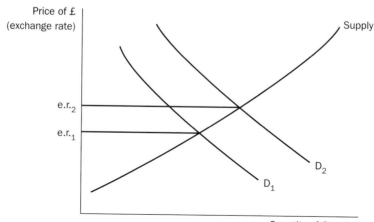

An increase in demand for pounds leads to appreciation

Floating exchange rates do have advantages.

- A balance of trade deficit, occurring when imports exceed exports by a significant margin, will lead to automatic adjustment. The high level of imports will create a large and growing supply of pounds (in the UK). This will lead to exchange rate depreciation. This will in turn make exports more competitive and imports more expensive, increasing exports and reducing imports (after a time lag). The deficit will diminish. So a floating exchange rate will, in time, bring about an automatic adjustment in the balance of trade.
- There is no need for potentially expensive central bank intervention to maintain the exchange rate at a fixed parity. Defending an unrealistic exchange rate can require the use of foreign exchange reserves and can be very costly.

The difficulty with a floating exchange rate is that it can be quite unstable. Firms may be unable to predict future profitability because they do not know what prices they can charge or how competitive they will be, if the exchange rate appreciates or depreciates. Furthermore, the exchange rate which results from market forces may be influenced more by *capital movements* than by trade. The euro has eliminated this uncertainty within the euro zone but not outside it.

flow: some variables are described as flows, others as *stocks*. Income is a flow: it comes in steadily, year by year. Wealth is a stock: it includes all sorts of assets (houses, bank deposits, shares and so on) which you hold, sometimes over a long period. Similarly, investment is a flow, while the stock of capital, the accumulated investments of past years, is a stock.

focus is the opposite of *diversification*. It means concentrating on core products, usually the ones in which the firm has the greatest competitive advantage. The firm will stick to its main line of business which is the one which it understands the best. Subsidiaries producing other products may be sold.

Food and Agriculture Organization (FAO): a constituent body of the United Nations. It undertakes research into agricultural methods and disseminates knowledge which can help to increase output of food products and improve nutrition.

footloose industries are able to locate in a wide range of places because their costs do not vary much between one place and another. Traditional industries are often tied to a location for historical reasons, such as past raw material or energy availability. Recently developed industries such as electronics are likely to be footloose.

Footsie (FT–SE 100): a measure of changes in the average level of share prices. It stands for Financial Times–Stock Exchange 100, because it is based on the share prices of the leading 100 firms. Price changes are weighted and an index is constructed on a continuous basis. A rise in the index suggests some optimism about future profitability generally, so the index is useful as a *leading indicator*.

forecasting: predicting future changes. Firms forecast likely future demand and other variables. Macro-economic forecasting uses sophisticated models to predict changes in the economy as a whole. Output, investment, inflation, employment and unemployment might all be the subject of forecasts. The models consist of a large number of equations which are used to represent the relationships between different variables in the economy.

foreign aid may be offered to developing countries with a low per capita income in order to help them invest. It may also be available to countries with serious famine problems. It may be bilateral aid, given by one government to another. Or it may be multilateral, given through an international organisation, often the World Bank or the European Development Fund. There have been strenuous efforts over the years to persuade the developed countries to give more foreign aid, almost always unsuccessful. A target of the 1960s and 1970s, that 1% of GDP should be given by each developed country, never came near to being reached and since then aid has tended to diminish rather than to grow.

Not all aid has been well used; some has been spent on prestige projects and military objectives which have not benefited poor people. There has been some evidence of corruption in the disbursement of aid and its usefulness has been further compromised by the tying of aid payments to a commitment to buy goods from the donor country. In some cases aid has been tied to the purchase of military goods.

foreign debt: the debts owed to foreign country lenders. These are most significant in the case of a number of developing countries which are heavily indebted. The lenders may be governments, banks, firms or international organisations. (See also *Debt Problem*.) Sovereign debt means debt owed by a government to a foreign lender.

foreign debt management refers to the problems of heavily indebted developing countries. Sometimes the *debt service ratio* is so high that after interest and repayments have been covered, there is little foreign exchange left to cover other needs. In these circumstances *debt rescheduling* may be considered. (See also *Debt Problem*.)

foreign direct investment (FDI) refers to investment by companies with their head office in another country, which are setting up factories or distribution outlets. In other words, it implies that the investment is in actual productive capacity which will generate output, rather than in financial assets such as shares or bonds. Many governments have been keen to encourage FDI. Within the UK, Wales has been particularly successful in attracting foreign investors. FDI has been important in helping some developing countries that have experienced rapid growth, e.g. Thailand.

foreign exchange may mean foreign currency, the medium of exchange of another country.

foreign exchange markets consist of the buyers and sellers of foreign exchange and the dealers who offer to buy and sell. Deals may be made in either the spot or the forward market. The spot market deals in currencies available immediately, while in the forward market deals are made which fix a price today for currency which will be available in the future, say in three months' time. Currencies are exchanged for trade reasons but also when there are capital movements. Money will be moved from one currency to another in order to get the best interest rate or for investment in production capacity overseas or perhaps to speculate on exchange rate changes.

foreign exchange reserves: the stocks of foreign currency held by the central bank and available if the exchange rate needs to be maintained at its existing level at a time when market forces are tending to push it downwards, i.e. to bring about a depreciation. The level of the reserves is important if there is either a *fixed exchange rate* or a *managed exchange rate*. Even if the exchange rate is floating, if it threatens to depreciate very rapidly, the central bank may want to try to stabilise its value by buying it, using the foreign exchange reserves.

foreign investment may take place in two ways:
- *foreign direct investment (FDI)* means spending in another country which will create production facilities

- *portfolio investment* means buying shares in companies based abroad or bonds issued by other countries' governments or moving money to bank accounts abroad.

formal economy: that part of the economy which is recorded in official statistics. So it includes all legally organised business and all government activity but excludes the use of resources which are not paid for such as voluntary and domestic work and work done for cash which is not declared for tax purposes. Some of the latter will be legal but some will not.

forward integration means creating a business which takes care of further processing and/or distribution and marketing of the final product, as well as its manufacture. It means that producers of intermediate goods may expand their business by taking the production process a stage further. Makers of computer chips might actually start to manufacture computers. The more likely route would be to buy or merge with an established business which has some expertise in the next stage of the process.

forward markets are the markets in which it is possible to buy a certain quantity of goods or foreign currency at a price agreed today, for delivery at a specific future date. This can act as insurance against unforeseen problems that may damage the profitability of an export order, such as a sudden jump in oil prices due to war breaking out in the Middle East. Contracts made in the forward market are known as *futures*.

franchise: a system by which independent businesses acquire the right to sell a branded product. The franchisee makes a payment to the owner of the brand, the franchisor. The franchisee is then entitled to sell the product and use the franchisor's marketing devices. These might include logos or the design of the premises or advertising material. In addition to the initial fee, the franchisee will also pay a percentage of sales revenue to the franchisor.

The advantage of a franchise is that the independent business can benefit from having a well-known branded product. Some of the advertising will be carried out by the franchisor. It may be much easier and less risky to go into business this way than to create and market a new product. The drawback is that the franchisor may strictly control the activities of the franchisee. From the franchisor's point of view, this may be one way to expand across a very wide area, maybe internationally, without having to acquire or finance all the outlets. Many retail outlets are franchised, such as Body Shop, Pizza Hut and McDonald's.

franchise monopoly: a franchise may be so arranged that the franchisee has a part of the market to itself. If the number of franchises is strictly limited and they are kept away from one another's natural territory, e.g. by making sure that they are a certain distance apart, the individual franchise will face less competition.

fraud means the use of misrepresentation in order to make money. It can include selling goods which are not what they appear to be, continuing to trade knowing that the business cannot pay its debts and generally taking money under false pretences.

free enterprise: a system by which individuals are allowed to set up in business without interference from governments, whether local or national. Free enterprise is commonly regarded as a good thing and it often is where there is strong *competition*. It can lead to there being lively and innovative producers who strive to meet real consumer needs and wants. If on the other hand producers acquire market power through monopolies or *cartels* they may be able to charge unnecessarily high prices. Or they may sell poor-quality goods against which the consumer has little protection. Regulation may be needed to protect consumers.

free entry refers to the situation in which entry is very easy for firms which seek to break into a new market. Where the market has a large number of small businesses, e.g. hairdressers, antique shops, accountants and so on, entry is usually fairly free. Manufacturing industries in which large potential economies of scale create barriers to entry illustrate the reverse situation. Free entry is used as a theoretical concept which helps to define **perfect competition**. Easy entry will always make for a more competitive market.

Free entry is important in that it is necessary in order to ensure that resources can be reallocated to adapt to changes in the pattern of consumer demand. Easy **exit** is also important in this respect, because it frees the resources needed by growing industries.

free goods are goods which have no price and no property rights associated with them and require no factors of production for their enjoyment. It is rather hard to find satisfactory examples because, increasingly, it has become apparent that the traditional examples such as fresh air and sunshine are not free at all. Hence the saying, there is no such thing as a **free lunch**.

free lunch: it is usually said that 'there is no such thing as a free lunch'. However, occasionally a policy will be found to benefit gainers while actually having no losers. This may be the result of deliberate efforts to compensate any losers. This situation is exceptional though: most decisions have an **opportunity cost**. The 'passports for pets' scheme might be a free lunch if none of them actually bring diseases home with them.

free market: a market in which there is no government interference. The concept of a free market underlies the **laissez-faire** principle, **capitalism** and the **market system**. In practice, a market with literally no government intervention would be totally chaotic, as there would be no legal system to ensure fair play. The term is used to describe markets where the government does not actually control decision making.

free market economy: one in which the government plays a limited role. All governments place some legal restrictions on firms, but if the government aims to avoid interfering in business decisions, the market may be reasonably free. This implies that the market mechanism is allowed to work, reasonably unfettered by excessive regulation. This can be a very grey area, politically.

free market policies are designed to reduce government intervention in the economy and ensure that decisions are made on the basis of market forces. Privatisation was a move in this direction and has led to closer attention being given to consumer preferences. However, many of the privatised industries – telephones, water, electricity and so on – are subject to regulation to ensure that they do not take advantage of their market power by overcharging.

free movement of capital is an important aspect of creating the **single market** of the EU, and important worldwide in facilitating growth and **globalisation**. It allows firms to invest in the locations where production will be most efficient and can lead to lower prices for consumers. They then have higher real incomes. Both they and the employees who find work in new locations get improved standards of living.

free movement of people: an important element in the underlying framework of the **European Union (EU)**. (The other two pillars of the system are free movement of goods and services and free movement of capital.) All EU citizens have the right to live and work anywhere in the EU and moves have been made to recognise qualifications across all member countries.

free rider problem: where there is a *public good*, no one can be excluded from benefiting from it and so no one has an incentive to pay for its installation or upkeep. Street lighting is a standard example; because of the free rider problem no individual will pay for it. All will wait for someone else to provide it, knowing that they will have the use of it without paying. This is why public goods must be provided by governments which have the legal right to tax people to pay for them.

free trade means trade which is not restricted by import controls such as *tariffs*, *quotas* or other methods. The theory of *comparative advantage* states that output can be increased when each country specialises in producing the goods and services with the lowest opportunity cost. The growth of free trade has in fact been associated with unprecedented economic growth and greatly improved standards of living.

The World Trade Organization exists to encourage free trade. Trade negotiations under its auspices have done much to reduce trade barriers, most recently in the Uruguay Round of negotiations. Many trade barriers still exist, however, and some of these are detrimental to the welfare of some of the world's poorest countries.

free trade area: a group of countries which allow free trade amongst themselves but retain a separate set of trade barriers against other countries. The most important free trade area is NAFTA, the *North American Free Trade Agreement*, which comprises Canada, the US and Mexico.

freight transport: facilities to move goods from one location to another.

frictional unemployment: the unemployment caused by the time taken to find a new job after one has come to an end. In many ways it is not serious in that time spent seeking an appropriate job, rather than taking the first which is offered, should improve the fit between the individual's personal qualities and the requirements of the job. Improved information can reduce frictional unemployment so the various contributions of Job Centres may be helpful. (See also *unemployment*.)

Friedman, Milton (1912–2006) was an American economist with an unusual devotion to the free market. He is closely associated with the view that governments should not involve themselves in business decisions.

His most important work concerned the relationship between the growth of the money stock and the rate of inflation. For this he was awarded the Nobel Prize for economics in 1976, after a lifetime of research and teaching at the University of Chicago. His view of monetary policy as the essential antidote to inflation was adopted by the Conservative government of 1979, though not very rigidly enforced. His followers, who advocated strict monetary policy, became known as *monetarists*. Their views were opposed by the *Keynesians*, who perceived a much stronger role for governments in preventing unemployment. Friedman's concept of the *non-accelerating inflation rate of unemployment (NAIRU)* and the *long-run Phillips curve* provided a helpful explanation for the tendency of economies in the 1970s to experience growing unemployment and accelerating inflation at the same time (*stagflation*).

fuel tax: excise taxes which raise the market price of petrol, diesel and heating oil. Initially the purpose of the taxes was to raise revenue. In the case of petrol and diesel, this was partly intended to cover the cost of building and maintaining roads. In the past fuel taxes have been raised to discourage consumption of fuels which generate greenhouse gases, but recently public opinion has tended to turn against this. The Department of Transport has estimated that a 10% increase in the real price of fuel will reduce quantity demanded by 3%, but governments have shied away from creating strong incentives to cut energy use for fear of losing popularity.

fuel tax escalator: the system by which fuel taxes were raised by more than the rate of inflation at each budget, so that the proportion of the price which was tax rose steadily. This was abandoned in the 2000 Budget due to its unpopularity with road users. This may have some impact on greenhouse gas emissions.

full-capacity output: the highest level of output which can be achieved in the economy as a whole, given the type of resources available and their existing location. *Aggregate demand* for goods and services in excess of this level of output will lead to accelerating inflation. However, there may at this level of output still be some *structural unemployment*. This will occur if the unemployed people do not have the skills which are required by employers or if they are located in areas other than the ones in which employers are recruiting. In other words, if they are *occupationally immobile* or *geographically immobile*, they may be unable to contribute to production.

full employment: the level of employment at which all those who wish to work have found jobs, with the exception of those who are *frictionally unemployed*. What level of unemployment in the UK now represents full employment is a matter of some debate. *LFS unemployment* reached its lowest rate for more than 20 years at 4.8% in 2004, having been around 5% since 2000. By the end of 2008 it had risen to 5.7% as recession set in.

Structural change, which includes an increasing rate of technological advance, has created considerable unemployment over the years and this can be slow to go away even when the economy is booming. Between 1999 and 2005, structural unemployment did appear to be diminishing.

full employment national income: the level of national income which would be possible if all resources were fully employed. It is a measure of what the economy is capable of producing.

function: a relationship between two variables, one of which depends on the other. The dependent variable is said to be a function of the independent variable. For example, consumption is said to be a function of income.

functional distribution of income: the shares of national income which go to *labour*, capital and land.

fundamentals: the underlying forces which determine how the economy performs. Many of the changes which take place are transitory and will be reversed later. Fundamentals determine the real long-term trends. The fundamental consideration in deciding how the level of exports is determined is the level of competitiveness, which is in turn determined by the exchange rate, incomes in other countries, the quality of the product and the costs of production.

futures trading is when commodities or financial assets are bought or sold for delivery at some time in the future, at a price agreed now. Commodities such as wheat, oil, wool and many other products can also be bought or sold 'forward' on the commodity exchanges. This can be purely speculative, but it can also be vital for a business to protect itself against possible exchange rate or commodity price fluctuations. (See also *hedging*, *derivatives* and *options*.)

G8: see *Group of Eight (G8)*.

G20: see *Group of Twenty (G20)*.

gains from trade: the benefits arising from trade which result in increased output from a given quantity of real resources. The theory of comparative advantage shows that trade allows countries to specialise in the goods and services which they produce most efficiently. By increasing efficiency, gains are made overall.

Galbraith J K (1908–2006): a Canadian-born economist who taught at Harvard University. He held views which contrasted with conventional *neoclassical economics*. In his writings he emphasised the dominating influence of big businesses. He saw them less as satisfying consumer preferences and more as moulding preferences for their own ends, primarily through advertising. He argued that large firms should be tightly regulated by governments to prevent abuse of their market power. He also emphasised the role of the public sector in providing goods and services which could prevent gross inequalities. He contrasted 'private affluence' with 'public squalor', which can be a result of the operation of a free market.

galloping inflation: see *hyperinflation*.

game theory applies when the bodies which are competing in the marketplace exhibit *interdependent behaviour*. This means that for each one, the actions of the other will have an impact on the decisions taken. For example, if one business decides to cut prices, its competitor may follow suit. Game theory can be applied in a range of oligopoly situations, whether the businesses are competing or colluding with each other. There may be gainers and losers or all may gain together.

Game theory uses formal models to analyse the alternative strategies that are open to competing firms. See also *first-mover advantage, prisoners' dilemma, profit pay-off matrix* and *zero sum game*.

Gates, Bill: the founder of Microsoft. Having started the business in 1975 he is currently the world's richest man. Microsoft provides an excellent example of a market leader and *dominant firm*. Bill Gates is still non-executive chairman of Microsoft but is not otherwise active in the general management of the company. He now dispenses large sums of money through the Bill and Melinda Gates Foundation, the largest transparently operated charity in the world, which has been particularly active in Africa.

GATT: see *General Agreement on Tariffs and Trade (GATT)*.

GDFCF is a statistical term, gross domestic fixed capital formation, which includes buildings, plant, machinery, vehicles (for commercial use), ships, aircraft and *infrastructure*. It is a measure of total investment in any one year.

GDP: see *gross domestic product (GDP)*.

GDP deflator: a price index which includes the prices of all the goods and services produced in the economy. It includes investment products as well as consumer goods. It is thus more comprehensive than the *retail price index (RPI)* or the *consumer price index (CPI)*, which measure the prices of consumer products. It is used to find the real value of total output and to decide on its real rate of growth.

gearing measures the relative importance of *loan finance* in relation to share finance (*equity finance*). It is important because a firm with a lot of debt will have to pay interest on it in good times and bad. If the firm relies more on share finance and if profits are poor, it can pay a lower *dividend* to shareholders or none at all.

General Agreement on Tariffs and Trade (GATT) was set up after World War II. It remained very small until it became the *World Trade Organization (WTO)* in 1995. Its objective was to encourage the growth of international trade by removing or reducing *tariffs* and *non-tariff barriers (NTBs)*.

Agreements under the GATT were reached after what were known as 'rounds' of negotiations, which often lasted many years. The last was the Uruguay Round which lasted from 1986 until 1994. It had considerable impact on trade in many products, including services.

GATT was instrumental in making the world trading environment very much freer than it was before World War II. It oversaw very large reductions in tariffs which in turn led to large increases in trade in manufactures.

general equilibrium refers to the type of economic analysis which examines the consequences of changes in all the markets which they might affect. In this way it takes account of the interrelationships between different markets. So partial equilibrium analysis would consider the impact of a change in demand for restaurant meals on their price and quantity sold, whereas general equilibrium analysis would go on to include consideration of the effect on demand for chefs and other *labour* market consequences, the impact on other producers in food processing and leisure activities and so on.

genetically modified (GM) foods: foods which have been grown or produced from new varieties based on changes in the genes which determine their attributes. These foods have enormous potential to cut costs and increase output but the wisdom of developing them is still hotly debated because of possible unknown effects on health and the environment.

In the long run, GM foods could eliminate food shortages in *developing countries*. New varieties could be created which will tolerate poor growing conditions in areas with low rainfall which are currently the scene of serious poverty. However, in order to make the new varieties available to people with low incomes, international organisations and governments will have to negotiate with the *multinationals* which are developing them.

geographical immobility occurs when people who have been made redundant are unable to move to areas in which jobs are available and thus remain unemployed. It is made worse when there is a lack of housing for rent at reasonable prices in the areas where jobs exist. Also differences in house prices, such that areas with high unemployment have low prices, make it hard for people without jobs to move to areas with jobs. Improved transport facilities can reduce geographical immobility.

Giffen good: a product for which quantity demanded rises when the price rises. This is so rare as to be almost a matter of theory. Potatoes during the Irish potato famine in the 1840s are used as an example. When potato crops failed, the price rose so spending on potatoes rose, leaving many people unable to afford anything other than potatoes and thus demanding more of them to satisfy their food needs. (You will only need to know this if you are studying for the AQA or IB courses.)

gilt-edged security: a loan to the government for the purpose of covering a budget deficit.

The term gilt-edged reflects the fact that the government can guarantee to pay the money back because of its legal right to tax. The shortened form, gilts, refers to the **bonds** which are the actual securities, i.e. pieces of paper stating the amount of the loan, the rate of interest and the maturity date (i.e. when it will be repaid).

Gini coefficient: a measurement of inequality in the distribution of income. It is the ratio of the area between the diagonal and the **Lorenz curve** to the total area under the diagonal. It measures the extent to which the distribution of income diverges from precise equality. Latin America has the greatest inequality with a Gini coefficient around 0.5. Developed countries typically have a Gini coefficient of around 0.3. In the UK, the Gini coefficient rose from 0.25 in the early 1980s to 0.37 in 2000, since when it has been fairly stable.

global brands are products with a brand name which is recognised all over the world. Some are tailored to local tastes but generally, such products are standardised. Coca-Cola is the archetypal example.

global imbalances: gradually, over many years, first Germany and Japan, and then China, developed large balance of payments surpluses. These had their roots in two factors – high levels of saving and at times, very low exchange rates, in the countries concerned. In 2007, their current account surpluses were respectively $253bn, $211bn and $372bn. For many years these surpluses were used to fund large loans to the deficit countries, the largest of which are the UK and the USA, both of which imported large quantities of the surplus countries' exports. Thus serious imbalances developed. So long as all countries were experiencing robust economic growth it was possible for their governments to ignore the potential problems. By 2009, however, it was clear that these imbalances had had a major role in the development of the financial crisis. The deficit countries need to cut spending so that they live within their incomes. However, this means much reduced demand for the surplus countries' products and the necessary adjustment could be very painful. The Chinese government recognises that it would be wise to encourage the Chinese people to consume more of their own products, but if they experience serious job cuts due to lack of demand, they may not be able to afford to. China is still a relatively poor country. At the time of writing the UK exchange rate is low and this may help UK exporters, which will reduce the external deficit.

This is a very complex story but A-level students should be aware of the problem of global imbalances and the fact that long-term changes will be needed to prevent them from leading to further instability. (See also **current account imbalances** and **balance of payments**.)

global warming is the rise in temperatures that is occurring as a result of the emission of '**greenhouse**' **gases** from industrial processes and vehicle exhausts. The likely consequences, climate change and rising sea levels, will probably have profound economic effects. Meantime, economic analysis can help us to understand the policies which might be used to combat the emission of greenhouse gases. (See also *fuel tax*.)

globalisation of the international economy refers to the process by which there is both an increasing world market in goods and services and increasing integration in world capital markets. This means that governments need to consult with their trading partners in order to co-ordinate their *macro-economic policies* and to avoid destabilising capital movements. Otherwise the success of their policies is likely to be compromised.

Globalisation has been associated with the rapid growth in world trade and has encouraged *economic growth*. It has improved standards of living for many people. It may also have increased the power of the multinationals. Some of the growth in trade has evolved as a result of efforts to make trade easier through the trade negotiations of the *World Trade Organization (WTO)*.

Globalisation has also made all economies more vulnerable to shocks elsewhere. The financial crisis of 2007–09 originated in the financial systems of the developed countries but had a serious effect on the developing countries because the fall in demand for manufactures and commodities reduced overall demand for their exports. The *IMF* was able to help some with loans but this usually requires policy changes that may be unpopular. Sharp falls in commodity prices were particularly difficult for poorer countries to deal with.

See also *global imbalances*.

glut: a quantity supplied which is well above the amount needed to satisfy demand at current prices. For example, an unusually large crop of tomatoes will lead to increased supplies in the marketplace and to fast-falling prices as producers try to get rid of the crop before it spoils. (See diagram below.) There can also be a glut of a mineral product (e.g. oil) if more has been produced than is being demanded. Depending on the extent to which the product has *inelastic demand*, the fall in prices will be higher.

Inelastic demand will mean a sharp fall in price if quantity increases significantly

GM foods: see *genetically modified foods*.

GNP: see *gross national product (GNP)*.

going rate: the current level of pay increases being negotiated.

gold: the precious metal now used in the financial system only as part of central banks' *foreign exchange reserves*. However, since it pays no interest, its role is diminishing further and central banks are selling it slowly. Gold is still used by some individuals as a store of value. They believe it can protect them from the effects of inflation and act as an emergency reserve. When other assets seem risky, as in 2008, gold prices tend to rise.

gold standard: a system for fixing exchange rates. Each currency had a fixed value in terms of gold. Until 1914 this was helpful in creating stability. Then the strains of World War I followed by the Great Depression made it impossible for most currencies to maintain the gold standard. The UK left the gold standard for good in 1931. By 1971 the last link between gold and the dollar had been abandoned. Gold reserves could not be expanded fast enough to finance the rapidly increasing levels of world trade.

golden rule: the idea that government budgets should balance over the course of the economic cycle, with borrowing used only to finance investment. During recession, incomes are falling and tax revenue will fall too. Unemployment is rising and benefit payments increase. The result will be an increasing *budget deficit*. As the economy recovers this process goes into reverse and it will be possible to generate a surplus which offsets the earlier deficit. Any borrowing which is additional to this should be spent on investment projects which have the potential to increase incomes in the future. This rule was important to the 1997 Labour government but by 2006 it appeared to be maintainable only by a changing interpretation of the data. (See also *fiscal rules*.)

good governance: all countries have institutions that exercise power and take decisions. Good governance implies that:
- there is *transparency* and openness so that information is freely available
- the *rule of law* is applied in a fair and consistent way
- governments both local and national respond to public opinion
- bribery and *corruption* do not have a significant impact on the decisions that are taken.

Where these conditions are not met, there may be a serious impact on standards of living generally and power hungry individuals may be able to appropriate resources for their own use on a scale that most people would regard as unacceptable. In recent years the World Bank and other agencies have sought to impose requirements relating to good governance when agreeing to aid packages. This has obvious relevance to some African countries but few governments are without fault.

Goodhart's law in its original form stated that where governments set a target for the money supply, the money supply figures will in time become distorted. This is because the banking system will find ways to lend that do not involve increasing their own deposits. If the money supply is tightly controlled in this way, then its usefulness as a measure of monetary conditions is reduced. This was observed in the late 1980s; the government changed from a money supply target to an inflation target which seems to work more effectively. The law has been extended since to refer to any variable that policy makers might want to target or manipulate. An example might be exam pass rates as used in school league tables. Some schools have targeted potential C-grade students and paid less attention to the rest. The usefulness of league tables has therefore been compromised.

goods are tangible products, in contrast to services. Goods are physical objects.

government: a political body which has authority over a group of people. It may be local or national in scope.

government borrowing is used whenever the revenue from taxation is less than total government expenditure. It can include sales of **bonds** (long-term borrowing), sales of **Treasury bills** (short-term borrowing) and the use of National Savings. (See also **bonds** and **budget deficit**.)

government debt: the total amount outstanding in terms of **bonds**, **Treasury bills** and National Savings bonds. (See also **National Debt** and **public sector net cash requirement**.)

government economic objectives are the main economic policy goals of the government of the day. All governments have at least some objectives in the four main categories of government economic activity.

- Provision of services – **public goods** (such as a police service and a legal system) must be provided by governments and **merit goods** (such as education and health care) may also be made available.
- Reallocation of resources is needed, to deter harmful activities (such as smoking) and encourage useful activities (such as setting up a small business).
- **Income redistribution** – taxing better off people and providing benefits and services for poorer people.
- Economic stabilisation – the use of **fiscal policy** to keep aggregate demand growing in a steady but sustainable way.

Conservative governments tend to want to reduce the scope of government economic policy by cutting both taxes and expenditure. They have in the past perceived inflation as a higher priority than unemployment. They tend to be less **interventionist**.

Income redistribution and the alleviation of poverty is always going to be a higher priority for Labour governments than for Conservative governments.

Economic objectives often conflict with one another. Tax cuts cannot easily be combined with increased spending on health care. (See also **conflicting objectives**.)

government expenditure: the sum total of all spending by both local and national government. The Labour government was committed to keeping this under 40% of GDP, but in recent years has obscured the reality by the use of **public private partnerships**. Support for the banking system after the 2007–09 financial crisis and the effects of recession are bound to raise the percentage considerably. The figures in the pie chart opposite are based on the 2009 Budget Statement but will change in response to circumstances. (See also **Budget**.)

government failure occurs when governments act to deal with **market failure**, but in the process create further **distortions** in the market. Very broadly, government failure may be said to occur when government intervention makes the situation worse rather than better. For example, **National Insurance charges (NICs)** raise revenue which can be used to pay benefits, but they also make it more expensive for employers to take on more **labour**. They thus tend to discourage job creation.

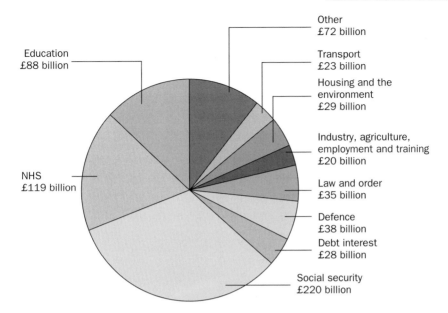

Education
£88 billion

Other
£72 billion

Transport
£23 billion

Housing and the
environment
£29 billion

Industry, agriculture,
employment and training
£20 billion

NHS
£119 billion

Law and order
£35 billion

Defence
£38 billion

Debt interest
£28 billion

Social security
£220 billion

Government expenditure. (Source: UK Treasury.)

government intervention is a loosely used term which usually refers to some way of influencing market forces and bringing about changes in production or consumption decisions. For example, the landfill tax is designed to give businesses an incentive to produce less waste and to use alternative forms of waste management, such as recycling. *Regulation*, tax incentives and government support for industry are all varieties of intervention.

government procurement: all governments buy goods and services from private sector suppliers. Tanks, bandages and the construction of motorways are among the many possible examples. In this way, the government is an important customer for many firms. In the past it has been customary for governments to buy from suppliers in the same country. Now the *EU* and the *WTO* are working to require governments to open up all procurement contracts to competition from any potential supplier. This could mean that governments will buy imported goods at lower prices, thus increasing efficiency.

government securities provide governments with a way of borrowing to cover any shortfall between tax revenue and government expenditure. They consist mainly of *bonds* and *Treasury bills*.

government spending: see *government expenditure*.

grant: a payment from the government or a charity given to fund a specific project or service.

Great Depression: the slump of the 1930s. It began with the Wall Street Crash in 1929. Many people lost money then and this made them less willing to spend. This had important consequences.

- Confidence was destroyed and investment was badly affected.
- The *downward multiplier* effects continued for some years.
- Government policies were not helpful. Many governments cut spending which further reduced *aggregate demand*.

- Exports fell as aggregate demand fell everywhere. Many governments retaliated by imposing **import controls** and competing with each other to devalue their currencies. This reduced international trade.
- Unemployment in the UK peaked at 20%. In the US and Germany it peaked at 33%. Those who were in work experienced reduced incomes.

By 1934 the worst was over but the recovery was slow and faltering and it was not until rearmament began in 1937 that the depression finally came to an end. Meantime, in Germany the depression had contributed to the conditions which helped bring Hitler to power.

The work of **J M Keynes** at this time offered real insights into ways of alleviating depression. The lessons which were learnt were put into practice after World War II in the creation of the **Bretton Woods** system and in the moves towards freeing international trade which followed. In the late 1930s the US government under President Roosevelt got the message that governments could help with **deficit spending** on investment projects.

green revolution: the improvement in agricultural yields which occurred in many parts of the developing world after technical changes. Research led to improved seeds which could yield more grain. To achieve the increased yields, farmers needed:
- rural credit schemes so that they could buy the new seeds
- appropriate irrigation and fertilisers
- extension workers from agricultural colleges who could explain the new methods to farmers
- crop insurance (because the new methods were usually riskier than traditional ones).

The green revolution brought about dramatic increases in food grain production, notably in India. The process started with wheat but other products have been favourably affected too. Similar progress with seeds and strategies suited to arid climates is still awaited; this would do much to help many African countries.

greenfield development: a term used for projects taking place on land not previously used for the same purpose. Usually it means that agricultural land is being used for industrial development or retail outlets.

greenhouse gases: the emissions of carbon dioxide and other substances which are leading to a build up of heat from the sun which cannot escape from the earth's atmosphere. The main causes are industrial pollution (part of it from power stations) and vehicle exhausts. Despite the work of many pressure groups, governments are so far unable to agree on the measures needed to reduce emission of greenhouse gases. Without an agreement which actually forces all governments to tax the activities which create the greenhouse gases, measures to reduce emissions are proceeding slowly and unevenly. (See also **fuel taxes**.)

Greenspan, Alan (1926–) was Chair of the US central bank, the Federal Reserve (the Fed), from 1987 until 2006. This gave him overall responsibility for all **monetary policy** decisions. He trained as an economist and then worked for a number of big businesses. From 1974 onwards he became an adviser to the US government. He was in charge during the long period of strong economic growth in the US, which lasted right through most of the 1990s and up to 2007. But he also presided over the huge increase in debt that led in time to the 2007–09 financial crisis. He enjoyed the confidence of all the US presidents during his term of office but recently admitted that he had made serious mistakes. His successor as chair of the Fed is Ben Bernanke.

green taxes can be levied on any good or service than leads to environmental externalities. The tax will increase the price of the product and reduce *overconsumption*. To achieve maximum efficiency, the tax should be equal to the marginal *external cost*. (See also *marginal social costs* and *benefits*.) Carbon taxes are a subset of green taxes, levied on products that involve carbon emissions.

grey market: an unofficial market which is legal. It can be seen in operation when retailers wanting to sell branded goods find a market where they can obtain them more cheaply than they can by buying direct from the manufacturers. This exposes the fact that the manufacturers are price discriminating. When discovered, they generally object but they have no legal basis for this.

gross domestic product (GDP) is the value of everything produced in the economy for the year. It is the most frequently used measure of national income and is used to provide economic growth rates and other important data. It is usually given 'at *basic prices*', which means that it is valued in terms of the costs of all inputs. Gross means total; domestic means it applies to everything produced within the economy, regardless of whether the producer is a foreign-owned business or locally owned, and product means output.

gross investment: the total of all investment in buildings, plant, machinery and vehicles and infrastructure, including both replacement investment and new productive capacity. (See also *net investment*.)

gross national product (GNP) is calculated by adding total output (*gross domestic product (GDP)*) to *net property income from abroad*. It corresponds to total spending power in the economy and is therefore a useful measure of the standard of living. Net property income from abroad is total interest payments, profits and dividends from money invested overseas, minus interest, profits and dividends earned by foreigners on investments in the UK.

gross profit is an accounting term which means sales revenue minus the costs associated with the actual production process (cost of sales). These do not include the overheads or *fixed costs* such as capital equipment, premises, management, marketing and so on. When these costs have been deducted, we have operating or net profit, which is closer to though not the same as the economist's definition of profit.

Group of Eight (G8) started out as the G7, which included the governments of the seven richest nations: Japan, the US, Germany, France, Canada, Italy and the UK. Then Russia was added to the list. Regular meetings allow matters of mutual interest to be discussed. Sometimes the governments work to co-ordinate their economic policies in order to try to stabilise the world economy. These meetings are widely reported in the press and can lead to significant progress in resolving world problems. The groupings of leaders that meet in this way fluctuate according to the political needs of the time. The need to include Russia is obvious for security reasons but a case can be made for including the other BRIC countries, Brazil, India and China. As these countries now have very large economies, their participation can be important.

Group of Twenty (G20) was set up in 1999 in recognition of the need to bring together important industrialised and emerging economies to discuss and co-ordinate their economic policies. At that time many Asian countries were grappling with acute financial problems which were affecting the whole global economy. The group has no administrative body but it provides for finance ministers and central bank governors to meet every year. The member countries are Argentina, Australia, Brazil, Canada, China, France, Germany, India, Indonesia, Italy, Japan, Mexico, Russia, Saudi Arabia, South Africa, South Korea, Turkey, the UK and the USA. In addition, the heads of the IMF and World Bank attend. A Leader's Summit was held in the UK in April 2009 to discuss the measures relating to the financial crisis.

growing populations: some economies have fast-growing populations. This means that their resources are increasing in quantity but also that they have more mouths to feed. In the US, population growth through continued high levels of immigration is a generally positive development. The increased *labour* supply helps to keep the economic growth process going. In Africa, high levels of population growth due to high birth rates have created some difficulty in improving per capita income and standards of living. The high rate of population growth may not continue in some countries if AIDS remains a serious problem.

growth: see *economic growth*.

growth rate: the percentage increase in GDP each year. This does tend to overstate the improvement in the standard of living because of the *costs of growth* which are not included.

Aiming for a grade A*?

Don't forget to log on to **wwwphilipallan.co.uk/a-zonline** for advice.

hard currency includes a number of currencies which are easily convertible and widely accepted in payment everywhere. The US dollar, the euro, the pound and the yen are examples. Indian rupees and Chinese renminbi (yuan) would usually be less acceptable because they are not fully convertible.

hard landing: it is quite likely that after any period of rapidly growing aggregate demand, *monetary* and *fiscal policies* will be used to slow the economy down in order to avoid accelerating inflation. Because there are time lags in this process and because it is difficult for the authorities to decide the precise amount of change required at just the right moment, it can happen that the rapid growth is followed by an abrupt loss of business confidence and a rapid fall in investment accompanied by falling demand for a wide range of products. This will precipitate a *recession* with rising unemployment. This would be a hard landing. A soft landing would entail a slowdown in the rate of economic growth which did not actually reduce income growth to nothing or entail rising unemployment.

hard loan: a loan given on normal commercial terms at the market rate of interest. In contrast, a *soft loan* would involve a lower rate of interest, perhaps with additional concessions. Soft loans are designed to assist developing countries. Projects with strong prospects of future profit can normally be financed with hard loans.

harmonisation in the European Union context means making all member countries' businesses subject to the same legal framework, i.e. harmonising laws and regulations. In this way the EU tries to create a 'level playing field' so that all firms compete on equal terms within the *single European market*. Harmonisation of the regulations governing actual products allows firms to standardise their production process and make one version of the product for the whole of the EU. This can lead to *economies of scale* and lower costs and prices.

Harrod–Domar model: a theory of *economic growth* which emphasises the importance of increasing capital inputs and therefore of generating savings which can be channelled towards investment in productive capacity. At the heart of the model is the constant capital output ratio.

Although the theory was originally devised in the context of developed countries, it has been widely applied in developing countries. The idea was that if you knew the capital output ratio, you could calculate the amount of capital needed to produce a given level of economic growth. It would then be possible to estimate the level of saving required to finance this level of investment.

Capital output ratios vary. Furthermore, it is clear that in parts of Asia, e.g. South Korea, growth has been greater than would have been expected on the basis of capital investment, even if investment in human capital is included. Other important contributing factors include technical progress and improved management techniques. No single growth model can be applied to all developing countries, although this particular model does offer some useful insights.

hazardous waste refers to the waste products of industrial processes which are harmful to people or the environment. In the past these have degraded soil and polluted water and air. *Regulation* of disposal is making this less likely. This means that firms are required to dispose of wastes safely and to bear the cost of doing so. This should mean that disposal costs become internalised (instead of being *external costs*) and are reflected in the price of the product. The desirable outcome is now occurring more often in developed countries. Developing and many emerging economies still have weaker legislation on this.

HDI: see *Human Development Index (HDI)*.

headline inflation is inflation as measured by the *retail price index (RPI)*. This includes some price changes which may be strictly temporary in their impact on the economy, such as mortgage interest payments.

headline unemployment is the total number of registered unemployed, as measured by the *claimant count*. This covers all those who registered as unemployed, i.e. those eligible for benefits. It will obviously exclude *disguised unemployment*. The figure for *LFS unemployment* will usually be higher.

health and safety legislation has gradually improved employees' working conditions over many years. This raises the costs of production but reduces the risks associated with accidents and industrial health problems. The laws are enforced by the Health and Safety Executive, a government-financed organisation which employs inspectors to investigate conditions in the workplace. Safety at work is now governed by the Social Chapter of the *Maastricht Treaty*, part of the 'level playing field' of the *single market* within the EU.

health insurance provides private health care outside the scope of the National Health Service to people who can and want to pay the premiums. It is quite often provided by employers as an additional element in the pay package, rather as they provide company cars.

heavy industry: this term does not have a precise definition but usually it refers to production of traditional, heavy products such as iron and steel, bulk chemicals, ships and vehicles on a large scale.

Heckscher–Ohlin theory of international trade predicts that countries with abundant, cheap labour will have a comparative advantage in labour-intensive products. Similarly, if capital or land are relatively abundant and cheap, the comparative advantage will lie with products that require more of those inputs. So it is no surprise that China and India have a comparative advantage in production of simpler manufactured goods, while research and product design activities are concentrated in the US. However globalisation has made comparative advantage more complicated. India has developed a highly competitive software industry; this is a labour-intensive activity but it also requires abundant human capital.

hedging is a way to minimise risks. Commodities or currencies can be bought now for delivery on a date in the future at an agreed price which removes some uncertainty. The importer who will need foreign currency at a date in the future will have it available at a known price. Similarly commodities which are known to be becoming available in the future can be sold in the future at a price which is agreed now. The alternative is to trade in the *spot market* at the current spot price and carry the risk that the price may change.

Contracts to buy/sell in the *forward markets* are known as *futures* contracts.

Her Majesty's Revenue and Customs (HMRC) is the agency responsible for collecting all taxes. Its old name was the Inland Revenue.

hire purchase: a way of buying on credit. It is used for consumer durables and also by firms investing in an item of capital equipment. Specialist companies, often subsidiaries of banks, provide the finance. Loans of this kind are less used now than in the past. Consumers can often get bank loans, which are cheaper if they are well known to the bank. Firms are more likely to go for *leasing*, which is more or less the same as renting the equipment.

historic cost is the actual price paid and usually refers to items of capital equipment used by a business and recorded in its accounts. If there has been significant inflation, it matters whether the accountant uses historic costs or current costs, which would give the replacement cost of the item. When interpreting company accounts, it is necessary to know how the *assets* have been valued.

hit-and-run competition comes from firms which enter the market expecting to make immediate profits and then make a rapid exit from the market. This works only if the fixed costs of entry are relatively low. A fashion for the product may attract hit-and-run competition. Profits for the stable producer who has been in the market for a long time may be much reduced by this.

hoarding occurs when people or organisations keep money which is not earning interest or being used in a productive way. Savings kept under the mattress is a traditional example. Excessive current account balances would be another.

holding company: a firm that holds shares in other companies. Normally, it will have a controlling interest, i.e. more than 50% of the shares, and will have control without involvement in day-to-day decisions. Control may be exercised with a very light touch or may involve participation in all strategic decisions.

homogeneous products are identical. It is impossible to know whether the product came from one firm or another. A homogeneous product is an important feature of the model of *perfect competition*. The more homogeneous the products are, the stronger the competition is likely to be in the marketplace. Examples include many agricultural products, e.g. wheat, and many mineral products, e.g. iron ore.

In contrast, many businesses spend a great deal of time and money trying to persuade consumers that their products are different from others; theirs are *differentiated products*, the opposite of homogeneous.

horizontal integration involves a merger or takeover where both firms are engaged in the same type of production. They could both be involved in a single stage in the production process or they could have very similar end products. The features of integration have pros and cons:

- **Rationalisation** will enable the firms to exploit potential **economies of scale**. The fall in costs may make it possible to cut prices and benefit the consumer. But it may also increase **market power** by reducing competition.
- The two firms combined may be better able to stand up to competition from foreign producers. But they may also have a large share of the domestic market and this may mean that they will be referred to the **Competition Commission**.

Horizontal integration has occurred in many industries. Hotels, chemicals and travel companies provide examples.

horizontal merger means the integration of two firms which supply very similar products. (See also *horizontal integration*.)

horizontal and vertical equity relate to equality of treatment under the law. Horizontal equity involves treating people in similar circumstances equally. So it requires gender and racial equality. Vertical equity concerns ways in which people should be treated differently in order to redistribute income more fairly. So different people may be taxed at different rates so that their disposable incomes will be less unequal.

host country: countries which attract foreign direct investment. Most governments are keen to be in this position because the investment creates jobs and income and may bring useful **technology transfer**. Foreign companies often provide training for employees. In the UK, Wales has been particularly successful as a host country and the employment generated has helped to fill the gap left by **declining industries**.

For developing countries, foreign investment has particular pros and cons.

- The investor may help to increase exports, bringing in much-needed foreign exchange. However, the profits will be repatriated to the parent company or its shareholders in developed countries, creating an invisible outflow in the balance of payments.
- Technology transfer may or may not happen. If it does, it will help to create a pool of new skills which will benefit the host country economy. But some multinationals set up in developing countries simply to take advantage of the cheap **labour** available, give little training and move on to other locations if wage rates rise.

hostile takeover bid: an attempt to take over a firm which is resisted by the existing board of directors. In order to fight off the bid, the board may recommend shareholders not to sell. There are stringent rules about how the battle may be fought. In early 2008 Yahoo managed to fight off a bid from Microsoft. Later in the year it forged a tie-up with Google, leading to a partnership agreement on search advertising. This improved its competitive position. However, at the time of writing this story is not over because the competition watchdogs of the EU may decide to investigate the effects of the agreement and Microsoft is continuing its complaints about unfair competition.

hot money: speculative flows on foreign exchange markets. It is possible to hold large cash balances in order to gamble on changes in **exchange rates**. For example, during the Asian financial crisis in 1997–1998, large quantities of yen and other Asian currencies were sold. As exchange rates fell, more and more holders of the currencies lost confidence and they in turn sold. Later, when the exchange rates had stabilised at a lower level, they bought the currencies again. Money which moves from one capital market to another in search of the best rate of return is termed hot money.

household: the basic economic decision-taking unit. Economists tend to talk about households rather than individuals because their consumption patterns have more in common than, say, those of a teenager living at home and a single person living alone.

house prices have a significant effect on the macro-economy. When they are rising there is a wealth effect – people feel better off and may choose to consume more regardless of income. When they are falling, some people may find that the outstanding loan is larger than the value of the property (*negative equity*). This reduces the demand for housing which has a downward multiplier effect on the economy.

housing association: a not-for-profit organisation which exists to provide low-cost housing. Flats and houses may be rented or sold on concessional terms or some combination of the two. Finance comes partly from the public sector, partly from charitable donations and partly from banks and other commercial sources.

housing benefit: a payment made on the basis of need to cover rent. Where rents are very high, as in London, housing benefit in combination with other welfare payments can contribute to the *poverty trap*.

HRM: see *human resource management (HRM)*.

human capital consists of knowledge and skills acquired by individuals. It may be acquired in a formal way through education or employers' training programmes. Or it may be the result of accumulated experience or on-the-job training, as with an apprenticeship. Investing in human capital makes people more productive and can increase their earnings, provided there is a demand for their particular skills and knowledge. It is an important element in the process of *economic growth*.

Some skills and knowledge are firm specific and of particular importance to the relevant employer.

Human Development Index (HDI): a measure of the quality of life constructed by the United Nations Development Programme. It takes into account not just income but also a range of other criteria such as literacy, life expectancy, clean water, inequality and gender issues. Canada and the Scandinavian countries usually rank among the highest. It can be instructive to compare the rankings with those based on GDP. Individual countries have a great variety of reasons for discrepancies between the two. In some countries where growth has been quite fast the distribution of income and wealth remains very unequal. Examples include Saudi Arabia and South Africa, where the HDI ranking is low compared to GDP.

human resource management (HRM): that part of the management process which involves the ways in which people are used and developed. Careful development and use of new skills can be very important in knowledge-based industries, so HRM has tended to become a higher priority for management generally in recent years.

hyperinflation: very rapidly rising prices. There is no precise dividing line between inflation and hyperinflation, but no doubt about when it is a real problem. Over 100% a year would probably be regarded as hyperinflation by most people.

Germany in 1923 experienced hyperinflation which peaked at 23 000%. At that level, people lose all confidence in money as a store of value. Zimbabwe had hyperinflation from 2006 to 2008, peaking at 231 million %. Soon after that most transactions in Zimbabwe dollars ceased as buyers turned to US dollars. Prices in US$ then began to fall but the economy was in great difficulty because there simply were not enough US$ to meet currency needs. Hyperinflation can have dire consequences because wealth is redistributed to those with debts and away from savers who are holding assets denominated in money terms, such as bank balances and building society accounts.

hypothesis: a theoretical connection between two variables, which can be tested against the facts. For example, we might suspect that the purchase of yachts is related to income. By examining the increase in real incomes which occurs when the economy is growing and comparing this with the trend in yacht sales, we might find that the hypothesis was supported by the evidence.

hysteresis can be used to describe a sequence of events in which a change takes place but there are difficulties and time lags in the adjustment process and, because of this, the outcome is not necessarily what we would have predicted on the basis of economic theory. For example, economic theory suggests that unemployment will lead to falling or slow-growing wage rates. Eventually this will provide employers with some incentive to hire *labour* again. However, people who have been unemployed for a long time may be deskilled and have great difficulty in finding work because of this, even when the economy has picked up.

A–Z Online

Log on to A–Z Online to search the database of terms, print revision lists and much more. Go to **www.philipallan.co.uk/a-zonline** to get started.

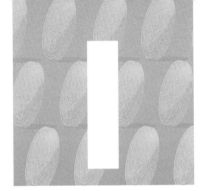

IBRD: see *International Bank for Reconstruction and Development (IBRD)*, commonly known as the World Bank.

ILO: see *International Labour Organization (ILO)*.

imbalances: see *global imbalances*.

IMF: see *International Monetary Fund (IMF)*.

immobilities occur when people are unable to take up a job which is available because they are living in another area (*geographical immobility*) or because they do not have the right skills for the job (*occupational immobility*). Immobilities are a form of *market imperfection*. They impede the process of reallocating resources in response to changes in consumer demand.

imperfect competition occurs when there are a number of competing firms, but the market lacks some or all of the features of *perfect competition*. Broadly there are three types of imperfect competition: *duopoly*, *oligopoly* and *monopolistic competition*. In a duopoly there are just two firms competing. Oligopoly describes a situation where there are several firms in the market. In both cases, the market will be characterised by *interdependence*: the competing firms will base their decisions on what the others are doing, or might do in the future. There is likely to be much non-price competition. Under monopolistic competition there are many competitors, each selling a *differentiated product*.

imperfect information is a market imperfection as a result of which competition is impaired by lack of easily available information. The consumer who does not know where to find a product at the cheapest price will pay more, and this protects the producer from the competition which might exist if information were fuller. Similarly, the firm which does not know where to find the cheapest inputs will have costs higher than necessary, which reduces efficiency.

imperfect knowledge: see *imperfect information*.

imperfect market occurs when there are *imperfections*, i.e. distortions in the market such that competition is not as forceful as it might be. An imperfect market departs in one or more ways from the conditions of *perfect competition*. It will generally not achieve *productive* and *allocative efficiency*. For example, firms which have a degree of monopoly within their markets may not be forced to seek the most efficient methods of producing and as a result, prices may be higher than they need be.

imperfections occur in an imperfect market, and include *immobilities*, *imperfect information*, *government intervention*, *barriers to entry*, small numbers of buyers or sellers and any other source of distortions which may interfere with the operation of competitive market forces. (See also *imperfect market*.)

import controls: *tariffs*, *quotas* or other controls which can be used to reduce imports. Tariffs are *import duties*: there must be a payment to the government before the products can be brought into the country. Quotas are physical limits for specific products, setting a maximum amount each year which can be imported. *Non-tariff barriers (NTBs)* include quotas and also many other regulations which have the effect of making it more difficult to import. For example, quality requirements may be used to exclude unwanted imports. Import controls have been generally reduced over the years by WTO negotiations.

import duty: a *tariff* levied on an imported item at the point of entry to the country. (See also *import controls*.)

import penetration: imports as a percentage share of the market for that product. For example in the pharmaceutical industry, import penetration in 2004 was roughly 26% for the UK.

import propensity: the percentage of total income spent on imports. A very open economy may spend a large part of total income on imports. For example, Belgium spends roughly 70% of GDP on imports while the UK spends roughly 30% and the US, 13%.

import substitution: some developing countries have sought to industrialise by reducing imports and developing domestic industries which would replace them. Although this has been occasionally successful, in general the protected domestic industries have never become efficient enough to compete on world markets. So the countries which concentrated on producing the goods in which they had a *comparative advantage* and exporting them performed better. Brazil was an exponent of import substitution for many years but has largely abandoned it in recent times.

imported inflation means a general rise in prices which occurs because prices are rising in other countries. This means that import prices will rise, thus raising the cost of imported inputs for the production process. The effect of these, together with price rises for imported consumer goods, will feed into the *retail price index (RPI)*.

imports: goods and services bought from overseas producers.

inactivity rate: the percentage of the population who are dependent in that they are very young or still in education, retired, disabled, or caring for family members.

inadequate capital accumulation can be a cause of slow growth and economic development. Raising the level of investment could speed up the development process, provided there are genuine opportunities to sell the products created.

incentives: financial and other rewards which can influence the decisions of firms and individuals. Favourable tax treatment of *investment* spending can induce firms to invest more. Increased taxes on tobacco give smokers an incentive to give up. On a wider level, the term may be used in connection with groups of people who, for example, lack the incentive to work because they are in the *poverty trap*.

Incentives can be vital in ensuring that the *allocation of resources* reflects the pattern of consumer demand. People may need an incentive to move from one kind of production to another; this could be a *pay differential* which encourages them to switch jobs.

incidence of taxation analyses the extent to which a specific expenditure tax falls upon the consumer or the producer. Depending on the *price elasticity of demand* for the product, the producer may or may not be able to pass the tax on to the consumer by raising the price.

A tax will shift the supply curve upwards by the exact amount of the tax. The more inelastic the demand is, the easier it will be for the seller to pass the tax on to the consumer in the form of a higher price (P_1 in the diagram below). If demand is elastic, then consumers will simply buy less of the product as the price rises and the producer will have to absorb at least a part of the tax (Ep minus F_2 in the second diagram). Taxes on items with elastic demand will reduce the quantity bought and have little effect on the price, while taxes on items with inelastic demand will discourage consumption relatively little but lead to an increase in price close to the amount of the tax.

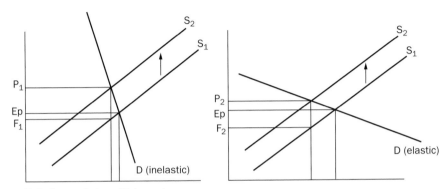

Ep is the market equilibrium price
P_1 and P_2 are the prices to the consumer after tax
F_1 and F_2 are the prices received by the producer after tax has been paid

Incidence of taxation

income is a flow of money which acts as a reward for the services of a *factor of production*. Wages and salaries are a reward to *labour* and are described as earned income. Unearned income includes rent, interest and profit: rent is a reward for the owner of land or property. Profit gives a return on capital invested and also rewards the efforts of *entrepreneurs*. Interest is a return on a capital sum which is loaned to someone else.

For firms, income comes from sales revenue plus the return on any investments. For the economy as a whole, income is the total income derived from all activities and is measured most often using GDP.

income distribution: see *distribution of income*.

income effect: when there is a change in a price, that change will have an income effect and a substitution effect. The *substitution effect* shows how quantity consumed changes in response to the change in that price compared to all other prices. The income effect shows the effect on consumption of the change in real income which occurs when a price changes. If the price of petrol rises, car owners will have to pay more for petrol and this will reduce their purchasing power. They will most likely buy less petrol but also spend less on other things too. This will mean a tendency for consumption of everything, not just petrol, to fall. Items with very low prices will have a very small income effect. *Inferior goods* have a negative income effect. (Unless you are studying the IB course you probably won't need this.)

income elasticity of demand measures the responsiveness of quantity demanded to a change in income.

FORMULA: $\dfrac{\text{percentage change in quantity demanded}}{\text{percentage change in incomes}} = \text{income elasticity}$

There are several important factors to consider in examining the income elasticity of demand for particular products.

Is income elasticity positive or negative?

- Positive income elasticity implies that as income rises, so does demand for the product. We can easily think up examples: people will want more weekend breaks, restaurant meals and books as their incomes rise. So a rise in income will lead to a rise in quantity demanded. Both the top and bottom of the formula will be positive, giving a positive income elasticity.

- With some products, there will be very little sensitivity to income changes. Take toothpaste, for example. A change in income will make no difference at all. Income elasticity will be zero.

- On the other hand, demand for some products will go down as income rises. Bus services, for example, faced decreasing demand as more people became able to afford cars. The formula gives a negative percentage for change in quantity demanded over a positive figure for change in income. The result is a negative income elasticity.

- Products with positive income elasticity, like cars, are called **normal goods**. Products with negative income elasticity are called **inferior goods**. These are relatively few in number compared to normal goods.

- Positive income elasticity may be high or low. For many products, rising incomes will lead to a modest increase in quantity demanded. Many food items would fall into this category, with income elasticity positive but less than one. For some products, a rise in income will increase demand greatly and income elasticity will be greater than one.

- Income elasticities can change significantly over time. The motorbike, for instance, was a great success in the UK as incomes rose to the point where people could afford one as opposed to a bicycle. As incomes rose further, a small car became affordable and the demand for motorbikes fell, making it an inferior good at this point. Then, as incomes rose to the point where the motorbike became a recreational vehicle, income elasticity became positive once more.

Businesses selling goods and services with low income elasticity will be less vulnerable during a **recession** than those selling goods and services with high income elasticities. Producers of biscuits might hardly notice a recession while producers of yachts may go out of business due to lack of demand.

Worked example

It has been estimated that a 10% increase in incomes will lead to a 3% increase in demand for fruit. What is its income elasticity of demand?

Income elasticity of demand $= \dfrac{\text{% change in euantity demanded}}{\text{% change in incomes}}$

so in this example $\dfrac{+3}{+10} = +0.3$

income redistribution means taxing high incomes much more than low incomes and providing benefits for those with little or no income of their own. The objective is to achieve a more equal distribution of income across society as a whole. *Progressive taxes* will achieve the first outcome. Providing more generous unemployment benefits, disability and child allowances and *income support* will achieve the second. *Means-tested benefits* may be used to ensure that the greatest help is given to the most needy.

Some income redistribution measures have been challenged on the grounds that they reduce the incentive to work. Where most benefits are means tested, there can be a *poverty trap* which is very difficult to escape. Recent policies on benefits have sought to address this by trying to ensure that everyone is actually better off working. The *Working Families Tax Credit* addresses this. (See also *income tax*.)

income support: a benefit payment designed to ensure that everyone has a minimum acceptable income. Income support is *means-tested* and supplements other kinds of benefits such as the state pension and unemployment benefit. For example, a person who is unemployed but has not made enough National Insurance contributions to qualify for unemployment benefit will be given income support.

income tax is a *direct tax* levied on the incomes of individuals. There is a personal allowance, which is tax free. Tax rates are announced annually in the Budget by the Chancellor of the Exchequer. The following example uses the bands and the tax rates set in the 2009 Budget.

Income between	Tax rate (%)
0–£6475	0
£6476–£37 400	20 (basic rate)
£37 401 upwards	40 (higher rate)

Worked example

	James earns £15 000 per year		Jane earns £50 000 per year	
	Tax %	Tax due	Tax %	Tax due
0–£6475	0	0	0	0
£6476–£37 400	20	£1705	20	£6185
£37 401 upwards	40	0	40	£5040
Total tax		£1705		£11 225
As % of income		11.4%		22.4%

Income tax is a *progressive tax*, which means that it takes a higher proportion of a higher income and a lower proportion of a lower income. (*Regressive taxes* do the reverse, while proportional taxes are neutral in this respect.) Income tax thus has a major role to play in *income redistribution*.

If tax rates are kept constant, tax revenues will vary with incomes and will fluctuate over the course of the *economic cycle*. Income tax plays a part in the operation of *automatic stabilisers*, which help to reduce fluctuations in the level of aggregate demand.

High marginal income tax rates are usually resented by those who have to pay them. It is sometimes said that they create a disincentive to work hard. There is no statistical evidence for this. Scandinavian countries have high tax rates and good economic growth rates over the long run.

Income tax is an important revenue raiser for the government, contributing roughly a quarter of total tax revenue at the present time. See also **tax revenue** for data on sources of revenue.

increasing returns to scale occur if output can be increased using a proportionally smaller quantity of inputs. It will tend to be associated with **economies of scale**.

indebtedness is the extent to which a business or a government owes money to banks or international organisations.

independent variable: where there is a relationship between two variables, one may be determined by something else and thus be termed independent. In the relationship between income and consumption, consumption is seen as depending on income, while income, the independent variable, is determined by a whole range of other things such as the level of **investment**, the level of **government spending** and the level of exports. It is therefore treated as being independent.

index linked means that the value in question will be changed in line with the retail price index. Pensions are now index linked so that their purchasing power is kept constant and keeps pace with inflation. Index-linked National Savings Certificates have their maturity values raised in line with the RPI. It is possible to index link wage rates but this is unusual because changes in supply and demand in the **labour** market make it desirable for wage rates to be more flexible.

index numbers can be created for any time series so that comparisons can be made more easily. A reference year is required and the value for this year becomes 100. In each subsequent year, the percentage change from the reference year is added to 100. There are many important indices.

- The **retail price index (RPI)** gives a measure of average price rises. It is built up from a large number of price changes for products which are frequently bought. These are made into a **weighted average** to ensure that the products which figure largest in the average shopper's buys are given the most importance in the index.
- The **consumer price index (CPI)** is very similar to the RPI but constructed in line with international rules so that it can be used for comparisons with other countries.
- Stock Exchange indices such as the **Footsie (FT–SE 100)** are also weighted averages, where the most frequently traded shares are given the largest weights.
- The **sterling exchange rate index** is a weighted average of exchange rate changes. The currencies of the UK's most important trading partners are given the largest weights.

These and other index numbers put a lot of complex information into a single series. They can be more easily interpreted than raw data.

Index of Sustainable Economic Welfare: a measure of the standard of living that attempts to quantify changes in well-being, not just changes in real income as given by GDP. The ISEW adds to GDP for the benefits that improve the quality of life (e.g. the value of services provided within the home, such as meals cooked). It subtracts from GDP figures for all the things that worsen the quality of life (such as estimated costs of climate change). It also deducts for defensive spending that covers the cost of cleaning up polluting activities. These raise GDP but simply maintain the existing standard of living for the future (e.g. by dealing with air or water pollution). Critics say that it is impossible to quantify the value of many of these additions and subtractions objectively.

indicators help to show what is happening in the economy. *Leading indicators* foreshadow changes to come: an increase in machine tool production might indicate that an increase in output is likely. The level of vacancies would show a sharp rise if skill shortages were developing in the *labour* market.

indirect controls: a way of controlling a variable by controlling its price. Pollution can be controlled directly by regulating the levels which are allowed and prosecuting firms which go over that level. Or it can be controlled indirectly by selling *tradable permits*. This gives firms an incentive to avoid polluting. In the past, the Bank of England would place direct controls on the amounts that banks could lend. Now the Bank just raises interest rates which discourages borrowers from wanting loans – an indirect control.

indirect taxes are paid when goods and services are bought, i.e. they are expenditure taxes. Examples include *VAT* and *excise duty*. In contrast, direct taxes are levied on income and profits. In general, an indirect tax will be a *regressive tax*, having a bigger impact on poorer than on richer people. However, VAT is less regressive than it appears because many necessities are exempt or zero rated.

individual bargaining, in contrast to *collective bargaining* with a *trade union* as intermediary, involves direct negotiations between employee and employer to determine pay and conditions. Some people, especially those with scarce skills, do not feel the need for a trade union to negotiate on their behalf. For some, there is no union readily available. Individual bargaining is on the increase.

individual savings accounts (ISAs): a type of tax-free savings scheme designed to encourage more people to save. ISAs can include cash savings, shares and life assurance policies. The interest received is not taxed.

indivisibility: a situation in which the different items of equipment needed for production come in different sizes, so that larger scale items are not used at full capacity. This can be a problem for small-scale producers, whose *average fixed costs* will be higher as a result. In this situation, expanding output would lead to *economies of scale*.

induced expenditure is spending, the level of which is determined by the level of income. Consumption, saving and tax revenue are all induced, within the framework of the basic Keynesian model of the macro-economy.

induction: a process by which relationships may be inferred from specific observations. The process may start with an examination of the data and from this a *hypothesis* may be worked out.

industrial action occurs when the workforce seeks to disrupt production as a way of bringing pressure to bear on employers. The objective is to secure better pay and/or conditions. Industrial action could take the form of a strike, a work to rule or a go-slow.

industrial democracy involves devising ways in which employees can participate in the decision-making process. Employees may elect a representative to sit on the board of directors. This person may or may not have voting rights. There may be a works council, which brings management and trade unions together at regular meetings. Provision for this is contained in the Social Chapter of the **Maastricht Treaty**. Some UK businesses have opposed this; others find the meetings useful.

The strongest form of industrial democracy is the **co-operative**. There, all employees have the right to participate in decision making, although in practice they may delegate this to a committee.

industrial dispute: a disagreement between management and trade union representatives. This will most often spring from negotiations about pay and conditions and may lead to industrial action if a ballot shows a majority of the workforce in favour. Alternatively, the parties may agree to go to **arbitration**.

industrial inertia refers to the way in which certain industries remain located in a particular region long after the original reason for their being there has ceased to exist. Manchester became an engineering centre during the industrial revolution. Renold plc, set up in 1879, making precision chains and transmission devices, still has its head office there and several factories, even though it sells in most industrialised countries and has other factories in Australia, Germany and the USA. Often the reason for industrial inertia lies in the **external economies of scale** which develop around an industry concentrated in one location. In many cases the main external economy will be a pool of skilled **labour** and local expertise; this is clearly important to Renold.

industrial location: the place in which firms choose to locate when setting up their production facilities. The location may be based on important cost factors such as:
- access to motorways
- locally based input suppliers
- a pool of skilled **labour**
- sources of raw materials
- nearby markets.

However, nowadays, many industries are **footloose**, i.e. they can locate in many places without their cost structures being much affected.

In some cases, industrial location is determined by factors which were important in the past (see also **industrial inertia**). In some of these situations, **external economies of scale** have become important, particularly if there is local expertise which could be a significant input.

Industries using advanced technologies cluster together in science parks, often located close to universities, e.g. Cambridge, where relevant research is under way. Then there is another kind of **cluster**, for which it is hard to find a logical reason. Antique shops are seldom found alone; they nearly always are one of a number up and down the high street, for example in country towns. It seems that if one is successful others will be attracted and together they attract people from further afield.

industrial policy can cover many different aspects of government economic policy.
- Regional policy can be used to regenerate areas which have suffered because **localised industries** have declined. Coal mining, iron and steel and shipbuilding have declined and left large areas with far fewer jobs than job seekers.

- Small firms policies can help to encourage firms to get started. Unemployed people with potential as entrepreneurs can get practical advice from **Business Link**.
- Technology policies can be used to fund **research and development (R & D)**. However, in the UK many commentators would hold that the government has not done enough.
- The **Private Finance Initiative** has been used to try to modernise UK infrastructure without relying too heavily on government funding. This was thought to offer a way of reducing the role of the government in the economy while still ensuring that services were provided.

industrial relations: the communication links which exist between employers and trade unions. Ideally, there will be some degree of trust between management and employees, which **employers' associations** and **trade unions** can build upon. In practice, old animosities can be a problem in some workplaces. Also some firms still pay the absolute minimum they can get away with, though others have come to see concern for employees as important in leading to a loyal and committed workforce.

industrial union: a trade union whose members are all from a specific industry. For example, the Communication Workers Union draws its membership mainly from employees in telecommunications. In contrast, a general union such as the Transport and General Workers Union (T&G) will have members from many industries.

industrialisation is the process by which a country may move from dependence on primary production to having a developed manufacturing sector. Many developing countries are in the process of this transition at the present time: for example, Mexico, India and Indonesia.

industry: an area of production defined usually by the product, e.g. the car industry or the chemical industry.

inefficiency: failing to maximise the value of output from a given quantity of inputs. If the quantity of output is less than it could be, **productive efficiency** is compromised. If the value of the output is less than it could be, the problem is with **allocative efficiency**. The problem then is that the output is not actually what consumers most want.

inelastic demand arises in situations where a change in price leads to a relatively small change in quantity demanded. Whatever the percentage change in price, the percentage change in quantity demanded will be less. **Price elasticity of demand** will be numerically less than one. This is shown in the diagram overleaf: inelastic demand can be represented by a fairly steeply sloping demand curve.

The change shown in the diagram indicates price elasticity of demand equal to 0.6, i.e. moderately inelastic demand.

There are two main reasons for inelastic demand.
- The product has few, if any, substitutes. When the price rises, people carry on buying the product because they cannot find a satisfactory substitute and they do not feel they can do without it. This would apply to bread, workclothes, and rail travel for commuters, as well as many other products.
- The product takes a small part of total income. This might apply to chocolates.

A 20% fall in price leads to a 12% increase in quantity demanded

Where there is inelastic demand, a fall in price will lead to a fall in total revenue. Quantity demanded will not increase very much and therefore the increased quantity sold will be insufficient to offset the decrease in price. In the diagram below, the shaded box showing lost revenue due to the price cut is larger than the shaded box showing revenue gained due to increased sales. Revenue gained through increased sales is less than revenue lost through the price cut. (See also **price elasticity of demand**.)

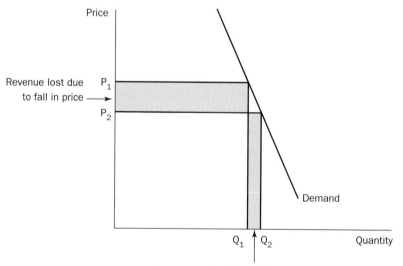

Inelastic demand means that a price cut involves falling sales revenue

inelastic supply: the quantity supplied has a relatively weak response to a change in price. If the price rises by a certain percentage, the quantity supplied will rise by less. Similarly, if the price falls, the resulting percentage fall in quantity supplied will be lower.

Inelastic supply is often an important factor in the short run, because producers have not had time to adjust to the price change. (See also *supply elasticity*.)

inequality: a situation in which there are large differences in incomes and wealth within a society. Most developed countries in Europe have a lower level of inequality than the USA does. Inequality has tended to increase everywhere in recent years. Inequality can be reduced by *progressive taxes* and social security benefits. (See also *equity*.)

infant industries: very new firms, starting up in an industry which previously did not exist in that country, may take some time to become competitive. They will not at first be able to reap the *economies of scale* which are a feature of production in countries where the industry is well established. If they are to survive they will need to be protected from competition from imports, by means of *tariffs* or other *import controls*. This argument is most often used in relation to new industries in *developing economies*. However, there are drawbacks to using import controls to protect domestic industries. There may be considerable difficulty in deciding when the industry no longer needs protection; in the meantime consumers will be paying more for the product than they would for imports. The cost of protection to consumers may be very high.

inferior good: a product with negative *income elasticity of demand*. This means that a rise in incomes will lead to a fall in the quantity sold. Consumers will choose to buy less of the inferior good and more of normal goods, which they are now better able to afford. As incomes rose, people opted less and less to take holidays in UK seaside resorts (the inferior good) and went instead to Spain or other sunny countries. Producers of inferior goods may do well during *recessions*, when incomes are falling. Could holidays in Spain become an inferior good in the future?

inflation is an increase in prices generally. Money loses some of its value because its purchasing power falls. If the process accelerates to very high levels, there is said to be *hyperinflation*.

The causes of inflation are complex. Until the 20th century, inflation was very infrequent and the price level was as likely to fall as to rise. Until the late 1960s, inflation remained at a relatively low level in most developed countries, most of the time. Then it became much more volatile, until the mid-1990s, when it settled at low levels until 2008, when it began to rise again (see graph overleaf).

The precipitating cause of accelerating inflation is *excess demand* in the economy as a whole. This occurs when *aggregate demand* is growing faster than the capacity of the economy to supply. At first there will be evidence of *skill shortages* and it will become clear that sellers can raise prices and still sell the goods. Firms will raise wages to attract the scarce skills they need to increase output. Trade unions and individuals will find it easier to negotiate pay rises.

Once inflation is accelerating it will tend to continue because of people's *expectations*. All employees will try to protect their real earnings by negotiating an increase equal to what they expect inflation to be. (See also *inflationary expectations* and *inflationary spiral*.)

The *monetarist* view of inflation holds that it is caused by excessive increases in the money supply. As bank lending increases, borrowers are able to increase spending, leading to the excess demand already described.

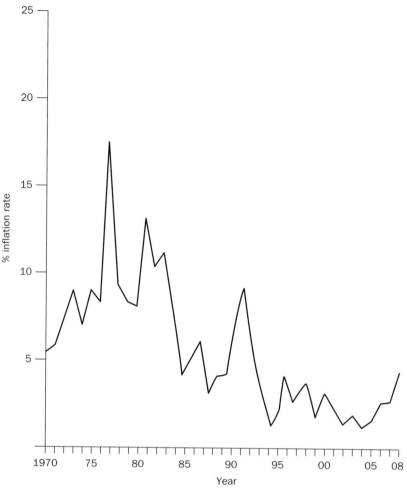

Inflation rate, 1970–2008. (Source: ONS.)

Inflation has numerous consequences:

- Borrowers gain. So for firms and households which have borrowed substantially, inflation makes the debt smaller in real terms. Incomes and sales revenue rise in line with inflation, while debt repayments stay the same, becoming more affordable. At various times during the past 30 years, home-owners typically made large capital gains as the value of their homes rose while the scale of their debt fell.
- Creditors and savers lose. When the money they have lent is paid back, it will have lost some of its value. The purchasing power of money held in the bank will be reduced. Interest rates may be too low to compensate for this (as in 2009).
- Inflation increases uncertainty. While a stable rate of inflation may appear predictable, in practice, the higher the rate of inflation, the more volatile it has proved to be. This makes planning difficult for firms and individuals.

Contractionary policies may be used to control inflation. Strict control of the growth of the money supply reduces aggregate demand and pressures in the **labour** market. In time, people's expectations of inflation will fall and they will accept lower pay increases. However, this process in the early 1980s and 1990s proved to be slow and to entail a considerable rise in unemployment.

At the time of writing, inflation was subdued by the recession but may accelerate if it turns out that there has been too much quantitative easing, or if commodity prices rise again. The low exchange rate could have an impact. The **Monetary Policy Committee** of the Bank of England comments on this regularly.

inflation targeting: when the **Monetary Policy Committee** was set up in 1997 it was instructed to adjust interest rates so as to keep inflation close to a target of 2.5%, as measured by the **consumer price index (CPI)**. This was later reduced to 2.0%. Because there is a long time lag between a change in interest rates and a change in the rate of inflation, the MPC examines detailed forecasts for inflation.

If the inflation rate deviates by more than 1% from the target, the MPC must write an open letter to the Chancellor of the Exchequer explaining the deviation and setting out its strategy for bringing the rate back under control.

The UK inflation target is a symmetric one, in that if inflation goes over 1% below the target, the MPC still has to explain to the Chancellor. This creates an incentive to avoid deflation, which could be associated with recession. This should mean that MPC policy has a stabilising effect in both directions.

inflationary expectations are the views which people may hold as to whether and by how much prices will rise in the future. Usually, people expect the rate of inflation to be similar the next year to what it was in the past year. So they will seek to obtain a pay increase which will maintain or improve their real incomes, i.e. keep pace with inflation. If inflation is accelerating this can be a real problem. As it rises, employees and trade unions will be increasing their demands for higher pay. This will in turn raise costs and prices. In order to get the rate of inflation down again, some way must be found to convince people that it will be brought down and that they should adjust their expectations. This is very hard to do. In the past accelerating inflation has been brought under control by large interest rate increases which led to painful recessions. The resulting unemployment caused people to adjust their expectations but only after a period of years.

inflationary gap: see *output gap*.

inflationary spiral describes the way price increases lead to demands for increased pay, which in turn raise costs, leading to further price increases. A period of buoyant demand in the economy can cause excess demand and rising prices. These create inflationary expectations with wage demands aimed at protecting the value of real incomes. Pay increases feed through into further price increases. (See also **wage–price spiral**.)

informal economy: that part of economic activity which is not recorded in official statistics. This includes all kinds of voluntary and domestic work and work done for cash payments which are not declared for tax purposes. Some of this is legal but some consists of tax evasion or leads to fraudulent benefit claims. The amount of income which is not declared is difficult to determine and estimates vary within the range of 5–10% of GDP. The value of voluntary work is impossible to quantify.

information asymmetry: see *asymmetric information*.

information failure can lead to a type of *market failure*. The *allocation of resources* may be less than optimal because people lack full information. Consumers may simply choose a selection of goods and services which omits items which would make them better off and includes items which make them worse off, because there are some things that they do not know about these products. For example, they may choose to curtail their education, not realising by how much it might increase future income. Or they may go on smoking because they underestimate the health effects. The allocation of resources can be improved if education is provided free as a **merit good** and if tobacco is taxed as a **demerit good**.

information provision: where *information failure* is responsible for *market failure*, governments can require sellers to improve the information given to buyers. For example, consumer protection law contains all kinds of provisions to ensure that labelling is accurate and not misleading. In some cases, the information which the consumer needs is very complex and it may be necessary to get advice, e.g. about mortgages and insurance policies.

infrastructure includes all the transport and communications links and the basic services which are used by firms and households. Gas, electricity, telephones, water and drainage are included along with roads, rail and air links. Lack of an efficient infrastructure raises costs for firms, as well as creating inconvenience. So the provision of infrastructure is an essential element in *international competitiveness*.

Infrastructure requires a great deal of *capital* investment both for construction and maintenance and for improvements, so it is hard for poorer *developing economies* to make progress in providing it. This puts local producers at an automatic disadvantage.

Most of the infrastructure is provided by regulated utility companies. Some items, e.g. roads, are provided directly by government.

inheritance tax is currently levied on estates of more than £325 000 at a rate of 40% (2009–10 figures). It thus works to create a more equal distribution of wealth. Where the estate is owned by a couple, the tax is payable after the second one dies.

injections are spending flows which add to the circular flow of money. They include investment, government expenditure and exports. When injections increase, there will be an increase in aggregate demand, which will have a *multiplier* effect on the economy. They are balanced by withdrawals (also called leakages) from the circular flow, namely saving, taxes and imports.

innovation means the development of a new idea so that it can be made into a new product or a new technique.

- Product innovation means a new product. It may be based on a new design or on new technologies or maybe just a new idea. Micro scooters provide an example. This is not exactly a new product – scooters have been made for children for generations. But new materials and technologies have transformed the scooter, making it lighter, faster and easy to fold up and carry. As such, consumer enthusiasm for it has been greatly increased.
- Process innovation means a new way of producing. Sometimes it involves the invention of new kinds of machinery which produce in a different way. Other kinds of process innovation might just involve a different way of doing things, different management strategies, new job descriptions or better ways of sharing responsibilities. Process innovation can lead to big cost savings and often to lower product prices. It is a major source of *competitive advantage* for individual firms.

Both product and process innovation play a major part in improving standards of living. The telephone is not a new product but today's instrument is very much cheaper and more efficient than its predecessors. Process innovation is of crucial importance in leading to the growth of *productivity* and ultimately to long-term *economic growth*.

inorganic growth can help a firm to grow larger by merging with or taking over other companies. The objective is to expand without having to undertake complex and costly investment projects.

inputs include anything used in the production process: land, *labour* and capital, raw materials, components, energy; the list could be extended.

insider dealing or trading: using inside information to make a profit. People often have information which they acquire at work which makes it possible for them to make profits for themselves. If you know that your employer is about to make a takeover bid for a company and that the shares are currently priced somewhat below the bid value, you could rush out and buy the shares and sell them later at a handsome profit. This is illegal, because effectively, you would be defrauding the original shareholder, who would get a relatively poor price for the shares.

insolvency occurs when a firm is unable to pay its debts. In technical terms, its liabilities are greater than its assets. In practical terms, it cannot raise enough cash to pay the bills as they come in. This will usually follow a period when losses have been made. It is illegal to continue trading once it becomes clear that the firm is insolvent. Under the insolvency laws, an official *receiver* may then be appointed. This person may be able to reorganise the business. If there is no way to save it, it may go into *liquidation*.

institutional investors are the pension funds, insurance companies and unit trust groups which invest their capital in shares. Because of the huge scale of their investments, they have enormous influence, far exceeding that of all the small individual shareholders put together. It is sometimes thought that they encourage firms to pursue short-term profit at the expense of long-term investment.

insurance is the principle by which risks are shared between all those who wish to protect themselves from unforeseen eventualities. To insure against a risk, a premium is paid. The insurance company then pays compensation if the risky event happens. The premiums paid provide the necessary funds for compensation, together with an amount which covers the insurance companies' administrative costs.

insurance companies provide different types of insurance cover. Their accumulated premiums are invested in a range of assets. This makes them very important as *institutional investors* on the Stock Exchange.

integrated transport policy: a policy which would develop a variety of transport facilities to meet the overall needs of the public to get from one place to another. Instead of responding to rising demand for roads, rail travel and so on in a piecemeal fashion, the government would produce an integrated plan which meshed developments so that provision could be made for pedestrians, cyclists, drivers, passengers and rail and air travellers, with fewer negative *externalities* developing than at present. Progress to date is disappointing because an effective integrated policy is likely to require some measures which will annoy motorists.

integration is a term used in two ways. It may refer to the bringing together of two or more companies, either by takeover or merger. (See also *forward integration*, *vertical integration*, *horizontal integration* and *conglomerate*.)

Alternatively it may refer to the way in which the economies of different nation states become *interdependent*. For example, the EU is a powerful force for integration within Europe.

intellectual property: ideas which have originated from an individual or firm. They can be protected by a *patent* if they involve a product or by copyright if they involve books, articles or music. Trademarks and logos can also be protected by law. The patented idea cannot be used without the permission of the owner of the patent. Anything which is original and has copyright cannot be copied without permission. Some of the hottest intellectual property issues currently concern the illegal copying of copyright musical items. Often, intellectual property rights can only be protected by legal action which may be difficult and expensive.

Intellectual property may give its owner some degree of *market power*. However, the protection given by the law is essential to preserving the incentive to innovate and produce new ideas. Few authors would bother to write if their work could not be protected by copyright. No drug companies would research new drugs if they could not be patented.

inter-bank market is the wholesale money market where banks lend to each other on a very short-term basis, to cover temporary deficits in their payments to each other. It reduces banks' need to hold large quantities of *liquid assets*. This market froze up during the financial crisis in 2008. Many such assets turned out to be much riskier than the banks had earlier supposed, so they became unwilling to buy them.

interdependence refers to the way in which the economies of nation states have become increasingly reliant on one another in recent years, through the growth of trade and capital movements. This integration means that they are more vulnerable to adverse events in the economies of their trading partners but they are also more likely to gain from positive trends. For example, as the US economy shrank in 2008–09, businesses in many countries experienced falling demand because the US is an important market for their exports.

interdependence between firms describes the way businesses in an *oligopoly* will each take decisions in the light of the behaviour, or the expected reactions, of the other firms in the industry. For example, if one firm cuts prices, others may follow suit because if they do not, they will lose market share.

interest is the return on *capital* which has been lent. The terms of a loan will usually specify a fixed percentage rate or they may provide for the rate to rise and fall with interest rates generally. Interest rations the amount of financial capital available amongst potential borrowers, in rather the same way as prices ration the goods and services available among competing buyers. Similarly, interest provides savers with the incentive to make their funds available to others. If they lend it (or deposit it in a bank which will lend it) they will be rewarded with interest payments.

interest rates define the amount which has to be paid in exchange for borrowing money. They will vary according to the riskiness of the loan. So, the highest interest rates are charged on unpaid balances on a credit card or on hire purchase loans. Bank loans are cheaper but the rate will depend on the bank's assessment of the risk involved. Mortgage rates are lower still, because the property can be repossessed in the event of default. Lowest of all are the rates charged by the Bank of England to the banks.

Lenders who are prepared to take some risks will get a higher rate of interest in return for the use of their funds than they would if they wanted to minimise the risk.

Interest rates are a key feature in many consumption and production decisions.

- If borrowing is for consumption, it is important to look at the total cost: the price plus the interest payable.
- A person who has funds but does not want to lend them will find that there is an **opportunity cost** – the interest which could have been earned.
- A firm which invests its **retained profits** in the business must be careful. The return on the investment should be at least equal to the interest rate which it could have got on this money if it had been placed in a bank account. This is the opportunity cost of the capital invested.
- A firm which borrows to invest must be sure that the returns on the investment will be greater than the interest payable on the loan.

Interest rates are the main feature of **monetary policy**. The Bank of England, in common with many other central banks, does not have any easy way of controlling the supply of money, i.e. the amount banks are prepared to lend. But through its control of interest rates, it can influence the demand for money, that is, the amount businesses and individuals want to borrow. This has a significant effect on the level of **aggregate demand**. See also **Monetary Policy Committee**.

intermediate goods are inputs to the production process which have already undergone some processing or are manufactured. They include all kinds of components such as car exhaust pipes and partly processed materials such as the bulk chemicals used to make plastic products.

intermediate technology can be used in situations where high-technology methods of production are not appropriate. For example, in developing countries where wages are low it is often not cost effective to use capital-intensive approaches. In addition, such an approach may worsen poverty by creating job losses. Intermediate technology uses imaginative ways of making people more productive but does not require expensive imported equipment. A wheelbarrow may be an improvement, for moving soil, on the traditional Indian method of a basket carried on the head. It does not reduce employment in the way that a JCB might.

internal costs are the costs that appear in the firm's accounts. In contrast, **external costs** are the ones which are paid for by third parties. So internal costs cover **labour** and capital costs and the cost of inputs. The external costs arise from any pollution or congestion caused by the production process and any other costs to the community.

internal economies of scale: the many factors which cause costs to fall as output rises. They originate within the individual firm.
- Technical economies arise when it is possible to use larger, more efficient machinery. Because new machines will be expensive, it must be possible to spread these high fixed costs across a large quantity of output. Also, large producers will encounter fewer **indivisibilities** as they combine equipment of varying scales into a single sequence of processes. Where storage is required, large containers work out cheaper than small ones: these are called economies of increased dimensions. (This arises because volume increases by more than the cost of the container's surface area.) Further technical economies may be possible if large organisations rationalise production facilities, concentrating different items in the product range at specific sites. The car industry does this, each plant specialising in one or two models which will then be shipped all over the EU. Lastly, technical economies can accrue to large firms which

can afford **research and development (R & D)** departments. The cost of these can be spread thinly across the large quantity of output.

- Managerial economies arise when growing firms can hire specialists, working to find and train exactly the right person for a narrow specialist role. Smaller firms need people who are versatile rather than specialists. A deeper **division of labour** is possible in larger firms.
- Financial economies mean that the larger firm can access funds for **investment** more easily and often at a lower rate of interest. Public companies can raise share capital from the public at large.
- Commercial economies are possible if the firm can benefit from bulk buying of inputs and bulk transport of the output. In this category there are also marketing economies. Big firms can afford national advertising campaigns, using the most effective medium for the product in question. The high fixed costs will again be spread thinly.

(See also **economies of scale**.)

internal finance: using funds for investment which have come from the firm's own activities. The main source of funds will be **retained profit**. This is sometimes called corporate saving. The funds may be accumulated over several years while expansion is being planned, then perhaps combined with **external finance** when the plan is carried out.

internal growth occurs when a firm expands its own output. The alternative approach, **external growth**, would involve taking over or merging with other firms. This is sometimes called **organic growth** and depends on the firm's ability to capture a larger share of the market.

internal market: the system within the National Health Service which requires individual sections of the organisation to pay other sections for the use of their facilities. The objective is to cut costs by allowing providers to compete. For example, GPs can choose which hospital will treat their patients.

internal trade: trade within the economy, as opposed to international trade. These two are similar in that there are buyers and sellers, transport costs and a process of **specialisation**. However, with internal trade all producers are competing under similar conditions. The legal system is well known to all, all use the same currency and all face the same situation as to **interest rates**, tax rates and the state of the macro-economy. With international trade there are exchange rate risks and transaction costs, the economic cycle in the other country may be different and so on. This is an interesting distinction because the EU is gradually becoming more like a single market and, within the euro zone, it could be argued that all trade is internal.

internalising externalities means finding a way to turn an **external cost** into an internal cost. For example, if a firm has been emitting harmful products through chimneys into the air, it can be required by law to clean up its emissions. It will have to install new equipment capable of doing this job and this will add to its costs of production – its internal, private, costs. Meanwhile the people who suffered from the air pollution will no longer be experiencing the external cost. This is an example of the operation of the **polluter pays principle**.

International Bank for Reconstruction and Development (IBRD) is the proper name of what is usually known as the World Bank. It was set up in 1947 along with the **International Monetary Fund (IMF)**. Initially it was designed to provide finance for the post-war reconstruction of Europe and Japan. Quite quickly its primary focus shifted to the *developing economies*. It borrows funds on Western capital markets and lends them to developing countries for projects of many kinds including infrastructure, agriculture, industry, education and health. It charges commercial interest rates, but lends for purposes and in countries which banks might usually find too risky. Loans are often conditional on the adoption of particular policies, which may be unpopular. However, this does mean that governments can shift the blame for necessary but unpalatable policies onto the World Bank.

Some of the World Bank's projects have been controversial. Although now anxious to promote environmentally sound policies, it has not always been so. Through its 'soft loan' arm, the *International Development Agency*, it lends to the poorest countries at concessional rates of interest. It also undertakes extensive research and advises developing country governments on economic policy.

international capital flows are large sums of money which are moved from one economy to another. There are two possible motives:

- Firms and individuals may be moving large bank deposits in the short run from one financial centre to another in order to take advantage of higher interest rates or to buy shares which have attractive profit prospects. (This is sometimes called *hot money*.)
- Firms may be investing directly in new productive capacities in other countries; this is a long-term flow. Many firms prefer to locate production overseas, close to the market. Alternatively, they may want to locate production in a country with lower *labour* costs, from which they will then import.

All international capital flows are liable to lead to exchange rate changes. A capital outflow increases the supply of the currency in question and encourages exchange rate depreciation. A capital inflow will have the opposite effect. (See *exchange rate determination*.)

international competitiveness depends on a wide range of factors and determines how successful a firm is in selling exports and competing with imports. Price may be an important consideration for some products. Prices relative to those of the overseas competition will be affected by differing cost structures and by exchange rate changes. If the exchange rate depreciates, export prices can be cut.

Other important factors include design, quality, reliability and after-sales service – all the component aspects of *competitive advantage*. For some producers an important question concerns how effectively they have tailored the product to the needs of the market in question.

For some countries competitiveness is based on low labour costs. But countries with very high labour costs continue to compete well by relying on design and quality advantages as well as technical expertise.

Some multinational firms locate the labour-intensive parts of the production process in countries where labour is cheap (e.g. component assembly can be carried out in the Far East) while the capital-intensive stages of production stay in the country where they are based.

International Development Agency (IDA) is part of the *International Bank for Reconstruction and Development (IBRD)* (World Bank), undertaking lending on concessional terms. Interest rates may be lower on these loans and they may be waived altogether for a period of time. These loans are available only to the poorest developing countries and some of the projects supported are not strictly commercial, although they may have an important role in the development process.

International Labour Organization (ILO): a member organisation of the United Nations, the ILO exists to help improve working conditions throughout the world. It maintains relationships with trade unions as well as governments and seeks to promote social justice in the workplace.

International Monetary Fund (IMF) was set up at the Bretton Woods conference in 1944 and was designed to co-ordinate the international monetary system. Until 1972, it oversaw the system of fixed exchange rates which was in operation. Its objectives were to ensure the stability of the system and provide adequate finance to support the growth of world trade. Stability can itself promote trade, because it reduces uncertainty and makes forward planning easier and less risky.

Member countries contribute funds in proportion to the size of their economies. If they have problems with a persistent balance of trade deficit, they may negotiate a loan from the IMF. This will help to finance the deficit in the short term and allow time for economic policies to produce a long-term solution. Usually the IMF sends a team of inspectors to the borrower country; they advise on the conditions upon which the loan is provided. These conditions are likely to include cuts in public expenditure and control of monetary growth. The availability of loans helps to ensure that exchange rate changes are not excessively destabilising.

Since 1972, most exchange rates have floated. The IMF has continued to act as co-ordinator of the international monetary system, ensuring that the growth of liquidity was sufficient to finance world trade. Its role as a source of loans has increasingly been confined to developing countries. It continues to provide surveillance of all member economies, acting as a source of information and advice. It has had an important role in organising the developed countries' response to the *Debt Problem*.

The IMF played an important part in planning the international response to the financial crisis in 2008–09. Many emerging economies needed loans to help with balance of payments deficits. At the G20 meeting in April 2009 the IMF agreed to provide US$250 billion in new *Special Drawing Rights (SDRs)* for this purpose.

international trade means importing and exporting. Through *specialisation*, countries are able to increase both consumer choice and the total quantity of output overall. The theory of *comparative advantage* shows how trade is associated with increased output.

In the long run, there is a very clear link between international trade and *economic growth.* (See the bar chart opposite. The dip in 2001 shows the impact of the *Asian financial crisis*.) Being able to buy a cheap imported substitute for a dearer domestic product can increase many people's purchasing power, giving them higher real incomes. However, in the short run, some people may lose out as growing international competition forces the less competitive firms out of business and makes their employees redundant. This can lead to *protectionism*, a movement to reduce trade through import controls.

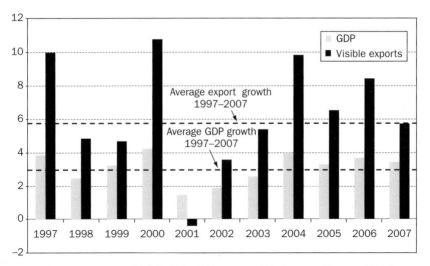

Growth in visible exports and GDP, 1997–2007, annual % change. (Source: WTO)

interrelationships between markets: many markets have connections, in that changes in one market will have some impact on other markets. Changes in some product markets will have an effect on the *labour* market – falling demand for seaside holidays in the UK, for example, has left many resorts with high unemployment. Falling demand for butter has been balanced by rising demand for margarine. Similarly rising wage rates affect cost structures and competitiveness in some sectors.

intervention (in foreign currency markets) occurs when a central bank steps in to buy or sell a currency in order to stabilise its exchange rate. (See also *fixed exchange rate*.)

interventionist: a person who supports action by the government to influence and control market forces. A lively appreciation of the forces lying behind the various types of *market failure* can lead people to support interventions, for example in the form of *employment protection* laws, subsidies to groups which pursue social and community objectives, and active involvement in the production process. Interventionists tend to be associated with left-wing political groups. (The Socialist Workers Party currently wants the government to take over loss-making manufacturing businesses so as to preserve jobs.) Conservative voters would be more likely to support a *laissez-faire* viewpoint.

interventionist policies are designed to manipulate or override market forces in such a way that a variety of political objectives can be achieved. Left to themselves, market systems tend to deliver marked inequalities in incomes, fluctuations in incomes over the course of the economic cycle and a variety of *market failures* which lead to long-term problems for society and the environment. The ultimate intervention was the nationalisation of many industries after World War II, so that the government was actually responsible for a considerable amount of production.

Although governments have become significantly less interventionist in recent years, some sectors are still subject to intervention. *Regulation* of utilities, *competition policy* and *environmental policies* are just a few areas where intervention is particularly visible. Nowadays, the intervention is often indirect, where it would in the past have been direct, influencing rather than controlling market forces.

Since 1979, many people have believed that government should stand back from the detailed working of the economy because markets are the most efficient way to allocate resources. On the whole, the government does not have a good track record for running businesses efficiently. Some good ways of encouraging efficient production have come from the ideas of **supply-side policies**.

invention means devising a new product or process. If it really is new, it can be **patert**, giving its owner some rights over its development. Invention is not the same as **innovation**, which means developing the product to the point where it is saleable.

inventory means stock. Stocks can be of inputs or outputs.

inverse relationship: when two variables are related, so that they move in opposite directions, they are said to be inversely related. For example, quantity demanded is usually inversely related to price. As the price rises, consumers will be discouraged from buying the product.

investment means spending now on something that can be expected to generate an income in the future. It is a term which is used rather loosely and in many different contexts.

- Most importantly, investment means spending on capital equipment which can be used to create products which will sell. Investment will increase **productivity** and may cut costs or contribute to improving quality.
- Investment may also be directed towards increasing **human capital**. Improved skills and knowledge bring high rates of return on investment in human capital.
- Just to confuse you, people talk about investing on the **stock market**. If they are simply buying shares from the previous owner, no real investment has taken place although there has been a change of ownership. If they are buying shares which are part of a new share issue, the proceeds of which will be spent on an investment in new productive capacity, then they are financing an investment by the firm from which they bought the shares.
- Investment in **stocks** and work in progress refers to the stocks of inputs and outputs which manufacturers must hold. These are an investment in that they can be sold in the future or at least they can be made into products which will sell.

On the macro-economic level, investment is important because it increases productive capacity and productivity and promotes **economic growth**. Investment spending is an **injection** into the **circular flow of national income** and will have an upward **multiplier** effect on income. Most governments want to encourage investment.

investment appraisal: the process of deciding whether a proposed investment will actually be worthwhile. For big projects, there are various ways of estimating the future income stream which can be expected. This must be compared with the **interest** payments which will be needed where loan finance is involved. Even where **internal finance** is being used care is needed to see that the returns are at least equal to the **opportunity cost** of the capital invested.

investment banks specialise in supplying financial services to firms, most often large ones. They are sometimes called wholesale banks: they do not usually provide day-to-day banking services. Their original role was in financing international trade, lending to firms which were exporting and therefore had to face a long gap between paying production costs and receiving sales revenue. They still do this. Other services offered include:

- long-term loans for capital investment
- advising on and organising share issues

- stockbroking
- providing venture capital, i.e. loans to relatively risky new ventures
- advising on and helping to organise mergers and takeovers.

There have been many mergers in the financial sector and merchant banks are often financial conglomerates. These are made up of many specialist departments offering different types of services.

investment income: income derived from profits and dividends or, if the *investment* is in property, rents. It can also include interest on loans and *bonds*.

investment trust: a company which invests its shareholders' funds in a range of different stocks and shares. This means that the shareholders get the benefits in terms of *dividends* and capital gains from the trust's choice of shares. But because they are holding a wide range of shares indirectly, they spread the risks.

invisible balance means the balance between invisible imports and invisible exports. In the UK the invisible balance is usually in surplus and helps to balance a visible deficit.

invisible export: the sale of a service to a customer based overseas. Financial services, insurance, air travel and tourism all generate revenue from invisible exports.

invisible hand: the term used by *Adam Smith* to describe how the market system allocates resources. A decrease in demand for a product will mean that stocks build up as orders fall, so the producers begin to make losses. In time they will cut production and fewer resources will be devoted to the product which has become less popular. The reverse happens when demand increases. There will be a rise in the price so that *profits* will increase. More firms will want to produce for the buoyant market. Resources will be attracted to the industry. In this way the *profit-signalling mechanism* in the marketplace will invisibly secure an allocation of resources which balances supply and demand.

invisible import: services bought from abroad.

invisible trade means imports and exports of services. Invisible trade is recorded in the balance of payments alongside visible trade. The invisible account includes financial services, insurance, tourism, shipping and air travel, interest, profit, dividends and personal transfers. For the UK, the net surplus on invisibles helps to offset frequent visible deficits.

involuntary unemployment includes all those unemployed people who have made determined efforts to find work and will accept what work they are offered. In contrast, voluntary unemployment refers to those who will refuse the work that is available because they do not consider it suitable or sufficiently well paid.

inward investment is *foreign direct investment (FDI)* which is coming in to the host country from abroad. Many *multinationals* have brought inward investment to the UK, including Nissan, Toyota, Hitachi, Ford, Peugeot and so on.

There has been a big increase in inward investment, which is one element in the process of *globalisation*.

inward-looking trade strategies emphasise self-sufficiency and the development of industries which can compete with imports. There may be a policy of *import substitution*, perhaps in the hope of creating jobs. These strategies are associated with *protectionism*. The resource cost of developing new industries in which the country does not have a *comparative advantage* can be very high. Some Latin American countries tried this approach in the past without great success.

irrational exuberance: *Alan Greenspan's* term for the way in which investors in shares pushed up their price. During the *bull markets* of the 1990s and 2000s, many of them bought enthusiastically at prices that seemed far higher than any reasonable expectations of profit. See also *animal spirits*.

irrigation: the use of extra water sources to supplement rainfall and grow crops which need more water than can be provided by the natural climate. Irrigation increases agricultural *productivity*, especially when used together with appropriate seed strains and fertilisers.

ISA: see *individual savings accounts (ISA)*.

Do you need revision help and advice?

Go to pages 326–46 for a range of revision appendices that include plenty of exam advice and tips.

Japanisation: the tendency of Western firms to adopt Japanese management strategies. These include emphasis on long-term planning, training and quality issues and *lean production*.

jargon: the language used by specialists to convey ideas. Certain words are given precise meanings which are somewhat different from those commonly understood. Some terms are invented to facilitate the identification of new ideas.

J-curve: the short-term response of the current account of the balance of payments to a sharp fall in the exchange rate. *Depreciation* makes imports dearer and exports cheaper. Other things being equal, exports will rise and imports will fall. However, this takes time and during the process of adjustment, as buyers react gradually to price changes, imports will cost more and exports bring in little more than they did before. So the current account may actually worsen before it gets better.

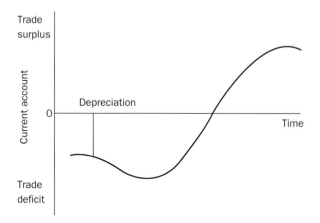

JIT: see *just in time (JIT)*.

job satisfaction: the level of enjoyment in work. Increased job satisfaction can be linked to raising *productivity*.

job security: the extent to which employees can rely on their jobs continuing. Jobs are likely to be much less secure during a recession.

jobseekers' allowance: the benefit paid to someone who is unemployed for the first six months.

joint costs: costs which are shared between two different products which are in *joint supply*. This makes it difficult to decide what the average cost of each product is. For example, diesel and petrol are produced from crude oil; apportioning costs is difficult.

joint demand occurs when two items are consumed together, i.e. are complements. Examples might be shoes and shoe laces or CDs and CD players. An increase in sales of one may lead to an increase in sales of the other.

joint supply occurs when the production of one good also entails the production of another. This often happens in the chemical industry where one chemical may be produced as a by-product of another. Meat and leather provide another example. A fall in the market price of one may affect the quantity supplied of the other.

joint venture: a collaborative project in which two separate firms set up production facilities which will be operated jointly. Each can contribute specialist knowledge or skills. It is often used to help firms set up in business abroad. Joint ventures have proved to be a useful way for developed country businesses to invest in developing countries with which they are not familiar (e.g. China and India).

junk bond: a fixed interest loan with a high interest rate but also a substantial degree of risk for the lender. Junk bonds were for a time used to finance takeovers in the US. Some of these were not successful.

just in time (JIT): an approach to organising stocks of inputs and output. With very careful planning, it is possible to arrange deliveries in such a way that production can continue with much lower levels of stocks. This saves the cost of financing and storing stocks. Computerised stock control and good relations with supplier companies make this approach easier. Pioneered in Japan, JIT has helped many firms to cut costs. Good industrial relations are essential, to ensure that production is steady and continuous.

Keynes, J M (1883–1946): an economist whose influence during his lifetime and after his death was really second to none. In 1919, he wrote the *Economic Consequences of the Peace*, which criticised the terms imposed on Germany after World War I. His warnings turned out to be prophetic. In 1936, Keynes published his *General Theory of Employment, Interest and Money*. This work grew out of his deep concern about the unemployment and the poverty brought about by the Great Depression.

Keynes's best-known work was built on his finding that a low level of **aggregate demand** did not necessarily correct itself and could persist for some time. This was in contrast to the classical view, which was that wages would fall during a depression until employers again began to take on **labour**. In this way unemployment would diminish on its own. To deal with the problem of **demand deficiency**, Keynes advocated deficit spending by the government. Expansionary **fiscal** and **monetary policies** could be used to increase aggregate demand. These ideas were influential all over the world, in particular during the period 1945–70. They have received further attention since 2007. (See also **Keynesian**.)

Keynes combined teaching and writing as an academic economist with advising the Treasury on the practicalities of economic management, over a very long period. But perhaps his most important contribution was in the thinking and negotiation which underpinned the creation of the international organisations that were set up after World War II (the World Bank and the IMF). He was instrumental in the setting up of the **International Monetary Fund (IMF)** just before his death. His approach to economic policy has had a lasting impact and is still visible from time to time in the policy pronouncements of politicians. His work on unemployment in the 1930s reflected a profound concern for the welfare of the unemployed. At the same time he was a strong advocate of prudent management of the monetary system.

Keynesian: people and ideas associated with the work of **J M Keynes**. After his death, many economists developed Keynes' ideas, seeking to apply them to new situations. In the process, they probably drifted some way from Keynes' original intentions. Certainly, the new situations they were analysing were very different from the world Keynes had analysed in the 1930s. The main thrust of Keynesian ideas included:

- a strong commitment to maintaining a level of **aggregate demand** at which unemployment rates would be relatively low
- active use of **fiscal** and **monetary policies** to control the level of aggregate demand. At one stage the process was known as **fine tuning** because it was believed that this approach could be used to promote economic growth and keep unemployment down without encouraging inflation or a balance of payments deficit.

Whereas the classical economists believed that unemployment would lead to falling wage rates, which would in turn increase the quantity of *labour* demanded by employers, and gradually eliminate unemployment, Keynes showed that a fall in wages might reduce consumption and so cause the economy to settle at an equilibrium level of output well below that of full employment. Hence the need for increased injections to raise aggregate demand. Increased government expenditure could be financed by borrowing until such time as the economy recovered.

For a time, Keynesians were at odds with the group of economists known as *monetarists*, who saw government expenditure as a source of inflationary pressures and emphasised the importance of controlling the growth of the money stock in order to prevent inflation from accelerating. During the early 1990s, the debate came to hinge upon the impact of rising aggregate demand on the labour market. Keeping large numbers of people unemployed can help to reduce inflationary pressures, but it also has serious implications for the welfare of the unemployed themselves. Improved understanding of the inflationary process and of the impact of *supply constraints* has made the debate between Keynesians and monetarists increasingly irrelevant.

Keynesian long-run aggregate supply curve: this stays horizontal across a wide range of output. While there is significant unemployment, output can be increased without raising wages, costs and prices. As supply constraints develop, employers have to pay more to get the labour they require so the curve slopes upwards. Eventually output cannot be increased at all because all usable resources are fully employed and the supply curve becomes a vertical line. (See *aggregate supply*.)

kinked demand curve: a theory which is used to analyse firms' behaviour in an *oligopoly* with no *collusion* between firms. It is observed that where there are just a few firms in competition with one another, raising product prices would mean a significant loss of sales because buyers would switch to competing products for which the price had stayed the same. This means that the upper part of the demand (or average revenue) curve would be highly elastic. However, a price cut would have little effect on sales because competing firms would follow suit with price cuts of their own. This would mean that the demand curve in this range would be very inelastic. The outcome of this analysis is a kinked demand curve and a tendency for prices to be quite stable as none of the firms in the industry has much incentive to change prices.

Kinked demand curve

Kyoto Protocol: an international agreement that sets targets for the reduction of emissions of greenhouse gases, signed in 1997. It was never ratified by the USA; powerful forces within the US were profoundly sceptical about the connection between climate change and the use of fossil fuels. Developing countries were reluctant to prejudice their chances of income growth while still suffering from widespread poverty. Developed countries were mostly reluctant to attack the problem energetically unless the developing countries also made progress. Only Denmark, Germany, Russia and the UK have actually reduced greenhouse gas emissions since the Protocol was agreed; other EU member countries have made progress. China, India and the USA have not. Negotiations for a new Kyoto agreement are continuing.

Aiming for a grade A*?

Don't forget to log on to **www.philipallan.co.uk/a-zonline** for advice.

labour: the factor of production which involves people working to produce goods and services. Labour involves both doing and thinking. Labour is often referred to as if it were a single type of resource. In practice there are many different categories of labour, depending on their respective capabilities, which are referred to as human capital. This can be increased through education and training.

labour, demand for: the demand for *labour* reflects the demand for the product and is thus a *derived demand*. There will be a demand schedule for labour just as there is a demand schedule for the product and the numbers employed will depend partly on the going wage rate. At any given wage, more labour will be demanded if the price of the product rises or if more can be sold.

If labour *productivity* rises, there are a number of possible outcomes. Costs will fall, so prices may be cut, sales may rise and more labour will be demanded. Alternatively, the increased productivity may make it possible to pay higher wages but in that case costs will not fall.

The demand for labour is thus closely related to the product market and changes in the pattern of demand work their way through the labour market into the overall allocation of resources. There is also a close relationship between the demand for labour and the price of capital. If wages rise relative to the price of labour-saving capital equipment, employers will tend to substitute capital for labour and the quantity of labour demanded will fall.

labour disputes: see *industrial disputes.*

labour flexibility: the extent to which it is possible for employers to use their workforces in a flexible way. This requires that:
- employees are trained for and capable of doing a range of different jobs
- they are willing to do different jobs as required and are not constrained by trade union agreements
- industrial relations in the work place are sufficiently trusting and amicable for flexible working not to be regarded as threatening.

Some employers have high expectations of employees in this respect. However, if it makes it possible to increase *productivity*, it may also be possible to raise wage rates.

labour force: the number of people available for work. This can be influenced by:
- birth rates in the past
- the number of people in education
- the retirement age
- the social security system and the extent to which poverty traps create disincentives
- the availability of child care.

When jobs are being created, discouraged workers and women who were not previously seeking work may rejoin the *labour* force.

Labour Force Survey: the quarterly government survey of employment and *unemployment*. It uses sample surveys to measure the number of people unemployed and actively seeking work and also the number of people who are not actively seeking a job but would like to work. It is thought to provide a more accurate measure of unemployment than the *claimant count*, which gives us the headline total for unemployment on a monthly basis, derived from the numbers claiming benefits.

labour intensive refers to production processes which use relatively more *labour* than capital. Typical examples of labour-intensive production include many services, arts and crafts production and some manufacturing processes in situations where labour is cheap relative to capital.

labour market consists of the demand for *labour* coming from employers and the supply of labour coming from individuals who want to work. The interaction of these groups creates market forces which determine the price of labour or the wage rate. Although we often speak of the labour market as a whole, in practical terms the labour market consists of a large number of separate but linked markets for different kinds of labour. The local authority looking for a competent computer specialist who can look after its networks is in a rather different market from the cleaning agency which makes office-cleaning arrangements for its clients. However, in many instances these smaller markets are interlinked. (See also *wage determination*.)

labour market failure refers to any imperfection in the *labour* market which impedes the movement of people away from the products with declining demand towards products with growing demand. The most important of these are *occupational immobility* and *geographical immobility*. Because they lack appropriate skills or live in a place where there is no demand for their services, people made redundant from a declining industry may be unable to find alternative work. Lack of information may also create imperfections.

labour market flexibility refers to the ease with which people are able to change jobs or adapt to changed circumstances in other ways. There are a number of examples:
- the trend towards greater *labour* market flexibility in recent years means that some people now have part-time contracts which allow the employer to vary the number and the timing of the hours worked
- improved education and training generally make individuals more flexible, so that they are relatively easily able to move to an alternative occupation
- any measure which improves *labour mobility* will be likely to increase flexibility. The US labour market is usually thought to be more flexible than the UK labour market. Within the EU, the UK and the Netherlands are thought to have the most flexible labour markets, but all are becoming more flexible.

Lack of flexibility can be due to *employment protection* law which may make it difficult for employers to make people redundant when demand for the product is falling.

labour market imperfections: see *labour market failure*.

labour mobility refers to the ease with which people can change jobs. Occupational mobility reflects the extent to which people can move to a different job. It depends on the ease with which they can be retrained and on their general level of education. Geographical mobility reflects the ease with which people can move from an area with limited employment opportunities to one with more jobs available. This depends on the availability of housing for rent, differentials in the cost of housing between the prosperous area and the area of high unemployment and people's willingness to move.

labour productivity: output per person employed, a measure of the efficiency of labour.

labour supply curve: the relationship between the quantity of *labour* supplied and the going wage. Higher wage rates can induce people to work longer hours. The supply of labour can be affected by the *participation rate*, by the structure of social security payments and by the rate of immigration. A growing labour supply has for many countries provided a stimulus to growth. Immigration into the US has always been seen as one of the strengths of the US economy. (See also *backward sloping supply curve of labour.*)

Laffer curve: the relationship between the rate of tax and the revenue derived from it, which makes a curve showing rising revenue as the rate is increased. The tax makes the activity in question less worthwhile so if rates are raised further the revenue falls again. This idea has been used in the past as an argument for cutting tax rates, because high marginal tax rates are sometimes thought to discourage hard work. This sounds plausible but there is no statistical evidence for it.

lagging indicator is an economic variable which changes after the event which caused it to occur. Unemployment is lagged in this way to the *economic cycle*, perhaps by about 12–18 months. Firms are often unwilling to take on more *labour* at the first signs of recovery; they want to be sure that the improvement will be sustained. Similarly, they wait as long as they can before making people redundant; by the time they do the economy may be well into recession.

lags may occur whenever a change in one variable has an impact on another, but after a lapse of time. It is usual for decision takers to take time to adjust to new circumstances. A change in prices will usually lead to a change in the quantity demanded but only after existing contracts have been completed.

laissez-faire: an approach to government intervention which favours minimal government involvement in the economy. All decisions are taken in direct response to market forces. If *perfect competition* were the rule in all markets, a laissez-faire approach would get the best allocation of resources for all. However, the existence of large numbers of *market imperfections*, distortions and market failures means that nowadays most people think that governments should have competition policies, environmental regulations and some degree of income redistribution.

During the 1960s and 1970s, a good deal of *government intervention* took place. However, during the early 1980s and since, there has been a swing back towards less interventionist policies, associated with Thatcherism in the UK and with the transition to market economies in Eastern Europe and Russia.

land: natural resources. Land can be used for agriculture or buildings. It can be improved, making it more productive, e.g. by drainage. It can be degraded, e.g. by overgrazing or pollution.

landfill waste tax: a tax on the amount of waste dumped in landfill sites. It was introduced in 1996, as a way of internalising an *external cost* to society: the polluter has to pay. It is being gradually increased, to provide bigger incentives to minimise waste.

law of diminishing returns: see *diminishing marginal returns*.

lead time: the time that elapses between one event and the next. For example, the lead time between the decision to design a new model of a car and its arrival on the market can be quite long. Japanese producers have developed an advantage because they have been able to shorten lead times, giving a swifter response to changes in market demand.

leading indicator means a variable which foreshadows subsequent events in the economy. The CBI Industrial Trends Survey collects data on business optimism, which can be a useful indicator of pessimism leading to falling demand for investment goods. Share prices similarly can foreshadow falling demand generally.

leakages are savings, taxation and imports, which leak out of the *circular flow of national income* and reduce aggregate demand. (See also *withdrawals*.)

lean production: the collection of strategies that have been broadly characterised by the term *Japanisation*. These include *just-in-time* stock control, emphasis on quality control, fast response to market changes and shorter lead times in product development. Usually these measures require a well-trained workforce and good *industrial relations*. For some firms, these approaches have brought substantial cost cuts.

Learning and Skills Councils: the bodies responsible for ensuring that local training opportunities meet local needs. They are composed of representatives of local businesses and work in collaboration with colleges of further education to set up appropriate courses.

lease: a contract giving a buyer the right to use something for a specified length of time. Usually this applies to property, most often to flats or industrial premises. The property reverts to the freeholder when the lease runs out.

leasing: a way of investing in new equipment without having to buy it. It involves a long-term contract to rent the equipment. It requires much less finance because the equipment will not be bought outright. Companies such as easyJet and Virgin have leased aircraft, particularly in the early days of their operation. Earth-moving equipment and vans are often leased.

least developed countries: the 49 countries identified by the UN as having the lowest per capita incomes. Thirty-three of the countries are in Africa south of the Sahara. The criteria for inclusion are:
- Per capita incomes average less than US$750 per annum.
- They are close to the bottom of the *Human Development Index (HDI)*.
- They are economically vulnerable in being prone to natural disasters, dependent on a narrow range of commodities with unstable prices and having few non-traditional sources of income.

leisure industries: an important sector in modern economies, which includes cultural activities, sport and entertainment. Generally speaking, the sector has enjoyed strong growth in recent years and is characterised by high *income elasticity of demand*.

lemon: a product which does not work as expected.

lender of last resort: an important function of the Bank of England (and other central banks), which guarantees to lend to banks which find themselves temporarily unable to meet their customers' requests for withdrawals. This process was much in evidence during the financial crisis, especially in 2007–08 when Northern Rock, Lloyds TSB, RBS and others needed to be recapitalised due to massive losses. In fact the system-wide crisis was so severe then that only the government could rescue the banks by taking a large share of ownership.

This does not mean that a central bank will bail out any bank at any time; a bank which has been mismanaged or involved in fraud may still fail or be sold, as happened with Barings in 1995, or with the US bank Lehmans, in 2008. But central banks will try to ensure the stability of the banking system as a whole.

level playing field: a situation in which all firms are competing on the same terms. Conditions which might make the playing field less level would include:

- government subsidies to some firms. This has been a particular problem in the iron and steel industry, where there has been world overcapacity and some governments have helped their domestic producers. The US has taken great exception to some European governments' subsidies
- health and safety requirements which raise firms' costs of production. Hence the harmonisation of employment law across the EU, as part of the *single European market* provisions. The single market is in fact an attempt to create a level playing field for all EU firms
- differences in fuel taxes. UK hauliers think that high fuel taxes in the UK put them at a disadvantage when competing with other EU hauliers who face lower fuel taxes.

There are a great many other ways in which playing fields are not level.

LFS unemployment refers to the measurement of unemployment based on the Labour Force Survey. (Headline unemployment is based on the *claimant count*.)

liability: a legal obligation to pay a debt. Liabilities appear in the accounts of banks and companies. They imply the existence of some form of loan or responsibility to cover debts in the future. (See also *limited liability (Ltd)*.)

liberalisation: movement towards a *free market* system. This means that market forces will become more important in determining the way decisions are taken. This can be important within the economy and also in international trade.

- In the domestic economy it is accomplished by allowing prices and quantities to be determined by *market forces*. The role of the government in production is reduced, e.g. by privatisation. Controls of any kind are avoided. Competition is encouraged. Perhaps the least liberalised market in the UK is that for agricultural products covered by the CAP. Guaranteed minimum prices mean that the impact of market forces is greatly reduced by EU action.
- Internationally, liberalisation means eliminating or reducing the impact of tariffs and non-tariff barriers. This brings us closer to free trade, in which decisions to buy and sell are based entirely on market prices. The World Trade Organization encourages liberalisation by organising worldwide negotiations to reduce import controls. This process has encouraged economic growth.

licensing: firms which have a *patent* or copyright may license other firms to use their intellectual property in exchange for a royalty payment. This is a good way to increase the returns on their investment without having to set up extensive production facilities in other countries.

life expectancy: the number of years that a person can expect to live. This is usually calculated for each country. It may be calculated as life expectancy at birth or at any later age. There have been big increases in life expectancy in a number of developing countries.

limit pricing involves selecting a price below the profit-maximising price. A company may choose to do this if it seems likely to discourage *new entrants* to the industry. This may help to preserve its competitive position. High profits could attract new entrants who would compete strongly. It is likely that this is an element in the pricing strategies of many firms producing consumer durables. The limit price will be lowest when entry is easy, indicating a *contestable market*. It will be higher if there are substantial *economies of scale* in the industry.

limited company: a firm that has limited liability. This means that the owners of the firm cannot be made to use their personal wealth to pay the debts of the business. This is important because without limited liability, many people who want to set up in business would be deterred by the risk to their families of losing all that they have. It is in society's interests to encourage entrepreneurship which creates incomes and jobs.

limited liability (Ltd) means that the owners of the company, i.e. the shareholders, can lose only the amount of money they put into the business if it becomes insolvent. They cannot be asked to pay the company's debts out of their personal resources. This limits the risks which people are taking when they invest in setting up a business or buy shares. (See also *private limited company* and *public limited company*.)

limits to growth and development: the constraints that prevent developing countries from raising incomes. They include lack of physical and *human capital, capital flight, corruption, Debt Problem,* difficulty in exporting competitively, difficulties with *good governance*, weak *infrastructure*, rapid population growth, *primary product dependency,* low *savings* and war.

liquid assets are either money or something that can very quickly be sold for money at a price which involves little or no loss. In the case of a bank, liquid assets would include cash and any kind of very short-term loan.

liquidation means that the firm has closed down, usually because it is *insolvent* and cannot pay its debts. Its assets will be sold for what they are worth. This may follow a court case brought about by a creditor asking for compulsory liquidation in an attempt to get debts paid. The court will then appoint a *receiver* who will sell either the firm or its assets in order to raise the necessary cash. Voluntary liquidation is possible if the owner of the business simply wants to cease trading.

liquidity: the extent to which a firm or an individual has an adequate supply of cash or of assets which can easily be sold and turned into cash. Assets which can only be sold at a loss or after time spent searching for a buyer are not regarded as being liquid. Firms need enough liquidity to pay their bills when they become due, as indeed do individuals. Insufficient liquidity may be the result of the bank being unwilling to lend any more.

liquidity trap: occurs when interest rates are so low that they cannot be cut any further. This means that any further attempt to ease lending conditions will have no effect because potential investors will wait until demand increases and expectations of profit improve.

listed company: a firm which is a *public limited company (PLC)* so that its shares can be bought on the Stock Exchange. This gives it access to finance from a large body of potential shareholders, but may make the business less easy to control than if it were a *private limited company*.

literacy rate: the percentage of the adult population able to read and write. Increasing literacy rates can be an important element in the process of economic development. The lifetime returns (in terms of increased pay) to learning to read and write are high.

living standards: see *standard of living*.

Lloyd's: the market for *insurance* in London. Its members provide insurance of all kinds all over the world. The risks are carried by the 'names', wealthy individuals who are prepared to cover potential losses. In normal circumstances, they make excellent rates of return but if losses are made, they may be very large indeed. Insurance contributes significantly to the UK's invisible exports.

loan capital: funds for investment which come from borrowing. In contrast, share capital (also called equity finance) comes from selling shares in the company.

local government is responsible in the UK for most school education, social services, local roads, planning and a range of other services. Changes in local government, and the trend towards unitary authorities (single authorities responsible for all locally provided services), may affect the way these services are organised.

local multiplier: when spending in one particular area increases, then a local multiplier effect will be observed. Extra spending will generate employment: if a new bridge is being built, people will be employed to do the building. These people will then spend some of their earnings locally, thus creating further demand and increased employment in the immediate area.

localised industry: where one area has a particular advantage for an industry, that industry will tend to develop there rather than in other locations. In the past the existence of coal often created an industrial area involving steel making and engineering. *Industrial inertia* may mean that these industries have continued to be located in the same place. Other possible local advantages include a supply of appropriately skilled *labour* with a tradition in the industry concerned.

location of industry: see *industrial location*.

long run: the period of time in which all factors of production can be varied. For example, it is possible to invest in new capital equipment and build new factories. Similarly, some businesses may enter or exit from the marketplace, so changing the size of the industry.

long-run aggregate supply: monetarist economists assume that the LRAS will be a vertical line, determined by the maximum capacity of the economy to produce. If there is a fall in demand, prices and wages will fall until the markets clear and full employment will be maintained. Over time, the line will shift to the right as investment and technical change increase productive capacity. (See also *aggregate supply*.)

long-run equilibrium under perfect competition: the equilibrium price and quantity produced, which will be at the point where average total costs are at a minimum. Only normal profit can be made. Price will be exactly equal to average total cost. (See also *perfect competition*.)

long-run Phillips curve: the long-run relationship between inflation and unemployment. (This is sometimes called the expectations-augmented Phillips curve.) The *short-run Phillips curve* shows an inverse relationship between inflation and unemployment, often associated with the *economic cycle*.

Normally, it is possible to see a trade-off between inflation and unemployment. When unemployment is high there is a relatively low level of aggregate demand in the economy and there will be few inflationary pressures. The reverse holds too: low unemployment indicates that labour resources are scarce, prices will be bid up by competing employers and inflation will follow. This is the relationship found in the **Phillips curve**.

Strong expectations of inflation cause people to expect large pay increases in compensation. This means that at any given level of unemployment, inflation accelerates. This pushes the Phillips curve upwards and to the right as shown in the diagram. The trade-off remains but at a new, higher rate of inflation.

In any economy there will be an **equilibrium unemployment** level at which wage rates are stable because employers can find the people they need without bidding up wages. This is called the long-run Phillips curve. It is a vertical line: unemployment can always be reduced by increasing aggregate demand, but this will lead to accelerating inflation. To get this under control it will be necessary to reduce aggregate demand and unemployment will rise again. So in the long run, the level of unemployment is constant and equal to that at which prices are stable. (See also **non-accelerating inflation rate of unemployment (NAIRU)** and **overfull employment**.) This level of unemployment will be close to the level of **structural unemployment**, which cannot be reduced in the long run by extra spending.

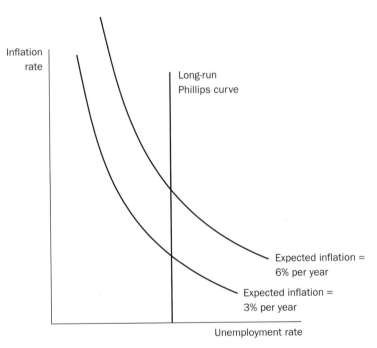

Long-run Phillips curve

long-run supply curve shows the quantities which will be supplied at a range of different prices in the long run. Firms can adjust fully to price changes in the long run. Whereas in the short run supply may be quite inelastic because there is not time to expand production in the most economical way, in the long run the supply of some products may be almost perfectly elastic, because firms can simply duplicate efficient facilities for production and expand to meet the demand.

long-run trend rate of growth: the rate of growth of output which can realistically be achieved over a long period. In the UK this has historically been about 2.2% per year. It is a moving average of growth rates over a period of time, typically the 30 years shown in the diagram below. It represents the average rate of growth of productive capacity for the whole economy. It is influenced by:

- the level of investment
- improvements in education and training
- increased technical knowledge
- innovation generally.

Improved management techniques can also have some impact. Shocks to the economy such as oil price changes or serious loss of business confidence, which lead to falling aggregate demand and recession on a serious scale, will tend to reduce the long-term trend growth rate. Counter-inflation policies can have the same effect. It follows that **macro-economic stability** can help to raise long-term growth rates.

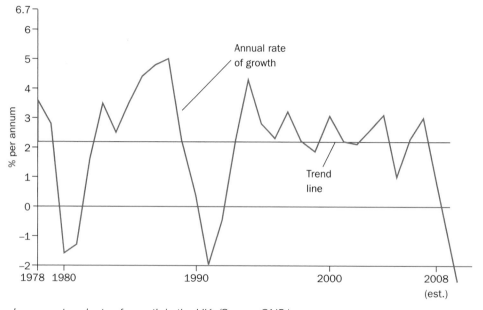

Long-run trend rate of growth in the UK. (Source ONS.)

long-term capital flows are international flows of money for capital investment, usually in productive capacity, e.g. car factories. (Short-term flows are usually in search of higher interest rates and may be used to buy **bonds**.)

long-term unemployed are people who have been unemployed for more than a year. The number or proportion of long-term unemployed has policy implications:

- they may become discouraged and cease to make active efforts to find work
- they may become deskilled or lose their work habits
- as a result, they may for practical purposes have dropped out of the **labour** market.

To the extent that these consequences have followed upon long-term unemployment, governments have to consider retraining or policies to reduce **geographical immobility**.

Lorenz curve: a graphical representation showing inequality. In the diagram, the Lorenz curve will run along the 45° line if the range of percentages of the population are the same as the share of total income which they receive. The more unequal the distribution of income, the more the Lorenz curve will be bowed out below the 45° line. For example, at point A, 24% of the population have 10% of the total income. So the closer the curve is to the 45° line, the greater is the degree of equality and vice versa. Lorenz curves can be used to compare other frequency distributions which are not equal, such as the number of firms and cumulative market shares. The **Gini coefficient** is the area between the Lorenz curve and the 45° line and gives a measure of inequality.

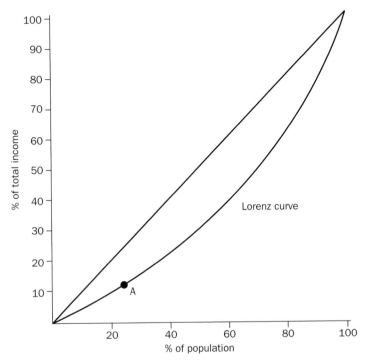

Lorenz curve

loss: the difference between total costs and sales revenue. Loss indicates that demand for the product is declining. The ***profit-signalling mechanism*** is working in reverse, indicating that resources should be reallocated away from the product in question. The product may have gone out of fashion or there may be a competing producer who can create and sell it at a lower price. The firm in question may cut production or it may exit from the marketplace. It may then switch to a more profitable product or go out of business altogether.

low-income countries are classified by the World Bank as those with per capita incomes of US$936 or less per year. 2.6 billion people live in low-income countries, a high proportion of the world's total population of 6.6 billion. The largest low-income countries are India and Indonesia. Many of the very poorest countries are in Africa south of the Sahara. China has moved into the bottom end of the middle-income group in recent years, but still has huge numbers of poor people living in the countryside rather than the more prosperous cities. For comparison, Portugal is rich enough to be classified in the high-income group.

Country	Per capita income, US$, 2007, GNI
USA	46 040
UK	42 740
Portugal	18 950
Ukraine	2550
China	2360
Indonesia	1650
India	950
Ghana	590
Uganda	340
Sierra Leone	260

Source: World Bank, World Development Report, 2009

While many African countries suffer from extreme poverty, many countries which are making the transition from central planning to a market economy are also in the low-income category. For many of the poorest countries, war is partly responsible for their plight. The data tells us nothing about the distribution of income within countries.

Ltd: see *limited liability (Ltd)*.

A–Z Online

Log on to A–Z Online to search the database of terms, print revision lists and much more. Go to **www.philipallan.co.uk/a-zonline** to get started.

Maastricht Treaty is named after the city in the Netherlands where it was negotiated in late 1991. It had five significant elements:

- Its main provision was the detailed plan for *Economic and Monetary Union (EMU)*.
- The funds which are used to assist poorer areas of the EU were expanded.
- It initiated the Social Chapter, a separate section of the agreement which created a system of regulations covering employee health and safety, workplace conditions, equal pay and employee participation.
- Provision was made to develop a common foreign and security policy.
- Arrangements were made to co-operate in matters of crime prevention, immigration and policing.

The Treaty came into force in late 1993. It marked a significant change in terms of the degree of harmonisation within the EU.

macro-economic equilibrium: in macro-economics, equilibrium is a situation in which *aggregate demand* is exactly equal to the level of planned output. Thus buyers wish to buy all that firms and other agencies intend to produce. There is no change in the level of stocks. If aggregate demand is greater than or less than output (i.e. there is disequilibrium), stocks will fall or rise to accommodate the difference. It is important to remember that a macro-economic equilibrium does not imply that the level of output will be sufficient to employ everyone who wants to work. It may well be associated with a high level of unemployment so that there is an *output gap*.

macro-economic performance: the progress made by the economy as a whole. An initial measure of performance would be the rate of *economic growth*. However, there is really more to performance than this:

- The *long-run trend rate of growth* would show how productive capacity is growing over time.
- *Inflation* and *unemployment* rates would give a guide as to how stable the economy is.
- Non-income measures of welfare would provide qualitative evidence, e.g. ownership of consumer durables and access to health care and education.
- Measures of *income distribution* would show whether all members of society are participating in improved standards of living.
- Data on the environment would clarify the extent to which economic growth is sustainable.

macro-economic policy aims to bring about desirable outcomes by influencing the economy as a whole. The objective might be to raise the rate of economic growth or to make

M

the economy more stable, by making adjustments in the level of **aggregate demand**. This could be done by making changes in:

- **fiscal policy**, using tax changes or government expenditure changes. Reducing taxes and increasing expenditure will increase aggregate demand and tend to stimulate the economy. Provided there are some unemployed resources, output will increase
- **monetary policy**, using interest rate changes to influence levels of spending on investment and consumer goods, will also affect aggregate demand and activity in the economy as a whole
- **exchange rate policy** may also be used because a falling exchange rate may stimulate demand for exports and discourage imports. Alternatively, a rising exchange rate may make imports cheaper and tend to reduce inflationary pressures.

In all macro-economic policy decisions, it is important to consider how close the economy is to **full-capacity output**. **Expansionary policies** used when the economy is close to full-capacity output and there are **supply constraints** will encourage inflation to accelerate. Equally, if **unemployment** is largely structural in nature, expansionary policies will not help. They may defeat the objectives which the government is aiming for. In these circumstances **supply-side policies** may provide a more appropriate strategy.

macro-economic stabilisation: market economies experience **economic cycles**, in which output fluctuates and unemployment and falling incomes can become a problem. Governments use macro-economic policies to stabilise the economy, attempting to avoid sharp fluctuations. Two types of policy can be identified:

- **Automatic stabilisers** may be in operation. As incomes rise, tax revenues rise, reducing the growth of aggregate demand in the upswing of the economic cycle. Similarly, unemployment will be falling and government expenditure on benefits will fall too.
- **Discretionary policies** allow governments to make an explicit decision to raise or lower tax rates or government expenditure. During a recession, they may choose to cut taxes and raise spending levels, as the Conservative government did in 1991.

The main difficulty with stabilisation policies is that it is not always easy for governments or central banks to gauge the precise amount of change which will have the desired effect. Statistical errors and time lags in the operation of policies make for uncertainty.

macro-economics relates to the economy as a whole. It is concerned with **aggregate demand** and aggregate supply and with total consumption, investment and expenditure. Aggregate demand is the total of demand from all sources, including consumption, investment, government spending and exports. Aggregate supply means total output for all producers in the economy. Important elements in macro-economics include:

- the **economic cycle** – the fluctuations in output over time which are a feature of most market economies
- **international trade** – the study of imports and exports and exchange rates
- the financial system including banking and the role of money.

The study of the macro-economy leads on to consideration of **macro-economic policy**. As there are areas of macro-economics which are still only partly understood, policy prescriptions can be controversial.

Malthus, Thomas (1766–1834): an economist who argued that population would grow faster than the capacity of the economy to provide food. There would be a long-run tendency for standards of living to fall. He was partly responsible for the view of economics as 'the gloomy science'. In fact, new technologies and falling birth rates have in many places improved standards of living hugely for most people. Parts of Africa south of the Sahara have not yet been able to join in this process, though many might in the fairly near future if peaceful conditions could be established.

managed exchange rate: a floating exchange rate may still be managed to ensure that day-to-day fluctuations are kept to a minimum. The central bank buys when the exchange rate is falling and sells when it is rising, so as to keep the exchange rate from deviating too far from its current market level. (See also *fixed exchange rate*.)

management buyout (MBO) occurs when the managers buy all of the shares in the company. For example, the managers of the Wensleydale Cheese factory in Yorkshire bought it when its then owners, Dairy Crest, were planning to close it down. Not only did they save the factory, they expanded production and set up a tourist attraction with strong links to Wallace and Gromit of *Wrong Trousers* fame. This was a highly successful MBO in which the new owners had a big incentive to try out new strategies. Other MBOs have been less successful, some based on excessive reliance on borrowed money. Sometimes the MBO is able to operate more efficiently because the original situation involved some *diseconomies of scale*.

managerial economies: see *internal economies of scale*.

manual worker: one who carries out practical tasks, such as might be found on a building site or a factory assembly line. The category is a very large one, including skilled, semi-skilled and unskilled employees.

margin: the amount of profit, usually defined precisely as profit as a percentage of sales revenue.

marginal analysis: economic theory analyses decisions taken at the margin. That is to say, people usually decide not whether to do something at all but whether to do a little more or a little less. They may produce, or consume, more or less. Producing a little more will bring in *marginal revenue* and have a *marginal cost*. The profit-maximising producer will carry on producing up to the point where these two are equal. This is economically efficient because the price a consumer is prepared to pay for that last unit is exactly equal to the real resource cost of producing it.

marginal concept: the idea that a small change in any variable will lead to small changes in other variables. This provides a way of analysing the size and direction of change, and of predicting the impact of change. (See also *marginal analysis*.)

marginal cost: the cost of one more unit of output. In the short run, only *variable costs* will alter, so for example the marginal cost of producing one more bicycle will reflect the extra *labour* and component costs of increasing output. In the long run, if factories are running at full-capacity, the marginal cost may reflect the *fixed cost* of building a new factory or assembly line. The marginal cost of one more hairdo will be almost entirely labour but if the shop is always fully booked, it may involve opening another shop. Normally, the term marginal cost is used to mean additional variable cost.

The formula for marginal cost can be used to focus attention on the additional cost of one more unit or of a batch of units.

FORMULA: $\text{marginal cost} = \dfrac{\text{change in total cost}}{\text{change in output}}$

Marginal cost may rise if firms are constantly increasing output with a given amount of capital. They may no longer be using labour and capital in optimum proportions. To get more of the relevant variable factors of production may mean paying more. To increase output, the firm may have to pay its employees at overtime rates, perhaps time-and-a-half pay.

The marginal cost curve always cuts the average cost curve at its lowest point. When MC is less than ATC, the latter will be falling. The additional cost of increasing output is so low that it increases efficiency. Similarly when MC is greater than ATC, it will be dragging it up – average cost will be above the minimum, i.e. the point at which **productive efficiency** is maximised.

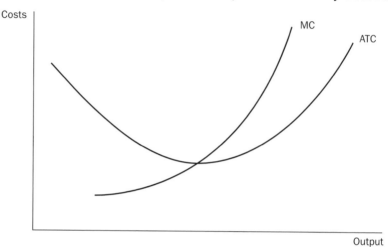

Marginal and average cost curves

marginal cost pricing: an item may be priced at its marginal cost, thus ensuring that the price is equal to the **opportunity cost** of the resources foregone in producing it. The drawback is that the price may fail to reflect some of the fixed costs of production and so lead to losses being made.

marginal factor cost: the extra cost of the **factors of production** needed to produce one more unit of output. In most cases the marginal factor cost will refer to the **labour** cost of increasing output.

marginal firm: if prices increase, marginal firms will be drawn in to the industry. For example, an increase in the price which people are prepared to pay for vitamin supplements will give potential producers an incentive to start making vitamin supplements. However, unless they are actually able to do this efficiently in the long run and compete with other firms, they may drop out again quite quickly, especially if the price falls again.

marginal land: some land which is used for particular crops or livestock will be of rather poor quality for the purpose. If the price of the product falls, that land will be withdrawn from production. Similarly, if prices rise, some marginal land will be brought back into production.

marginal physical product (MPP): the number of units of output resulting from a small increase in the input of a factor of production. (See also **marginal product**.)

marginal product: the extra output generated by the input of one more unit of a factor of production. For example, if a firm producing micro scooters takes on one more employee, the extra output they can produce is the marginal product of the additional **labour**.

marginal productivity theory gives one explanation of how wages are determined. The theory is that wages will be equal to the value of the marginal product of **labour**. Profit-maximising employers will hire people up to the point where the cost of doing so (the wage) is just equal to the value of the output added. Although this can be quite helpful in giving an understanding of the forces underlying the demand for labour, it has little practical useful-ness in that it is usually rather hard to tell exactly how much output one particular person has added to the total. (See also *marginal revenue product (MRP)* and *wage determination*.)

marginal propensity to consume (MPC): the proportion of an increase in income which will be spent on consumption. It is important within the Keynesian model of the macro-economy because, along with the *marginal rate of tax* and the *marginal propensity to import* (i.e. the *marginal rate of leakage*), it helps to determine the size of the *multiplier*. The higher the marginal propensity to consume, the larger the multiplier will be.

marginal propensity to import: that proportion of an increase in income which is spent on imports.

marginal propensity to save: that proportion of an increase in income which is saved.

marginal rate of leakage: that proportion of an increase in income which leaks out of the circular flow of national income in the form of savings, taxes and imports. The marginal propensity to consume and the marginal rate of leakage together are equal to one by defini-tion. So a high marginal rate of leakage will be associated with a small multiplier.

marginal rate of tax: the proportion of an increase in income which is taken in tax. This may be used as a macro- or a micro-economic concept.

marginal returns refers to the extra income generated by increasing production or investment.

marginal revenue: the extra revenue which comes from selling one more unit of output. In a highly competitive situation this will usually be the price of the product. Where the firm has some monopoly power, it may be less than the price, because selling one more unit of output may entail reducing the price. (See also *profit maximisation*.)

marginal revenue product (MRP): the extra sales revenue generated by the input of one more unit of a factor of production. This will be equal to the *marginal physical product (MPP)* multiplied by the price of the product, provided the firm is operating in competitive markets.

  FORMULA: MRP = MPP × price

The MRP of *labour* can be important in determining how many people will be hired.

Marginal revenue product

187

In the previous diagram, the MRP slopes downwards to the right because each extra person using the existing quantity of fixed factors will lead to diminishing increases in output. It pays employers to take on more labour up to the point where MRP is exactly equal to the going wage rate. Below this level of output, MRP will be greater than the wage rate and profits could be increased by taking on more people. It follows that the MRP curve is also the employer's demand curve for labour.

The demand for labour is a **derived demand**, which depends on the demand for the final product. A rise in the price of the final product will increase MRP and cause the MRP curve to shift to the right. At any given wage rate, more labour will be demanded.
(See also **wage determination**.)

marginal social benefit: includes all the extra benefits which result from an increase in the output of a particular product, whether they are felt by the person who bought the product or by some third party. It thus takes in any **positive externalities**. If you spend money on extra clothes, you get a marginal private benefit from feeling good in them. There is a marginal social benefit to anyone else who appreciates your appearance. The marginal social benefit of devoting additional land to sheep farming in mountain areas includes the private benefit of the meat and wool produced and also the benefit to people who like to see the countryside farmed in the traditional way. In the diagram, Q shows the social optimum equilibrium. The existence of social benefits indicates that the free market equilibrium would be at a lower level of output and sales. There would be **underconsumption** in the case of the extra clothes, and **underproduction** in the case of the meat and wool. (See also **welfare gain**.)

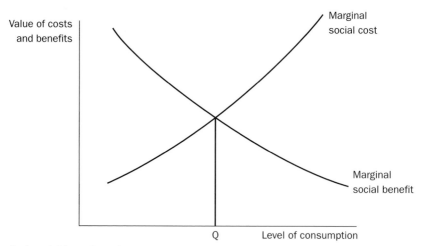

Marginal social benefit and cost

marginal social cost includes all the costs of producing one more unit of output, whether they be the costs of production incurred by the business or the **external costs**, which may be borne by third parties. So the marginal social cost of producing more electricity in coal-fired power stations includes the cost of the coal and other inputs and also the cost to people in the neighbourhood of the increased atmospheric pollution. This may show up in health problems or any other problem caused by pollution. Social cost will exceed private costs and there will be overproduction at the free-market equilibrium output level, which will be greater than Q in the diagram above.

Marginal social costs and benefits can be compared diagrammatically. If output is below the level Q, the marginal social benefits of extra consumption would outweigh the marginal social costs. From the point of view of society, it would make sense for output to be increased.

market: all the buyers and all the sellers of a product and the way in which they are able to interact. A market may be located in a particular place or it may merely have a way for buyers and sellers to communicate. The market will allocate resources among competing buyers. The interaction of buyers and sellers will lead to an *equilibrium price* at which *market clearing* will take place. Markets will be created wherever there are people who have a product which potential buyers want. In recent years markets have developed in Internet banking and new kinds of recreational drugs. Some markets are generally left free to operate according to market forces, others are often regulated or controlled by governments. (Try making a list of markets in each category.)

market access: in general, most sellers have access to markets for their products. However, some markets may be closed because of distance, *trade barriers* or inability to compete effectively. Lifting trade barriers can create much larger markets for some producers, e.g. within the EU.

market capitalisation: the value of a firm as measured by the number of shares it has multiplied by their current market price.

market clearing: the process by which price changes until the amount which sellers wish to sell is exactly equal to the amount which buyers demand. If this process does not occur, then there is said to be market failure. The market clears at the equilibrium price, by definition. Situations in which the market does not clear are known as *excess demand* or *excess supply*, depending on the circumstances.

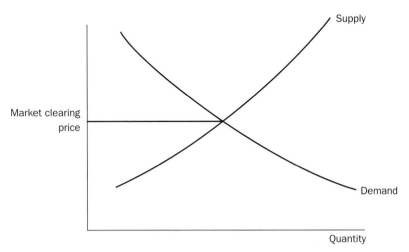

The market clears at the equilibrium price

market concentration: see *concentration ratio*.

market demand: see *demand* and *demand curve*.

market distortions occur whenever prices fail to reflect marginal social costs and benefits. They may be caused by *externalities*, taxes or monopoly. For example, when a firm with monopoly power restricts output and raises its prices, consumers choose to buy less of the product than they would if its prices where roughly equal to the long run average cost of producing it. Underconsumption results.

market dominance: the situation in which a single firm dominates the market. This means that it will be a *price leader* and all other producers in the field will tend to adapt their decisions to the behaviour of the dominant firm. This is likely under *oligopoly* conditions, where the dominant firm has a large market share. Competition will be rather limited. This may be because of significant economies of scale, such that the market is not large enough to make more than a few producers profitable (as with wide-bodied aircraft). Or the firm may have important patents, as with the biggest pharmaceutical manufacturers. In order to continue to dominate the market, a firm may have to put a lot of resources into research so as to maintain its advantage.

market economy: an economy in which the majority of decisions about the allocation of resources are taken in response to market forces. The *price mechanism* shows when and where people are prepared to pay more for a product and this creates an incentive for firms to produce and sell more. A market economy will have a number of attractive features.

- The price mechanism will operate in product markets and also in the markets for factors of production. Prices will signal the value of each resource to both buyers and sellers. These prices will be the basis for individual and firm-level decisions.
- The price mechanism will guide resources towards their highest value uses, i.e. those where buyers are prepared to pay the highest price for them. So, for example, the most profitable retailers will offer the highest prices for high street retail outlets.
- Competition ensures that costs are kept down to a minimum and *productive efficiency* is encouraged, with products available at lowest possible prices to consumers.
- High prices will signal the existence of profitable markets. Firms will respond to the incentive and enter the market. The increase in quantity supplied will satisfy consumer demand and eventually prices will drop back to around the minimum average cost (provided the market is competitive). How much do you think the price of mobile phones has dropped between their initial introduction and the present time?
- Changes in the pattern of consumer demand will lead to changes in the allocation of resources. *Consumer sovereignty* will ultimately determine the allocation of resources and there will be *allocative efficiency*.

The problem with markets is that they do not always work as hoped. They provide no guarantee that everyone will enjoy a reasonable standard of living. Many markets are not competitive. There are all kinds of reasons for *market failure*.

Some leaders have opted for *centrally planned economies*. However, these proved to be disappointing in terms of the extent to which they were able to improve standards of living, as well as in greatly limiting personal freedoms. The current conventional wisdom is that market economies produce the best rate of economic growth and governments can regulate markets to reduce the worst excesses associated with *market failure*.

market equilibrium: the point at which the quantity sellers wish to sell is equal to the quantity buyers wish to buy. The equilibrium price equates supply and demand and brings about market clearing. There is no *excess supply* or *excess demand*.

market failure occurs when market imperfections lead to an allocation of resources which is less efficient than it might be. For example:

- *Imperfect competition* can lead to firms not striving to minimise costs and prices, especially if buyers have imperfect information.
- Some goods may not be produced at all unless the government steps in – these are *public goods* such as the legal system.
- *Merit goods* such as education and health care may be consumed in smaller quantities than would be most effective from society's point of view, if available only through the market. (See *underconsumption*.)
- *Externalities* may lead to high *social costs* which affect third parties, who are not producers or consumers of the product.
- The market may fail to clear, as is the case where large numbers of people are unemployed; this may be partly due to labour immobilities.

Government intervention can correct market failures but does not always do so in the most efficient way due to *government failure*.

market forces are the forces of supply and demand in the marketplace. When demand is growing, other things being equal, the price will rise. If supply is rising but demand is constant, prices will tend to be pushed downwards. Market forces lead to price changes which reflect underlying changes in demand and supply. They influence the *allocation of resources* so that production is in line with consumer demand and reflects the real resource cost of production.

market imperfections come in many forms, each of which is a departure from the conditions of *perfect competition*. The main ones are:
- few firms in the market
- differentiated products
- imperfect information
- immobile factors of production.

market leadership refers to the way in which a *dominant firm* may be able to lead the market in setting prices and sometimes by determining the design and quality of the product. This is most likely to happen where there is an *oligopoly*, with one firm which has a particularly large *market share*.

market mechanism is the process by which *market forces* determine prices, which in turn determine the decisions that are made by firms and households. Prices reflect both the strength of consumer demand and the total costs of production. Levels of production reflect the quantity demanded at a price which is sufficient to cover the full costs of production.

The outcome is an *allocation of resources* which is both productively efficient and allocatively efficient. However, this holds true only if the market mechanism is working under conditions of *perfect competition*. Market imperfections will tend to reduce the efficiency of the allocation of resources in practice.

market model: the theory which explains the working of supply and demand in competitive markets. It analyses market forces and their interaction, taking in the resulting consumer decisions and the response of firms.

market orientation: a tendency on the part of the firm to tailor the product and the way it is sold to the precise needs of the buyer.

market period: the period of time in which the quantity supplied cannot be altered. For example, the quantity of a crop product such as potatoes cannot be altered until the next season. This means that supply is perfectly inelastic, i.e. the quantity is fixed. The length of the market period will vary from product to product. For some manufactured products it will barely exist.

market power: a firm may have power over its market. This means that to some degree the seller is able to determine the price charged. Market power develops when:

- a seller is able to distinguish what is offered for sale from that which is on offer from other producers (*product differentiation*)
- there is little competition from other sellers
- there is a *monopsony* buyer which has more influence in the market than the seller does.

A person with scarce skills which are in strong demand will have some power in the *labour* market because buyers of those skills are competing to hire the few people who have them.

Marketing strategies can be used to increase market power and reduce the threat from competing products. Market power opens up the possibility of being able to determine the price at which the product sells and is a feature of *oligopoly*, where a small number of firms each have a significant *market share*. The **Competition Commission** exists to reduce market power wherever it threatens to work against the interests of the consumer.

Several sources of market power can be seen in the position of the large supermarket chains. Typically, they have market power in relation to suppliers because they can negotiate very favourable prices. Most of their suppliers will be operating in much more competitive markets, being relatively small-scale producers. They also have some market power in relation to consumers because many of the latter have only limited choices about where they can shop. Market power can develop wherever competing substitutes are hard to find. It will always mean that price elasticity of demand is relatively low.

market price is the price prevailing in the market. The implication is that the price has been determined by market forces, i.e. supply and demand, and is not influenced by government intervention of any kind.

market saturation occurs when almost everyone owns the product in question. It applies to washing machines and other products where normally each consumer wants just one. Once this point has been reached, future demand will be for replacement only. The market will be smaller than it was when new customers were buying.

market segment: a section of the market with specific features, e.g. a particular age group or income level, or a common hobby.

market share: a firm's percentage share of the total market. Where there are many competitors this will be insignificant. In an *oligopoly* situation, several firms may have a significant percentage. In the UK, a monopoly is legally defined as a firm with 25% or more of the market. Many firms strive to increase market share because this can increase their *market power*.

market share maximisation: a possible goal for firms, which in some cases may be more important than *profit maximisation*. Economists usually assume that all firms strive to maximise profits and in some cases this is undoubtedly broadly true. However, increased market share can bring many benefits:

- firms may improve their position relative to that of a particular competitor
- they may establish a reputation which is conducive to long-run profitability and survival

- they may increase their *market power*
- managers may relish the personal power and influence that comes with a substantial market share.

market-sharing agreement: an arrangement by which a group of firms agree to avoid competing directly in some markets. Normally this would only happen if there is an oligopoly and there are *barriers to entry* preventing *new entrants* from coming into the market.

The agreement might take the form of a geographical share-out. Each firm would be able to sell in a particular area without facing strong competition. Or the firms might each sell a limited range of products so that there would not be too many close substitutes.

Market-sharing agreements are defined by the Office of Fair Trading as *restrictive practices* and are illegal under competition law. Only in exceptional circumstances are they tolerated. Cement manufacturers have in the past tried to maintain agreements but have been prosecuted successfully.

market size: the total market, i.e. the maximum possible level of sales if all potential buyers are included. Markets grow when:

- new technologies are making it possible to reduce prices
- tastes are changing in favour of the product
- incomes are rising (if the product has income-elastic demand)
- competing substitutes are becoming more expensive.

market structure refers to the number of competing firms in the market. There may be:

- *perfect competition* or something resembling it in many respects, as with many farm products
- *monopolistic competition*, for example hairdressers
- *oligopoly*, as with supermarkets
- *duopoly*, for example most soap products come from one of two suppliers
- *monopoly*, as with water supply.

These are theoretical structures and in practice, a much fuzzier picture emerges. For example, it is possible to argue about whether the computer hardware industry is an oligopoly or whether it really has important elements of monopolistic competition.

market system: the form of market organisation in which the decisions of firms and households are made on the basis of the market forces of supply and demand. A *market economy* will allocate resources largely on this basis, although some government intervention and regulation will also be important and will influence market conditions.

market value is the price which an item might fetch in the open market. In other words, it is what someone is prepared to pay for the item in question. It tells the owner the price at which it might sell. It is important to remember that a resource may have some perceived intrinsic value, especially to its owner, yet have a market value of absolutely nothing. An old easy chair, for example, may still be comfortable to sit in but will not sell at any price because no one else wants it.

marketing: the process by which firms seek to ensure that they actually sell as much output as possible. In a few cases, firms seek out a particular market rather than try to maximise sales. For example, they may concentrate on a market in which they can charge high prices.

Business success often depends upon a close understanding of the market and this can lead to serious efforts actually to provide the types of products most wanted by consumers. However, much marketing effort is actually aimed at exploiting **market imperfections**:

- products may be increasingly differentiated from one another, in order to capture some consumer loyalty
- advertising may become an important part of **product differentiation**
- pricing policies may be designed to drive competitors from the marketplace.

Marshall-Lerner condition states that for an exchange rate devaluation to be successful in improving the balance of payments, the sum of the demand elasticities for exports and imports must be greater than one (ignoring the minus sign). Elasticities are important in determining the outcome of a devaluation (or a depreciation). If the demand for exports is price inelastic, the percentage increase in quantity demanded of exports will be lower than the percentage decrease in price. This means that export revenue will fall. If the demand for imports is price inelastic, people will tend to carry on buying them even though the price has risen. The import bill will rise. If the combined elasticities of demand for imports and exports are between 0 and –1, the balance of payments deficit will actually get larger after devaluation/depreciation. If demand is more elastic, the deficit will fall.

Marx, K (1818–1883) perceived capitalism as one stage in economic development, because it would eventually bring about its own destruction. It would create the conditions in which revolution supported by workers would overthrow capitalism and replace it with the collective ownership of the means of production. Workers would be paid according to their needs rather than their market power and in this way capitalists (owners of capital) would no longer be able to exploit their employees by paying them less than the value of what they produced.

The development of communism in Russia (from 1917) and later in Eastern Europe and China (from 1948) was based on Marx's thinking. In all cases communist revolutions created much more egalitarian societies than those which preceded them. But most of the countries involved experienced rather low economic growth rates. They were unable to reduce poverty as effectively as many capitalist economies had done. When free elections were held in Russia and Eastern Europe in 1989, the communist party did badly and the new governments began the transition to market systems. China, Cuba, North Korea and Vietnam still have communist governments but are becoming steadily more market oriented.

Marx was banished from his native Germany in 1849, for his political activities, and settled in London where he did most of his writing in the Reading Room of the British Museum. He died long before his ideas came to fruition.

mass production: manufacture of a standardised product which can be carried out on a large scale, reaping significant **economies of scale**. Typically it might involve an assembly line making a product which can be widely advertised. Henry Ford was the famous initiator of mass production with the Model T car assembly line in Detroit, USA, later set up at Dagenham, UK, also.

Computer-controlled manufacturing has made it much easier and cheaper to vary the features of the product and sometimes, to produce only to order. Mass production of standardised products is therefore much less prevalent than it was. **Flexible specialisation** has to some extent taken its place.

massaging statistics: the process of creating intelligible data series. Data is often inconsistent, with changes in the way it is collected and items that are missing altogether. Statisticians use their skills to construct reasonably comparable data series with as few inaccuracies and gaps as possible. Unfortunately, some governments sometimes use this process as an opportunity to make the data give a message of which they approve. This may diverge somewhat from the most truthful approach. Governments with no democratic foundations and no free press are particularly suspect.

mature economies are those which have been fully industrialised for some time and are now experiencing a shift of resources into the service sector. The USA and the UK are examples of economies where the manufacturing sector has tended to shrink while a number of services have shown above-average growth rates. Financial services, tourism, health care and a variety of personal and professional services have all been growing over the long term. (See also *deindustrialisation*.)

maturity date: the date on which a *bond* becomes due for repayment.

mean: see *arithmetic mean*.

means-tested benefits are social security payments which are available only to those whose incomes are below a certain level; for example income support.

measures of development are indicators that usefully supplement the standard GDP and HDI data. They include school enrolment, access to clean water, energy consumption per capita and access to mobile phones. Examination of the range of economic activity and how it is divided between primary, secondary and tertiary *sectors* is also important.

median: the middle observation in any data series. It is an important measure of the average in data series which have many extreme values. For example, the median income is sometimes more useful than the arithmetic mean income because it is not distorted by very high incomes which drag the mean upwards.

mediation: see *conciliation*.

menu costs are the costs to a firm of adjusting prices as a consequence of inflation. Price tags, price lists and advertising material all have to be adjusted. The term has widened in usage to mean any administrative cost of inflation.

merchant bank: a bank which specialises in supplying financial services to firms. See *investment banks*: this is the US term for them, which is more commonly used in the UK now.

merger: the combining of two firms under one management. Whilst a *takeover* may involve a hostile bid by one company for another, which may be bitterly opposed by the one which is going to lose its independence, a merger is normally brought about by mutual agreement. A merger may have a number of advantages, depending on the nature of the companies concerned.

- A *horizontal merger* involves two firms operating in the same market. It will increase *market share*, possibly giving the merged company some *market power*. It may therefore be referred to the *Competition Commission*. Rationalisation of production facilities may make it possible to reap *economies of scale*. The merger of SmithKline Beecham and Glaxo Wellcome in 2000 to form the giant pharmaceutical company GlaxoSmithKline provides an example. By merging their research efforts they could cut costs and further savings became possible from rationalisation. But the resulting company was so large that the US competition authorities created stiff conditions for the merger to be approved.

- A vertical merger may give the new company control over more of the production and distribution process. A manufacturer may merge with a supplier company or a distribution network.
- A *conglomerate* merger involves firms with very different products. The assumption is that the new firm will have an advantage in terms of management skills or access to finance. In the past this has not always turned out to be of real benefit and some conglomerate mergers have ended in *divestment*.

merit goods are provided by the government for those who are deemed to need them. Examples include health care, education and social services. The logic for government provision is that there is likely to be *market failure* in that there will be *underproduction* and *underconsumption* of these goods and services if decisions are based on market forces. Many of the people who would benefit from health care and education would have insufficient income to buy the services for themselves. Yet it is in the interests of society as a whole that the population have good health and education. Government provision ensures that everyone likely to benefit does so.

methodology: the range and structure of thinking processes which are used to make the subject clearer. In economics, methodology relates to the formation and testing of hypotheses and the development of theories about relationships between variables.

micro-economic models are theoretical systems of thinking which help to explain the working of markets. Each model consists of a set of relationships which can be used to analyse changes in the marketplace. If the relationships have been defined accurately in terms which match reasonably closely to the real world, it is possible to predict the outcomes of a variety of different possible changes.

micro-economics studies how the component parts of the economy work. It includes price theory, the theory of the firm and the study of *labour* markets. It provides a theoretical framework for analysis of decisions made by firms and individuals concerning consumption, production and the way factors of production are to be put to use. Analysis may be of one particular market or it may involve the interrelationships between different markets (*general equilibrium* analysis). The former would, for example, look at the way an increase in demand for bicycles might affect the price and quantity of bicycles sold, while the latter would go on to look at the impact on numbers employed in the industry and their wage rates and the secondary effects on any other products.

Micro-economics can be used to address a wide range of questions:
- What should be produced?
- What factors of production should be used in the production process?
- How do consumers choose what to consume?
- What determines the level of income received by individuals?

microfinance refers to the provision of small-scale loans to poor people living in very deprived circumstances in developing countries. It enables them to set up small businesses. Originally pioneered in Bangladesh, the provision of microfinance has been found to be a cost-effective way of providing development assistance. Often, the credit has been targeted specifically at women, who have generally proved reliable about paying it back. The schemes set up to administer the loans are often co-operative in nature. Successful schemes are now operational in rural China and a number of other countries. It is beginning to have a significant impact in Africa.

middle-income countries are those with per capita incomes lying between the low and the high-income categories. They account for just under half the global population and many who live in them still have less than US$2 a day to live on. (Some countries have very unequal income distributions.) Many are growing very fast (though this will be much affected by the 2007–09 financial crisis). The World Bank divides into lower middle-income countries ($936–$3705) and upper middle income countries ($3706–$11 455). These figures are for 2007.

migrants' remittances: migrant workers who go abroad often send quite large sums of money back to relatives in their country of origin. For some countries, these remittances are a valuable source of foreign exchange. For example, Bangladesh, Egypt and India all receive substantial inflows.

migration occurs when people move from one area to another or from one country to another with the intention of working. People tend to move from areas where incomes are low to areas where some employers are having difficulty recruiting at the going wage rate. Some international migration is illegal; where this is the case *labour* laws will not apply to those that find work and pay and working conditions may be very poor.

minimum and maximum prices: where prices are set by governments, they may be above or below the equilibrium prices and lead to *excess demand* or *excess supply*.

minimum efficient scale (MES): the lowest level of output at which costs can be kept at their minimum. In the diagram below this is the lowest output at which average total cost is minimised. For most goods, efficient production is possible across a range of output levels, so the average total cost has a flat-bottomed U-shape and the minimum efficient scale is on the extreme left of the bottom of the curve.

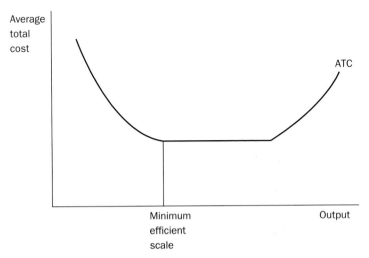

Minimum efficient scale

minimum guaranteed prices may be used where there is government intervention in a market, with the objective of increasing the market price. For example, the *Common*

Agricultural Policy (CAP) of the EU requires intervention in the markets for farm products in such a way that the price cannot drop below a certain level.

minimum unit cost: at a certain level of output, costs of production will be the lowest possible.

minimum wage: the minimum rate of pay per hour which must by law be paid by employers. This was introduced in 1999 at £3.60, rising to £5.73 in 2009. The rate for those aged 18–21 is £4.77 and for those aged 16–17, £3.53.

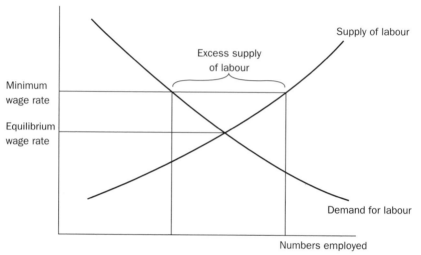

Minimum wage rate may reduce employment

The impact of the minimum wage varies greatly from one region to another. Few employers will be able to hire even unskilled people in London at the minimum wage anyway but it may have more impact in less prosperous regions. The objective is to prevent employers from paying very low wages.

Economists have tended to argue that a minimum wage will reduce the level of employment if it is above the equilibrium wage rate. It may lead to an excess supply of *labour*. At lower wage rates, employers might take on more labour. (See diagram above.) However, there is no strong evidence yet that the introduction of the minimum wage in the UK has significantly reduced employment. After it was introduced, unemployment fell anyway. Employers interviewed since then mostly say their employment levels have not been affected.

A minority of economists argue that the minimum wage will give employers more incentive to train employees so as to increase their *productivity*. If true, this would improve *competitiveness*. Minimum wages cannot raise the incomes of those who are not in work, who are likely to be among the very poorest.

misallocation of resources occurs when the composition of output is not the optimum in terms of prevailing supply and demand conditions. This may be because of *market failure*, or *government failure*. There may be people who would be willing to pay for certain products at a price reflecting the true costs of the resources needed to produce them, but find that they are not available. Normally the price would then rise and firms would have an incentive to produce them. Or there may be a glut of a product that no one wants to buy at the price being charged. A wide variety of measures could be used to restore *allocative efficiency*.

missing markets occur where a good or service that would have a positive effect on consumers' lives is not provided. This could be the case for *public goods*, where the *free rider problem* makes it impossible to set a price for all who benefit. However, some economists have shown that extending *property rights* can create new markets. For example, there is no market for the right to fish from the sea. This gives rise to overfishing. If property rights could be created for the right to fish, then it would be possible to charge an amount for them that would ensure that fish stocks were safe. These rights could be owned by governments on behalf of all of us and traded. But getting agreement and enforcing the arrangements would be very difficult, perhaps impossible. New markets will emerge in the future as economies deal with their problems.

mixed economy: one in which there is both a *public sector* and a *private sector*. In practice all economies are mixed economies. It is difficult to imagine a country where all allocation decisions are taken on the basis of market forces and even the remaining *centrally planned economies* now allow some market forces to operate.

The relative proportions of activity falling into the private or the public sector vary very much from one country to another. China still has a very large number of state-owned enterprises but even there, there are plans to sell off many of them. Most European countries have drastically reduced their public sectors since 1980, mainly through *privatisation*. In the US, the public sector has always been much smaller than it was in the EU.

As public ownership has diminished, regulation has increased. This means that the private sector makes production decisions on the basis of market forces but within the constraints created by employment and competition law and other forms of regulation.

mobile phones have had a significant impact on the development of economies in poor countries that do not have extensive fixed-line systems. It can be much cheaper to buy a mobile phone than to get a land line installed. For example, poor farmers in India can use mobile phones to check the local market prices of their products and sell when they judge the best prices to be available. In Africa, mobile phones have made it possible for markets to develop in a wide range of useful products, where previously markets did not exist. Many opportunities have been created for small-scale entrepreneurs. Everywhere, it is likely that mobiles have increased *productivity*.

mobility refers to the extent to which people can move from one job to another and also from one location to another. The more mobile people are, the more flexible the *labour* market will be. A *flexible labour market* makes it easier for resources to move out of one less profitable line of production and into another more profitable activity. It increases *allocative efficiency*. *Occupational immobility* and *geographical immobility* both can lead to *structural unemployment* and an economy which has difficulty in adjusting to changes in the marketplace.

mode: the middle observation in a data series.

model: a simplified structure which mimics real-world trends in a way that makes them easier to analyse. The structure is based upon assumptions which allow us to isolate each individual change and analyse it without the complication of several different trends operating at once. The model is defined by a set of relationships which can be set out as equations or represented on a graph. For example, models which describe what happens in a market will use the relationship between price and quantity demanded as a starting point.

Macro-economic models involve a great many variables and equations and are very complex, requiring large computers to generate their predictions. (See also **Treasury** model.)

Models do not necessarily have to be realistic in order to be useful. Neither the model of **perfect competition** nor the model of **comparative advantage** is in the least realistic, but both perform a useful function in providing insights into the way the world works. Perfect competition provides a yardstick against which the competitiveness of individual markets can be assessed. Comparative advantage makes a link between international trade and economic growth and has some explanatory power.

monetarism: an approach to the analysis of macro-economic trends which emphasises the link between the money supply and the rate of inflation. It suggests a very direct relationship between the two. The strongest proponent of monetarism was the American economist **Milton Friedman**.

Monetarists tend to be rather pessimistic about the government's chances of bringing about any improvement in economic management. They see the control of inflation as a far more important objective of government policy than reducing unemployment. Their views have been contrasted with those of the Keynesians, for whom unemployment has generally been the top priority. The differences of view hinge on the question of the extent to which monetary growth should be controlled.

In practical terms, strict adherence to monetarism involves very careful control of the money supply. This requires willingness to raise **interest rates** very sharply if inflation threatens to accelerate. High interest rates will discourage spending and reduce aggregate demand and may lead to **recession**. During the 1980s there was much debate as to whether wage demands would automatically moderate in response to high interest rates. Monetarists held that they would. In contrast, the Keynesian view was that they would not, until unemployment rose substantially. When interest rates were raised in 1980, unemployment did increase greatly in the UK, over a period of years.

The useful thing that monetarism accomplished during the 1980s was to draw attention to the role of expectations in determining rates of inflation. This made for clearer thinking about the problems. There is no doubt that monetary policy has been made to work better as a result of monetarist influence. Equally, raising interest rates significantly does increase unemployment substantially, so keeping inflation at bay is much less costly than trying to reduce it once an inflationary spiral is in operation.

monetarist model: the macro-economic approach which defines the money supply as being a crucial determinant of the rate of inflation. (See also **monetarism**.)

monetary base: the amount of cash held by the public and by the banking system, including banks' balances with the Bank of England. This serves as the basis for the expansion of bank lending.

monetary policy uses changes in **interest rates** to control the demand for money and hence the rate of increase of bank lending. This in turn will influence the level of demand in the economy as a whole. High interest rates discourage borrowing for consumption, investment and house purchase.

The Bank of England, in common with other central banks, has for some years found it difficult to control the supply of money (the amount of credit created) directly, so the thrust of monetary policy has been through control of the demand for money. If inflation is threatening, the Bank will announce an increase in its official interest rate, the **bank rate**. Borrowers will economise and reduce their demand for loans as fast as they are able. The growth of bank credit will be reduced. This means that borrowers, be they investors or home buyers, bear the brunt of a tight monetary policy. Interest rates were raised in 2006 when food and commodity prices were rising fast (see chart).

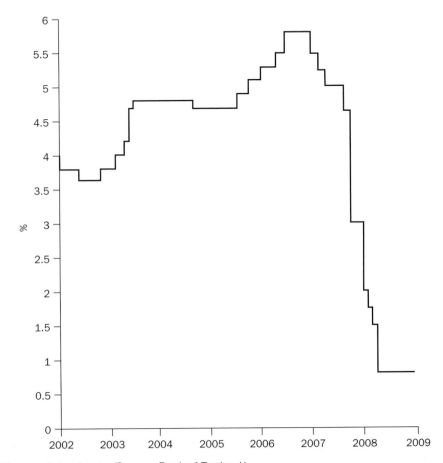

Changes in bank rate. (Source: Bank of England.)

The 2007–09 financial crisis led to major adjustments in monetary policy. The inflation that threatened from 2006 to early 2008 reversed itself as **recession** took hold across the world. Central banks cut interest rates aggressively in order to help firms to survive and consumers to continue spending. When they realised that the recession was rapidly deepening and interest rates were already close to zero (0.5% in the UK from March 2009), they tried **quantitative easing**, which is a way of increasing the supply of money. The government put pressure on the banks to continue lending, but the huge losses that banks were suffering because of debt defaults made them very cautious. At the time of writing, this was obviously an area of great difficulty.

It is important to remember that monetary policy will always operate with a time lag. Most spending decisions take time and the full effects of a change in interest rates may take up to two years to work their way through the economy. If the exceptionally loose monetary policies of 2009 continue for a short time after the economy has begun to recover it is quite likely that the next problem will be accelerating inflation. (If this has happened by the time you read this, please e-mail the publishers and tell them you need a new edition of this book.) But it may be that the Bank of England and other central banks will be smart and reverse their policies at just the right moment.

In 1997 the Chancellor of the Exchequer made the Bank of England much more independent of the government. Monetary policy is now decided by the **Monetary Policy Committee** of the Bank of England. (See also **inflation targeting**.) The financial crisis forced the government and the Bank to collaborate, because the scale of the loans needed to keep the banks operating was beyond what the Bank could achieve on its own. This may have long-term implications.

Monetary Policy Committee: the group of nine Bank of England officials and independent experts which decides **monetary policy**. The committee meets monthly to agree any change to interest rates. If it wishes rates to change it will announce a change in the official interest rate. The Governor of the Bank of England takes the chair and minutes are published two weeks later. The votes of individual members of the committee will be recorded in the minutes. This ensures that monetary policy can be decided without political interference.

The MPC's target for the underlying rate of the inflation is currently 2.0%. If the rate diverges by more than 1% from this, they will have to write to the Chancellor of the Exchequer explaining why and what should be done. The MPC itself has decided that earnings growth must be kept below 4.5% if inflation is to be kept low.

monetary squeeze describes a monetary policy which attempts to restrict spending in the economy by raising interest rates and thus limiting the amount of credit.

monetary system: the structure which provides the money needed to make the economy function effectively. The component parts of the system are:
- the banking system
- the central bank
- the body which supervises the banking system, which in the UK is the Financial Services Authority (FSA).

monetary transmission mechanism: the process by which changes in monetary policy affect the real economy. A cut in **bank rate** causes interest rates generally to be adjusted downwards (sometimes after a delay). Borrowers have to pay more for loans. Investors will scale back their plans or abandon them. Consumers will borrow less and consume less. Falling demand for investment goods and consumer goods will lead firms to cut output. In time, they will reduce the size of the workforce by zero recruitment (**natural wastage**) or redundancies. The newly unemployed people's incomes will fall so that consumption falls again. As spending falls, the circular flow of national income is reduced and there is a **multiplier** effect. Competition for scarce jobs may lead to pay cuts but even if not, employees who keep their jobs are very unlikely to demand significant pay increases. If costs of production fall or even stay the same, firms will be able to survive. In time inflation, and people's expectations of inflation, become much reduced.

The reverse process can be employed when aggregate demand is low and there is much unemployment. However, its success will depend on whether firms can see good reason to start investing again. (See also *monetary policy*.)

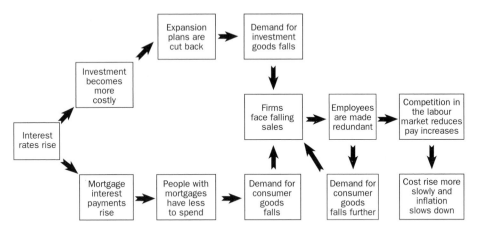

The impact of rising interest rates

monetary union: see *Economic and Monetary Union (EMU)*.

money: anything which is generally acceptable as a means of payment. Money is usually defined according to its functions. These are: a medium of exchange, a unit of account, a store of value and a standard of deferred payments. Keep in mind that these functions may be affected when money loses its value during a period of rapid *inflation*.

In the UK, money is measured in two ways, *narrow money* and *broad money*.

money income means income measured in money terms without allowance being made for inflation. In contrast, *real income* means income measured in terms of its purchasing power (i.e. in constant prices). The amount of the adjustment required depends on the rate of inflation.

money laundering occurs when people who acquired money in an illegal way want to disguise its origins. Drug dealing, tax evasion and other crimes lead people to move money around until it appears to have been generated by a legitimate activity.

money market: the market for short-term loans of various kinds. There is no particular place for this: most communications will be by telephone or electronic.

money multiplier: the amount by which bank lending can be increased if there is an increase in the *monetary base*, i.e. the amount of cash in the banking system.

money supply means the amount of money available to the general public and the banking system. This is an important macro-economic variable because it can affect the capacity of firms and individuals to spend. It includes *narrow money* and *broad money*.

The money supply must be allowed to grow in line with output. The figures have to be interpreted with caution because they can be affected by a wide range of events and there is often considerable uncertainty about their true meaning. This makes monetary policy difficult at times.

monopolistic competition occurs when there are many firms in the industry, each selling a slightly *differentiated product*. The market is characterised by easy entry and exit, so that small businesses can easily be set up and there is thus strong competition. Yet each has a small degree of monopoly power because the differentiated product allows consumers to choose to buy from a particular producer. Restaurants, hairdressers, estate agents, potteries and many others illustrate situations of monopolistic competition. It merges into oligopoly if there are relatively few producers or a few large ones and many smaller ones. Building societies provide an example of the latter situation.

Easy entry and strong competition ensure that in the long run there can be no super-normal profit under monopolistic competition. Firms will produce at the profit maximising output, but average revenue (price) will be equal to average total cost. This indicates that there will be excess capacity. Firms could expand and reduce ATC. However, the higher output would mean lower prices and losses would be made. The diagram illustrates the output at which profits are maximised but no super normal profit can be made. (You may not need to know this diagram.)

Under monopolistic competition average revenue just covers average cost

monopoly means a market in which there is a single supplier. In practice, this is unusual because in most markets there are alternatives or substitutes. However, if you consider Microsoft for a moment, you can see that some producers do have a great deal of monopoly power.

Monopoly is at the extreme end of the *spectrum of competition*. At the other end is *perfect competition*. Both ideas are fully expressed in theoretical models which define the precise conditions of each and predict how prices will be determined. However, the term is also used in connection with the legal definition of monopoly. In the UK, a firm with 25% of the market is said to have a monopoly and this will mean that it will be investigated by the *Competition Commission*.

The monopoly model has the following features, which can be shown diagrammatically.

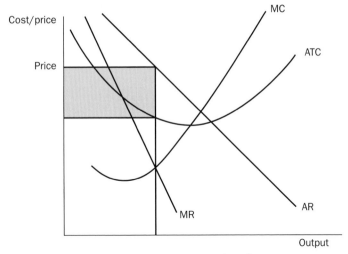

The shaded area shows the monopolist's supernormal profit

- In a monopoly, the demand for the firm's product is the market demand. So the demand curve (which is also the average revenue or AR curve) slopes downward to the right. The monopolist can choose the selling price and sell more or less, accordingly.
- The marginal revenue (MR) curve also slopes down and is always less than the average revenue. This reflects the fact that a price cut will always mean that average revenue falls.
- The profit-maximising output is at the point where marginal cost (MC) is equal to marginal revenue. If marginal cost is greater than marginal revenue, it will pay the monopolist to reduce output and raise the price.
- It follows that monopolists will have an incentive to keep output lower and prices higher than they would be under competitive conditions.
- The supernormal profit made by the monopolist is shown by the difference between total revenue and total cost or, as on the diagram, by the space between the price charged and the average total cost (ATC).
- Monopolists have no incentive to strive for efficiency, since they can sell the product even if production costs are higher than they really need to be.
- They have little incentive to strive for quality, again because they have a captive market.

Monopolies may end in taking advantage of consumers. The underlying logic of the monopoly model can be used to show why **competition policy** provides important protection for consumers. Equally, where **natural monopolies** are concerned, **regulation** will restrict their power.

monopoly costs and benefits: the costs centre on the likelihood of prices being higher, and quantity sold lower, than would be the case if the industry were competitive. (See **monopoly**.) The benefits come from **economies of scale** and the lower prices that may result and the incentive to undertake research and develop **innovations**. These can be considerable. Pharmaceutical companies have justified their monopoly profits on the grounds that they are constantly producing new and better drug treatments. Only recently have they thought about collaborating with government bodies to decide which drugs are the most valuable to society.

monopoly legislation covers the full range of laws which restrict the ability of firms to develop monopoly power. It is operated through the **Office of Fair Trading (OFT)** and the

Competition Commission and also through the EU. As well as providing for the investigation of mergers and anti-competitive practices, the OFT deals with restrictive practices and restrictive trade agreements.

monopoly power: the *market power* which the single or dominant supplier has, in terms of being able to set prices. By restricting output, the monopolist may be able to set a higher price and increase both revenue and profit. (See also *monopoly.*)

monopoly profit: the *supernormal profit* which a monopolist can earn by virtue of the capacity to raise prices by restricting output. This is profit in excess of the full opportunity cost of all the resources used. (See also *monopoly.*)

monopsonistic labour markets exist in areas where there is not much choice of jobs. They may exert *monopsony* power over their employees. This may enable them to hire people at lower wage rates than would be possible if they were competing for *labour* with other employers. The National Health Service is in some areas a monopsonistic employer of nursing staff.

monopsony: a single buyer. As with monopoly, it is unusual to find the extreme case of a single buyer but much less so to find a buyer with a dominant position in the marketplace. Large manufacturers are often in a dominant position with respect to their component suppliers and can force them to reduce their prices or accept rising costs when quality improvements are made. Supermarkets may do the same with small-scale food producers.

moratorium: a temporary halt to the requirement to make interest payments or repay loans. This may happen if the lender prefers to allow the moratorium because this is the only way in which the borrower is going to be able to cope with the payments anyway. Rather than forcing the borrower into bankruptcy, it may seem better to wait for the debts to be paid. Borrowers then stand some chance of obtaining extra finance to tide them over. This usually applies to developing country governments but it can apply to individuals who are unable to make mortgage payments.

mortgage: a loan made for the purpose of buying property. The property will act as security in the event of the borrower being unable to make interest payments or repay the loan.

movement along the demand curve: a change in price which leads to a change in quantity demanded but does not alter the position of the *demand curve*. A likely cause of this would be when the producer is able to cut costs, for example by investing in new technologies. This will shift the supply curve to the right (from S_1 to S_2 in the diagram) but the general conditions of demand and the demand curve itself will remain unchanged.

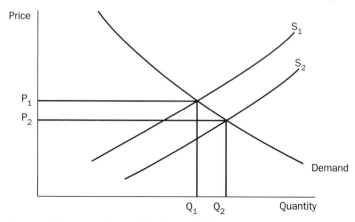

The fall in price leads to a rise in quantity demanded

movement along the supply curve occurs when the demand curve shifts to the right or left, showing changing levels of demand for the product at any given price. Supply conditions are unchanged but costs may rise if the equilibrium quantity rises, just because the supplier has to find more resources to meet the demand.

moving average: an average which shows a long-term trend by calculating an average value for a number of years together and doing this for each successive year. A three-year moving average would average out the values for the year in question, the year before and the year after. This will smooth out the short-term fluctuations so that the long-term trend is more easily visible.

multilateral negotiations or agreements involve a number of governments. Trading blocs such as the EU or the ***North American Free Trade Agreement (NAFTA)*** require multilateral negotiation as do the rules of the ***World Trade Organization (WTO)***.

multilateral trade involves trade, which need not be reciprocal, between a number of countries. For example, if China buys office equipment from the UK, while the USA buys toys from China and the UK buys computers from the USA, multilateral trade has taken place.

multinational: a firm which operates in a number of different countries. It could have retail outlets (like Body Shop) or manufacturing plants (like Nissan). Multinationals are usu-ally involved in ***foreign direct investment (FDI)***, which may be very welcome to the ***host country***. They bring both advantages and disadvantages. However, most host countries want their multinationals to stay.

- The investment increases productive capacity and provides jobs in the host country. This raises local incomes substantially but the multinational may depart again if wage rates rise or other conditions become less favourable. Nissan for a time threatened to stop producing in the UK if there is a decision to remain outside EMU.
- Multinationals in developing countries may facilitate technology transfer or they may just use unskilled ***labour***, pay low wages and maintain poor working conditions.
- Profits may be repatriated to the country where the multinational has its head office and various ways may be found to avoid paying taxes in the host country.
- Many consumers all over the world get the products they want at lower prices because multinationals choose the cheapest location at which to manufacture them.

multiplier: the amount by which an increase in ***injections*** into the ***circular flow of national income*** will increase total income in the economy. If investment (I) or consumption (C) increases, this adds to aggregate demand and many firms will be able to sell more invest-ment goods or consumer products. For example, a number of firms may start off large new investment programmes involving much new plant and machinery. As the producers of these investment goods expand, they will take on more ***labour***. The newly employed people will have rising incomes and will consume more. This will again add to aggregate demand and many firms will now expand. The increased demand will proceed around the circular flow of national income for some time.

However, each time demand increases, some of the increase in income will be used to increase savings (S) or tax revenue (T) or imports (M). These are all ***withdrawals*** from the circular flow of national income and will reduce successive increases in aggregate demand.

The size of the multiplier will depend on the extent to which increasing incomes leak away into savings, taxation or imports.

A decrease in withdrawals may have the same effect. Similarly, increased withdrawals or reduced injections will lead to a downward multiplier effect, with a cumulative fall in income.

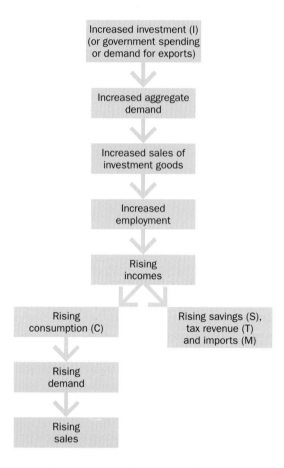

multi-skilling means that employees will be capable of doing a range of different tasks. This contrasts with the traditional situation in which people tended to have one craft skill and carry out only jobs associated with that skill. This sometimes requires more training but it means that the workforce will be more flexible and better able to adapt to changing circumstances, including changing patterns of demand.

NAFTA: see *North American Free Trade Agreement (NAFTA)*.

NAIRU: see *non-accelerating inflation rate of unemployment (NAIRU)*.

narrow money generally means the measure of money which is mainly cash. In the UK this means M0, which consists of notes and coin held by the public and in cash machines and banks' balances with the Bank of England.

National Debt: the sum total of all past debt accumulated by the UK government. It has tended over the long run to rise sharply during times of war. In relation to national income, it has fallen during periods of rapid inflation. It is currently rising, due in part to increased spending on health and education during the period 2002–06, and significantly due to *recapitalisation of banks* in 2007–09. It is still low by international standards. However, it is set to rise much further, to an estimated 78%. The ONS argues that three banks, Northern Rock, Lloyds TSB and RBS, should be classified as public sector organisations; their debts would then be part of the National Debt.

Country	Year	National debt as % of GDP
UK	1946	150
UK	2002	30
UK	2007	37
UK	end 2008	48
Japan	end 2008	194
USA	end 2008	74

Source: UK Treasury

national income is a term used in two ways. It is often used quite loosely to mean total income for the whole economy. To find out what this is you might well select *GDP* figures, or *GNP* if you wanted to include *net property income from abroad*. However, it also has a precise statistical definition: net national product. This is GNP at *basic prices*, minus depreciation (*capital consumption*). (Check your specifications before worrying about this.)

national income statistics cover all the accounts on the macro-economy, drawn up by the Office for National Statistics, which show all the components of national income. The ONS has overhauled both its statistical approaches and its terminology in recent years.

National Insurance is the scheme by which the UK government provides pensions and sickness and unemployment benefits. Its revenue comes from National Insurance charges (NICs) paid by employees, employers and the self-employed. Very low incomes are exempt. The rest pay a percentage of income, up to a certain maximum. Effectively, NICs are a tax. However, they are not sufficient to pay all the costs of social security payments, which have risen over the years. Pensions threaten to take a larger share of government spending as the population ages. Unemployment payments rise and fall with the rate of unemployment. When it was set up in the late 1940s, the scheme was intended to be self-financing but that is impossible now.

National Insurance charges (NICs): the payments made by employees and employers as their contributions to the funds needed to cover benefit payments. Employers' contributions raise the cost of employing *labour*. They may create some disincentive to employ people and thus contribute to unemployment so some attempts have been made to make them less onerous to employers. The employee's contribution effectively raises the marginal rate of tax: a pay increase will lead to higher tax payments and a higher NIC.

national minimum wage: see *minimum wage*.

national pay bargaining: negotiations between a trade union and an employers' association concerning a rate of pay which will apply across the country. It used to be the case that large numbers of employees had their pay determined in this way but many employers now negotiate directly with the union in the workplace or with individuals.

National Savings offer opportunities for people to save by lending to the government. In return they get a modest interest rate but total security and easy access to their money through post offices. From the government's point of view, National Savings provide a reasonably cheap source of finance.

nationalisation: the process by which governments take firms and industries into the *public sector*. The Labour government of 1945–51 nationalised a number of industries. The objective was to run the industries concerned in the public interest. The nationalised industries included the railways, steelmaking, coalmining, British Airways and BP. Later shipbuilding, Rolls-Royce and British Leyland (which became Rover) joined the list.

In time it became apparent that civil servants were not necessarily best placed to make the necessary business decisions. Many of the nationalised industries were prone to large losses and not just because many were declining industries. After 1979 the then Conservative government began a programme of *privatisation* which returned most of the nationalised industries to the private sector.

Currently a proposal to part privatise the Post Office is under discussion. A 30% share would be sold to the private sector, opening up possibilities for increased investment. This is badly needed because the Post Office is losing business and recently losses have been running at around £200 million a year. However, employees and unions are not happy about the proposal.

Ironically, though the government involvement in production generally has been vastly reduced, the *recapitalisation of banks* has greatly increased the size of the public sector. Many economic analysts described this as the 'least worst' solution. We cannot know how long this will last although the government says it will return the banks to the private sector as soon as possible.

natural environment: the physical resources that surround us, as opposed to the business environment. The latter includes all the institutional structures which affect firms' decisions, the legal system and the state of the economy as a whole.

natural monopolies occur where a single supplier has an enormous cost advantage such that to have competing producers would actually raise costs. The most obvious example is water: two complete sets of mains water pipes would involve duplication of resources and raise costs. People used to use gas and electricity as examples of natural monopolies but firms are now competing, albeit in a regulated market. The existence of a natural monopoly has been used to justify **nationalisation** in the past. Now, it is the reason why privatised utilities all have **regulators**, which are supposed to protect consumers from the monopoly power of the utility companies.

natural rate of unemployment is a monetarist term for the **non-accelerating inflation rate of unemployment (NAIRU)**. Sometimes it is described as **equilibrium unemployment**.

natural resources: include land and supplies of basic raw materials such as oil reserves. They may also include sites with development potential, which may for example be turned into deep water ports or hydro-electric schemes.

natural wastage: the inevitable fall in the number of people employed by a firm, as people retire or leave of their own accord. It can be used as a painless way of reducing the **labour** force without compulsory redundancies.

needs and wants: the preferences for particular consumer goods and services that people use as their basis for making the decisions that create a demand for various products. They figure in the process of **choice** which is necessary because people have unlimited needs and wants but a limited income with which to buy them. This is the fundamental feature of scarcity, with which economics as a subject is deeply concerned.

negative equity can be found when people have borrowed to finance a house purchase, only to find that house prices subsequently fall. The size of their loan may then be greater than the value of the property.

negative externalities occur when an economic activity affects third parties, i.e. people other than the producers or the consumers, in some way which reduces their quality of life. For example, a polluting factory creates a negative externality for people living in the area affected by the pollution. They may encounter health problems which are a cost to the community. This cost is not borne by the producers or the consumers. The price of the product to the consumer is lower than it would be if it covered all of its **social costs** and the producer's profits may be higher than they would be if the social cost were included in the costs of production. (See also **externalities**.) It is difficult to put a money value on some negative externalities, especially when they relate to health or personal well-being.

negative income tax: a unified tax and benefits system, such that people could be taxed or receive benefits according to a single set of rules. Its attraction is that it could be used to eliminate the **poverty trap** which sometimes means that people lose money by taking a job. Although the UK does not at present have a unified system, it is moving in that direction with the **Working Families Tax Credit** which reduces the impact of the poverty trap.

negative relation: an inverse relationship, such that as one variable rises the related one falls. For example, generally speaking, as the price of a product rises, the quantity demanded will fall.

negotiation is a method of reaching agreement, used where both parties have some bargaining power. The obvious example concerns a trade union and an employer, who will negotiate in order to agree an acceptable wage rate.

neoclassical economics: a set of economic ideas developed by a number of economists in the 1870s and further refined by Alfred Marshall. The general thrust of neoclassical economics lies in the study of market forces, supply and demand and the theory of competition. This approach analyses the way individuals achieve their objectives and how firms maximise profits. The price mechanism is seen as the fundamental determinant of the way in which the optimum *allocation of resources* is achieved. Heavy use is made of *marginal analysis*, in order to study the way in which markets create an optimum allocation of resources. (See also *productive efficiency* and *allocative efficiency*.)

neo-Keynesians: those economists who have generally followed the teaching of *J M Keynes* and sought to develop his ideas in the context of recent economic conditions. There is some debate about how closely Keynesians have in fact adhered to the original ideas of Keynes.

net exports means the amount by which exports (both visible and invisible) exceed imports. If imports are greater than exports net exports will be negative.

net foreign assets means all assets held overseas by UK residents less all assets held in the UK by people living abroad. These assets include bank balances, shares, factories, retail outlets and any other production facilities. In many cases the owners will be companies rather than individuals. For example, the Japanese company Nissan has a big factory in Sunderland while the UK company BP has extensive oil production facilities in Alaska.

net investment is gross (i.e. total) investment less *replacement investment* (also known as *capital consumption*). Net investment thus represents the value of the addition to total productive capacity which has taken place over the year. It gives a good indication of the extent to which the economy is able to increase *aggregate supply* in the future.

net profit is defined as *gross profit* less overhead costs (which are usually similar to fixed costs). An alternative approach defines it as total sales revenue less total costs. It is often called operating profit in company accounts.

net property income from abroad is a term found in the *national income statistics* which refers to interest and profits on foreign investments. It means total interest and profit received by UK residents on their foreign investments, less total interest and profit paid to foreign residents on their investments in the UK. (See also *gross national product (GNP)*.)

net savers: people who save more than they borrow (e.g. through their mortgage).

net wealth: an individual's total *assets*, less any debts.

New Deal: a policy to deal with youth *unemployment* and long-term unemployment, introduced in 1998. It is a requirement for continuing to receive benefits for

- people aged 18–24 who have been unemployed for more than six months
- people over the age of 25 who have been unemployed for more than eighteen months.

Under the New Deal, lone parents, disabled people, partners and musicians each have specialised programmes. Each individual has a personal adviser who will help and support them in improving their existing skills, acquiring new ones and finding employment.

There is some evidence to suggest that the New Deal has been an improvement on the previous system. For many years after 1998, unemployment decreased steadily. However, it is not clear whether it is a cost-effective way of reducing unemployment. Part of the problem is that it is difficult to keep track of everyone who has passed through the scheme for long enough to assess the impact it has had on their lives. It will certainly be difficult to find employment while redundancies are at the high levels seen in 2008–09.

new entrants: firms which set up in business in a particular industry for the first time. Usually they will be attracted by potential profits. These may arise because there has been an increase in demand for the product. This is part of the *price mechanism*, which creates incentives for firms to produce goods and services for which there is a demand. New entrants may be new businesses or well-established businesses venturing into a market which is new for them.

new technology: new ways to:

- raise the level of output by investing in new machinery and other ways to produce
- bring new products to the marketplace
- improve the quality of existing products
- improve management techniques so that costs, and also prices, can be cut.

Innovation is one of the most powerful ways of increasing *productivity* and fostering *economic growth*. The implementation of new technologies has a critical effect in improving standards of living. Sometimes new technology is equated with advanced technology. In fact, some new technologies may be *intermediate technologies* put to new uses in situations where they were not previously in use. In some developing countries good results have been obtained with cookers built according to new designs and requiring less fuel. This economises on firewood, reducing the effort required to collect it and the environmental damage caused by too much cutting.

newly industrialised economy (NIE): an economy which has recently experienced a high level of growth of manufactured output.

- Typically, a large part of manufacturing output will be exported.
- Low wage rates attract *foreign direct investment (FDI)*.
- Investment may be encouraged by a high rate of domestic saving (as in Singapore and South Korea).
- *Labour* moves quite rapidly out of agriculture and into the *secondary sector* (as currently in the eastern provinces of China).
- New skills are acquired and a larger range of goods is produced.

The classic example of NIEs used to be the Asian tigers: Taiwan, Hong Kong, Singapore and South Korea. Singapore now has a very high per capita income and the rest are not far behind. The NIEs today are numerous, still heavily concentrated in Asia, but including also some from Latin America such as Brazil and Mexico.

NIEs are characterised by their high level of manufactured output. As they continue to grow they will tend to develop larger service sectors.

NGOs: see *non-governmental organisations (NGOs)*.

Nikkei Index is Japan's Stock Exchange Index, equivalent to London's Financial Times Stock Exchange (FT–SE 100) index (Footsie).

nominal GDP means *gross domestic product (GDP)* at current prices. This means that no allowance has been made for *inflation*.

nominal value means value in money terms. No allowance is made for *inflation*. Nominal wages will increase over time. Some of this increase will be nominal, reflecting the current rate of inflation. The rest of the increase will be a *real* increase, reflecting an increase in the purchasing power of the wage.

Sometimes nominal value means face value: this can apply to shares which have a face value derived from their initial price and a current market price which may be higher or lower.

non-accelerating inflation rate of unemployment (NAIRU): the level of unemployment at which inflation is stable. Once unemployment falls below a certain level, some skills will be in short supply and there will be a tendency for wages to be bid up and for inflation to accelerate. This is known as **overfull employment**. It will be below the NAIRU level but may not last long before inflation becomes a problem. This type of argument is particularly associated with **monetarism** and with the work of **Milton Friedman**. But much of it has been widely accepted by economists who would not describe themselves as monetarists. NAIRU is often now referred to as **equilibrium unemployment**.

Higher rates of unemployment (above NAIRU) induce people to settle for moderate, or no, pay increases or even a pay cut. So there is still a trade-off between inflation and unemployment (the **Phillips curve**). Competition for scarce jobs will gradually bring down pay increases and the rate of inflation. In extreme cases (as in Japan in 2001–02) prices will fall.

Structural unemployment, which is long term by its nature, tends to continue even when aggregate demand is sufficient to buy all of the current output. This is the main component of NAIRU. The existence of structural unemployment has little effect in forcing down pay rises. It is determined by the nature of the labour market. If there are labour **immobilities**, it may persist for a long time.

There is some debate about the actual level of NAIRU in the UK. It certainly rose during the 1970s and 1980s, probably because of the increasing pace of **structural change**. It is thought to have fallen during the late 1990s. It may have been affected by:
- improved support and training embedded in the **New Deal**
- increased incentives to work provided by the **Working Families Tax Credit**
- availability for work tests used in the administration of unemployment benefits.

Structural unemployment can be reduced by training in areas of skill shortage and other measures which make it easier for people to suit themselves to the jobs available.

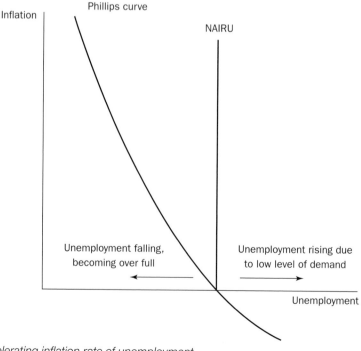

Non-accelerating inflation rate of unemployment

See also *Phillips curve*. The graph on page 235 shows the way in which inflation and unemployment data have moved and how the nature of the trade-off has changed over time.

non-collusive oligopoly: a situation in which there is a small number of producers competing strongly with one another and making no attempt at collaboration or at *tacit collusion*. The market will exhibit interdependent behaviour in that each producer will be observing and reacting to the strategies of the other producers. There are three possible outcomes:

- The firm will assume that competitors will not react to its actions. It will do its best to maximise profit with a strategy which does not depend on competitors' reactions.
- The firm will assume that competitors will react to its actions. This could lead to a situation in which there is a *kinked demand curve*. The firm will try to predict the reaction, using its own past experience, and allow for this in its forward planning.
- The firm will try to predict what competitors will do and will devise a profit-maximising strategy which allows for new possibilities in the marketplace. This outcome will correspond to a *game theory* type of approach.

In practice, oligopolies often lead to price stability. However, there can be short periods of intense change, as when there is a *price war*, in which these types of market behaviour can be observed. For example, Woolworths traditionally had 20% of the Easter egg market and when it closed down in November 2008, it had already ordered 20 million eggs for 2009. Tesco bought up all the eggs that were exclusive to Woolworths and launched a price war by saying it would sell these eggs at prices well below what Woolworths had planned. Asda and Sainsbury's then bought all Woolworth's stock of other brands and joined in with more price cuts. As a result, eggs were available at prices around 19% less than their 2008 level.

non-excludability: a feature of *public goods*, the consumption of which by one person does not exclude consumption by others. The security provided by the police force is one example. Provided there is a police force, all will benefit regardless of whether they have contributed to its financing.

non-executive directors are appointed to the board of directors of a public company on a part-time basis. Their purpose is to provide an independent voice and to observe and advise on the actions of the full-time managers. They have the potential to prevent fraudulent or dubious decisions. In practice, they are sometimes the cronies of the management.

non-governmental organisations (NGOs) are bodies which are associated neither with governments nor with firms in the private sector. For the most part they are charities or *pressure groups* which are non-profit making. Oxfam is a well-known example. They can be big spenders worldwide, although their local projects tend to be small scale. They are a significant presence at some meetings of international organisations such as the UN and the *WTO*, where they will normally have observer status. Some non-governmental organisations have been very critical of the process of globalisation on the grounds that it allows multinational corporations to pay low wages in poor countries. There is a long-run debate between those who focus on the way globalisation has created jobs and those who hope to see working conditions and pay improved through regulation and international agreement.

non-inflationary growth: rising output which does not lead to accelerating *inflation*. Economic growth can lead to a rise in demand for particular types of *labour* with scarce skills.

This can bid up wages as employers compete for the available people. Costs of production then increase and these may be passed on to consumers in the form of higher prices.

Economic growth may not lead to inflation if:
- the supply of labour is growing
- training procedures are being improved
- labour is being used more efficiently and productivity is growing.

This can be shown diagrammatically with long-run aggregate supply increasing at the same time as aggregate demand.

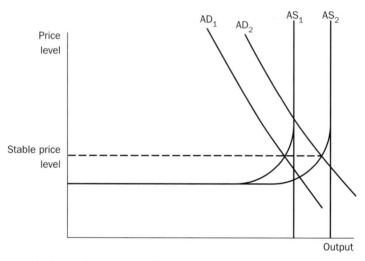

Aggregate supply rises to keep pace with aggregate demand

non-marketed activity: economic activities the products of which do not appear on any market. This includes housework and caring activities within the home, DIY activity, voluntary work and some health, education and personal social services provided free of charge by governments.

non-material progress: improvements in the standard of living which are not captured in GDP data. In developing countries these might, for example, relate to:
- longer life expectancy
- higher literacy rates
- improved water supplies
- fewer environmental hazards.

non-pecuniary advantages are the elements in the package of rewards for working which are not quantified in money terms as pay. They might include a company car, private health insurance and other similar rewards. They can create incentives to change jobs or undertake particular types of work.

non-performing debt: a debt upon which no *interest* is being paid and repayments are in arrears. Lenders will sometimes carry a non-performing debt on the books for some time before they give up hope of debt service payments being resumed. This problem featured in the financial crisis 2007–09 and in the long period of economic difficulty experienced in Japan over the past twenty years.

non-price competition involves any kind of competitive activity other than reducing the price. It is a particular feature of market structures which fit the pattern of an *oligopoly*. It can mean competing on quality or design, through advertising or packaging or special offers of any kind. Oligopolists often use non-price competition because it reduces the risk of lower profits associated with price competition. Branding is a particularly visible form of non-price competition, in its attempts to enhance customer loyalty.

non-profit making organisations are run without profit as an objective, although they may try hard to cover all their costs. They include charities, some schools and a range of other organisations designed to operate in the public interest.

non-renewable resources: see *finite resources*.

non-rivalry refers to *public goods* which can be consumed by an unlimited number of people because the presence of one consumer does not exclude the enjoyment of the product by another. Public parks provide an example: people are generally not in competition with one another in order to consume their benefits. A number of people can enjoy them at the same time.

non-tariff barriers (NTBs) include *quotas* and other restrictions on trade which do not involve taxing imports. Many of them are contrary to either the spirit or the letter of international regulations under the *WTO*. Quotas involve an upper limit on the level of imports. Also included in the category of non-tariff barriers:

- a particular type of quota called a *voluntary export restraint (VER)*. This is negotiated with the exporting country's government
- technical regulations which force exporters to make specific changes to the product so that it is acceptable in that particular market. This raises costs for the exporter.

Because barriers to trade tend to reduce the level of trade, they also reduce the real incomes of the countries which employ them, by depriving consumers of cheap substitutes for domestically produced goods. They may be popular with voters, though, because they are thought to protect the jobs of domestic producers.

non-tradables are products which will not normally figure in international trade. They include some sorts of services which are unlikely to be consumed much by tourists and some very heavy construction materials. Usually, the markets for non-tradables are rather less competitive than those for tradable goods and services. Prices may be rather higher because there are fewer substitutes.

normal goods are those for which demand will increase when incomes increase. In other words, the *income elasticity of demand* for them is positive. They include a huge range of products, such as foreign holidays, restaurant meals, theatre visits, golf clubs and so on. In contrast, inferior goods experience falling demand when income rises. Examples include maincrop potatoes, basic models of consumer durables and so on.

normal profit: that level of profit which is just sufficient to keep the resources employed in making a particular product from being used for some other purpose. Any profit in excess of that amount, termed *supernormal profit*, will tend to attract additional resources into the industry; in other words there will be entry into the industry by new firms. If less than normal profit is earned, some resources will leave the industry to exploit more profitable opportunities producing other things. Normal profit is an important feature of *perfect competition*. The theory predicts that under perfectly competitive conditions, only normal profit will be earned in the long run, because the entry of new competitors will force prices back down to the level which just covers the costs of all resources used in production. (See also ***profit-signalling mechanism***.)

normative: involving a value judgement. A normative statement is one which cannot be tested against the facts. It is likely to be a matter of opinion. It contrasts with a positive statement which can be tested against the evidence. 'The Chancellor ought to raise taxes and increase pensions' is a normative statement, because different people will have different opinions on it, depending perhaps on their age and values.

North American Free Trade Agreement (NAFTA) consists of the US, Canada and Mexico. As a ***free trade area***, it is different from the EU because it does not have a ***common external tariff*** against the rest of the world. Also it does not on the whole attempt to harmonise its regulations. However, it has been successful since its inception in 1993 in increasing trade between member countries. As a major trading bloc, it has potential to influence future trade negotiations quite strongly.

no-strike agreement: a negotiated agreement between employees and management not to go on strike. This will usually be in return for some concessions as to pay and working conditions, as well as a commitment to go to ***arbitration*** in the event of a dispute which is not easily resolved.

Do you need revision help and advice?

Go to pages 326–46 for a range of revision appendices that include plenty of exam advice and tips.

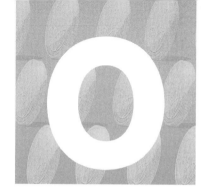

obsolescence: when a product or a process is going out of date. While not yet completely obsolete, it is becoming so. For example, a piece of machinery may still be usable in the production process, but may be more expensive to operate than the latest technology.

occupational immobility occurs when people have been trained in a skill which is no longer in demand and have difficulty in retraining in a skill which is in demand. This may result in their being unemployed. This type of unemployment is known as *structural unemployment*. Policies to deal with it include projects such as the *New Deal*, which gives help in finding work as well as additional training.

OECD: see *Organisation for Economic Co-operation and Development (OECD)*.

offer curve of labour: see *backward sloping supply curve of labour*.

Office for National Statistics: the body responsible for collecting statistics in the UK. Its parent organisation, the UK Statistics Authority, is a government department with overall responsibility for all statistics. In 2007 it was made independent of the government of the day and it reports directly to Parliament. This is to safeguard it from government interference which might put pressure on it to begin *massaging statistics*.

Office of Fair Trading (OFT) was set up in 1973 to oversee all of the UK's competition policy. It operates in a range of areas. It:

- monitors changes in *market structures*, collecting data and investigating merger activity generally
- decides whether to refer takeovers to the *Competition Commission* for further investigation before approval can be given
- responds to complaints about anti-competitive activities (which usually come from competing firms)
- takes care of many aspects of *consumer protection*, including trades description.

The OFT was greatly strengthened by the 1998 Competition Act, giving it the power to stage a *dawn raid* if a firm might try to obscure important evidence. Also, it gave firms immunity from fines if they inform on other members of a *cartel*. The Enterprise Act of 2002 made forming a cartel a criminal act and allows the OFT to fine firms which collude up to 10% of their UK turnover for up to three years.

The OFT first used its power to bring criminal charges in 2007 against a cartel of British, Swedish and US producers of marine hoses. The operation was carefully co-ordinated with the EU Competition Commission and the US Department of Justice. Eight people from the three companies involved were arrested in the US, in order to avoid extradition problems. They were accused of rigging bids, fixing prices and allocating markets. A Japanese competitor was the whistleblower.

Official Bank Rate: see *bank rate*.

official development assistance (ODA) is the *foreign aid* given by governments to developing countries in the form of grants and loans. This may come in the form of bilateral aid, from one government to another, or multilateral aid, from an international organisation funded by many countries. It does not include charitable donations or private investment.

official finance transactions are payments made by the Bank of England to offset inflows and outflows on the *balance of payments*.

official reserves are the reserves of foreign exchange held by the *central bank*. They may be used to defend the exchange rate if market forces are pushing it down. (See also *fixed exchange rate*.)

offshoring: setting up a company in a foreign country or tax haven in order to take advantage of low tax rates or light touch regulation. An offshore investment fund is based in an offshore centre for tax or other reasons.

OFGEM, the Office of Gas and Electricity Markets, is the regulator for the gas and electricity industries. The industry has been regulated since *privatisation* in the late 1980s. OFGEM regulates the extent to which gas and electricity prices can be raised and also the value-for-money which customers get. It can require suppliers to restrain their activities in order to ensure that the market remains competitive. Because both industries are to some extent *natural monopolies*, regulation is needed to protect the interests of consumers.

Since 1999, neither British Gas nor the electricity suppliers have had a monopoly position; consumers can choose where to buy. *Regulation* has at times brought OFGEM into dispute with shareholders. To the extent that suppliers' profits may be reduced, shareholders sometimes object when prices cannot be raised.

OFCOM is the regulator for UK communications industries. It has been instrumental in opening up the telecommunications market to many competing suppliers. By creating much stronger competition it has helped to bring down the cost of phone calls. It covers radio, television, telecommunications and wireless communication services. It set price controls for BT until 2006 but this is no longer necessary. (See also *regulatory capture*.)

OFT: see *Office of Fair Trading (OFT)*.

OFWAT is the regulator for the water industry, set up at the time of privatisation in 1989. In spite of its efforts to hold down price increases, many people think that the water companies continue to act like monopolies. Water remains a true *natural monopoly* in that it is not usually possible to choose between competing suppliers and the need for a pipe network makes duplication of facilities wasteful and inefficient. In fact, prices have risen in part because of the need for extensive investment in improved water supplies. It is hard to tell how effective regulation has been in this case.

oil crisis: a situation in which supplies of oil are threatened and prices rise as it becomes more scarce. The precipitating cause could be war in the Middle East, as in 1973. *OPEC* has in the past been able to restrict production with a view to raising prices. Protesters have at times succeeded in blocking supplies by picketing the refineries, when attempts were made to raise taxes to discourage greenhouse gas production.

Because demand for oil is very inelastic, a relatively small fall in production can bring about a much larger increase in prices. Shortages are likely to disrupt economic activity because of the crucial role of oil in industry and distribution.

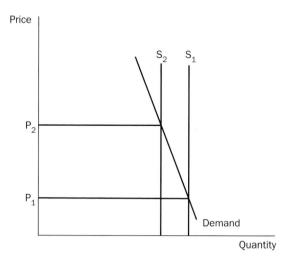

A small fall in quantity supplied leads to a large increase in price if demand is inelastic

oil price: the price of oil in the wholesale market, which is a significant indicator of future pressures on production costs and sometimes of impending *inflation*. The price is usually quoted in US dollars.

oligopoly: a market in which there are a few large firms competing with one another. It is characterised by:
- *differentiated products*, sometimes with well-known and easily distinguished brand names
- *barriers to entry*, such that it may be difficult or impossible for *new entrants* to come into the market
- the fact that firms may make *supernormal profits* in the long run, because of the barriers to entry
- the relatively small number of competing firms, which is likely to include *price makers* and *price takers*. The former will tend to set prices and the latter will tend to follow.

Oligopolies can have very stable prices, because firms will often favour *non-price competition*. They may seek to expand their market share on the strength of design or advertising. There may be *tacit collusion*, with no price cuts but intense efforts to promote products in other ways.

Occasionally, though, a price war may break out, in which one firm begins aggressive price-cutting strategies and others follow, each trying to undercut the other in a bid for increased market share. This is good for consumers in the short run but may lead to the least profitable firm going out of business. Then competition is reduced and a return to tacit collusion is likely. Petrol provides occasional examples of price wars.

Interdependent behaviour is an important feature of oligopoly, because the small number of competing firms watch each other closely, devising strategies which take into account the likely reaction of the others.

Some oligopolies have a number of large competitors, as with Coca-Cola and other major soft drink suppliers, together with a large number of comparatively small suppliers which are price takers. (See also *concentration ratios*, *kinked demand curve*, *anti-competitive activities*.)

ombudsman: a person or body which investigates complaints from consumers in either the public or the private sector. Banking and insurance both have ombudsmen whose findings are not legally binding, but who can give the consumer view some strength.

ONS: see *Office for National Statistics (ONS)*.

OPEC: see *Organization of Petroleum Exporting Countries (OPEC)*.

open economy: an economy in which foreign trade is important. Exports contribute significantly to aggregate demand and imports are a significant proportion of total purchases. For example, the UK economy is a more open economy than the US. Luxembourg is even more so.

operating profit: the main accounting measure of a firm's profit. Total costs will be subtracted from total sales revenue so this is the accounting measure which comes closest to the economist's view of profit. However, the costs which are included may not cover all of the resources used so there is still a difference in the two concepts.

opportunity cost represents cost in terms of what could have been had as an alternative to the item actually chosen. For example, the opportunity cost of a new economics textbook might be two cinema tickets which you could have had instead. So opportunity cost is the best or highest valued alternative that must be foregone.

The idea of opportunity cost may be applied in any situation where choices are being made. For example, consumers' decisions involve choices between items; one will be chosen and the one foregone is the opportunity cost. Similarly *labour* market decisions may involve choices between work and education or between two possible jobs. And the government may find that the opportunity cost of, say, more money for the NHS is less money for roads or social services.

Opportunity cost is also important in considering alternative investments. Even if the firm is using its own *retained profits* to fund the investment, it must allow for the interest which could have been earned if this money had been left in the bank. This is the opportunity cost of investing in, say, a new machine or office furniture. An investment which cannot equal the rate of return on a bank deposit is not a good use of funds.

optimise: to strive for the most favourable outcome. This could mean *profit maximisation* or maximising market share or any other objective.

optimum means simply the best possible outcome, i.e. buying your first choice of product, getting the best paid job possible for you, making the most profit you can.

optimum currency area: the best size for a single currency area. There is no simple answer to what this might be.
- A small currency area such as the UK will have to carry the risk of an unfavourable exchange rate change. Firms will face uncertainty: the exchange rate may float up, making export prices rise and leading to difficulties in maintaining competitiveness.

There will be transactions costs associated with every trade deal. But the government will retain the option of allowing a *depreciation* which will enhance competitiveness. It will have a wider range of macro-economic policy choices. It will be able to set *interest rates* to suit the needs of the economy at any given time.

- In a large currency area such as the *euro zone*, all producers will know the price at which they can sell across a very large market. There will be much less uncertainty and no transactions costs. But if one member country loses competitiveness compared to other member countries, e.g. because of inflation, it will not be able to depreciate as a means of adjusting and regaining competitiveness. Interest rates will be determined by the *European Central Bank (ECB)* with reference to the area as a whole and not to the needs of individual member countries.

In practice, large and small currency areas exist side by side. Think of the US and Switzerland, both with high standards of living and both able to compete very success-fully with the rest of the world in their own specialist areas. West Virginia does not seek its own currency despite having rather low incomes relative to the rest of the US and Switzerland seems quite unlikely to seek to join the euro.

option: the right to buy or sell a *commodity*, *bonds* or currency at a specific time in the future, at a price agreed now.

order book: means literally the book in which a firm's orders are recorded. The term 'a long order book' means that the firm has enough work already arranged to last for a substantial period. It is an indication that the firm is working close to *full-capacity*.

ordinary share: a way of buying a small part of a *public limited company*, i.e. one which offers its shares to the general public. The firm gets finance for investment, while the shareholder gets a *dividend*. However, the shareholder runs the risk that the share price will fall or the company will become insolvent, in which case the money will probably be lost. Then again, the company may turn out to be profitable, the share price may rise and the dividends may offer a good rate of return.

organic growth: an expansion of the firm which is based on building up new production capacity within the existing business, rather than through merging with another firm.

Organisation for Economic Co-operation and Development (OECD) is a group of 30 member countries, mainly those with relatively high incomes. In recent years some *transitional economies* have joined, including Mexico, South Korea, Hungary, Poland and others. More countries will join soon, including Russia. In the longer term, Brazil, China, India, Indonesia and South Africa may join.

OECD is located in Paris and does much useful work in producing consistent data which can be used for international comparisons. Its main functions are:
- acting as a forum for discussion and co-operation in international economic policy, supported by research into economic problems; meetings are attended by finance and trade ministers
- co-ordinating the provision of bilateral aid by the donor countries to the developing countries.

organised labour means the trade unions and their membership. In contrast, employees who choose not to join a union and negotiate independently or accept the going wage are not part of organised labour.

Organization of Petroleum Exporting Countries (OPEC) is the group of oil-exporting countries drawn from the Middle East, South America and Africa. Its objective is to control supply in order to maintain prices but in this it has had very varied results. The US, Russia and European producers do not belong to OPEC. In 1973 and in 1979 it operated as a very effective *cartel*, reducing supplies and forcing up oil prices so that producer countries' revenues were greatly increased. However, this price increase made new oilfields such as those in the North Sea and Alaska economic to develop, thus reducing the market power of the OPEC cartel. To a degree, Saudi Arabia is still able to influence the quantity of oil supplied. In 2008 when oil prices soared it increased production for a while as part of an international effort to stabilise prices.

other things being equal: see *ceteris paribus*.

output: the end product of a firm, resulting from an economic process. Output can be valued according to its price in the market or stated in volume terms. **Productivity** means output per person employed and is a measure of efficiency.

output gap: the difference between actual output and the potential output of the economy when it is working at full capacity. By looking at real GDP over time and comparing it with the *long-run trend rate of growth*, it is possible to see when there is a divergence. In 2007 the UK economy grew by 3%. The long-run trend rate of growth in the UK is about 2.2%, so real GDP was above its underlying trend and the output gap was positive. With a growth rate in 2008 of 0.8%, there was clearly a negative output gap. Central banks attempted to close this gap with low interest rates and **quantitative easing**. For 2009 this gap was estimated to be 9% for the USA and probably no less for the UK.

The diagram below shows a negative output gap. The level of expenditure is less than the capacity of the economy to produce. There will be a deflationary situation with a significant amount of unemployment and idle capital equipment. This may be eliminated by using expansionary fiscal and monetary policies.

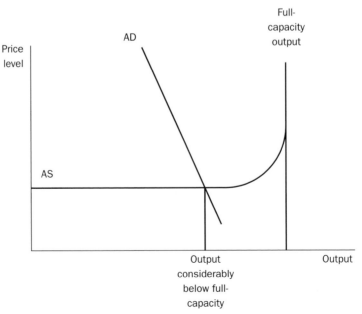

A negative output gap: aggregate demand is insufficient to buy all that the economy can produce

If there is a positive output gap, expenditure has risen above the long-term capacity of the economy to produce and there will be inflationary pressures. Policies to reduce expenditure will be needed.

outsourcing is the process by which firms buy services, component inputs or even finished products from independent suppliers, rather than produce them themselves. This practice increased as many businesses have found it cheaper to rely on other producers than try to do everything themselves. Sometimes new cheap sources of inputs can be found overseas; this has been an important element in *globalisation*.

outward-looking trade strategies: trade policies which encourage exports and allow imports. These have become important in *developing economies* because some of the countries which adopted such policies have been very successful. Singapore is an example, now having per capita income near to the highest in the world and a very high percentage of output exported. In contrast, countries which adopted *import substitution* policies have tended to grow more slowly.

overcapacity occurs when demand for the product is less than the capacity of the firms in the industry to supply. Usually this happens because demand has fallen, as with the steel industry. As alternative materials displaced steel and new producers became competitive, much capacity had to be closed down.

There is currently world overcapacity in the car industry; this started well before recession set in. In the US, the process started with the import of Japanese cars that were smaller, more fuel efficient and more reliable. US manufacturers carried on producing big cars and SUVs, which in time went out of fashion. For some years, Ford, GM and Chrysler have been trying without much success to rationalise production so that they might become profitable again and meet consumer demand effectively. In the UK, Ford Dagenham closed down in 2007. The US car companies finally took their medicine as a condition of getting some support from the US government, but the actual outcome remains uncertain.

Meanwhile, many new producers have come on stream, e.g. in China, Korea and Eastern Europe. Tata in India has come up with the Nano, the $2000 car. The demand for cars is growing but the older US and European companies have not adapted to the competition. If this continues, more will close down.

overconsumption occurs when the price of the product does not reflect the full costs of the product. Prices may not include *external costs*. For example, it can be argued that cigarettes are overconsumed because buyers do not take full account of the health effects of smoking and the price does not fully reflect the health care costs of tobacco-related illnesses. Taxes go some way towards this, of course. We may be overconsuming petrol because we are not allowing for the long-term environmental effects of our behaviour. Overconsumption can be associated with *information failure* and also with *demerit goods*.

overdraft: a loan facility which allows individuals or firms to borrow from the bank only just the amount they need at any time. If borrowing needs vary from day to day this arrangement saves interest payments when loan needs are low. Usually the bank will set a maximum limit on the size of the overdraft.

overfull employment: a level of employment which is going to lead to inflationary pressures. Unemployment will be low, and less than the *equilibrium unemployment* level *(NAIRU)*, by definition. At this level of unemployment, employers are competing for people with scarce skills and they will tend to bid up wages in an attempt to get the people they want in order to expand production. Costs will increase and this will be passed on to consumers in the form of higher prices. There is **excess demand**. Any further growth in aggregate demand will lead to accelerating inflation rather than rising output because aggregate supply cannot increase fast enough to keep pace.

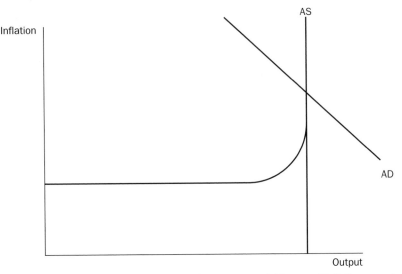

Aggregate demand exceeds aggregate supply, wages are bid up and inflation accelerates

overheads are similar to **fixed costs** in that they are not related to the level of output. They include salaries of people not actually involved in production, capital equipment, rent, heating and lighting.

overheating occurs when **aggregate demand** exceeds **aggregate supply**. The **excess demand** which results reflects the fact that **supply constraints** are preventing producers from increasing output. There will be a tendency for **inflation** to accelerate and for imports to rise as the pressure of demand increases. (See also **overfull employment**.)

overmanning: using more **labour** in the production process than is strictly necessary. It can occur when firms are run inefficiently yet survive because they have a degree of monopoly power. Or it can occur when agreements are made between unions and management not to make people redundant. This means that employees are kept on the payroll even though it would be possible to supply the existing quantity of the product without their help.

overproduction occurs when there are **external costs** which are not included in the cost and price structure of the product. For example, a producer which manages to keep costs down by emitting polluting waste into the air or rivers will have accounting costs which are lower than the full **social cost** of production. This will make the product look artificially cheap and firms will be able to sell more of it than they would if the price reflected the externality. Internalising these costs by making the firm clean up its emissions will raise the internal costs and prices and lead to an equilibrium output which reflects demand at the resulting price level.

overshooting: when the economy is changing fast, some variables have a tendency to overshoot, i.e. adjust more than is necessary. For example, if there is a glut, prices may actually fall too far and a temporary shortage will follow. An overvalued exchange rate may also fall too far, down below the level needed to balance imports and exports. Share prices may do the same. In each case, markets fail to clear, there is then a price adjustment but initially it overshoots, leading to a later correction which adjusts prices more closely to the long-run equilibrium.

overtime: time spent at work in addition to the hours which are part of the normal working week. Typically, the working week will be 38–40 hours and any time spent over that will attract overtime payments for manual workers and some clerical occupations. Managerial groups and professionals seldom get overtime payments.

overtime ban: industrial action that allows a normal working week but bans any overtime. This leaves wages close to normal but may disrupt the production process if employers would have required overtime.

overvalued currency: an *exchange rate* level which is above that at which exports and imports would automatically balance. Export prices will be high and firms will have difficulty in competing. Similarly import prices will be low and people will increase their imports. There will be a current account deficit.

In time, the resulting low level of demand for the currency, and high level of supply, will tend to push the exchange rate down again if it is floating fairly freely. Market forces will create downward pressure. This may or may not be counteracted by central bank action to maintain the exchange rate by buying it and so supporting its value. The pound was probably overvalued in 2007. (See *exchange rate index*.)

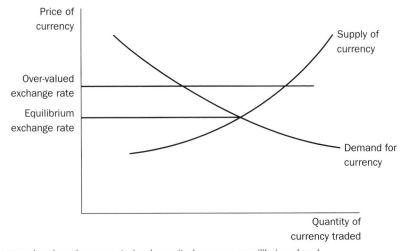

The overvalued exchange rate is above its long-run equilibrium level.

owner occupation: ownership of the property by the person who is living in it. In the UK this is the commonest form of housing arrangement.

ownership rights usually allow owners to decide how their property will be used. This works well with a tin of soup – you can decide when to consume it. It is more complex with land – you will have to get planning permission to develop it. If you own a property, you will be taxed on the rent from it. Ownership rights are an important aspect of the *free market economy*.

packaging: one of the elements in *non-price competition*. Along with advertising, product design, quality and customer service, it can be a part of the competitive process in an *imperfect market*.

paradox of thrift: when people start to save a larger part of their incomes, the resulting withdrawal from the *circular flow of national income* has a *downward multiplier* effect on aggregate demand, which eventually leads to a fall in the level of saving. This is a prediction of the basic Keynesian model of the macro-economy, in which saving is directly related to income because a rise in the rate of saving implies a fall in consumption.

parallel imports are branded goods which are imported by a distributor who is not connected with the manufacturer. These importers look for price differences between countries, buying where the product can be obtained most cheaply. They will then be able to sell at a higher price in countries where the 'official' distribution network charges more. Parallel imports encourage price competition, e.g. in the car market where prices have tended to be higher in the UK than on the continent. They are not to be confused with *pirate products*, which are illegal copies of branded goods, e.g. expensive perfumes. However, they are very unpopular with manufacturers because they reveal their efforts at *price discrimination*.

Pareto efficiency, or Pareto optimality, refers to a situation in which it is impossible to make anyone better off without making someone else worse off. This means that there must be an optimal *allocation of resources*, such that inputs are used in the most efficient way (*productive efficiency*) and output yields the maximum possible utility to consumers (*allocative efficiency*).

Pareto, Vilfredo (1848–1923): an Italian professor of economics who set out the Pareto criterion for efficiency. His work centred on the workings of the market economy and on the ideas of *productive* and *allocative efficiency*. The Pareto criterion states that there is a clear improvement in welfare if at least one person can be made better off without making anyone else worse off. This idea has provided an important foundation for later work in *welfare economics* and *cost–benefit analysis*.

Pareto's reasoning does not take into account the distribution of income. Also, it assumes a situation of *perfect competition*; nevertheless, it provides important insights into the way markets work.

parity is a term used in the context of exchange rates. We may speak of a fixed parity, meaning a value for the exchange rate which will be kept fixed.

partial market failure occurs where a market exists but produces too much or too little of the good or service. It can apply to *merit goods* or *demerit goods*, where the market on its own will lead to production of less or more of the product than would be socially optimal.

Imperfect or *asymmetric information* is likely to be a factor in many such cases. (See *overproduction* and *underprovision.*)

participation rate: the proportion of the population which is either in work or registered unemployed. It is thus a measure of the size of the total workforce available and the extent to which the population is economically active. This in turn depends on the age at which people cease full-time education, the retirement age and the extent to which parents take time out from employment to look after children.

partnership is a type of business organisation owned by two or more people. They will be able to raise more capital together than they could as *sole traders*. But they will not have *limited liability (Ltd)*, so they may have to meet all of their debts out of their own resources if the business is not successful. This means that trust between the partners is essential. Partnerships are common in accountancy and the law.

par value: see *nominal value*.

patent: a legal right to the *monopoly* of a new product or process. The newness of the invention must be demonstrated in the application to the Patent Office. Once the patent is obtained, the holder can use the process or manufacture the product, or license other firms to make it, for up to 20 years.

Patents can be very valuable, as with certain drugs for which pharmaceutical companies hold the patent. Pfizer is seriously worried about the likely effect on its profits when the patent for Lipitor runs out in 2011.

Patents are economically important because they provide a significant incentive to innovate. Without patent protection, few innovations would be developed and *productivity* would probably grow much more slowly than it has. However, the patent holder must be prepared to defend the right in court, which can be expensive. Patents are one element in the general term *intellectual property* rights.

pattern of trade: the way in which an economy trades with different parts of the world and in different products. The UK pattern of trade has the following features:
- increasing trade with the EU
- the US and Germany are the two single most important trading partners
- a high proportion of exports consist of services, particularly financial services.

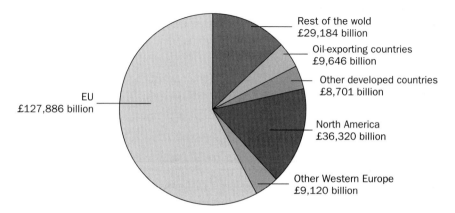

Exports from the UK by destination, 2007, £ million. (Source: ONS, Annual Abstract of Statistics, 2008.)

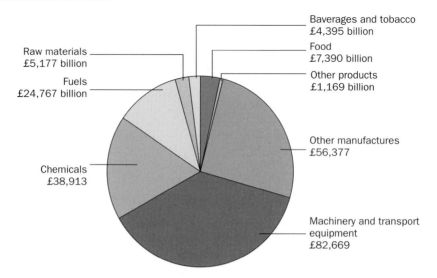

Raw materials
£5,177 billion

Fuels
£24,767 billion

Chemicals
£38,913

Baverages and tobacco
£4,395 billion

Food
£7,390 billion

Other products
£1,169 billion

Other manufactures
£56,377

Machinery and transport
equipment
£82,669

UK visible exports, by commodity, 2007, £ million. (Source: ONS, Annual Abstract of Statistics, 2008.)

pay differentials: the differences in wages and salaries between specific occupations and industries. Differentials reflect education and training which lead to differences in **productivity**. They are also important indicators of market forces in the labour market. They create important incentives. High pay sends a signal to the market that more people are required in that particular occupation.

- Pay can act as an incentive to move into an occupation for which demand is growing. Some computer programmers are very highly paid because they possess very scarce skills. The high pay should in time act as an incentive which will attract more people to get the appropriate training.
- Pay differentials between regions create an incentive to move. Higher pay in South East England attracts more people into the area.
- Low pay indicates declining demand and sometimes encourages people to retrain or move to another region.

Pay differentials do not always perform their function of reallocating resources very efficiently. Sometimes the differentials are insufficient to compensate for the bother of retraining or moving, so that excess supply and demand in the labour market may persist.

Differentials can reflect innate abilities. **Labour market flexibility** requires that differentials do actually induce people to move to where they are needed.

PAYE stands for 'pay as you earn'. It is the system by which employers deduct income tax from pay at source.

payroll tax: a tax paid by the employer which rises with the number of employees. The common example is the social security taxes which exist in most countries of the European Union. In the UK these are called employers' **National Insurance charges**. They have the effect of raising the costs of employing **labour**. They therefore have the potential to reduce employment if the employer is likely to look for labour-saving ways of producing.

peak pricing may be used where there are substantial variations in demand over the course of time. For example, rail fares are set in such a way that it costs more to travel during the rush hour. This is a way of raising revenue and charging higher prices to those customers who put the most pressure on the capacity of the organisation to provide for them. (See also *price discrimination*.)

pension funds are *financial intermediaries* which channel money from the premiums of people who want pensions into a variety of investments in firms. Payments are paid monthly into pension schemes by large numbers of people who have occupational pensions. The pension funds invest in shares, property and government bonds, spreading the risks associated with any one investment. Along with insurance companies and investment trusts, the pension funds are known as *institutional investors*. They are a very important source of funds for investment and have considerable influence with the firms of which they are shareholders.

per capita means 'per head', as in *per capita income*, meaning income per person. It is usually used as an average of the whole population.

per capita income means income per person and is an important measure of the standard of living. In *constant price* terms, it is widely used for international comparisons. It is based on either GNP or GDP so it must be interpreted with the caution required for all standard national income measures. In particular, care is needed where exchange rate changes have occurred. Allowance may have to be made for environmental degradation or deterioration in the quality of life as measured in other ways.

percentile: a one-hundredth part of a set of observations. A person who is among the highest 1% in terms of income earned may be said to be in the top percentile. The 50th percentile corresponds to the median observation, and so on.

perfect competition is an economic model of a market situation characterised by a large number of firms all making the same product. Many markets for farm products such as cauliflowers or wheat are broadly similar to perfect competition. Some commodity markets also have many similarities to it. The model itself has the following features:

- Many buyers and sellers, all of whom are *price takers*. They are able to sell as much as they can produce at the going market price.
- No one seller's product is distinguishable from another's. All produce a *homogeneous product*.
- There is *free entry* to and exit from the market. New firms can start up production easily and there are few or no *barriers to entry*.
- There is *perfect knowledge*, meaning that all buyers and sellers have full information about products and prices. All producers have access to the same technologies.
- Factors of production are perfectly mobile – they are able to move from one line of production to another without difficulty.
- In the long run, only *normal profit* can be earned. Any *supernormal profit* will be competed away by *new entrants* to the market, forcing prices down to the minimum average total cost.

Productive efficiency can be achieved under perfect competition because there will always be many sellers competing and they will need to keep costs to a minimum in order to survive. *Allocative efficiency* can be achieved because free entry to the market means that there will always be a producer seeking to meet consumer demand at a price which reflects costs of production.

As with all firms, profit is maximised where **marginal cost** is equal to **marginal revenue**. Marginal revenue is always equal to price.

Many of the important features of perfect competition can be shown diagrammatically. The diagram shows the long-run equilibrium.

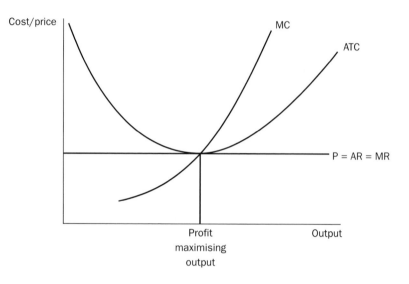

In looking at the diagram, keep in mind that:
- firms can sell all they produce at the going market price. This means that the firm faces a horizontal perfectly elastic demand curve, which also corresponds with the marginal and average revenue
- competition forces firms to minimise costs, so all firms will produce at the point on the average total cost curve where costs are at a minimum. This will be the lowest possible price at which they can stay in business
- in the long run, prices will always be forced down to this level by competition. At this point, marginal cost will equal marginal revenue and this will be the output at which profits are maximised. So the long-run equilibrium price under perfect competition will be the minimum average total cost of the product.

New entrants will always force the price to the level of minimum average total cost, so that only normal profit can be earned. (See also **short-run equilibrium under perfect competition.**)

perfect knowledge is a condition of **perfect competition** implying that both consumers and producers are fully informed about the conditions in the market and about the best ways of producing. Consumers know all about the prices and availability of the products they may purchase and producers are all able to use the best technology available at the time.

perfect market: a market in which the conditions are those of perfect competition, with many suppliers, a **homogeneous product** and **perfect knowledge**.

perfect mobility is a condition of *perfect competition* and means that both *labour* and capital can move from one use to another. People will be able to move from one occupation to another without difficulty and also move to a different geographical area. Funds for investment will be able to move out of a less profitable use and into a more profitable activity.

perfectly contestable market: a market where entry is free and practically costless. Firms already in the market will be aware of the ease with which competitors can enter the market and will keep their prices at levels where they are likely to make no supernormal profit, so discouraging new entrants. This means that consumers benefit from economies of scale but can buy the product in quantities and at prices that reflect the true cost of production.

perfectly elastic demand: sellers can sell all they produce at the going price. For each one, the market is very large compared to the size of the firm. This is one of the conditions of *perfect competition*.

perfectly elastic supply: the quantity supplied is theoretically limitless. In the long run, the supply of many products can be increased indefinitely. There is no problem about finding the resources to expand production at the same price. Some manufactured products are like this, e.g. plastic toys. However, this would only be the case in the long run. The long-run supply curve would be a horizontal line.

perfectly inelastic demand: consumers demand a fixed quantity. Price has no effect on this quantity. At any reasonable price, this applies to kitchen salt. The demand curve will be a vertical line, at the single quantity demanded.

perfectly inelastic supply means that there is a fixed supply. This holds for many products in the *market period*. Prices will be entirely demand determined. The supply of housing is fixed in the short run, because it takes time to build or convert more. In the long run, high prices would induce builders to expand supply.

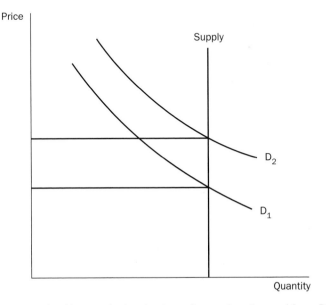

Perfectly inelastic supply of homes in the short run; increasing demand from D₁ to D₂ will drive up prices

233

performance-related pay (PRP) means linking pay to some measure of performance, e.g. sales or output. This can act as an incentive to achieve particular business objectives. In the period preceding the 2007–09 financial crisis, bankers' bonuses encouraged them to pursue profit at the expense of prudent management, leading to the creation of quantities of bad debt. There are calls for employers and remuneration committees to reward performance without encouraging reckless disregard for likely default.

perks: those items within a pay package that are additional to the financial sum, e.g. a company car, private health insurance or free lunches.

permanent income hypothesis: a theory of the determination of the level of consumption, which holds that consumption is directly related to expectation of income over the long run. This theory was set out by *Friedman* and contrasts with the view of *Keynes*, who saw consumption as depending on current income.

personal allowance: the amount of an individual's income which is free of income tax. This amount is usually raised in line with inflation in the *Budget*, unless the Chancellor wants to increase the real level of tax revenue.

personal disposable income is the income which remains to individuals to spend as they wish, after all direct taxes have been deducted.

personal preferences: individual consumer choices which determine the level of *demand* for each product.

personal sector: that part of the economy which consists of transactions made by individuals. The corporate sector involves all decisions by businesses and these two and the financial sector together constitute the private sector.

petroleum revenue tax is levied on the profits from the production of oil within the jurisdiction of the UK government. The oil companies can offset the cost of exploration against the tax.

Phillips curve: the name given to the trade-off between *inflation* and *unemployment*. The nature of this trade-off is complex and sometimes also controversial. It rests broadly on the experience of the *economic cycle*, in which periods of accelerating inflation tend to be associated with falling unemployment during a boom. During recession inflation will usually slow down and unemployment will rise.

The relationship between inflation and unemployment was first studied in detail by A W Phillips (1914–1975). In 1958 he published his investigation of annual data for the previous 100 years, showing a strong inverse relationship between the two. During the period of high unemployment in the 1930s, prices had actually fallen so the relationship looked broadly like the diagram on page 235.

During the 1970s, the idea of a straight trade-off between inflation and unemployment fell into disrepute because the two increased together for a time. This happened when oil prices were rising and there were expectations of accelerating inflation. For more detail see the entry on *long-run Phillips curve*. (This is tricky to follow and you may not need to know it in detail – check your specifications.)

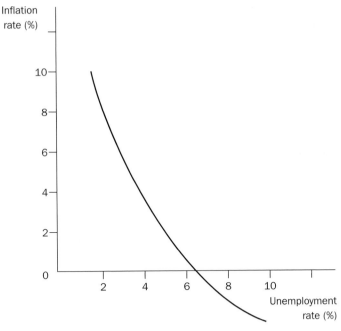

The Phillips curve

The problem of the 1970s – **stagflation** – was eventually defeated by the very tight monetary policies of the 1980s, which were closely associated with high and rising unemployment. From about 1980, you can begin to see a trade-off emerging again in the annual data.

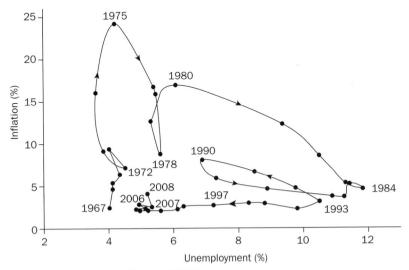

Inflation and unemployment. (Source: ONS.)

The relationship between inflation and unemployment is important in policy making but it keeps changing. Just to keep us all puzzled, in the period 1995–2004 unemployment fell without inflation accelerating. It is likely that there is still a short-run trade-off between inflation and unemployment, but it may be at a lower level of unemployment than in the 1980s. Think about the points on the graph for 2009 onwards. Where are they and what do they suggest?

physical capital means tangible investments in production facilities of all kinds which will bring in an income stream in the future. They include buildings, shops, tankers, machinery and office equipment, along with many other examples. In contrast, *human capital* is embodied in the skills and education of people.

picketing means standing outside a place of work and discouraging people who want to carry on working during an *industrial dispute*. It is strictly controlled by law, which tends to limit the powers of trade unions.

pirate products: imitations of famous brands. These are illegal because brands are generally protected by trademarks which can only be used for the genuine article. The *intellectual property* rights of the owner of the trademark are being infringed and legal action may follow. However, many firms find it very difficult to identify the sources of pirate products. They may come from countries with low wages and weak systems of commercial law.

planned economy: an economy in which all the resource allocation decisions are taken by government departments. So decisions about what is to be produced, and how, and how it will be distributed, all become a matter for the bureaucracy. Of the remaining centrally planned economies, China and Vietnam have large private sectors and North Korea and Cuba are opening up some areas of their economies to market forces. Many countries' governments still plan some parts of economic activity centrally, e.g. the NHS in the UK.

planning permission involves getting permission from the local authority before starting to build new homes, factories or retail outlets. The objective is to protect the countryside and ensure that designs are appropriate to the location. In practice, the process has made building land much more expensive than agricultural land. In some places the scarcity of land for development raises prices a great deal. High property prices in areas where *labour* is scarce can deter people from moving away from areas of high unemployment to places where they would be more likely to find work.

plant is capital equipment which is fixed in place in a factory or other production facility. It is a term usually used to describe facilities and machinery which have a very specific use, as with a chemical plant or car assembly line.

ploughed-back profit means profit retained within the firm. In contrast, the rest of the profit will be distributed to shareholders in the form of *dividends*. It is an important source of finance for investment in the future.

policies for economic development include investment in physical and *human capital* and *infrastructure*, creating incentives (e.g. through ensuring realistic prices for farm products), *debt relief, trade liberalisation* and *good governance.*

policy: a course of action planned by the government or by other decision takers.

policy conflict: it is frequently the case that policies conflict with one another in that the effect of one policy is to make another policy harder to achieve. For example, policies which are likely to reduce inflation are also likely to increase unemployment. Policies to persuade more firms and individuals to use the railways are likely to entail raising the cost of road use. This conflicts with the objective of keeping road use costs at a level acceptable to public opinion. There are many other examples. As Abraham Lincoln said, you can't please all the people all the time. (See also *macro-economic policy*.)

policy instrument: the means used to carry out a particular policy.
- Interest rates are the instrument used to implement *monetary policy*.
- Taxes and government expenditure can be used to create incentives and provide goods and services. *Incentives* are sometimes called *indirect controls*, because they work through their effect on people's decisions.
- Regulations are called *direct controls*, because they actually force people into a particular way of doing things, e.g. health and safety regulations.

policy package: some economic problems cannot be solved with a single policy. Supposing the government wanted to reduce air pollution by 50%. The causes of air pollution are quite varied so a range of policies would be required to deal with ozone, carbon monoxide, particulates and so on. The broader the policy objective, the more likely it is to require a policy package. Poverty, for example, has to be tackled in a whole range of ways.

poll tax: a fixed amount of tax which must be paid by each person as an individual.

polluter pays principle is the idea that polluting emissions should be taxed so that the businesses which create the pollution carry the full cost, i.e. both the private and the *social cost*, of the pollution they create. This involves internalising an external cost.

pollution: impurities which are allowed to escape into the environment. Air pollution comes from vehicles, power stations and industries. Water pollution comes from farms, sewage and industries. Efforts are being made to ensure that polluters clean up more effectively. *Business responsibility* is often now described as entailing a commitment not to pollute or to control the level of pollution. In practice there is still much to be done.

pollution charges can be used to discourage pollution. Usually, such charges will be taxes on polluters, levied in proportion to the scale of their emissions. The climate levy in the UK forces firms to pay escalating amounts as pollution rises above set levels. This gives them an incentive to install equipment which will reduce the amount of pollution.

pollution permit: a licence given by the government which allows a firm to emit polluting substances up to a certain level. By allowing less than the amount of pollution currently occurring, the government can reduce pollution overall. Over time, levels allowed by the licences can be reduced. (See also *tradable permits*.)

population: all the people within a defined area or group. Most commonly it refers to countries or regions, but it can be used to refer to a more closely defined group, e.g. car owners or NHS users.

population change: a change in the number of people in a given population. Changes may occur because of:
- immigration or emigration. Immigration can be stimulating to an economy. Immigrants are often looking for work and can increase the supply of *labour*. They may relieve known labour shortages. Some may bring entrepreneurial vigour to a market system. It is clear that this happened to the US in the 19th century
- changes in birth rates and/or death rates. Falling death rates have typically had a big impact on the populations of developing countries. Between 1990 and 2006, life

expectancy in India rose from 59 to 63. Over the long run, this kind of change can make a big difference to populations.

During the development process, birth rates are at first high but infant mortality rates fall as incomes rise and health care improves. So families often become larger. In time, rising incomes lead people to want fewer children. They can be fairly sure their children will live. They may become eligible for welfare payments in old age. The critical need for children, as an insurance policy against poverty, diminishes. Birth rates fall. This process is advancing rapidly in many Asian developing countries, followed closely by some Latin American countries. In large parts of sub-Saharan Africa it has yet to appear.

population control: in countries with high birth rates, limiting population growth is very important because it can raise per capita incomes. Different strategies have been tried in different places. China has the one-child policy, which has been a success in urban areas but not in rural areas where two thirds of the population still live. The Indian government has tried to promote vasectomy. However, these types of measures have really had limited success until people's incomes rise fast enough to improve their standards of living significantly. Then they seem to manage to control family size regardless of government policy. Italy, Japan, Germany and a number of other developed countries are likely to face falling population trends in the future unless they decide to encourage immigration. At the present time there are many countries with *ageing populations*. (See also *population change*.)

population growth: the rate at which the population increases. This may come from immigration or from a rising birth rate or a falling death rate. (See also *population change*.)

portfolio: the full range of assets held by an individual or a firm. A wealthy individual or firm might have property, *shares*, bank balances, perhaps held in more than one currency, and fixed interest securities such as *bonds*. Many individuals might have a selection of these types of assets and a pension plan of some value too. A major objective would be to spread risks, sometimes described as not having all one's eggs in the same basket or *diversification*. For this reason, most people would hold shares in several companies rather than just one.

portfolio investment means buying *financial assets* rather than direct investment. The latter would involve actually setting up productive capacity such as factories or retail outlets. The former involves buying shares, property, bonds or other financial assets.

positional goods are things which by their nature are fixed in supply and therefore, ultimately, accessible only to those who can afford to pay rising prices if demand increases. Examples include quiet beaches and unrestricted rural views. As population pressures and economic growth continue, demand for such things increases while supply diminishes, pushing the price up and limiting access to the relatively few people who can buy themselves a privileged position. Another example might be a seat on the centre court at Wimbledon or any other item the desirability of which is increased by its scarcity.

positive externalities are the external benefits that may result from a course of action. Sometimes they are called spillover effects because they bring some benefit to a third party, someone who is neither a producer nor a consumer of the product. The firm which builds an office block of some architectural merit improves the appearance of the neighbourhood. In this way it benefits anyone who appreciates the improvement. (See also *externalities*.)

positive statements can be checked against the facts in order to decide whether they are true. They contrast with *normative* statements, which involve value judgements and will reflect personal opinions.

post-tax profit: profit after *corporation tax* has been deducted. This can be kept as *retained profit* to finance future expansion or distributed as *dividends* to shareholders.

potential output is the maximum amount that can be produced when all of the resources in the economy are in use. Also known as *full-capacity output* or full employment output.

poverty is a situation in which people's *standard of living* is low. It may be measured in either absolute or relative terms. *Absolute poverty* means that a person's basic human needs for food, clothing and shelter are not being met and a poor standard of health may also result. This applies to people suffering from malnutrition or without homes. *Relative poverty* depends on the standards being applied and implies that within a particular society a given standard of living is unacceptably low. So people may be described as living in relative poverty if they are unable to participate in activities which are considered normal in that society, even though they have enough to eat and somewhere to live. Thus poverty may mean having basic needs satisfied but being unable to go to a football match or spend a short time at the pub or pay for children's books or outings.

There is some evidence that poverty is on the increase because *income distribution* has widened in the past 15 years, worldwide, under the impact of market forces.

poverty cycle: the sequence of low incomes leading to low savings, implying limited resources available for investment to increase output, low productivity and continuing low incomes. This can be seen in the *least developed countries.*

poverty line: an arbitrary dividing line which defines the income below which people are said to be living in poverty. This will vary from one country to another because exchange rates and prices do not necessarily coincide and because standards as to what is acceptable vary.

There is no single widely acceptable definition of world poverty but an income of less than US$1.25 per day is seen as unambiguously poor. Substantially reducing the number of people with incomes below this level has become a target for many organisations concerned with poverty, including the UN. There are currently around 1.4 billion people with less than $1.25 a day, mainly living in rural areas. This is 20% of the world population. 1.72 billion are living on less than $2 a day, 27% of the total.

In the UK, the income level at which benefits such as *income support* become available has been described as the poverty line. However, many people would argue that this level of income is insufficient to allow people to lead a normal life.

poverty trap: a situation in which a person may be worse off working than living on *means-tested benefits* because the marginal rate of taxation and the rate at which benefits are lost in combination remove the incentive effects of the earnings. This results from low *tax thresholds* combined with a sharp tapering off of means-tested benefits as income rises. Incentives have increased with the introduction of the *Working Families Tax Credit*.

PPP: see *purchasing power parity (PPP)*.

PPPs: see *public private partnerships (PPPs)*.

predatory pricing occurs when one firm sets its prices lower than those of its competitors, in the hope that one or more will be driven out of business because it cannot follow suit without making a loss which forces it to leave the market. The original firm can then raise prices to their old level again. Normally the price cutter will be a *market leader* with a chance of eliminating smaller competitors from the field and gaining *market power*. In 2005 BT was accused of predatory pricing of cordless phones. *OFCOM* investigated but found that BT had not abused its dominant position in the market even though its market share had increased in the relevant period.

premium can mean either an insurance premium or an extra amount paid for a particularly attractive product or asset. An insurance premium is the amount paid for the insurance policy, i.e. the right to reimbursement if the event insured against actually happens.

present value is the name given to the current value of a future income stream. This may be calculated using a *discount rate* when an investment project is being considered. (See also *investment appraisal*.)

pressure group: an organisation which represents the interests of a particular group of people. Oxfam is a pressure group which works to reduce poverty in developing countries. Its members are all people with a particular concern about the issues involved. Pressure groups include *employers' organisations*, *trade unions*, community organisations and charities. They bring pressure to bear by lobbying wherever help towards their cause may be obtained. Oxfam lobbies government organisations and international organisations such as the *WTO*.

price: the money value of anything which is bought and sold in the marketplace, including goods, services, assets and factors of production. In competitive markets price is determined by market forces, i.e. supply and demand. Businesses with some monopoly power may be able to decide prices within limits. In some cases prices are decided by governments, e.g. prescription prices in the UK or all prices in a *centrally planned economy*. Mostly, prices are displayed and known in advance. In some cases, they may be negotiated, depending on the quantity bought or the means of payment, or there may be a haggling process in which the price emerges as a compromise.

price agreements are generally illegal under *competition law* but may be arrived at by a group of firms (a *cartel*) trying to reduce the impact of competition on each other. They may agree to keep prices above a certain minimum level. So long as they all stick to the agreement, they will be acting collectively like a *monopoly* and will be able to keep quantities sold lower and prices higher than they would be if there were strong competition. A participant in a price agreement can go to the OFT with information so that it faces lower fines than the rest of the group if the OFT decides to prosecute.

price ceiling: a maximum price set by law. Most often this occurs where there is *regulation*, as with a *public utility*. In the past, rent controls have prevented rents from rising. The risk with a price ceiling is that if it is below the market clearing equilibrium, quantity supplied will in time be reduced.

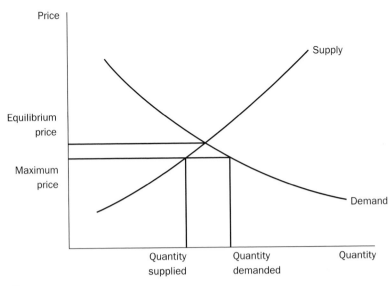

Price ceiling

price competition means the rivalry between firms which use price as a way of attracting consumers. It contrasts with non-price competition, which involves other ways of attracting consumers, e.g. through advertising.

price controls can be used to prevent prices from rising. However, they are seldom used because they tend to lead to excess demand which cannot be satisfied because there is no incentive for firms to increase output.

price deflation means generally falling prices.

price discrimination: charging different prices in different markets where there are different price elasticities of demand. For example, rail operators charge commuters much more than they charge travellers who start out after the morning rush. For commuters, demand for rail services is very inelastic because there is usually no substitute: alternative ways of getting to work would take too long or it may be impossible to park a car. Keeping the price high means high sales revenue.

Other travellers have choices. They may be able to travel by bus or by car or avoid travelling altogether. There are substitutes and demand is price elastic. Low fares may induce them to travel by train, so maximising revenue. The marginal cost of taking an extra passenger in the middle of the day is usually zero, so offering low fares means extra revenue at no extra cost. (See also *price elasticity of demand* for diagrammatic explanation.)

Price discrimination will not work unless it is possible to separate the two different markets effectively.

price elastic: a change in price leads to a proportionately larger change in quantity demanded. (See also *price elasticity of demand*.)

price elasticity of demand measures the extent to which a change in price leads to a change in quantity demanded.

FORMULA: $\dfrac{\text{percentage change in quantity demanded}}{\text{percentage change in price}}$

For example, if the price of a good rises by 10%, and the quantity demanded then falls by 20% price elasticity is: $-20\% \div +10\% = -2$

If the number is greater than one the product is said to be price elastic. A number between zero and one is said to be price inelastic. If price elasticity is zero, it is termed unit elasticity of demand.

A straight-line demand curve does not indicate constant elasticity of demand: it will vary all along the line.

Price elasticity of demand is a negative number because an increase in prices causes a fall in quantity demanded and vice versa. There is an *inverse relationship*. As this is always true the minus sign is sometimes ignored in discussing the value of price elasticity. It should never be ignored when doing calculations.

Price elasticity of demand has a number of features:

- The most important factor in deciding elasticity of demand is whether **substitutes** are available. If there are, people will shop around and if the price rises, they will switch to an alternative. If there are no good substitutes, the demand will be inelastic. Often the elasticity depends on how tightly defined the product happens to be. The demand for toothpaste is inelastic because there are no acceptable substitutes so far as most people are concerned. But the demand for Colgate toothpaste may be quite elastic because a price rise may lead people to choose another brand.
- A second factor of relevance in determining price elasticity is the amount spent on the product in question. Where the price is low relative to the income available, demand is likely to be inelastic. Demand for a packet of crisps or a box of matches is usually inelastic.
- Time can be another factor. Sometimes information about price changes takes time to reach people. Then it may take a while for people to adjust to a price change. In the short run, a big increase in the price of petrol will make only a little difference to the demand for it. People who have cars will continue to use them for journeys they consider essential, getting to work, shopping and visiting family. In the long run, demand may be less inelastic. Some people will find alternative ways to travel and the car makers will have a bigger incentive to design fuel-efficient cars.
- There is a link between price elasticity of demand and sales revenue. If demand is elastic and prices rise, the greater-than-proportionate fall in quantity sold will mean that sales revenue will fall and vice versa. In the diagram, the box showing lost revenue is larger than the box showing gained revenue. With inelastic demand, a price increase will result in a rise in sales revenue. In the diagram that follows, the box representing revenue gained is larger than the box representing revenue lost.

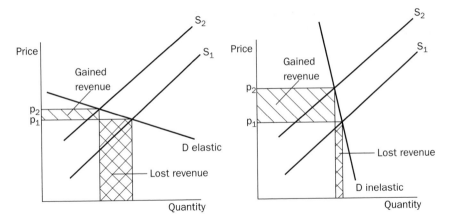

- Price elasticity of demand is of considerable significance because it may affect decisions about price. Raising the price of an item which has elastic demand may not help to cover rising costs. Also price elasticity affects the impact of certain indirect taxes, e.g. those on petrol, alcohol and tobacco (see also *tax incidence*) and of *tariffs* and *quotas* on imports.

price elasticity of supply: see *supply elasticity.*

price fixing occurs when two or more firms agree to charge a minimum price. This is defined as an anti-competitive activity. (See also *price agreement*.)

price floor: a minimum price set by law. The commonest example comes from the guaranteed prices of the *Common Agricultural Policy (CAP)* of the EU. Farmers receive a set price for most of their crop and animal products. The CAP authorities guarantee to buy all that is produced. If this is above the equilibrium market price, the outcome will be an excess supply which has to be bought and stored (in the diagram, Q_S–Q_D). In the past this has made the CAP very expensive and has raised food prices above the world level. Now the level of guaranteed prices has been reduced somewhat.

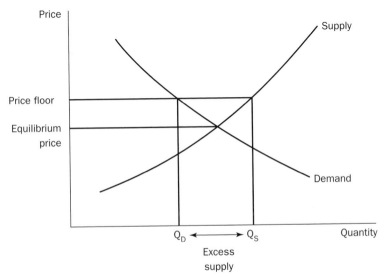

A price floor leading to excess supply

price index: a way of measuring changes in the general level of prices using index numbers. The *retail price index (RPI)* measures inflation generally. The wholesale price index measures changes in wholesale prices and provides a useful leading indicator of inflation. The *consumer price index (CPI)* measures inflation in a way that allows international comparisons.

price inelastic: see *inelastic demand*.

price leader: a firm with sufficient market power to decide on a price change which its competitors will tend to follow. This will be the *dominant firm* in the industry and perhaps also the largest. Often, all the competitors will be facing similar changes in costs and all follow the lead given by the price leader. This would be likely to occur in an *oligopoly* situation.

price level: the average level of prices of all consumer goods and services. This is measured by the *retail price index (RPI)*.

price maker: another term for *price leader*. It contrasts with *price taker*, the firm which follows the price leader.

price mechanism is the means by which resources are allocated in a *market economy*. Price rations the available resources among competing buyers. Rising demand tends to push up prices. This gives producers higher profits, which act as an incentive to increase the quantity supplied. Similarly, falling demand leads to lower prices and lower profits. If a loss is made, some producers will close down and the quantity supplied will fall.

The price mechanism works in the market for factors of production as well. If, for example, *labour* becomes scarce, wages in the occupation concerned will rise and costs of production will rise too. Producers will seek to pass the cost on to consumers in higher prices. Some people will switch to substitutes or reduce consumption. This may lead to lower levels of production.

As wages rose generally, the price of hiring servants rose. Quantity demanded fell. People did their own cleaning, in time switching to vacuum cleaners and other machines. A whole occupation more or less disappeared, changing the allocation of resources dramatically, though over a long period. (See also *profit-signalling mechanism*.)

price rigidity: the tendency of prices to stay the same and to change very little over time. This is most likely to happen in an *oligopoly*, where firms may try to avoid competing on price. Instead they will engage in non-price competition.

price sensitive means that the product is *price elastic*. A given change in price will lead to a proportionately higher change in quantity demanded. Some products are much more price sensitive than others. Compare the likely change in quantity demanded resulting from a 10% increase in price of petrol and skiing holidays.

price stability means that the price level rises slowly and the rate of inflation does not fluctuate greatly. The current target for the UK inflation rate is 2.0% per year. The Bank of England is charged with ensuring that it stays within 1% of this target. A low rate of inflation (rather than a zero rate) is generally thought to provide the best conditions for a flexible economy. Wage rates and prices often rise in response to increases in demand, creating incentives for resources to move into products for which consumer demand is increasing. Because both wages and prices tend to be sticky downwards at times, an increase of less than 2.0% (i.e. a relative fall) may be easier to achieve than an actual cut. It will still give the same useful signal of changes in demand which require resources to move from a declining industry into a line of production for which demand is growing.

price stickiness: the tendency for prices to rise but not often to fall. This does not really apply to individual products, where price cuts may be found. It refers to the tendency of the average price level to rise. (See also *price stability*.)

price subsidy: a payment to producers from the government which will enable them to charge a lower price for the product. Subsidies are often used to help sell EU exports of agricultural products. (See also *subsidy*.)

price supports are used where governments want to keep prices above their free market level. This can be done if the government is willing to buy the surplus which develops. The *Common Agricultural Policy (CAP)* of the European Union provides an example of the extensive use of price supports. (See also *price floor*.)

price system: the mechanism which causes prices to rise when demand exceeds supply, and vice versa, so ensuring that prices send signals to producers about the nature of changes in consumer demand. This in turn enables the *allocation of resources* to change in response to consumers, thus preserving *consumer sovereignty*. (See also *price mechanism*.)

price taker: a firm which sells at the price prevailing in the market. It will face strong competition and will not be able to sell its product at a higher price. This may be because there is a *price maker*, a large and powerful producer, in an *oligopoly* market. Or it may be because there are many quite small producers, all competing strongly.

price theory: the area of economics which is concerned with the determination of price, through the study of demand and supply and their interaction. The focus of price theory is on *equilibrium* and disequilibrium prices and it seeks to predict the outcome of a variety of possible changes in the marketplace.

price transparency: a situation in which it is easy to compare the prices of different competing producers. The euro makes for greater price transparency within the euro zone, than when prices were given in different currencies. This may be important in the car market, for example.

price war: a series of competing price cuts which are likely to lead to losses for some or all of the competitors. Price wars are usually associated with an *oligopoly*. They may be started by a dominant firm with a *predatory pricing* strategy and an objective of driving one of the smaller players out of the market. They occur from time to time among newspapers, package holidays and petrol companies, among others. They usually do not last very long because profits are likely to be reduced for all. They will be followed by a much longer period of *price rigidity*.

prices and incomes policies were used in the past as a way to reduce the rate of inflation. Actual upper limits on rises were set by the government. The policies were not very successful.

primary product dependency arises when *developing economies* have to rely upon primary product exports for most of their foreign exchange needs. Many of them have large primary sectors, relative to their *secondary* and *tertiary sectors*. They have few if any manufactured products in which they have a *comparative advantage*. But many primary products have fluctuating prices and some of these exports therefore are not a very reliable source of revenue.

primary products are produced directly from natural resources in agriculture, fishing, forestry, mining and quarrying and oil extraction.

primary research is gathered directly from its source, rather than looked up in books and databases created by others. Firms often carry out their own market research using interviews: this is primary research. Investigating sources of data already collected is called desk research.

primary sector: all producers engaged in agriculture, fishing, forestry, mining, quarrying and oil extraction.

principal–agent problem: consumers and firms often need to employ agents, for example to give professional advice that the principal needs in order to make a good decision. The problem is that there may be **asymmetric information** and the agent may not act in the principal's best interests. For example, you may go to an estate agent to buy a home, precisely because you do not know much about the local housing market. But the agent may conceal information about a property, without your realising, and may do so in order to achieve a speedy sale. In a firm, the principals may be the shareholders, who employ the management to run the business, or the management, where the agents are the employees lower down the ladder. The agents may choose to run the business in a way that takes little effort, where the shareholders would prefer an energetic search for profit. The latter may be unable to get the information needed to show that this is happening.

printing money refers to the ways in which **central banks** can increase **liquidity** in the economy. This is currently called **quantitative easing**. It may involve lending money to banks and buying bonds and other assets. It has for long been a dirty word because it can be associated with inflationary policies and excessive government borrowing. However, inflation will not accelerate if aggregate demand is less than aggregate supply, as in 2009. (See also **output gap**.)

prisoners' dilemma: a **game theory** idea, based on the situation of two prisoners who must decide whether to confess, without knowing whether the other will or not, when confession carries the possibility of a lighter punishment. This is akin to competitors in a duopoly. They are not allowed to collude by law, but they will be greatly affected by each other's pricing strategies.

A **profit pay-off matrix** shows what will happen in all four different outcomes.

private benefits are the benefits which accrue to the individual buyer and seller of a product. In contrast, the **external benefits** are those which accrue to third parties. For example, if a large new factory is built, shopkeepers close to the area where employees of the new factory live will probably find that their profits are rising because of the increase in incomes in the area.

private costs are the costs of production which are borne by the business which produces the product. For example, private costs will include wages and salaries, interest and the costs of raw materials and components, as well as any research and development costs. They do not include **external costs**, i.e. those which are borne by third parties. These might be the costs to health and welfare of pollution which results from the production process.

private enterprise includes all economic activities which are undertaken for **profit** within the **private sector**. The owners of the business will be individuals operating as sole traders or as shareholders or other private sector organisations. In contrast, **public enterprise** involves the government. Private enterprise is normally subject to market forces, with decisions being made according to conditions of demand and supply.

Private Finance Initiative (PFI): a strategy begun in 1992 to invest in UK *infrastructure* using a mixture of private and public sector funding. The objective was to modernise the infrastructure without being committed to a big increase in government spending. It has been used to encourage private sector approaches to increasing the efficiency of building programmes in health, education and transport. Projects are run by private sector contractors, using private sector funds. The public sector body concerned undertakes to pay an annual fee for a given length of time (sometimes 20 years) which covers the costs. The most controversial plan is to modernise the London Underground through a PFI. It is still too soon to say whether the costs of PFIs are worth the benefits. Some projects have delivered on time at reasonable cost while others have not. (See also *public private partnerships*.)

private goods: items bought and consumed by individuals for their own benefit. Most goods and services come into this category. The distinguishing feature of private goods is that there is *rivalry* in consumption. Once consumed by one person they cannot be consumed by another. Other people are said to be excluded from consumption. There is rivalry in that consumers are competing with one another to obtain the goods they want. In contrast, *public goods* are those which must be provided by the public sector if we are to have them at all. No one will be excluded from benefiting from them and there will be no rivalry in consumption.

private limited company: a business set up under company law with shareholders and *limited liability (Ltd)*. It is private in that the shares cannot be bought or sold without the consent of all the existing shareholders.

private marginal cost: the extra cost of producing one more unit which is borne by the producer. (See also *marginal social cost*.)

private property: *assets* and goods owned by individuals who have a right to use them as they please which is recognised by the law. In contrast, public property is owned by local or national government. The right to use private property as the owner pleases is usually constrained to some degree, for example through planning permission.

private sector: all the firms which are owned by shareholders or individuals. Within the private sector, decisions are made on the basis of *market forces*, with businesses responding to the conditions of supply and demand so that changes in consumer demand will be reflected in decisions about what to produce. Approximately 60% of economic activity is conducted in the private sector, with the other 40% being public sector activity. Some activities, e.g. street cleaning, are financed by local or national government but actually carried out by the private sector.

privatisation: transferring economic activity out of the public sector and into the private sector. Privatisation was an important element in the policies of the Conservative government elected in 1979 although it took several years to get under way. Privatisation took several forms:

- The nationalised industries were sold to the public, mainly from 1984 onwards. During the late 1940s, many industries had been nationalised, including coal mining, the railways, British Airways, BT, gas, electricity and water. Iron and steel had been nationalised in 1966. Some of these which did not necessarily face strong competition were given regulatory bodies to protect the interests of consumers, e.g. OFGEM.

- Tenants of council houses were given the right to buy their homes at favourable prices. Between 1979 and 1997, 1.4 million dwellings were sold.
- Some public services were contracted out to the private sector, e.g. buses, school meals and refuse collection. Many homes that were not bought by their tenants were sold to housing associations, voluntary sector bodies that may be able to run them more efficiently.

Many of the nationalised industries were actually declining and privatisation made it somewhat easier to close down parts of them. Others were very profitable, e.g. BT, and their sale sparked off a big increase in the number of people who owned shares. On the whole the privatised industries have become more efficient when subjected to market forces.

There are still many controversial issues pertaining to privatisation. Much depends on the way in which the *regulators* operate. The Post Office may soon be part privatised but this is opposed by the workforce and the trade unions involved.

process innovation: improvements in the way a product is produced, arising from new technologies. This is a powerful way to cut costs and become more efficient for many businesses. It can lead to big increases in *productivity*.

procurement means the purchase of goods and services by governments. Very large contracts are involved, e.g. for aircraft for the defence forces. In the past it has been quite normal for governments to favour domestic producers, but procurement contracts are being gradually opened up to competition within the EU. The issues may be discussed further within the *WTO*.

producer goods are goods bought as inputs into the production process for consumer goods and services.

producer objectives: see *business objectives*.

producer price index: an average measure of the prices of goods and services sold on a business-to-business basis. There are two distinct types:
- the average price of inputs to firms' production processes
- the average price of output sold wholesale.

These indices give an early warning of rising costs which could feed through into accelerating inflation.

producer surplus: the difference between the amount that buyers are willing to pay and the amount needed to induce the producer to continue supplying them at the same level. This is actually the same as profit – total revenue minus total cost. The supply curve shows the amounts producers are prepared to supply at a range of prices. The firm will stop increasing output if the price is just equal to the marginal cost of production. Any more than that would entail a loss on the extra output. But for all the output up to that point, the producer is getting a price above the marginal cost of production; this is the producer surplus. If there is an increase in price because the demand curve has shifted rightwards, producer surplus will increase.

Producer surplus can be calculated using the price and quantity data on the diagram. (Most readers will not need to do this.)

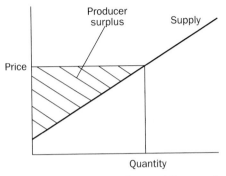

Producer surplus is the area between the price line and the supply curve

product differentiation: see *differentiated product*.

production means the use of real resources to contribute to the creation of a final product. It applies to both goods and services. In practice, however, it is most often used when considering *primary products* and manufactures.

production costs: see *cost*.

production function: a mathematical relationship which links the quantities of inputs to the production process to the quantity of output.

production possibility curve: see *production possibility frontier*.

production possibility frontier: within an economy, real resources are finite and scarce in relation to demand. *Scarcity* means that *choices* must be made. The PPF is based on a two-product economy and shows the range of combinations that may be chosen if all resources are being fully utilised. It is usually shown in diagrammatic form as a curve which is concave to the origin, because resources vary as to the efficiency with which they can be used to produce particular items.

The curve shows the *opportunity cost* in terms of loss of one product if it is decided to produce a little more of the other product. Giving up some of one product may be possible but may not lead to much more of the other product being produced, if all the resources suited to its production have already been used.

Combinations of products outside the frontier (e.g. at point A on the diagram overleaf) are impossible because they require more resources than are currently available. Combinations of products inside the frontier (e.g. at point B) entail unemployment of **labour** or capital or both. If the quantity of resources available increases, e.g. as a result of investment, then the frontier may shift outwards, allowing more of both goods to be produced, i.e. economic growth.

If it is possible to increase output of just one of the two products, the curve will show a skewed shift.

(If you are studying the WJEC course, you need to know that a straight-line PPF indicates that all resources are perfectly capable of producing either product and can be substituted for one another without any change in the opportunity cost.)

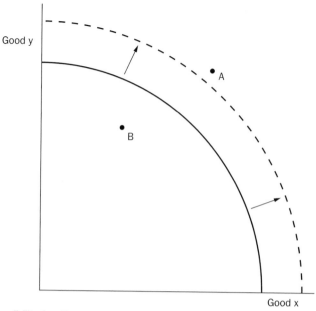

Production possibility frontier

productive capacity refers to the ability of the economy to produce. An increase in productive capacity, which might result from an increase in investment, implies that it will be possible to increase output.

productive efficiency: a production process is said to be productively efficient if the costs of production have been minimised by economising in the use of real resources. It is one element in *economic efficiency* and is achieved when average total cost is at its minimum point. Achieving productive efficiency involves using the lowest cost resource inputs in the most effective way, e.g. by avoiding wasted inputs and co-ordinating production to avoid wasting time. *Economies of scale* are often important in achieving productive efficiency.

productive potential: see *productive capacity*.

productivity measures the efficiency with which resources are used. The most commonly used productivity measure is output per person employed. When people speak of productivity, this is usually what they mean. However, it is possible also to measure output per unit of capital employed – the productivity of capital. Productivity can be measured within the individual firm or for the economy as a whole.

On the international level, differing levels of productivity growth (efficiency) are important in explaining variations in industrial performance and rates of economic growth. These in turn have a major impact on standards of living. In recent years, productivity growth in the UK has improved. Productivity grows for a number of reasons including:
- increased capital investment, so that *labour* inputs are working with better quality or larger amounts of capital equipment
- technological change, so that production processes are more efficient
- improved management techniques, so that people work more effectively together. Examples of the possibilities would be *multi-skilling* and *teamwork*.

Rising productivity can cause unemployment, which may persist for a number of years, if demand does not rise as fast as the productivity gains. Despite this, it is difficult for an economy to grow healthily in the long run without productivity improvements. In the past, UK productivity grew very slowly compared to other developed countries, but since the early 1990s, productivity has much improved, though there is still concern in some industries.

Productivity increase, annual average growth, 2001–07

US	Japan	France	Germany	Italy	UK
2.0	2.1	1.7	1.3	-0.1	2.1

Source: OECD

productivity bonus: a cash incentive to keep production at or above a target level. Some employers try to link pay increases to productivity in order to keep *unit costs* from rising and stay competitive.

productivity deal: part of a pay negotiation which links the pay increase to productivity improvements. These may involve changed ways of working which help to use the workforce more efficiently.

profit: a simple definition of profit is what is left from sales revenue after costs have been deducted. Profit is also a return on capital invested: it compensates the owner of the capital for the loss of the capital for any other potential use.

Economists distinguish *normal* and *supernormal profit*. The former is that amount of profit which is just sufficient to keep the resources employed in their current use. The latter is profit in excess of this amount and indicates that buyers are prepared to pay a price above the costs of all the resources used in production. In time this will attract more resources into production and increase output in line with consumer demand. (See also *profit-signalling mechanism*.)

FORMULA: revenue − costs = profit

profit and loss account: part of a firm's annual report and accounts which gives a record of costs and revenues for the year. *Gross profit*, *operating (or net) profit*, profit before and after tax and *retained profit* will all be shown.

profit margin: profit as a percentage of sales revenue.

profit maximisation: in economic theory it is usually assumed that firms always maximise profits. Although many firms do have other objectives, profit is necessary for survival and is also likely to be a consequence of pursuing these other objectives. So the assumption can still give useful predictions. In practice:

- many firms look for long-term profit and may not maximise profits in the short run. Sales maximisation may be their main objective in the short run and this may bring with it increased *market power*
- other firms may take quite the opposite view, neglecting long-term planning in order to maximise profit in the short run. This is sometimes called *short-termism*
- another possible strategy is *satisficing* – earning enough profit to stay comfortably in business. Small businesses sometimes ignore opportunities to expand because they are comfortable with their existing scale of production.

The theoretical profit-maximising output for any firm will be at the point where **marginal cost** is equal to **marginal revenue**. Under **perfect competition**, marginal revenue will be equal to price (diagram A). Under **imperfect competition**, marginal revenue will tend to fall as output and sales increase, because prices will fall (diagram B). In both cases, at point A on the diagram, profits are less than they could be if output was increased, because the extra output would cost less than the revenue brought in. At point B profits are less than they could be (and losses may be made) because output above the profit-maximising level costs more to produce than it gains in revenue.

Diagram A

Diagram B

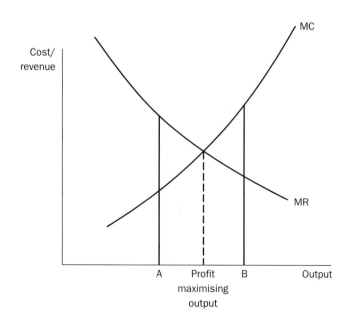

profit motive: the objective of the *entrepreneur*, who will seek sales revenue over and above the level of costs of production, as a reward for taking risks and organising the business. Economic analysis usually rests on an assumption that all entrepreneurs are motivated by profit. In fact, although it is important to make a profit to ensure long-term survival, many businesses have other motives as well. (See also *profit maximisation*.)

profit pay-off matrix: this is a game theory tool which can be used in a *duopoly* or *oligopoly* situation to show how each firm's best strategy depends on the reactions of competing firms. Firms are said to be interdependent.

Using the diagram below, within the matrix, firm X has the lower triangle in each quadrant and firm Y the higher triangle. HP is the high price strategy and LP the low price strategy. If both firms X and Y maintain high prices, profits will be 10 each, as in the top left quadrant of the diagram. If X thinks Y may keep to the high price, it will be better off cutting its price. It will make profits of 14, while Y will make 2. Alternatively, if Y takes this position and X maintains a high price, the position will be reversed. If in fact both cut prices together, both will have reduced profits of 6 each. (This is the *price war* type of outcome.) The least risky course of action is to stick to a high price strategy – hence *price rigidity* is very likely in this situation.

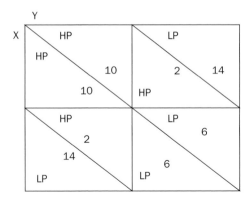

profit-related pay: earnings which are directly related to the *profit* levels of the employer. While this can give employees an incentive and a stake in the company, it may be hard for them to see their role in increasing profits.

profit-signalling mechanism: when demand for a product is increasing, prices will tend to rise and the product therefore becomes more profitable. This encourages entrepreneurs to expand output in profitable lines of production by moving resources into them. When losses are being made the reverse happens: resources will be moved out of the unprofitable lines. In this way profits signal the existence of unsatisfied consumer demand and ensure that the allocation of resources falls into line with the pattern of consumer demand. This link between the pattern of demand and the allocation of resources is an important element in the working of the *market system* (see diagram overleaf).

Profit-signalling mechanism

progressive tax: one which takes in tax a higher proportion of high incomes than it does of low incomes. The most important example is *income tax*. Having a tax-free allowance means that people on lower incomes are taxed on a smaller proportion of their incomes than people on higher incomes.

property rights: all economic goods are associated with property rights and their owners have the right to decide how they may be used. Owners of *assets* have a right to charge people who want to make use of those assets. For example, owners of fishing rights may charge for the use of them by other people. The term is often used in connection with *intellectual property* rights such as copyright and patents. Extending property rights can be useful in correcting market failures. For example, if it is established that those who suffer from pollution (e.g. from a local chemical plant) have the right to be free of it, polluters can be required to pay compensation.

proportional tax: a tax which takes an equal proportion of income whatever the person's income level.

protectionism involves any policy which protects domestic producers from international competition. Measures used might include any barrier to trade: *quotas*, *tariffs* and *non-tariff barriers (NTBs)*. These will raise the price of the imports to which they apply, so reducing the threat to domestic producers.

Protectionism can reduce the benefits of free trade in terms of consumer access to cheap products and enhanced economic growth. It is therefore discouraged by WTO rules and has been reduced through international trade negotiations. There are still many protectionist measures operating in some countries and it has a significant effect on the trading prospects of some of the *developing economies*.

The most notorious period of protectionism was between the two world wars, during the *Great Depression*, when country after country put up barriers in the hope that unemployment would not increase. The barriers made unemployment worse: they reduced exports for all concerned. At international meetings in early 2009 world leaders said that they would not make this mistake again.

Despite the benefits of trade generally, people with vested interests in certain industries are sometimes able to bring pressure to bear on their MPs or Congressional representatives so that they will support protectionist measures. For example, at times the EU and the USA have required *voluntary export restraints (VERs)* on imports from the Far East of cars, steel and electronic goods. Sometimes *anti-dumping measures* are used to exclude imports.

proven reserves: known amounts of crude oil which are underground (or under the sea) which would be economic to extract at current oil prices. There is much more oil which could be retrieved economically if the price were to rise.

PSDR: see *public sector debt repayment*.

public borrowing means borrowing by the government to finance current and capital expenditure. (See *public sector net borrowing*.)

public choice: the choice of goods and services to be provided by the government. Overall, this is a matter of great complexity. Governments respond to public opinion and to media views to a degree, but many of the more complex decisions have to be made in the context of the relationship between the government and the civil service.

public corporation: the legal basis for the formation of a *nationalised industry*. The BBC is an example.

public enterprise refers to state-owned organisations, i.e. *nationalised industries*, which produce for the market, for example the Post Office (for now).

public expenditure is spending by the government, for example on social security, defence, education and health. Public expenditure in recent years has been averaging around 42% of GDP. (See also *fiscal policy* and *government expenditure*.)

public finance refers to government expenditure and the ways in which it is financed through taxation and *public sector borrowing*.

public goods are items which must be provided by society as a whole for two reasons. No one can be excluded from benefiting from them. (If provided by the private sector, *free riders* would benefit.) And their consumption by one person does not prevent their consumption by someone else, i.e. they are non-rivalrous. Examples include street lighting, defence and the police force. These are pure public goods.

Quasi or non-pure public goods *could* be provided by the private sector if a way can be found to exclude free riders, e.g. by charging for their use, as with roads like the M6 toll road that skirts round the north of Birmingham. But a case can be made for providing any non-rivalrous product or facility free of charge so as to avoid *underconsumption*. Another example would be picnic table in a public park. However, these kinds of resources can become congested and then rivalry is present. Think of a hot day on the beach.

The provision of public goods by governments can be affected by *government failure*. Market intervention always requires accurate information both about the problems arising from free market decisions and about the likely impact of the government response. Full information is seldom available in advance. Furthermore, there may be uncertainty as to the value of the government's chosen solutions.

public interest: the interests of society as a whole. The term is usually used in relation to the actions of the public sector, in particular of the remaining nationalised industries and the regulatory bodies set up to monitor the privatised industries (e.g. *OFGEM*). These are charged with acting in the public interest. This needs constant reinterpretation in the light of changing circumstances but can be loosely defined as protecting the consumer and the community from hidden or unnecessary costs.

public limited company (PLC): a company with *limited liability (Ltd)* and shares which can be bought by the general public. PLCs are the only type of company which can be quoted on the *Stock Exchange*. The drawbacks of being a quoted company are illustrated by Richard Branson of Virgin. He decided that having become a public company he wished to return to the status of *private limited company* again to avoid the loss of control and the share price fluctuations which accompany quotations on the Stock Exchange. (See also *divorce of ownership and control*.)

public ownership refers to *nationalised industries*, which produce for the market but are owned by the government and are therefore part of the *public sector*.

public private partnerships (PPPs) can be used by governments to induce private sector companies to contribute to investment in the development of public services. For example, regeneration of run-down areas can involve government agencies in planning a variety of developments alongside private building projects. In return for planning permission or a share of the revenue, the government may persuade private sector firms to contribute new roads or other assets useful to the community. PPPs have also been used to fund school and hospital buildings and to develop public transport. (See also *Private Finance Initiative*.)

public sector: that part of the economy which is organised directly or indirectly by national or local government. It includes the civil service, the NHS, all the services run by local government (e.g. education and refuse collection) and the few remaining *nationalised industries*. Decisions will tend to be made in the public interest, rather than on the basis of profitability, although some activities are required to cover their costs (as with the Post Office and the BBC).

public sector borrowing: total borrowing by the *public sector*. *Public sector net borrowing* shows the amount of borrowing needed in the current year to cover the government deficit when expenditure exceeds taxation. The *National Debt* is the total loan outstanding, accumulated over many years. If there is a surplus of tax revenue over government expenditure, there will be a PSDR, *public sector debt repayment*. This will reduce the National Debt.

public sector debt repayment (PSDR): if government expenditure is less than tax revenue, then the government will be able to pay off some of its debts. This occurred from 1987–1990, partly because the government was receiving large payments for shares in the privatised industries. It occurred again in 1999–2000 as the economy grew and tax revenues rose.

public sector net borrowing is the amount by which *government expenditure* exceeds revenue from taxation and other income. It varies from year to year, depending on government policies at the time and on the state of the *economic cycle*.

The mechanism for borrowing may be the sale of Treasury *bonds* or *bills* or the encouragement of *National Savings*. High levels of borrowing may necessitate high interest rates, in order to encourage people and organisations to buy Treasury bonds. This can be a problem if the result is to make borrowing more expensive for businesses that want to invest. It also means that there is a link between the way government expenditures are financed and **monetary policy**. High levels of borrowing can make it difficult to pursue prudent monetary policies in order to reduce inflation. Borrowing increases in times of **recession** as tax revenues tend to fall and expenditure on benefits increases. The reverse may happen in a boom.

Public sector net borrowing as % of GDP

2003	2004	2005	2006	2007	2008	2009 (est)	2010 (est)
3.0	3.4	3.0	2.3	2.4	8	10	9

Source: HM Treasury

The Budget of 2009 revealed a massive increase in public borrowing which will be very difficult to deal with. In order to borrow so heavily, interest rates on bonds will probably have to rise.

A negative figure would imply that there is a **public sector debt repayment**. Some governments at times have difficulty in keeping borrowing under control. One of the requirements for entry to the EMU is that borrowing be less than 3% of GDP per year. The various rules which have been applied to levels of public borrowing are usually relaxed in times of recession.

public sector net cash requirement (PSNCR): a technical term that means much the same as *public sector net borrowing*.

public spending: see *government expenditure*.

public utility: the suppliers of basic services to homes and businesses, including water, gas and electricity. These are *privatised industries* with *regulators* to protect consumers from the *market power* of the companies.

public works: expenditure by the government on *infrastructure* or socially useful projects, which may be of particular value in times of high unemployment.

pump priming: a term used much in the past to describe government spending which may be able to increase economic activity in a depressed area. For example, building new roads creates jobs for unemployed people; it may also improve communications and have a *multiplier* effect.

purchasing power: the real value of a given sum of money in terms of what it will buy. Inflation causes the purchasing power of the currency to fall.

purchasing power parity (PPP): an approach to international comparisons of standards of living which takes into account price levels in different countries. It uses exchange rates which have been adjusted to give accurate comparisons of purchasing power.

quality assurance: all measures taken to ensure that quality standards are actually reached.

quality control: checking the quality of a product. Usually this term is applied in manufacturing processes, meaning checking that both inputs and outputs are made to the correct specifications.

quality of life: recent research into the cost-effectiveness of particular medical treatments now measures quality of life achieved. This is an improvement on merely measuring mortality rates because it takes into account what people can do as a result of their treatments and not just whether they are alive.

quango: see *quasi-autonomous non-governmental organisation*.

quantitative easing was proposed in 2008 as a way of providing an additional monetary stimulus to reduce the impact of recession. Interest rates had already been reduced as far as they could be, and banks were still finding it difficult to maintain lending. Early in 2009, the Bank of England began buying bills and bonds, exchanging them for cash which would increase bank deposits. This has the effect of increasing the money supply and giving banks more liquidity. Many other central banks implemented similar policies at the same time. (In the US it is called credit easing.)

This is sometimes described as *printing money* and, if carried too far, it could lead eventually to inflation. But at the time it was introduced there was a significant risk of deflation occurring, which could turn out to be even more problematic.

quantity demanded: the specific amount of a product which consumers want to buy at a particular price. This is different from *demand*, which refers to the amounts demanded at a range of different prices (the *demand curve*).

quantity of money: the amount of money available in the economy. (See also *broad money* and *narrow money*.)

quantity theory of money: the theory which links the quantity of money in circulation with the rate of *inflation*. The simplest version of this is given by the *equation of exchange*. This states that MV = PT, where M is the quantity of money, V is the *velocity of circulation*, P is the price level and T is the number of transactions. (In itself, this is in fact an identity: it is true by definition.) The theory holds that if M rises while V and T are constant, P will also rise.

This theory was important in economics in the early part of the 20th century but was superseded when Keynes and other economists observed that V and T might not be stable. It was replaced by a more sophisticated theory relating money and prices, developed by the proponents of **monetarism**, of whom the most notable was **Milton Friedman**. These ideas were influential during the early 1980s and became associated with Margaret Thatcher's time as prime minister. The policy prescription which resulted from monetarism was one of strict monetary control which would bring down the rate of inflation.

The quantity theory of money may offer some useful insights when the economy starts to recover from recession.

quartile: the observation which lies one quarter of the way through the population being studied. It is similar to the median or middle observation. The upper quartile will be three quarters of the way through the population, in ascending order. The lower quartile will be one quarter of the way through. This means that, say, people with incomes below the lower quartile level will be the quarter of the population with the lowest incomes.

quasi-autonomous non-governmental organisations (quangos) are bodies appointed by the government which are nevertheless independent of it. Their objectives are clearly laid down by the government but they are not subject to regular interference by it in their actual operation. They have been used to try to reduce the size of central government. The Equality and Human Rights Commission is an example.

quasi-public goods: goods which have some features of **public goods**.

quintile: the observation one fifth of the way through the population. So the lowest quintile would be the observation 20% of the way up a population arranged in ascending order. The term is also often used to refer to fifths of the total population.

quota (IMF): the money paid into the **International Monetary Fund (IMF)** by each member country. This will determine its voting power and the amount which can be borrowed in the event of a balance of payments emergency.

quotas (import): an **import control** which places a fixed limit on the quantity of the good which can be imported. The objective is usually to protect domestic producers. The supply of the imports will be reduced and the price will usually rise.

The more inelastic the demand for the imported product, the more the price is likely to rise. Above the level of the quota, the supply is fixed and the price is demand determined (see diagram overleaf).

A common form of quota is the **voluntary export restraint (VER)**; these have been placed on imports of cars, electronic goods and steel to the EU and the USA from the Far East. Quotas are strongly discouraged by the **WTO** but are nevertheless widespread in some product areas. This is because there has been support in recent years for protectionist policies on the grounds that they may save jobs. In reality it is likely that the loss of output caused by the restraint on trade is more serious for standards of living than the loss of jobs.

The effect of a quota

quoted company: a firm that has its shares listed on the *Stock Exchange*.

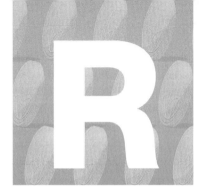

R & D: see *research and development (R & D)*.

race relations legislation makes it illegal to discriminate against people at work on grounds of colour, race, ethnic or national origin. The *Equality and Human Rights Commission* can investigate and pursue employers or *trade unions* which are thought to discriminate.

racial discrimination means refusing a job or a promotion to someone on grounds of race. Although it is illegal, recent studies show that it is still occurring. It is sometimes difficult to prove in individual cases. Unemployment rates amongst different ethnic groups are too large to be explained entirely by differences in qualifications.

random sample: a sample selected at random from a population being researched, so that it is likely to be representative of the population as a whole.

rate of interest: the amount which will have to be paid annually for the loan of funds. This will be higher for risky borrowers than it is for known, reputable borrowers. The lowest interest rates are those used by banks when they lend to each other. (See also *interest rates*.)

rate of return: a measure of the profit earned in relation to capital invested. Various definitions of profit may be used and comparisons of different investments may be made in order to determine which is most profitable.

rate support grant: the old name for *revenue support grant*.

rates are taxes paid by businesses to the local authority in their area and are usually known as the *Uniform Business Rate*. Rates used to be payable on all properties but now individuals pay *council tax*.

rating agencies are firms that specialise in assessing risks. Banks use them to provide risk ratings. They have been blamed for giving excessively favourable ratings to debts that turned out to be very risky indeed, during the run-up to the 2007–09 financial crisis. This meant that potential asset buyers were given very inaccurate information and made decisions to buy what became known as *toxic assets*, which, if fully informed, they might not have wanted to buy. The two biggest agencies involved are Moody's and Standard & Poor's. Many of the ratings were based on unrealistic assumptions, such as that house prices would continue to rise indefinitely.

rational expectations: an economic theory which holds that because people learn from past experience, their reactions can be predicted, for example in relation to inflation. The theory was an important element in the body of thinking known as *monetarism*, which was particularly influential in the early 1980s. After that it became clear that people sometimes take some time to learn from past experience and therefore there may be long time lags in their reactions.

rationalisation: closing down parts of a firm which duplicate functions. This often happens after a merger but may happen wherever the firm is trying actively to cut costs. When the Royal Bank of Scotland bought the National Westminster Bank, rationalisation (i.e. closing branches) was planned in areas where both banks had branches located close together.

Sometimes rationalisation is used as an excuse for redundancies which the employers wanted anyway.

rationing: a limit on the amount that can be consumed. This term appears in a number of contexts, for example:

● when essential consumer goods were rationed by the UK government, during World War II
● when referring to the way the *price mechanism* rations consumer goods according to ability to pay
● in relation to the NHS, which is forced to ration certain health-care procedures because there is not enough money for everyone to have all the treatments from which they might possibly benefit.

Rationing can lead to the development of alternative markets. During World War II, the rationing system was respected by most people but *black markets* did develop, selling foodstuffs which had been produced on the quiet. NHS rationing does send some people off to the market for private health care, through which they can get faster treatment.

Economic theory predicts that if there is someone who wants to sell the product and someone who wants to buy it, a market will develop.

raw materials: *commodities* in an unprocessed state which will be inputs to the production process.

real means that the item in question is being expressed in a way which removes the effects of inflation. (See also *real incomes*.) For example, real earnings show the actual change in the *purchasing power* of what people are earning. In contrast, *nominal values* are expressed in money terms, without allowance for inflation.

real disposable income: the amount of money that people have to spend after all taxes have been paid and any welfare benefits have been added.

real GDP means a figure for total output in the economy which has been adjusted to allow for *inflation*.

real incomes are money incomes adjusted to allow for inflation. The figures must be deflated to constant prices using *index numbers*.

$$\textit{FORMULA:} \quad \text{real income} = \frac{\text{money income} \times \text{base year index}}{\text{current year index}}$$

Worked example

If money income has increased by 20%, from £20000 to £24000, while the price level has risen by a total of 15%, how much has income increased in real terms and in constant prices?

To convert the new money income to the base year prices, it must be deflated using a price index. This means the index for the base year is 100. For the current year it is therefore 115.

$$\text{Real income} = \frac{£24\,000 \times 100}{115} = £20\,870$$

real interest rates reflect the actual rate of interest paid on a capital sum after allowance for the effects of inflation. Usually, the rate of *inflation* is deducted from the actual (nominal) interest rate, to arrive at the real rate of interest. Some of the nominal interest rate is in fact compensation for the fact that the capital sum is losing some of its value each year because of inflation. What is left is in fact the real rate of interest.

> *FORMULA:*   real interest rate = nominal interest rate − rate of inflation

So a nominal rate of interest of, say, 7% with a rate of inflation of 2% implies a real rate of interest of 5%.

real national income: total income for the economy as a whole adjusted to *constant prices* to allow for the effects of rising prices.

real resources are all the things which can be used to create products for which there is a demand. So they include the *factors of production*, *land*, *labour* and *capital*, *human capital* and *natural resources*.

real terms: the use of *constant prices* to give values in terms of their purchasing power, making due allowance for the rate of *inflation*. Output in money terms can be deflated to constant prices in the same way as *real income*.

real values show changing values over time with the effects of *inflation* removed. This means they will be expressed in constant prices, using a base year. (See also *real incomes*.)

real wage unemployment occurs when trade unions or professional organisations drive up wages so that they are above the market clearing level. The quantity of labour demanded by employers will be less than it would be at the equilibrium wage rate. (See also *equilibrium unemployment*.)

recapitalisation of banks began in 2007 and continued through 2009. First the *Bank of England* took Northern Rock into public ownership. This bank was heavily committed to sub-prime mortgages, including many loans of 100% or more of the value of the homes on which they were secured. As house prices fell, concern about bad debts led depositors to withdraw their funds and bank failure was imminent. Nationalisation looked like the least bad option. The government guaranteed the capital and the taxpayers got to own the bank. Eventually the intention is to sell it back to the private sector, possibly at a profit to the taxpayer.

By 2008, many banks were in difficulty and the UK government offered support to UK banks. The offer was taken up by Royal Bank of Scotland and Lloyds TSB; both received a large amount of capital while the government received shares of equal value. These shares can eventually be sold back to the private sector; meantime both banks are substantially nationalised. The objective was to ensure that banks would continue to lend to firms which might otherwise be *insolvent* and have to close, with serious effects on output and employment.

In the US, President Bush set up TARP, the Troubled Asset Relief Program. The necessary money was a long time being approved by Congress and was finally pushed through by President Obama. The funds were used to buy bad debts, often known as *toxic assets*, that resulted from excessive mortgage lending at the time of steeply rising house prices. Other central banks came up with similar policies. *Quantitative easing* will also help to recapitalise the banks.

receiver is appointed when a firm becomes *insolvent*, i.e. it does not have enough *assets* to cover all of its debts. The receiver will try to sell the company or as much of it as possible in order to raise money to pay off the debts. Receivers are sometimes called insolvency practitioners.

recession is the downswing of the *economic cycle* during which aggregate demand is growing slowly, if at all, and may be beginning to decline. There will be little sign of business confidence, so investment will be falling. *Inflation* will slow as people compete to get the few jobs available and pay increases become smaller. *Unemployment* will start to rise after a time lag. In the UK, there was a severe recession, with output actually falling, during 1991. Aggregate demand was well below the level needed to absorb all of *full-capacity output* and unemployment was growing quite fast. From 1993 until 2007, the UK and the US enjoyed steady and fast economic growth.

Recession hit right across the world as the financial crisis developed in 2008. The fall in output and international trade was very dramatic during 2008–09. Unemployment rose sharply in 2009. It might have risen even faster except that many employees were willing to go without a pay rise and some accepted a pay cut in order to save their jobs. This helped many firms that were having difficulty getting loans to tide them over.

The Bank of England reduced interest rates dramatically, to 0.5% in early 2009 and the government cut VAT in an attempt to maintain the level of consumer spending. This was also helped by the reduction in mortgage interest payments for many households.

reciprocity is the principle by which countries agree to grant the same trade concessions to their trading partners as they are receiving from them. When governments are negotiating trade arrangements through the *WTO* this principle is often important in securing agreement.

recovery is the upswing phase of the *economic cycle*. At first *aggregate demand* and output will grow slowly. *Investment* will begin to recover from its previous very low level. There will be little inflation at this stage. For a while, *unemployment* may continue to rise because employers will be reluctant to take on more people until they are certain that the rise in demand will be sustained. (There is a time lag of 12–18 months between changes in output and changes in employment.) Later in the recovery, optimism returns and investment grows faster. There will be a *multiplier* effect.

At the time of writing it is impossible to say when and how the world economy will recover from the recession associated with the 2007–09 financial crisis. This may happen earlier in some countries than in others.

recycling means reusing existing resources, rather than using raw materials. It usually applies to paper, plastic or metallic products. The decision whether or not to recycle usually entails careful consideration of the costs and benefits of doing so. Waste products have to be collected, sorted and processed and the cost of these processes can be more than the cost of raw materials.

redeployment means moving to a different job offered by the same employer. When *structural change* is under way and people are being made redundant, redeployment can reduce the number of actual *redundancies* required. It may happen as a result of *rationalisation* or of declining demand for one product when the firm has other products for which demand is stable or growing.

redistribution of income: see *income redistribution*.

redundancy: job losses that result from fewer employees being needed. It may be the result of declining demand for the product or of *rationalisation*. Sometimes the firm will be investing in new equipment which is more efficient than the old. There will be a shift to more *capital-intensive production*. This will increase productivity and wages may rise but fewer people are needed. If redundancy payments are attractive enough it may be possible for some or all of the redundancies to be voluntary.

reflation means stimulating aggregate demand by using *expansionary policies* in order to increase the rate of economic growth and reduce unemployment. These could be *fiscal policies* such as tax cuts or increases in government spending or *monetary policies* such as reducing interest rates.

Regional Development Agencies (RDAs): the bodies responsible for implementing *regional policy*. Scotland, Wales and Northern Ireland have had them for some time; the nine English RDAs were set up in 1999. The objectives are to enhance competitiveness within each region and to create job opportunities in areas where they are scarce.

regional policies are designed to address inequalities between regions. Incomes and unemployment vary considerably. In particular, the policies aim to address the problems created by localised industries' decline. The policies are administered partly through the government's regional offices and partly through the *Regional Development Agencies (RDAs)*. The amount of money spent on regional assistance by the UK government has declined over the past 20 years. The decline in the UK budget reflects concerns about the costs and effectiveness of regional policies.

regional trading blocs or regional trade agreements (RTAs) are groups of countries that negotiate to trade more freely with each other than with the rest of the world. NAFTA is the best known, uniting Mexico, the USA and Canada. There is also Mercosur, which includes Argentina, Brazil, Paraguay and Uruguay. These allow freer trade, achieved with less lengthy and painful negotiation than worldwide attempts at liberalisation. They may be a step towards freer world trade, or a source of difficulty in achieving it.

regional unemployment is one element of *structural unemployment*: It is associated with the decline of localised industries which have in the past been big employers and have experienced a fall in demand for their products. Shipbuilding, iron and steel and coal are the industries most affected; in all three cases production was concentrated in locations which had been very favourable in the past. Another example comes from Merseyside, where

100 000 jobs were lost on the docks between 1970 and 1990. Shipping traffic gradually shifted away from Liverpool towards air transport and towards the ports facing Europe rather than the US. The unemployment has persisted: it can take a long time for the local economy to adjust.

regressive tax: a tax which takes a larger proportion of low incomes than it does of high incomes. Expenditure taxes are all broadly regressive. To the extent that people on lower incomes are likely to save less, poorer people will find that expenditure taxes take more of their total income. Everyone who smokes 100 cigarettes a week will pay the same tax; it will be a large proportion of a poor person's income, a smaller proportion the higher the income.

The regressiveness of *VAT* is greatly reduced by the fact that it does not apply to food prepared and eaten at home, housing and public transport.

regulation covers a wide range of legal and other rules which apply to firms. Some come from national governments, some from the EU and some from trade associations which guarantee certain standards for their member firms. Regulation includes:

- health and safety regulations which might apply to electrical goods or to toys
- *consumer protection* which requires sellers to maintain standards
- employee protection which provides some guaranteed rights in the workplace
- competition law which requires firms to compete freely with one another
- rules for the privatised industries set up by their *regulators*, which watch prices and value for money.

Firms often complain of excessive regulation but modern societies have numerous reasons for maintaining extensive sets of rules. *Compliance costs* can be high but the rules protect large numbers of people. There is less regulation in the UK than in many other developed countries.

Bank regulation is currently under review as a consequence of the 2007–09 financial crisis. It is certain that it will be tightened in order to prevent the excessive lending that caused the problem; probably this will be to some extent a matter of international negotiation. Very big banks (those described as too big to fail) may be broken up. (See also *bank supervision*.)

regulator: an independent body set up by the government to ensure that privatised industries with an element of monopoly in their markets do not exploit consumers by overcharging and do make strenuous efforts to keep their costs down. Important elements in their approach have included the monitoring of prices, price caps and performance targets. For example, the Office of Rail Regulation (ORR) requires rail operators to comply with a huge range of conditions, relating to pricing, punctuality and safety. ORR is responsible for licensing train operators; these licenses are reviewed regularly. National Express lost the right to run the east coast railway line in 2009. (See also *OFGEM, OFCOM, OFWAT*.)

regulatory capture: it is possible for regulators to be influenced by the firms they are supposed to regulate. This may make them prone to favour the interests of the industry rather than those of the consumer. It has been suggested that the US *Federal Reserve* (central bank) has been subject to regulatory capture. Unlike the *Bank of England* or the *European Central Bank (ECB)*, it has responsibility for regulating the US banking system. It may have listened too carefully to the anxieties of the bankers and paid insufficient attention to the stability of the wider economy.

relative export prices: export prices compared to those of competitors or to world prices. Low relative export prices indicate a high degree of *competitiveness*.

relative inflation rates involve a comparison of *inflation* rates between countries. A high inflation rate relative to those of competing countries will mean that the exchange rate will become overvalued. As prices rise, exports will become dearer and are likely to fall while imports will become cheaper and may rise. *Depreciation* may follow.

relative interest rates involve a comparison of interest rates with those offered by other *financial intermediaries* or with those in other countries.

- Interest rates may be high or low in general but vary between one bank or building society and another and between different sorts of loans. Interest rates on very risky loans will always tend to be relatively high.
- Where one country has a higher interest rate than other countries, it will tend to attract deposits from abroad (provided its currency is one which the depositors are willing to hold). There are large amounts of capital which can be moved at short notice if an interest rate differential opens up, making the change worthwhile. (See also *capital inflow* and *capital outflow*.)

relative poverty means lacking the income needed to lead a normal life in the society concerned. It reflects the variations in expectations between countries. In developing countries there may be large numbers of people who are living in *absolute poverty* and so do not have the basic necessities of life: nourishing food, clothing and shelter. In *developed economies* almost everyone has these basic necessities, but many people do not have opportunities for leisure pursuits or reading books; their housing may be damp or in an area where safety is questionable. In the UK it is estimated that one fifth of all children are living in relative poverty which will have an adverse effect on their opportunities as adults.

relative price: a price may stay the same in money terms but rise or fall in relation to that of another good if the price of the other good changes. Prices change in relation to one another because of market forces. These will vary from one market to another depending on changes in the pattern of consumer demand and in supply conditions. For example, prices of British-grown flowers have tended to move with inflation, while prices of Dutch-grown flowers have stayed the same or gone down. This has reduced demand for British growers' flowers. Changing relative prices make competing products look more or less attractive and are a part of the *price mechanism* which determines the *allocation of resources*.

relative wage rates mean wages in comparison with those in other occupations, with other employers or with the price of other inputs such as capital. They reflect differentials between different jobs, which are important in determining how *labour* is allocated between different possible products. Changing patterns of demand and changes in supply conditions will work through prices to affect the relative cost of wage rates and the allocation of resources.

For example, wage rates may stay the same while the price of capital equipment may fall due to technological developments. Decisions about how much capital to acquire and how much *labour* to employ depend on their relative prices. The fall in capital prices and the relative rise in the wage rate may lead to capital being substituted for labour in the production process and fewer people being employed. Production will be more *capital intensive*.

Differences in **unit labour costs** can be important in determining where production is located and may lead to **outsourcing**.

relocation of labour refers to measures which might encourage geographical **mobility** of **labour**. These could include:

- relaxing restrictions on planning permission in areas where work is plentiful, so that more houses could be built
- offering more council housing in areas with job vacancies
- improving transport systems so that longer journeys to work become practical.

renewable energy certificates are designed so that green energy producers get a subsidy. They are used in the USA where certain states require energy companies to produce a certain percentage of their energy from renewable sources and individual consumers can opt for carbon-neutral energy to be supplied to them. The certificates are given to the producers and can be sold on the open market. They provide an incentive to use renewable sources.

renewable resources are natural resources which can be regenerated. For example, forests which are regularly replanted after felling has taken place are renewable and hydro-electric power is renewable because it is continuously available. In contrast, electricity from a gas- or coal-fired power station is not a renewable resource because fossil fuels which have been used are not replaceable – they have been taken from the earth's crust. Wind power is controversial. It is available whenever the wind is blowing so is theoretically renewable but wind farms do spoil the view, which is not so easy to renew.

rent is the payment made for temporary use of a property. Income from rent is the return on the capital invested in the property. **Economic rent** has a specialised meaning: it is a payment made for a factor of production which is fixed in supply and therefore receives more than its **transfer earnings**. The economic rent reflects its scarcity in relation to the demand for it.

rent seeking: looking for ways to persuade the government to change the rules and regulations so that more profit can be made. This might involve trying to get the OFT to agree to some kind of **restrictive practice** being allowed or to negotiate a subsidy.

replacement investment: the level of investment needed to maintain the existing stock of capital equipment. This is sometimes known as **capital consumption**. **Gross investment** less replacement investment gives the level of net investment. This is the addition to the capital stock, which takes place each year.

repo rate: the interest rate charged to banks which borrow from the Bank of England whenever they are short of funds. Repo is short for 'sale and repurchase', the mechanism by which the Bank lends. This rate is now universally referred to as 'bank rate'.

repossession: when a borrower is unable to make interest and debt repayments on a loan which has been given specifically for the purchase of a home or a consumer durable the property is security for the loan and may be taken back by the lender to cover the outstanding debt.

resale price maintenance describes the way in which manufacturers sometimes try to set a minimum price for the product. It was made illegal to try to enforce these prices in 1964. This brought about much stronger competition between retailers, which generally favoured the large supermarket chains and caused small shops to suffer.

research and development (R & D): scientific research followed up with the development of products or processes which are either new, better or cheaper. R & D is an important aspect of innovation and of the process of **economic growth**, leading to rising standards of living as quality products become more accessible. The UK has in the past spent relatively little on R & D, which may explain why **productivity** growth sometimes lagged behind that of competitor countries. Recently an R & D incentive scheme has made a difference.

Some economists argue that the firms most likely to spend on R & D are the ones in an **oligopoly** situation, where new product development can confer significant advantages. Some innovations can be protected by **patents** and this creates another type of incentive.

reserve assets: the assets held by banks which are very liquid and available for use when people want to withdraw their deposits. They include cash balances and very short-term loans.

reserve requirements: the reserve asset ratios which specify how much money banks must keep easily accessible in the form of liquid **reserve assets**. Central banks can vary these requirements. They are used in the **bank supervision** process which is an essential aspect of banking **regulation**.

reserves is a term usually used to refer to the foreign currency reserves held by the **central bank**. These may be used to manage the level of the exchange rate, so that its value is kept stable.

resource allocation: see *allocation of resources*.

resources: sources of inputs available to the economy for use in producing goods and services. Ultimately, the quantity of real resources available depends on the quantity of land, **labour** and capital and the extent to which changing technologies can improve the ways in which they are used.

restrictive practice is a term used in two different contexts. It can be:
- any method of interfering with the free play of market forces. Firms may try to reduce the market supply, which will tend to drive up prices. Or they may try to make a **market-sharing agreement**. This will reduce the amount of competition and again, help to keep the price high. However, it will only be legal if it can be justified to and registered with the **OFT**
- regulations which prevent employers from using their employees in flexible ways. For example, there may be job demarcations which mean that certain jobs are reserved for employees with specific craft skills, e.g. electricians. This is much less common than it used to be because firms have negotiated flexible working arrangements with trade unions and have given employees extra training to bring about **multi-skilling**.

restructuring means changing the departmental organisation of the firm or **rationalising** production. The objective is usually to cut costs but it may also involve reducing the output of some products which are not very profitable and increasing the output of others which are more so. It may involve closing down some factories or branches.

retail banks: the banks which cater for the needs of individuals and small businesses. They include the traditional banks, Barclays, Lloyds TSB and HSBC and a number of banks which used to be building societies, such as Birmingham Midshires (this eventually became part of Halifax and then Lloyds TSB). The remaining building societies also offer many retail banking services. In contrast, **investment banks** deal mainly with the long-term needs of large businesses.

retail co-operatives were set up to give consumers better value for money at a time in the 19th century when prices in the shops were much less competitive than they are now. Profits went to the customers themselves, who were members of the co-op.

retail price index (RPI): the main measure of inflation in the UK. It is a *weighted average* of price changes based on average levels of spending on a wide range of consumer goods and services. It is used for uprating pensions, benefits and indexed bonds, and in pay determination.

The Expenditure and Food Survey carries out regular surveys of prices and spending patterns, using a representative range of different types of households. From this weights are calculated. For example, with weights totalling 1000, food is given 105 and clothing 44, while fuel and light takes 39 and housing 238. These weights are changed every year to give a true reflection of spending patterns.

The base (or reference) year is given the value 100; 1987 is the current base year. Price relatives are constructed for each product included, showing the price change from the base year. These are combined with the weights to arrive at the weighted average for the overall change in prices.

A number of different price indices are constructed for particular purposes. The RPI is the main measure. In addition there are:

- the Pensioner Price Index, which uses a different selection of goods and services which reflect pensioner habits and excludes housing, reflecting the prices which actually have most impact on pensioners
- RPIX, which measures inflation but without mortgage interest payments. This makes it possible to measure price changes without the impact of changes in interest rates which can distort the overall change
- RPIY, which measures inflation without mortgage interest payments and also excludes changes in council tax, VAT, import duties and the taxes on cars, airport use and insurance
- the CPI, consumer price index, which is constructed slightly differently and is used for macro-economic policy making and international comparisons. It differs from the RPI in including a wider range of population groups, and in excluding council tax and mortgage interest.

retained profit is profit kept by the firm rather than being distributed to shareholders as *dividends*. It will usually be used to finance new investments or the replacement of worn-out equipment. This is known as *internal finance*.

retraining: giving people who are part of the way through their working lives different or improved skills which are likely to be in demand in the future. Where people are *occupationally immobile*, this can enable them to take the jobs which are available.

return on capital employed (ROCE) is profit as a percentage of capital employed. It provides a measure of the rate of return on capital invested.

returns to scale: the relationship between the level of output and the quantity of inputs needed to produce it. If there are possible *economies of scale*, there will be *increasing returns to scale*. A given increase in output will require a proportionately smaller quantity of inputs in order to produce it.

revaluation refers to a rise in the value of the currency in relation to all other currencies. This might occur if there is a fixed exchange rate. It is likely to happen if the country has a long-standing surplus on the current account of the balance of payments.

revenue is the total value of sales made within a given period.

FORMULA: revenue = price × quantity sold

revenue maximisation is one possible goal for a firm operating under imperfect *competition*. It may wish to expand its market share and therefore prefer revenue maximisation to profit maximisation. It will expand output up to the point where the marginal revenue is zero. This will be higher than the profit-maximising output. To sell all it has produced, the firm will need to reduce prices below what could be charged at the profit-maximising level of output. However, depending on its market power, it may still be able to make **supernormal profit**.

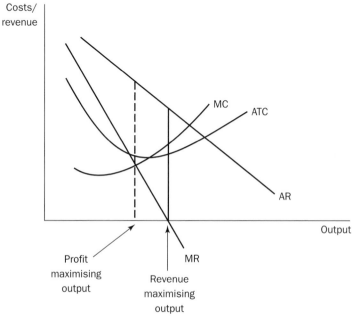

Revenue maximisation

revenue support grant: the block grant from central government to local authorities. It means that not all of local spending needs to be financed by local taxes (i.e. by **council tax** and the **Uniform Business Rate**). It also allows the government to provide extra money to those areas with the greatest needs. In recent years it has been reduced somewhat. (It used to be called the rate support grant.)

Ricardo, David (1772–1823): an economist whose most enduring contribution was the Theory of Comparative Advantage. This shows how each country will have a **comparative advantage** in producing different goods and services and if each specialises in the products in which it has the comparative advantage, it will be possible to increase total output, thus making everyone at least somewhat better off.

rights issue: an opportunity given to existing shareholders to buy more shares. From the firm's point of view this may be a relatively cheap way to raise extra finance. From the shareholder's point of view the outcome depends upon what happens after this to the share price.

risk: the possibility that events will not turn out exactly as expected. Risks are quantifiable, and probabilities can be assigned to them. Sometimes it is possible to insure against them, the insurers using the probability of their happening as a basis for setting the insurance premium. In contrast, uncertainty is not quantifiable. During the 2007–09 financial crisis it became clear that although risks are quantifiable, mistakes had been made in the way that risk was calculated.

rivalrous marketing: where a small number of firms are competing fiercely, their marketing strategies may be quite clearly targeted at each other's products. Advertising may be designed to invite unfavourable comparisons. Products may be designed so that they compete directly. This type of behaviour is very typical of an *oligopoly*, where a small number of large firms compete on price and on a number of non-price features.

rivalry: a term used in two contexts:
- Competition between firms may lead to intense rivalry as each seeks to outdo the other in the marketplace. This is a likely outcome where there is an *oligopoly* or a *duopoly*, where each firm is using both price and *non-price competition* and is intensely preoccupied with increasing market share.
- Rivalry in consumption refers to the fact that *private goods* can only be used by the household that bought them. Other people are excluded from consuming them. In contrast, *public goods* such as defence or street lighting are not rivalrous in this way. Once they are provided, everyone can benefit from them.

road pricing: a system for ensuring that the costs of road use are paid for entirely by the road users. The technology for tracking road use now exists but it is unpopular with many motorists. Some cite potential invasion of privacy.

It has a number of advantages:
- Vehicle users would be paying for road use at a level closer to the full social cost. It can be argued that using roads free of charge leads to both overconsumption and overproduction.
- Prices could be set at a level which discouraged users from driving their cars in congested places unless the benefits to them outweighed the costs, so reducing the total amount of traffic.
- Congestion would be reduced and traffic would move faster, saving the economic costs of delay caused by congestion.
- Funds raised could be used to improve public transport.

The London Congestion Charge has reduced traffic jams but remains unpopular with many. Voters in Manchester rejected a similar scheme in 2008, despite serious congestion problems.

ROCE: see *return on capital employed (ROCE)*.

RPI: see *retail price index (RPI)*.

RPIX and RPIY: RPIX is the retail price index excluding mortgage interest payments, thus giving a measure of inflation which is not distorted by interest rate changes. RPIY excludes *indirect taxes* as well as mortgage interest.

rule of law: where this prevails, business decisions are subject to much less uncertainty because *contracts* can be enforced if necessary and government actions are predictable. In the absence of *good governance*, business becomes much riskier. So some economic developments that make good sense will not happen.

sacking: dismissal by an employer. This may be for a breach of contract or **redundancy**.

salary: monthly payment by an employer. From the point of view of economic theory, salaries are exactly the same as wages, i.e. a payment for the services of **labour**.

sales maximisation: the highest output possible without making a loss. This can be an objective for the firm in certain circumstances.

- It may happen in an **oligopoly**, when a firm engaged in a price war has to decide by how much it can afford to cut its price, with a view to maintaining market share.
- *Satisficing* could also produce this result. Imagine a firm with a local market, very much a part of its surrounding community, which could present its product as an expensive, upmarket item but instead chooses to produce all it can with the facilities it has and sell it at a price which makes a **normal profit**.

In the diagram, output will be at the level where average revenue is exactly equal to average total cost.

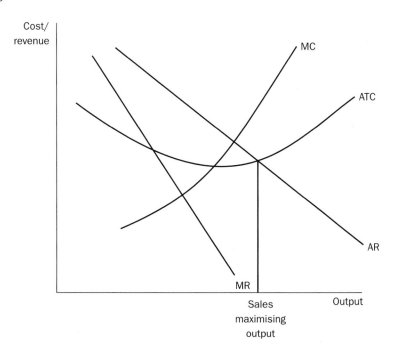

sales promotion: bringing the product to consumers' attention. It is particularly visible in an *oligopoly*, where there is much non-price competition. It includes:

- advertising and packaging, both of which can be used to create an image for the product which eventually may become an element in the product itself
- branding, which can be used to promote the product on quality expectations, style or reliability
- personal selling, which may persuade consumers
- free offers, competitions etc. which may be used briefly to attract customers who, it is hoped, will then develop some brand loyalty.

sales revenue: the total value of output sold.

> *FORMULA:*   quantity sold $\times$ price $=$ sales revenue

Sometimes sales revenue is called total revenue or just revenue. When prices change, revenue will be affected and the size of the effect will depend on the price elasticity of demand. (See also *average revenue*.)

sales revenue maximisation: see *revenue maximisation*.

sales tax: a tax on goods sold which is included in the price to the customer. Examples include VAT and excise taxes.

sales turnover: an everyday business term for *sales revenue*.

sanctions: rules made by international organisations or pressure groups which prohibit trade with countries which are behaving in ways which are considered unacceptable. The United Nations may place sanctions on a country which is considered to be behaving aggressively, as for a time with Serbia and later Iraq. South Africa was eventually forced by economic sanctions to abandon overtly racist policies in the early 1990s.

satisficing: taking business decisions which lead to an adequate *rate of return*, rather than *profit maximising*. There are a number of reasons why this *business objective* may seem to be the best option.

- Small businesses may not want to grow, because the owner of the business is happy making a living and does not want the risks and anxiety of a more dynamic approach.
- Very large firms in an *oligopoly* situation may prefer not to be seen to be making very high profits. These could attract *new entrants* to the market, which would intensify competition. (This is the situation in a *contestable market*, where barriers to entry are relatively low.) High profits might also attract the attention of the OFT, which may leave well alone if the firm is offering good value for money.

saving: the amount of *disposable income* which is not spent on consumption but kept for the future. Saving is a withdrawal from the *circular flow of national income*. In the short run an increase in saving will reduce *aggregate demand*, other things being equal. Saving is normally measured by the *savings ratio*.

Saving can provide finance for investment. Over the long run this can be important in promoting economic growth. Japan, Taiwan and other Asian countries have high savings ratios which have contributed to high levels of investment.

In the basic *Keynesian* model, saving is directly related to the level of income. (See also *average propensity to save* and *marginal propensity to save*.) At very low levels of income, there will be dissaving – past savings will be run down in order to provide funds for essential consumption. At higher incomes, if consumers save more and spend less then aggregate demand may be insufficient to sustain business confidence and output may fall.

savings gap: the difference between the savings ratio and the desirable level of investment that would lead to improved rates of economic growth. Many less developed countries have low savings ratios because people there are too poor to save much. They may also lack access to banks. High savings ratios in Japan, South Korea and other Asian countries have been a significant factor in their economic success.

savings ratio measures the rate of saving, i.e. saving as a proportion of GDP. In the long term, the growth of an economy depends upon a high rate of saving, although in the short term a rise in the savings ratio can cut consumer spending and reduce *aggregate demand*.

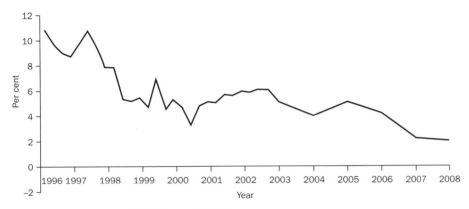

The savings ratio in the UK. (Source: ONS.)

In the past savings were thought to be at least partly determined by interest rates. That link now appears rather weak. Savings could be determined by expectations, so that the threat of rising unemployment might make saving increase. However, this has proved to be a weak link too. A stronger connection can be made between the savings ratio and the rate of *inflation*. A higher rate of inflation can erode the value of money-denominated assets and therefore lead people to save more for a while in order to rebuild the real value of their assets.

Low savings ratios in 2006–07 can be linked to the rise in consumption, imports and indebtedness at that time.

scale of production: some production, e.g. of cars, will be undertaken on a large scale, because mass production is cheaper – there are *economies of scale*. For other products, small-scale production works quite well. For some products, production may work well on either a small or a large scale. Pottery can be produced by one person skilled in the craft, making hand-made pots, or in a factory with a large output.

As output increases, it is possible for the producer to encounter *diseconomies of scale*, which will mean that average costs are rising.

scarce resources: *factors of production* and *raw materials* which are scarce in relation to the scale of human needs and wants. The scarcer they are, the more the price will tend to rise as people compete to obtain what they want.

scarcity: the term used to describe the fact that people's wants and needs always exceed the resources available to satisfy them. In practice, choices must be made and those choices determine the *allocation of resources*.

Schengen countries: most EU member countries have opted to eliminate border immigration controls on their internal frontiers. Only the UK, Ireland, Romania and Bulgaria have stayed outside this agreement. The fundamental principle of free movement of people wanting to live and work in other parts of the EU is not affected by this. Norway and Iceland are non-EU Schengen members.

science park: industrial estates located close to universities. Easy access to expert knowledge can provide *external economies of scale* for the firms in the science park.

SDRs: see *Special Drawing Rights (SDRs)*.

seasonal adjustment removes regular seasonal changes from data so that the underlying trend can be seen clearly. *Unemployment* figures are usually seasonally adjusted so that monthly figures show the changes which are brought about by macro-economic factors.

seasonal unemployment: unemployment which rises and falls according to a seasonal pattern. Wintry weather can lead to *unemployment* of construction workers or of people employed in tourism.

secondary sector: all manufacturing, energy production and construction activities. However, the term is often used to describe manufacturing alone. In relation to manufacturing, several trends have been discernible in the UK:

- The secondary sector faces competition from imports. Some products lose their *comparative advantage* as developing countries become cheaper sources of standard consumer goods and semi-manufactures (processed raw materials).
- Other products have lost their comparative advantage to imports coming mainly from developed countries, such as cars.
- Some manufacturers compete very successfully and have expanded exports in a wide range of products, such as speciality chemicals.
- Most manufacturing has become more *capital-intensive*. Productivity has increased. Employment in the secondary sector has fallen dramatically.
- In developing countries, it is common for the secondary sector to be growing fastest.

(See also *sector*.)

sector: the economy can be divided up into sectors, each of which consists of a group of decision takers with features in common. For example, one distinction is between the *private sector*, the *public sector* and the overseas sector. The economy can also be divided up into the personal sector, the corporate sector and the government sector. The personal sector consists of all individuals, the corporate sector of all businesses.

Importantly, production is divided into sectors:

- The primary sector – farming, fishing, mining and quarrying (including oil production), approximately 3% of total production.
- The secondary sector – manufacturing, energy production and construction, 22% of the total.
- The tertiary sector – services, including health, education, social care and government administration, 75% of the total. It is normal for developed economies to have a large service sector.

securities is a general term covering financial contracts such as **bonds**, **shares** and *derivatives*. In each case, a sum of money changes hands in return for an income stream which may be in the form of interest or dividends. Often, owners of securities take some risk as to possible changes in capital value, should they wish to sell them.

segmented labour markets: the *labour* market consists of a number of different occupational groups, between which there is relatively little movement because of *occupational immobility*. This means that pay differs quite substantially between groups, depending on the bargaining power of each group. Some professional organisations, e.g. the British Medical Association for doctors, have some monopoly power and are able to keep pay high.

self-employment refers to people who work freelance or in their own business, either alone or with some employees. The numbers involved tend to increase during a **recession**, as jobs with employers become harder to find. In late 2008, 13.1% (3.8 million) of the UK *labour* force was self-employed.

self-fulfilling prophecy: a situation in which the expectation of an event may actually help to bring it about. The best example concerns the increase in **investment** which follows upon resurgent confidence during the recovery phase of the **economic cycle**. During recession, firms' expectations are gloomy. Demand is stagnant or perhaps falling, new production capacity is not needed and investment is very low. In time, however, **aggregate demand** will begin to rise and firms' expectations will become more optimistic. Investment will seem worthwhile and will start to rise, so there will be an upward **multiplier** effect and incomes will rise by more than the initial injection into the circular flow of national income. Investment will increase again, fulfilling the promise of the expectations.

self-regulation means that the industry itself imposes standards and codes of conduct which encourage firms to act in a responsible way. It is essentially a form of consumer protection which is operated by the firms themselves. Sometimes self-regulation is the industry's response to the threat of regulation by the government.

sellers' market: a market in which there are more buyers than sellers, so that the sellers can raise the price and still sell. The term applies most often in a housing boom, when prices are rising steadily.

separation of ownership from control: see *divorce of ownership and control*.

services: products which consist of something done, rather than a tangible object. They include retailing, hotels and catering, hairdressing, transport, technical services and financial services, among many others. The line between a good and a service can be blurred. As I write this book I am part of a long process in manufacturing it. It is a good and if someone throws it at you, it will hurt. But the ONS would probably think I am offering professional services to the publisher.

service sector: see *tertiary sector*.

set-aside: the scheme by which farmers are paid not to cultivate a portion of their land. The **Common Agricultural Policy (CAP)** of the EU currently has a set-aside policy, as does the US government. This is to ensure that farmers in the country concerned do not produce so much that farm prices fall and farm incomes are reduced.

sex discrimination means preferring men to women applicants for a job or for promotion. Although it is illegal under the Sex Discrimination Act of 1975, it is still clear that it is happening, particularly in some sectors. Part of the problem is that proving it is difficult. Employers who discriminate are missing the opportunity to appoint the best person for the job and may have higher costs of production as a result. There is ample evidence that on average, full-time women employees are paid less than their male equivalents. The difference is not explained by differences in qualifications.

share: a contribution to the capital needed by a firm, by virtue of which the shareholder becomes a part owner of the firm in perpetuity. A share certificate is issued, entitling the shareholder to a *dividend*. This will normally be paid once or twice a year and will vary depending on the profits earned during that year. (In a very bad year it may be zero.)

Shares in a *public limited company* can be sold on the *Stock Exchange* but the price will be uncertain and will depend on expectations of future profitability or likely growth in the share price. Some high-technology shares, e.g. Microsoft, seldom pay dividends but may offer some prospect of capital gains due to a rising share price.

Shares in a *private limited company* can be sold with the permission of the rest of the shareholders.

share options are opportunities for particular employees to buy shares in the firm at a price fixed on a certain date. If the share price rises, the employee can exercise the right, making an immediate capital gain. If the price falls, they lose nothing. This can provide a substantial incentive to key employees. It can also lead to enormous rewards to managers who may in fact have contributed no more to the success of the firm than has the workforce as a whole.

share price index: a measure of the average change in share prices over time. In London, the most important is the Financial Times Stock Exchange 100 Share Index (the Footsie), a weighted average of equity prices for the 100 biggest publicly owned firms. It is calculated from a base of 1984 = 1000; the firms included are updated quarterly and the index is updated every minute. In Japan there is the Nikkei index. New York has the Dow Jones and the NASDAQ index, which is part of the National Association of Securities Dealers Automated Quotation system, which competes with the New York Stock Exchange.

shareholders are the legal owners of the firm. They receive a share of the profits in the form of dividends. They are also entitled to go to the *annual general meeting (AGM)* of the firm where they will approve the accounts, elect directors and get the opportunity to ask questions. Many shares are owned not by individuals but by financial intermediaries such as insurance companies and pension funds. Individual shareholders often do not exercise their rights to ask questions but some buy a few shares with the main intention of using their rights to question the directors on the firm's *ethical policy*.

shift in aggregate demand: an increase in the amount of aggregate demand at all price levels. This is likely to happen because consumption, investment, exports or government expenditure, or some combination of these, has changed. If there is an increase in aggregate demand, it will be possible for output to increase so long as the appropriate resources are available (AD_2). If the economy is approaching *full-capacity output* (AD_3), pressure on resources will cause inflation to accelerate as *supply constraints* develop.

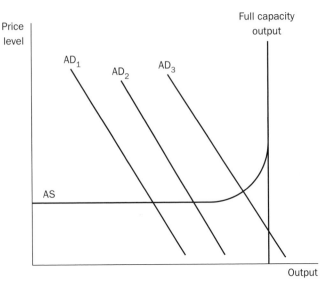

Shift in aggregate demand

shift in aggregate supply: a change in the potential of the economy to supply goods and services. Usually this will increase over time as technology and *investment* create new productive capacity. (See also *economic growth*.)

shift in the demand curve: the demand curve, which shows the relationship between price and quantity demanded, will shift if there is a change in market conditions. This might result from a change in incomes, a change in the price of a substitute product or a complement or a change in tastes or fashion. For example, an increase in incomes will shift the demand curve for designer clothes to the right. More will be sold at any given price. (See also *demand curve*.)

shift in the supply curve: the supply curve shows the relationship between price and quantity supplied. The curve shifts if there is a change in costs of production. For example, an improvement in technology or investment in new capital equipment will shift the supply curve to the right. A larger quantity will be supplied at any given price. There may also be a shift in the supply curve if some other product becomes more profitable, diverting resources towards the most profitable items. (See also *supply curve*.)

shift work means that different teams of employees work one after the other, using the same space and equipment for two or three eight-hour shifts in each 24-hour period. All essential services work like this. In manufacturing, shift work makes sense if the equipment is very expensive relative to other costs, because it makes the fullest possible use of the large capital *investment*. It may also be used if orders are coming in faster than one day shift can handle. Work during anti-social hours will usually have to be compensated at higher rates of pay, so the decision to work shifts requires a careful evaluation of the costs. The car industry may or may not work shifts according to the level of demand.

shocks are unexpected or unpredictable events which have a major impact on the economy. Examples include the reunification of Germany in 1989 and the oil price rises of 1974 and 1979. A change in commodity prices will be a major shock for a country which depends on export revenue from the sale of that commodity. The financial crisis of 2007–09 brought a widespread shock to the world economy. Shocks can initially affect demand or supply, or both. The financial crisis had a massive effect on aggregate demand. An oil price change affects supply in that it changes the cost of many inputs to the productive process. Natural catastrophes may affect supply. Once the impact of the shock is felt, both demand and supply will usually be affected.

shortage: a situation in which demand exceeds supply. Usually, with a *market system*, the shortage will cause prices to rise, creating an incentive for producers to supply a larger quantity, and *equilibrium* will quite quickly be restored. A shortage will persist if for some reason the price cannot rise. (See also *excess demand*.)

short run: a time period in which only some variables may change. For example, the short run may be the time in which inputs only of *variable factors of production* can be altered. The input of fixed factors cannot be changed. So more employees might be put to work with the same stock of equipment. In contrast, in the long run, inputs of all factors of production may be changed. The definition of the short run may change according to the context in which it is being used.

short-run aggregate supply may increase in the short run, so long as there are unemployed factors of production, labour and capital that can be put to work to increase output. In the long run however it will be fixed, or capable of growing slowly, as more resources become available or managers learn to use the existing resources more productively. (See *aggregate supply*.)

short-run equilibrium under perfect competition is a situation in which demand has changed, so that the price is not at its usual level. This is a signal that consumers want to buy more or less of the product. There are many firms under *perfect competition* and *entry* and *exit* are easy, so a change in profits will bring a fairly swift change in output, restoring the system to the long-run equilibrium.

If your exam board requires diagrammatic detail on this, read on.

- If demand has increased, price and *marginal revenue* rise. There is a new, higher short-run equilibrium at the output where marginal cost is equal to marginal revenue. Firms already in the industry will make *supernormal profit* (sometimes referred to as *economic profit*) which is over and above the long-run opportunity cost of the resources used. In the diagram, it is the shaded area between price and average cost. This will attract *new entrants* to the industry, so that added competition will force the price back down to its long-run equilibrium level, P_1.

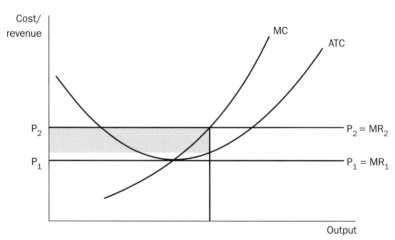

Short-run equilibrium after an increase in demand

- The converse may happen. Demand has decreased and the price has fallen. Firms will be making losses (equal to the difference between ATC and price). There will be a new short-run equilibrium where the price is equal to or more than the level of average variable cost. So long as their fixed factors of production keep on running, firms will continue to produce because their variable costs (AVC) are covered. As their fixed factors of production wear out, some of them will go out of business rather than replace their capital equipment. As firms exit the market, competition will be less forceful and the price will gradually rise to its long-run equilibrium level, P_1, at which both fixed and variable costs are fully covered.

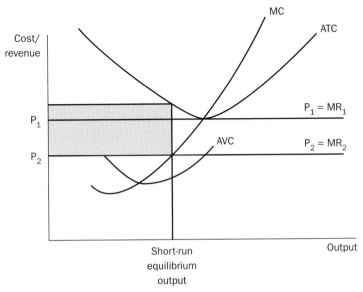

At the short-run equilibrium output, variable costs are covered

(See also **perfect competition**.)

short-run Phillips curve: the trade-off between inflation and unemployment which can be observed over a period of a few years. This term is used when it is assumed that the long-run Phillips curve is a vertical line which corresponds to the **non-accelerating inflation rate of unemployment (NAIRU)**. (See also **Phillips curve**.)

short selling means selling shares when their price is falling or expected to fall, with a view to buying them back at a lower price a short time later. Opinions differ as to whether this practice makes financial markets more or less stable. (See also **speculation**.)

short-term capital flows consist of large money balances which their owners can move from one bank or one currency to another. This may be a response to interest rate changes. Big investors often keep some footloose funds that can take advantage of more favourable interest rates as and when they appear.

If investors suspect that one currency will depreciate, they may sell it and move into another which is likely to appreciate. Of course, if many people sell the currency which is expected to depreciate, this is just what will happen – there will be a **self-fulfilling prophecy**. Speculative capital flows can create major problems for central banks and governments but they cannot be stopped without disrupting normal capital movements as well. They draw attention to the importance of confidence in keeping economic systems reasonably stable. (See also *speculation*.)

short-termism describes a tendency on the part of firms to plan for short-run profit maximisation rather than long-run growth. The main problematic consequence will be to reduce investment in projects which pay off only in the long run, and in research and development. This may mean that quality and technical prowess are threatened. Sometimes the shareholders are blamed for wanting to see good results quickly.

short-time working: during a *recession* or a period of reduced demand for any reason, firms may reduce the length of the working week to perhaps three or four days.

shutdown point: the level of output at which total sales revenue is only just equal to total costs. As soon as costs exceed revenues, losses will be made and production will cease if no improvement can be expected.

simulation: the use of a model of a firm or of the economy, which imitates what happens in the real world. It can be used to explore the effects of a variety of changes. Simulations are usually based on a set of equations which describe the relationships between different variables.

single currency: the *euro* is the single currency of the 16 EU countries which have joined together in the *Economic and Monetary Union (EMU)*. In 2002, national currencies went out of use and the *European Central Bank (ECB)* issued notes and coins. The costs and risks associated with foreign exchange transactions were eliminated within the member countries. The UK, Sweden and Denmark remain outside the euro area but only the UK has an opt-out agreement. The costs and benefits of the single currency are still hard to determine conclusively.

single European market: the agreement to create a unified market across the European Union. The overall objective was to make it genuinely possible for goods, people and capital to move around freely. Part of this entailed the removal of restrictions encountered when crossing member countries' borders. The overall effect of the measures was to make the EU much more like a single economy. They came into force at the start of 1993. Specific changes included the following:

- Foreign exchange controls were abolished, making financial integration much easier, so that capital could move around. This opened up the financial markets of all member countries to all the banks.
- Many *regulations* were harmonised, so that firms could produce to specifications common to all member countries. This meant that products could be standardised for the whole of the EU. It removed many *non-tariff barriers (NTBs)* to trade.
- Qualifications which are recognised in one member country are generally recognised throughout the EU.
- Common systems were established in the fields of transport and communication.
- Qualified majority voting was introduced in the *Council of Ministers* and the *European Parliament* was given added powers. This reflected the general view that closer economic integration would require more effective political systems.

In many respects, the single market is still incomplete because full harmonisation has not yet been achieved. However, movement towards the single market has been significant.

skill shortage: even when there is substantial unemployment, shortages may develop of people available for work and possessing the skills required. This is likely to happen if the economy has been growing and the employment of skilled people has been increasing.

Employers may offer higher pay in order to attract the type of people they require. Where skills are scarce, appropriately qualified people are in *inelastic supply*. An increase in pay may provide an incentive to acquire the skills but this will be a long-run process. This will help to reduce *occupational immobility*.

skills: any job-related competences possessed by an individual, who can use these to help produce a saleable product.

skills mismatch: a situation in which the people available for work have skills which are not those required by the employers who are seeking to hire people. This will be associated with *occupational immobility*. It occurs because people have been made redundant from *declining industries*. The skills required by growing industries are different. This is a feature of *structural change*.

slump: the low point of the *economic cycle*. *Recession* brings a slowdown characterised by gloomy expectations, low levels of investment, rising unemployment and eventually falling *aggregate demand* and output. If falling output persists for more than two quarters, there is said to be a depression or a slump. Output fell in late 2008 and in 2009. The government responded with a substantial fiscal stimulus, involving a much-increased public sector deficit in order to revive demand.

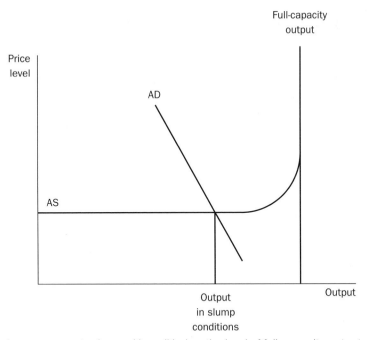

During a slump, aggregate demand is well below the level of full-capacity output

small and medium-sized enterprises (SMEs) are defined as all firms with less than 250 employees. Small firms are those with less than 50 employees; medium-sized have between 50 and 250. These firms are thought to be very important in creating new jobs.

Smith, Adam (1723–1790) was a Scottish professor of moral philosophy who pioneered much of the thinking in classical economics and laid down the fundamentals of the working of market economies. In his book *The Wealth of Nations*, published in 1776, he explained the process of specialisation and the **division of labour**. He showed how the market mechanism could promote productive and allocative efficiency. He wrote about the **invisible hand**, which allocates resources amongst alternative uses, and showed how self-interest pursued in a free market would lead to consumer satisfaction. Although in using this reasoning, Smith was assuming that markets would be highly competitive, he was well aware of the tendency among producers to collude in order to secure a higher price.

snouts in the trough is an expression designed to highlight the way human beings can be impelled by greed. It has been freely used in describing the disquiet of people who object to senior managers receiving pay rises much larger than those awarded to the workforce. There have been suggestions in the press that these pay rises may not actually be necessary in order to secure the most talented managers.

social benefits are all of the benefits from consumption of a particular item, not just those received by the buyer. They therefore include the **external benefits** which may be obtained by third parties, i.e. people who neither bought nor sold the item. For example, the social benefits of a pretty front garden include the benefits obtained by the owner of it, together with the benefits of any passers-by who happen to enjoy looking at the garden.

> FORMULA: internal benefits + external benefits = social benefits

(See also **marginal social benefits**.)

social capital: *infrastructure* which is provided by governments and is very necessary for economic growth, but cannot always be provided on a profitable basis by the private sector. It includes education, health care and some transport and communications facilities.

social cost measures the cost to the whole of society of a production process or business decision. This means that not only are the firm's **internal costs** accounted for, but also the costs imposed on society as a consequence of the action (such as pollution or unemployment). These latter costs are external to the company.

> FORMULA: internal costs + external costs = social costs

(See also **marginal social costs**.)

social development refers to the need for improvements in the social infrastructure of developing countries. It is related to important elements in the improvement of welfare such as the availability of clean water supplies, of health care and of education. These are generally seen as part of the social development process.

social exclusion is about the way in which some members of society seem to be permanently excluded from benefiting from rising standards of living. This problem develops because people who are living in poor housing with few job prospects often have children who are at a real disadvantage too. There is a cycle which is hard to break.

socially efficient level of output: the level at which the marginal social benefits of the last unit of output is equal to the marginal social cost. (See also **marginal social cost**.)

social responsibilities refer to a firm's duties towards its employees, customers, society and the environment, which it may or may not accept. Some firms see social responsibility as being very much in their own interests in the long run. Others will try to evade responsibility with a view to maximising short-run profits.

social security is the system by which governments provide for people in need. Unemployment benefits, pensions, income support and various other income supplements are payable to people in certain circumstances. Payments may be **means tested**, as with income support, or handed over as of right, as with pensions. Social security payments have increased enormously in all developed countries in recent years, partly because of ageing populations and partly because **unemployment** has been higher since 1980 than it was before.

Social security is part of what is called the **welfare state**. Increasing numbers of benefits are now being means tested because of rising expenditure on **universal benefits**.

social welfare concerns the well-being of people and how it may be improved. It involves **normative** aspects of economics which are directed towards deciding the way in which resources should be allocated so as to maximise welfare.

socialism is a social and economic system which involves collective ownership of the means of production and a major role for the state in the provision of services which can improve people's welfare. In its extreme form of communism it dominated the **centrally planned economies** of Eastern Europe until 1989. In its social democratic form, socialism has been an important underlying principle for a number of left-of-centre political parties in Western Europe.

soft currency: a currency which is not always completely freely convertible. This means that countries will not want to hold the currency as part of their foreign exchange reserves.

soft landing: if a prolonged period of economic growth has led to accelerating inflation, policy makers will aim for a soft landing, i.e. a downturn which leads to a slower, sustainable rate of economic growth but not a recession.

soft loan: a loan which is made on concessional terms, so that the interest rate is lower than the market rate or there is a 'holiday' during which no repayments are necessary. Soft loans are made to developing countries as part of their aid packages.

sole trader: an individual who runs a small business, who may or may not have employees, but does not have **limited liability (Ltd)**.

solvency: a situation in which a firm has enough assets to cover all of its outstanding debts. In contrast, insolvency implies that the firm cannot cover its debts and may be forced into **liquidation**.

sources of finance: businesses which are investing need finance, which may be internal or external. **Internal finance** can come from retained profit, working capital or the sale of assets. **External finance** may come from bank loans or from a new issue of shares.

sovereign debt: debts owed by governments rather than by private sector organisations. Many developing country governments have borrowed from banks. These debts are different from loans to the private sector because the borrowers cannot be pursued through the courts if they do not pay the interest or make repayments. (See also the **Debt Problem**.)

sovereign wealth funds have developed in countries that have large foreign exchange reserves, originating from growing exports. Some oil exporters figure prominently, e.g. Abu Dhabi and Saudi Arabia. The funds may be managed by a central bank, state pension fund or official investment bank. Some have bought into Western banks and other financial institutions.

spare capacity: a situation in which a firm has equipment which is not fully utilised. It could expand output very quickly if there was a demand for it.

Special Drawing Rights (SDRs): IMF member governments can use SDRs to settle debts with each other. They are a form of international money which exists only on paper and only for use by the IMF and governments. They are used to help countries with balance of payments problems. In 2009 the quantity available was increased in response to the financial crisis.

specialisation: the process by which individuals, firms and economies concentrate on producing those goods and services in which they have an advantage. Further specialisation is possible as production processes are broken up into a sequence of different tasks. This was described by *Adam Smith* in his account of the *division of labour* at the pin factory where each employee had a different job.

Specialisation has the potential to increase the output that can be obtained from a given quantity of resources. It is closely connected to the theory of *comparative advantage*. Scarce resources can produce more when specialising in the type of production to which they are best suited. For example, a farmer who specialises in arable crops such as wheat and sugar beet, because the land is most suitable for these, will probably make more money than when the farm also had dairy cattle. Aiming for self-sufficiency (as subsistence farmers must) is probably the least efficient and least profitable approach.

Taken to extremes, specialisation can involve some jobs becoming very repetitive and boring, for example, assembly processes in manufacturing. One management response to this has been *teamwork* and *multi-skilling* – which can provide employees with more variety and the firm with a more flexible *labour* force.

specific tax: an indirect tax which is a fixed amount per unit of output. Petrol, alcohol and tobacco – the products with excise taxes – are taxed like this. In contrast, an ad valorem tax is one with a percentage rate, like VAT.

spectrum of competition: the range of market systems which can be anything between *perfect competition* and *monopoly*. At one extreme there is the situation of many competing producers with easy entry into the market; hairdressing would be one example. At the other extreme there is the single business which dominates the market and cannot be challenged because *new entrants* to the market have difficulty in getting started because of *barriers to entry*. Microsoft is currently the best-known example.

Perfect competition	Monopolistic competition	Oligopoly	Duopoly	Monopoly

speculation involves buying or selling something in the expectation of a price change and so making a profit. For example, foreign exchange dealers who expect the *exchange rate* to fall will sell quickly, then when the price has fallen they can buy back the currency at a much lower price than they sold at, so making a profit on the deal. Speculation may be suspected whenever a financial asset such as a share or a property is bought and then sold a short time later. (See also *short selling*.)

speculative capital flows: see *short-term capital flows*.

spillover effects: the effects of certain production decisions which have an impact on third parties, who are neither producers nor consumers of the product in question. They are the same as *externalities*.

spot market: a term used to describe a commodity or foreign exchange market where the deals are made and completed there and then and delivery is immediate. In contrast, in the *forward market* deals are made in which the price is agreed now, but the delivery of the goods concerned takes place perhaps three months later.

spot price: the price in the *spot market*. This means the price which must be paid for a consignment of a commodity for delivery immediately.

stabilisation policy aims to keep the economy growing in a sustainable way and prevent a cycle of *boom* and *recession*. It uses *fiscal* and *monetary policies* to influence the level of aggregate demand and prevent both overheating and rising unemployment. Stabilisation policies are not always successful because the time lags in the economy and weaknesses of some of the data can make it very difficult to predict how much policy change is required. Stabilisation policies can be used for electoral reasons in ways which are ultimately destabilising, but this has been made much less likely since the Bank of England became responsible for monetary policy in 1997.

Stability and Growth Pact: the EU framework that provides for economic policy collaboration between member states. It has particular importance for the euro zone countries but the UK is involved simply as part of its commitment to EU co-operation. The objective is to promote fiscal co-ordination, and allow member countries to achieve sustainable growth by encouraging a flexible response to shocks that may occur. The basic rules follow the *convergence criteria* in stipulating a fiscal deficit of no more than 3% of GDP over the course of the economic cycle and total government debt of no more than 60% of GDP.

stagflation means a combination of *stagnation* and *inflation* happening together. This was a phenomenon associated with the 1970s. Whereas normally there is a trade-off between inflation and unemployment, stagflation led to the two rising together. Because trade unions expected further inflation, they wanted to negotiate pay rises big enough to preserve and increase real incomes. But at the same time, unemployment was rising because of recession. Competition in the *labour* market might have depressed pay rises. In this instance, efforts to maintain real incomes overrode competition from unemployed people for the available jobs. This experience led to detailed study of the role of *expectations* in the determination of inflation and a fuller appreciation of their impact.

stagnation: a situation in which the economy is growing very slowly or not at all.

stakeholders: people with a strong interest in a particular firm, including employees, shareholders, consumers, suppliers and the community. Firms which take *business responsibility* seriously recognise obligations to all of these groups.

standard of living refers to the well-being of the population but does not have a precise meaning. A serious attempt to assess progress in this area requires inspection of a wide range of data, including:
- measures of real income such as GDP at *constant prices*, to assess the economic component of the standard of living
- per capita income, if population growth is rapid

- measures of social welfare such as mortality rates, life expectancy, participation in education, access to health care and clean water and so on
- in some cases, data for the *distribution of income* would add detail to the picture. The presence or absence of a *social security* system may also be relevant.

International comparisons of the standard of living can be confused by exchange rate variations. The World Bank produces data based on *purchasing power parity (PPP)* which gives a clearer picture. The UN's Human Development Index also provides useful data.

standardised products are those which are mass produced to uniform specifications. This type of production opens up possibilities of reaping economies of scale. For example, the use of standardised parts in vehicles reduces stockholding costs and design costs. Paradoxically, computer-controlled manufacture has made it easier for firms to manufacture small batches of items, so cars now come in a bewildering array of models with many variations, many of which are produced more or less to order. These two trends are occurring side by side.

state-owned enterprises include all the organisations which sell a good or a service for a price and are in the public sector. This category was large until many such enterprises were privatised from 1981 onwards. The best remaining example in the UK is the Post Office although there are proposals to sell one third of it to private sector buyers.

state planning: the process by which, in a *centrally planned economy*, decisions are made about how resources will be allocated. This will be an administrative process which overrides market forces as to both prices and quantities.

state provision covers all the goods and services provided (i.e. paid for) by the public sector. The actual delivery of these goods and services may be undertaken by either the public or the private sector. Refuse collection is provided by the local authority and may be carried out by it too, or it may be put out to *tender* with the private sector. Many home helps now come from private operators working for the local authority.

static efficiency refers to improvements in efficiency that could be made by reallocating existing resources. (Dynamic efficiency is concerned with strategies for increasing the availability of resources.) So *productive efficiency* and *allocative efficiency* are static concepts because they involve ways of reallocating existing resources so as to avoid waste in production and to fit the output of products more closely to consumer preferences.

statistics: the data which record events in the economy and can show trends in a range of important variables. They make it possible to predict likely levels of growth, inflation and unemployment but may be subject to errors and uncertainties and may only become available with a *time lag*.

sterling: another name for the pound, the UK's currency.

sterling exchange rate index: a measure of change in the foreign *exchange rate* which takes a weighted average of a basket of currencies. These are weighted according to their importance in the pattern of trade. It provides the simplest way of measuring competitiveness.

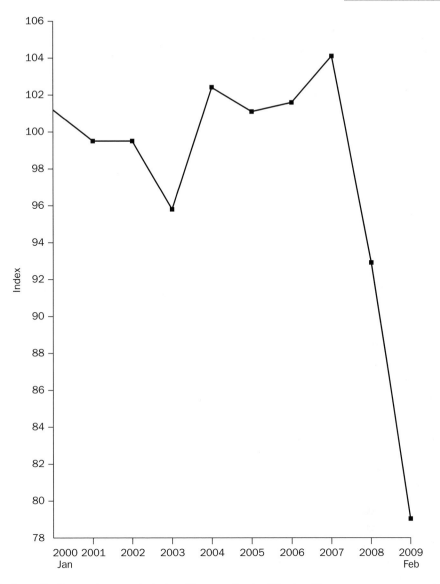

Sterling effective exchange rate index. (Source: Bank of England.)

Stern Review: a report written in 2005 by the then head of the Government Economic Service for the Treasury, on climate change. He concluded that the economic risks associated with climate change are potentially very serious, but that if 5% of world GDP were to be devoted to tackling it, it would be possible to reduce greenhouse gas emissions by 80% from their present level. He concluded that costs of managing climate change were significant but manageable, if a quick start could be made. The report was very influential. It is not clear how any action that might have been taken will be affected by the aftermath of the 2007–09 financial crisis.

sticky wages: a term which refers to the tendency of wages to go up but not down. *Trade union* negotiators will try to see that wage rates rise each year by the rate of *inflation* plus a real increase. In non-unionised occupations with no bargaining power, money wages may sometimes be held constant but this will mean that their purchasing power will go down by the rate of inflation. It is very rare for money wage rates to fall. Sticky wages can make the economy less flexible because they can obscure signals that *labour* should be being reallocated away from declining industries and towards products for which demand is growing.

stock: this term has three meanings:

- A stock, as opposed to a *flow*, means an amount held. Wealth is a stock, while income is a flow. Savings are the stock of past saving, whereas saving is a flow, i.e. the extra saving added this year to the stock of past savings.
- Stocks may be of inputs, work in progress or output. When aggregated for the whole economy, the level of stocks is important because it may reflect changes in the level of *aggregate demand* relative to output. Also, changes in stocks may impact upon the level of output. If demand has been falling, stocks will rise and destocking may become necessary. This means that the level of output will for a while fall below the level of demand and this may reduce the demand for *labour*, leading to rising unemployment.
- Stocks is another term for bonds in the UK, or for equities in the US.

Stock Exchange: a market on which *shares* and *bonds* (*securities*) can be bought and sold on a second-hand basis. This means there is always a way in which securities can be exchanged for money, although the price will not be known much in advance. Shareholders do not have to hold their shares indefinitely unless they want to.

The London Stock Exchange is very large, competing for international business with Frankfurt, Tokyo and New York. Stock exchanges help to ensure that funds are made available to firms to invest. A steady flow of investment finance is an important element in the process of *economic growth*.

stock market: see *Stock Exchange*.

stocks and shares: investments which can be bought and sold on the Stock Exchange. *Shares* or equities imply part ownership of the company by the shareholder; they pay *dividends*. The term 'stocks' in this context is thoroughly confusing; they may mean the same as shares (in the US) or they may mean a fixed interest loan like a *bond* (in the UK).

strike: a situation in which workers stop work in order to exert some power in an *industrial dispute*. Most often, this will be over pay but it can be about redundancies or unfair dismissal. Strikes may be official, i.e. sanctioned by the trade union, or unofficial. They are much more likely to occur in larger firms than in smaller ones. In recent years strikes have been fewer in number, partly because of the fear of unemployment and partly because the law now requires a secret ballot of union members as to whether they want to strike.

structural adjustment: a set of policies which has become associated with the *International Bank for Reconstruction and Development (IBRD)* (the World Bank) and the *International Monetary Fund (IMF)*. The package of policies will depend upon the circumstances of the country concerned, but is likely to include:

- *devaluation/depreciation* of the currency
- cuts in government expenditure and reform of the tax system which will reduce the public sector deficit
- reduced trade restrictions and the encouragement of market forces in a number of contexts, sometimes through *privatisation*

- improved incentives to encourage increased agricultural production
- export incentives.

Often the World Bank and the IMF are in a position to dictate the policy prescription because of the country's need for development finance. Some of these measures have proved unpopular at times.

structural change is the process by which resources are reallocated away from the production of items for which demand is falling and towards items for which it is rising. This reallocation of resources leads to changes in the composition of output. It also entails major changes in employment patterns. Where a *localised industry* declines, it can cause whole communities to be affected by increased *unemployment*, often for many years. Coal and shipbuilding both provide examples of serious structural problems. However, without structural changes, the economy does not adapt to new patterns of demand and *productive efficiency* may be compromised as well.

structural unemployment occurs when people are made redundant from *declining industries* but lack the appropriate skills to enter a growing industry or are located a long way from the jobs available. Many declining industries such as coal and iron and steel are localised, so that the large excess supply of *labour* in a place with limited opportunities becomes a real problem.

Occupational immobilities and *geographical immobilities* make it difficult for people to find alternative jobs. Supply-side policies such as training and retraining may be needed to deal with these. *Regional policy* and regeneration measures can be helpful too. There has been a long-term and substantial increase in structural unemployment in many developed countries which governments have had little success in reducing. Unskilled people are particularly vulnerable and despite recent improvements, the problem remains grave in many parts of the EU.

structure of industry: the composition of output.

subcontracting: buying in inputs from another firm, rather than creating them in-house. Another term for this is *outsourcing*.

sub-market: see *market segment.*

subsidiarity involves taking political decisions at the lowest appropriate level. In theory it should lead to a strengthening of the role of local authorities, which may be responsive to local needs. It may prove useful in the EU context in preserving the democratic process in distinctive regions. At present in the UK there is a tendency, despite devolution, to deal with some local issues at the central government level. Subsidiarity may be a good idea but it hasn't made a great deal of progress.

subsidiary: a firm that is owned by another firm (the holding or parent company). The subsidiary may be fairly independent of the parent company or it may be effectively controlled by it. There may be no independent accounts published so that the subsidiary's performance is hard to evaluate.

subsidy: a sum of money paid by a government to a producer, so that the price to the customer will be lower than it otherwise would have been. This may be done either for social reasons (e.g. to a railway as a provider of an essential service) or to raise incomes (e.g. hill sheep farmers) or to keep down prices of essential goods.

In the UK the biggest subsidies go to farmers. Oxfam says that these subsidies cost each household an average of £832 per year. Effectively they protect farmers from competition from lower cost producers overseas, including many very poor farmers in Africa.

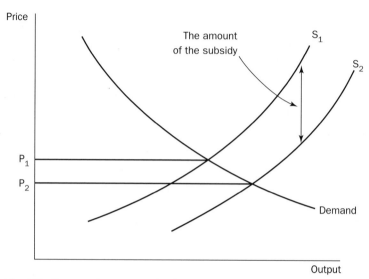

The subsidy shifts the supply curve to the right, making it possible for producers to charge a lower price, P₂

subsistence agriculture: a system in which farmers supply all or most of their daily needs by their own efforts. They have little or no surplus which they can exchange for goods and services produced by others. They are likely therefore to have a very low standard of living.

subsistence level: an amount of real income which provides only just enough to keep the person alive in the long run.

substitutes: goods and services which are possible alternatives for the consumer, so that a change in the price of one will have some impact on demand for the other. Some substitutes will be much closer than others. For example, an own-brand tin of baked beans is quite a good substitute for a tin of Heinz beans. But a cauliflower, although it is another vegetable product, is probably not a very close substitute for any tin of beans. (See also *cross-price elasticity of demand*.)

substitution effect: a change in price will lead to a substitution effect. If there is a fall in the price of housing (either because of interest rates or because of low levels of demand), some people will choose to buy a larger house rather than have an expensive holiday. This is the substitution effect of a fall in price. There will also be an *income effect*: because people actually have more real income as a result of the fall in the price of housing, they may buy more of a number of products, including housing.

sunk costs: costs which have already been paid for and which no longer figure in the decision-taking process. For example, once the product is brought to the market, research and development costs are sunk costs. The likelihood of sunk costs in some industries (e.g. mining) may mean that economies of scale are present.

sunrise industry: one which is expected to grow quite fast. It may be one in which new technologies are important.

sunset industry: one which is declining because of lack of demand, perhaps caused by competition from new products.

supernormal profit: profit which is in excess of the amount needed to keep the resources in the industry, i.e. the full *opportunity cost* of all the resources used. When demand is rising, it will often be possible for the firm to make supernormal profit because it can raise the price and still sell the goods. This situation will continue until more firms have moved into the industry, thus competing and driving prices back down to the level where *normal profit* only is made. If there are *barriers to entry*, then the firm may make supernormal profit in the long as well as the short run, because the level of competition is reduced. In fact, any kind of market power will allow supernormal profits to be made; for example, brand names, such as Levi's, create loyalty which reduces the power of competition to force down profits. (See also *perfect competition* and *monopoly*.)

supplier relationships are important to firms which buy in many of their inputs from other businesses. In the context of a good relationship, it will be easier to negotiate quality improvements or *just-in-time* stock control procedures.

supply is one element in the market system: the market forces contributed by supply and demand together determine prices and quantities and the *allocation of resources*. Firms will supply goods and services in a range of quantities, depending on the price they can get for them. At any given price level, quantity supplied will be affected by input costs in general, by technological change and by government policies which affect taxes and subsidies. Supply can be affected by producer cartels, e.g. OPEC. (See also *supply curve*.)

supply chain: the sequence of processes by which a final product is created. For many products, the supply chain takes in many different suppliers, often located in different countries. Many sophisticated manufactured products are built up in developed countries using intermediate products assembled in *developing economies* where wages are lower.

supply curve: the curve showing the quantities producers wish to supply at a range of different prices. It is normally shown sloping upwards to the right. This is because a higher price gives a business more of an incentive to produce and indicates possible higher profits (as at p_2 and q_2 on the diagram overleaf).

The supply curve will shift if there is a change in costs and it may then change its shape as well. For example, new technologies will tend to make the supply curve shift down and to the right, reflecting the fact that costs have fallen and possibly also *economies of scale* have been reaped. Then it may be possible to produce the larger quantity (q_3 in the diagram) at the original price.

Shifts in the supply curve may also be caused by changes in indirect taxation, or subsidies. (See also *tax incidence*.)

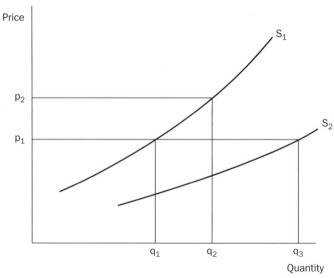

Supply curve

supply elasticity: the responsiveness of quantity supplied to a change in price. The formula is:

$$\textit{FORMULA:} \quad \text{elasticity of supply} = \frac{\text{percentage change in quantity supplied}}{\text{percentage change in price}}$$

Inelastic supply will be less than one, while elastic supply will be greater than one. Supply may be perfectly inelastic (i.e. equal to zero) in the market period simply because there has not been time to mobilise the resources needed to increase supply or to disband them if the price is falling (see diagram opposite). In the short run, supply can be increased by the addition of variable factors of production to the production process. In the long run, fixed factors of production can also be increased. So supply becomes more and more elastic the longer the time period. Housing is usually in inelastic supply: it takes time to build more; equally, if demand is falling the existing stock of housing will continue to stand for some time. This means that changes in demand may produce sharp fluctuations in price. Another example of inelastic supply occurs when scarce skills are in demand; it will take time to train more people and in the meantime the supply of the skills will be very inelastic.

If very scarce resources are needed to produce the item, then costs may rise as output increases, thus making supply rather inelastic. As depletable resources of mineral products are exploited, the price will rise and this means that supply is inelastic. In contrast, the supply of most manufactured products in the long run is highly elastic.

Firms will respond to a change in prices in different ways over time. In the market period they cannot change the quantity supplied but in the short run they can use more or less of the variable factors of production to increase or decrease output. The long-run response will take advantage of all possible ways to adapt to new conditions.

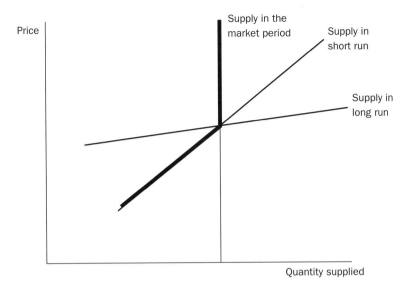

supply of labour: the number of people available for work. The *participation rate* gives the percentage of the people who are working or available for work. The number of people who are actively looking for work depends on rates of pay, the likelihood of finding a job and the level of benefits paid to those out of work. Also important is the immigration policy at the time.

The supply of *labour* in any one occupation is greatly affected by pay. Higher pay will enlarge the number of people prepared to move to a new occupation or to retrain for it. It will also encourage those already working to work longer hours.

supply schedule: see *supply curve*.

supply-side policies are based on the notion that economic growth can best be encouraged by helping markets to work more efficiently. They actually work to increase supply from a given quantity of real resources. This contrasts with the so-called *Keynesian* policies which are designed to influence the level of demand in the economy. Supply-side policies were originally favoured particularly by *monetarist* economists, who believed that policies to increase *aggregate demand* were potentially inflationary and could destabilise the economy. There are many possible supply-side measures.

- Policies which make the *labour* market more flexible: these involve restriction of trade union activities, which has led in the past to overmanning and demarcation problems. Supply-side enthusiasts also argue for some reduction in *employment protection*.
- Training and retraining: these address directly the *supply constraints* which usually exist to some degree, increasing the supply of skilled labour able to respond to job vacancies.
- Competition policy: by encouraging competition, it is possible to force firms to organise their production systems more efficiently, increasing the output from a given input.
- Reducing disincentives to work: some people have suggested reducing unemployment benefit and income support to this end. Marginal tax rates can be reduced, but the evidence that this actually makes people work harder is difficult to come by. In recent

years the government has introduced new measures, such as the Working Families Tax Credit, to try to ensure that people with families are always better off working than not.
- Financial incentives to promote spending on research and development and encourage investment.
- Promoting competition in the financial sector, to encourage it to work more efficiently at channelling funds towards profitable opportunities.
- Privatisation: reducing the extent of the involvement of the public sector in economic activity can help to increase general efficiency in the industries concerned.

Many supply-side measures have in fact secured widespread support from all political parties. Support is not confined to the original Conservative monetarist enthusiasts of the 1980s. Measures such as improving training and retraining, helping people to find jobs, and spending money on research and development can all help to increase *productivity* and employment, as well as fostering growth.

supply-side shocks: noticeable changes which have an impact on the quantity of goods and services supplied and the general price level at which they are available. The oil price rises of 1973 and 1979 were shocks in that many producers found their costs of production rising and prices were raised in turn. Oil-users' purchasing power was reduced. The impact of the changes was very considerable. A pleasanter kind of shock concerns the rapid impact of new technologies in the US during the late 1990s. This led to big increases in *productivity* in the industries concerned and increased prosperity for many people.

surplus: the amount by which revenue exceeds costs in *non-profit making organisations*.

surplus on current account: the amount by which visible and *invisible exports* together exceed visible and invisible imports.

sustainable growth is a term used in two different contexts:
- Growth which can be kept up at a steady rate over the long term is said to be sustainable. In contrast, unsustainable growth requires resources which will become increasingly scarce as growth proceeds. In particular, shortages of scarce skills will develop and when they do, wage rates will be bid up, costs will rise and *inflation* will accelerate. This will lead the government to damp down the growth process and the result may be a swing into *recession* which will last until such time as people's inflationary expectations have adjusted under the impact of the threat of unemployment. (This sequence of events was experienced in the UK between 1987 and 1992.) So sustainable growth must be at a rate such that the resources available at the time can meet the aggregate demand without input prices (including wages) being bid up through increasing scarcity.
- In the context of the environment, sustainable growth means growth which does not rely on exploiting resources which cannot be replaced. For example, the use of *depletable resources* such as oil can probably not be sustained indefinitely unless the rate of use can be slowed dramatically. The exploitation of hardwood forests cannot be sustained indefinitely unless the rate of use slows and more attention is given to replanting.

sweat shop: a workplace where the wages on offer are very low indeed and little attention is paid to the need for good working conditions. Unemployment may be high so that employees have little choice but to put up with the conditions. There will normally be no trade union and the employees may have difficult circumstances which reduce their capacity to resist *exploitation*. Sweat shops can probably be found more often in developing countries but there are still instances of such situations in some developed countries.

symmetric inflation target: the type of target used in the UK which gives equal emphasis to deviations from the 2.0% target whether they are above or below it.

synergy means combining the positive qualities of two entities, so that their economic prowess emerges greater than the sum of their parts. It is often advanced as an argument for a merger, where the two firms have complementary strengths. Mergers sometimes disappoint in this respect and the outcome may be a *demerger* or divestment process.

Aiming for a grade A*?

Don't forget to log on to **www.philipallan.co.uk/a-zonline** for advice.

tacit collusion means that an understanding has developed between two competing firms, but without any kind of personal contact or formal agreement. It is characteristic of an *oligopoly*. The sellers will simply not take action in any way which might increase the level of competition between them. Because there is no actual agreement, this is hard to prevent, even though it may have considerable impact on the buyer. It is possible for a long period of tacit collusion to follow a *price war* which the participants have found very damaging. They may just set their prices at similar levels and avoid further price competition.

In 2006, fifty independent schools were investigated by the *OFT*. The problem was that they had exchanged sensitive information about the level of the fees they were planning to charge in future years. They admitted that this had distorted competition but denied that it had had any effect on fees. There was clearly no agreement on what fees to charge, but the information gave each school crucial detail about what fees the market would bear. There was no overt collusion but the sharing of information created an opportunity for tacit decisions to be made.

takeover: one firm buys a controlling share (i.e. at least 51%) of the shares of another firm. A takeover may be hostile or friendly, according to the attitude of the management of the firm taken over. These *acquisitions* are an important means by which firms can grow in size without having to go to the trouble of expanding their own operations. This is known as *inorganic growth*. It is often an easy way for the firm to increase its market power and its market share. Some takeovers may create so much market power that the OFT considers whether to refer the takeover to the *Competition Commission*.

takeover bid: the opening offer by a firm for the shares which it hopes to buy in order to achieve control of another company. To be successful, the bidder will have to make an offer better than the current market price for the shares. It may offer cash, some of its own shares or a combination of the two. If the response from the shareholders is insufficient to give it full control, the firm may make a higher bid. Sometimes there will be two competing bids for the target company.

target savers: there is some evidence that savers have a target level of savings that they will seek to rebuild if for any reason the value of their savings goes down. This can be an important determinant of the *savings ratio* in times when inflation is a problem.

targets give specific objectives for economic policies, thus focusing the minds of those who will implement the policies. They provide some clarity as to what is expected. However, they may become an end in themselves so that the target becomes the objective, rather than the expression of a significant underlying improvement. (As for example, with the target percentages for five A*–C GCSE grades, which encouraged teachers to concentrate on the needs of those on the C–D borderline.) (See **Goodhart's law**.)

tariff: a customs duty on an imported good. The effect of this tax is to make the price of the import higher, so competing domestic products will be relatively cheaper. The domestic producer will benefit from some **protection** against foreign competition.

The tariff can be an **ad valorem** or a **specific tax**. Import tariffs are discouraged, and some are banned, under **WTO** agreements. They raise prices to consumers and can reduce real incomes, especially if the exporting country decides to retaliate with tariffs of its own. This will reduce trade all round, reducing demand for exports generally.

The impact of tariffs depends on the elasticity of demand for the product. If demand is elastic, this implies that there are competing substitutes available from domestic producers and the tariff will cut imports considerably, as in diagram (a). It may be impossible for the importer even to pass on the full amount of the tariff to the consumer. An example of this might be a tariff on steel products. If, on the other hand, demand is inelastic, as in diagram (b), the price increase brought about by the tariff will be quite high but the fall in quantity demanded will be less than proportional because people carry on buying the import as they see few or no satisfactory substitutes. This might happen with a tariff on sound systems.

The general principle on which tariffs work is the same as that of **tax incidence**.

The impact of tariffs with elastic and inelastic demand

tax allowance: a specific amount which may be deducted from income before tax is calculated.

tax avoidance means reducing the tax bill by legal means. People with businesses can reduce their liability by deducting legitimate expenses. Firms and individuals may keep some of their assets in tax havens, where tax rates are much lower. **Transfer pricing** allows multinationals to avoid some profits tax by setting the prices of goods transferred from one country to another at levels which minimise the overall tax bill.

tax base includes all the sources of tax revenue. For example, profits are taxed to provide *corporation tax*, individuals are taxed to provide income tax and products are taxed to provide *VAT* revenues. Widening the tax base means devising ways of raising revenue which rely on different sources.

tax burden refers to the total amount of tax. When taken as a proportion of GDP, it is possible to compare the tax burden in different countries.

Current tax revenue as % of GDP, 2007

Australia	30.6
Belgium	44.4
France	43.6
Germany	36.2
Italy	43.3
Netherlands	38.0
Sweden	48.2
UK	36.6
US	28.3

Source: OECD

tax evasion means paying less tax than is legally due. For example, a person might not declare all of their income and thus pay less income tax than they should. Or they may claim allowances to which they are not legally entitled.

tax haven: a country with low rates of *income* and *corporation tax*, such as the Cayman Islands.

tax incidence: see *incidence of taxation*.

tax rate: the marginal percentage rate at which an income or an expenditure tax will be levied. (See also *income tax*.)

tax relief: a reduction in tax which is designed to create an incentive. For example, deducting investment expenditure from total profit can reduce tax payable on profits and encourage firms to invest.

tax revenue is the money which is paid to the government in tax. The total is important because it influences both the amount which the government may spend and the amount which has to be borrowed (*public sector net borrowing*).

The expected revenue from taxation is determined by the policies laid out in the **Budget**, usually in March. For 2009–10, income tax, VAT, National Insurance and corporation tax revenues were all forecast to fall because of the recession. The figures are shown on the pie chart opposite. The figure for borrowing shows the extra amount needed to cover total expenditure.

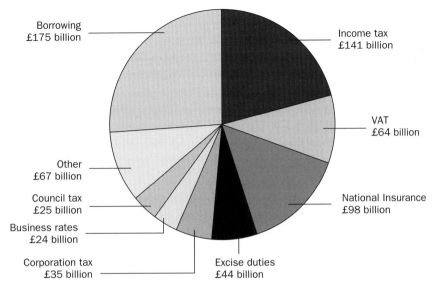

Expected tax revenue, 2009–10, £ billion. (Source: UK Treasury.)

tax thresholds are determined by the size of the personal tax allowance, which is the amount of income people are allowed to earn before tax becomes payable. An increase in the personal allowance means that the tax threshold rises. There is another threshold at the point at which the person becomes liable for tax at the 40% rate.

tax yield: the revenue raised by a tax, less the cost of collecting it.

taxation: the process of raising finance for government expenditure through the use of direct and indirect taxes. *Direct taxes* are those levied on incomes, profits or wealth, while *indirect taxes* are levied on expenditure. The pie chart shows the relative importance of each tax. Excise taxes are those levied on specific products such as petrol, tobacco and alcohol. (See pie chart above.)

taxation principles provide the basic framework for creating an effective tax policy. They are set out in the UK Code for Fiscal Stability. They include:

- transparency – objectives should be clearly stated and based on realistic estimates of the likely outcomes of tax changes
- stability – policies should minimise fluctuations in output and employment
- responsibility – in terms of use made of available resources and the need to avoid future problems
- fairness – so that ability to pay is taken into consideration
- efficiency – constructed so that any incentives they create are in line with the rest of government policy (e.g. they should not create a disincentive to work).

teamwork: the system by which production is carried out by teams of people who co-operate in order to achieve efficient ways of working. It may be associated with *multi-skilling*, whereby some members of the team can carry out a number of different tasks. Teamwork can help to alleviate the boredom of repetitive tasks, associated with too extreme a *division of labour*.

technical economies: see *internal economies of scale*.

technical efficiency: see *productive efficiency*.

technical or technological change refers to the process by which both products and the processes of production are developed and improved, as a result of increased scientific knowledge and the application of that knowledge to production.

- A technical breakthrough may make a new product development possible. Mobile phones are a relatively recent new product. This is product *innovation*.
- Equally, technical change leads to new and cheaper methods of producing and this leads to costs falling and sometimes also falls in relative prices. Telephone calls have recently become cheaper because of improved equipment. This is process innovation.

Technical change provides a substantial impetus to the process of **economic growth** because it makes it possible to increase **productivity**, e.g. to reduce the quantity of real resources needed to produce a particular item. The gains from technical change are most obvious in manufacturing, but there have also been major increases in productivity in the **primary sector** and in the **service sector**, for example as a result of using computer systems.

technological unemployment occurs where people have been made redundant as the business invested in labour-saving capital equipment. However, they will only remain unemployed if they are also affected by *occupational* or *geographical immobility*.

technology transfer occurs when countries acquire techniques they did not have through contacts with other countries that are technically more advanced. It can arise when there is *foreign direct investment (FDI)* taking place, via the technical assistance element in *foreign aid*, education abroad or the *licensing* of patents.

teleworking means working at home, often by using electronic communications. This can benefit the employer by reducing the fixed costs per worker and may suit the employee personally. Teleworking has some potential to create a more flexible *labour* market because it provides a range of options to suit different situations.

tender: a system by which a number of competing firms will bid for a contract, saying exactly what they will provide and giving a price. The lowest price or best value bid will be accepted. Local authorities, central government and a variety of businesses all use the system from time to time, e.g. for building projects or provision of school meals or home helps.

terms of trade: the price of *exports* relative to the price of *imports*. It is measured by the terms of trade index.

FORMULA: $\text{terms of trade index} = \dfrac{\text{index of export prices}}{\text{index of import prices}} \times 100$

The terms of trade improve if it becomes possible to buy more imports with the proceeds of a given quantity of exports, i.e. if import prices fall or if export prices rise. For example, if the price of copper rises, Zambian copper producers will receive a higher price for their exports and will be able to buy more imports. Similarly, if the price of copper stays the same but the price of imports rises, Zambia's terms of trade deteriorate.

There will be a change in the terms of trade if there is a change in the exchange rate. A *depreciation* leads to lower export prices and higher import prices. This implies a deterioration in the terms of trade. This leads to confusion, because the terminology suggests that deteriorating terms of trade are a bad thing. In fact, a depreciation may have the beneficial effect of making producers more competitive and lead in time to an improved trade balance.

The Prebisch–Singer hypothesis suggests that developing countries will experience falling commodity prices over time, while prices of manufactured imports will tend to rise. This will lead to steadily worsening terms of trade. This is certainly the case during a recession. (In summer 2008, the copper price peaked at $9000 per tonne. By December 2008 it was down to $3000.) However, when the world economy was booming in 2006–08, commodity prices rose steadily. Increasing pressure on natural resources as Asian countries expand manufacturing production seems likely to benefit commodity producers in the long run.

term structure of interest rates means the whole range of *interest rates* which apply to all the different types of loans that exist. Broadly, interest rates depend on the length of the loan and the degree of risk associated with it. Money lent to the government when a *bond* is bought will have a very low rate of interest because it is certain that it will be paid back and that the interest will be paid in full and on time. Similarly money lent within the banking system overnight will also have a very low rate of interest. A credit card loan will have a very high rate of interest: non-repayment is quite likely. Loans to firms for investment purposes will lie somewhere in between.

tertiary sector: all the firms in the economy which produce services. It is much the largest sector in the UK, as also in the US. (See also *secondary sector*.)

Thatcherism: the set of policies, and their underlying philosophy, developed during Margaret Thatcher's period as Prime Minister (1979–90). Her objective was to set the economy free from government intervention and allow *market forces* much more of a role in determining the *allocation of resources*. The main policies were:
- *privatisation* of the nationalised industries
- the use of *monetary policy* to control inflation, a high priority at the time
- reduction of the power of the *trade unions*
- increases in incentives through tax cuts
- strengthening of *competition policy*
- *deregulation* of the private sector.

Of these, the implementation of the first three had substantial effects. The tax cuts certainly redistributed income towards the richer part of the population.

theory: a set of principles used to explain real-world events. Economic theory aims to provide insights into the nature of economic problems by simplifying sequences of events so that stage-by-stage analysis is possible. For example, the theory of *perfect competition* defines the nature of a very competitive market, allowing us to pinpoint the extent to which real markets diverge from the competitive model.

theory of the firm: a branch of economics which seeks to explain price and output decisions. It uses *marginal analysis* to explain the profit-maximising output of the firm. It examines the nature of the various market forms, covering *perfect competition*, *monopolistic competition*, *oligopoly* and *monopoly*. In recent years it has been extended to analyses of relationships between firms through *game theory*.

third parties: individuals or groups which are not the main parties in a transaction, but are affected by it. For example, if a paint factory is polluting the atmosphere and people living nearby are affected by the pollution, those people are third parties in the transaction which takes place between the producer and the consumer of the paint.

third world countries: another term for *developing economies*.

tied aid: aid given by developed countries to developing countries which carries a condition that it be spent on exports from the donor country. Sometimes this considerably reduces the value of the aid to the recipient. The donor's products may not be the ones most suited to the recipient country's situation.

Tier 1 capital assets: the funds provided by shareholders to banks. These funds underpin their lending capability. The capital adequacy requirements of the regulators are that these should be 4% of total assets.

tight fiscal policy means using a tax increase and/or government expenditure cuts to reduce *aggregate demand* in the economy. This could be used if the economy has been growing unsustainably fast and *inflation* is accelerating. It could be combined with a *tight monetary policy*. The success of such a policy depends upon its being implemented at the right moment (rather than too late) and therefore upon having accurate forecasts about likely future changes. This is important because there will be *time lags* between the policy decision and its effect upon the economy, probably of between one and two years.

tight monetary policy involves high interest rates, so that borrowers will try to keep their loans down to a minimum. This is usually associated with *counter-inflation policy*. As borrowers try to reduce the amount they spend, aggregate demand will fall (or grow more slowly). Demand for the products of many firms will fall and they will cut production. In time they will reduce employment and incomes will fall. Consumption then falls, so that the process is repeated, with a downward *multiplier* effect. Competition for the few jobs available will reduce demands for pay increases and the inflation rate will fall again but only after a time lag.

The success of such a policy depends upon its being implemented at the right moment (rather than too late) and therefore upon having accurate forecasts about likely future changes. This is important because there will be time lags between the policy decision and its effect upon the economy, probably of between one and two years. (See also *monetary policy*.)

time lag: a delay in the reaction of one *variable* to a change in another variable. For example, during the *economic cycle*, *unemployment* may start to fall only 12–18 months after output starts to rise at the end of a recession. An increase in *interest rates* will also have a delayed effect, spread over a period of perhaps a year, during which borrowers adjust their plans in response to the change.

time series data covers a period of time, so that a sequence of events can be described. Inflation data for a 20-year period would provide a time series. In contrast, cross-section data provides a series of observations drawn from a single time period. Rates of inflation in one year for 20 countries would be cross-section data and would enable international comparisons to be made.

total cost: all the costs of production to the firm, including *fixed costs* and *variable costs*.

total fixed cost: the full cost of all *fixed factors of production*, which include land and capital.

total revenue: sales revenue, for which the formula is:

FORMULA: total revenue = price × quantity sold

total variable cost: all the variable costs to the firm, which will include *labour*, raw materials, component inputs, energy and any other costs which vary with the level of production.

toxic assets: loans made by banks to borrowers that are highly likely to default, i.e. be unable to pay them back. They are therefore likely to contribute to bank losses. The fall in US house prices meant that the underlying finance for mortgages was tied up in assets that had insufficient collateral in case of default. The value of the property if it was sold would be less than many of the mortgages. This was one of the fundamental causes of the 2007–09 financial crisis.

tradable permits: these allow certain businesses the right to pollute the atmosphere or water up to a certain point, but no more. The EU (and governments elsewhere) can cap the total amount of pollution allowed, gradually reducing the total. The permits are divided amongst the firms participating in the scheme.

The emissions trading system allows firms that can reduce their polluting activities below the level of the permit to sell it to another business, enabling it to pollute more. Allowing the permits to be sold to the highest bidder ensures that they go to the users that benefit most from the polluting activity. This means that 'the polluter pays'.

This scheme uses the price mechanism to turn an *external cost* into an internal one. Firms have an incentive to pollute less. However, the success of the scheme depends heavily on the number of carbon permits issued. The EU issued so many that their price fell up to 2007, i.e. for the first two years of the scheme. This ensured acceptance by the participating companies but greatly reduced the incentive to reduce pollution. However, if the allowable level of pollution is reduced over time, the system could become effective. Costs to firms will rise as firms adopt cleaner technologies, prices will rise, quantity of the products demanded will fall and pollution will diminish.

tradables: goods and services which figure in *international trade*. In fact, most goods and services can be traded to some degree, if only by being bought by tourists when visiting the country or, as in the case of education and health care, bought by people who travel to obtain them. The exceptions include some heavy building materials and some kinds of services, including government-provided social services and administration.

trade agreements: international agreements about the rules under which trade takes place. These have all happened under the auspices first of GATT and then its successor, the *WTO*.

The agreements cover *tariffs* and *non-tariff barriers (NTBs)* and dispute settlement mechanisms. The most important grew out of the three major 'rounds' of negotiation, the Kennedy Round in the 1960s, the Tokyo Round in the 1970s and the Uruguay Round in the 1990s. These brought about successive reductions in the level of barriers to trade in many manufactured goods and made trade much freer. Only with the Uruguay Round was agricultural protection seriously addressed and much protection still continues untouched. An important principle in trade negotiation is that of **reciprocity**, meaning that countries must offer equal access to each other's markets.

From 2001 until 2008, WTO members met regularly as part of the **Doha Round**. The foremost items under discussion included issues relating to agriculture and services, which had been neglected in previous trade negotiations. The agenda as a whole focused on the problems of developing countries but discussions are currently stalled.

trade barriers impede the trading process and include **tariffs**, **quotas** and other **non-tariff barriers (NTBs)**. Tariffs tax imports. Quotas place a physical limit on imports. **WTO** aims to reduce trade barriers over time. (See also **import controls**.)

trade creation occurs when a new **trading bloc** has been set up and businesses begin to take advantage of the opportunities arising from **free trade** between member countries. Because there are fewer **trade barriers**, new markets open up and businesses will try to extend into them. There will be increased **specialisation** and more trade.

trade credit: firms which are selling their products to other firms will often give them time to pay. This credit is interest free. It may be given to retailers who will find it hard to pay for the goods until they have been sold. The availability of the credit is one element in the value for money of the product being sold.

trade cycle: see **economic cycle**.

trade deficit occurs when visible **imports** are greater than visible **exports**.

trade diversion: when a new **trading bloc** is created, trade diversion takes place because some member countries will shift to buying more from other member countries rather than from non-member countries. For example, when the UK joined the European Union, it began to buy more butter from France and less from New Zealand. The absence of **trade barriers** between member countries and the **common external tariff** give people an incentive to switch. NAFTA, the **North American Free Trade Agreement**, is demonstrating trade diversion at the present time, as people in the USA, Canada and Mexico will tend to buy more from each other and less from outside the area.

trade gap: a deficit on the **balance of trade**.

trade in goods: visible exports and imports which include primary products and semi-processed raw materials and manufactures.

trade in services: **invisible exports** and imports including tourism, financial services, transport services, education and so on.

trade liberalisation: the process of limiting and reducing **trade barriers** and drawing closer towards a situation of free trade. The impetus for this has come from the **GATT/WTO** and it has been carried out through the various **trade agreements**. It has resulted in reduced tariffs on a wide range of goods and services and restrictions on the use of quotas and other non-tariff barriers. It has been a substantial element in the process of **globalisation**.

trade-offs: in making decisions people often have to consider that having more of one thing may mean having less of another.

- An important trade-off in **macro-economic policy** is between inflation and unemployment. It is often the case that lower unemployment can be achieved but at the price of accelerating inflation. Other ways to reduce unemployment need to be found, e.g. *supply-side policies*.

- Another trade-off involves *equity* and *efficiency*. Increased wage *differentials* lead to improved incentives but less equity in the *distribution of income*.

In making a decision which involves a trade-off, there will be an *opportunity cost*. This is obvious when considering trade-offs as they affect consumers.

trade sanctions: see *sanctions*.

trade surplus occurs when the value of visible *exports* is greater than the value of visible *imports*.

trade union: an organisation that represents employees who can gain more from collective negotiation or action than from individual negotiation or action. Trade unions can ensure that their members have some redress when faced with an employer who is unconcerned about working conditions. In recent years a number of unions have amalgamated. Often a single union, e.g. Unite, will represent people from a wide range of occupations.

Trade unions can operate at the level of the individual workplace or within a region or nationally. They represent their members in the negotiation of pay and conditions where collective bargaining is appropriate. They take a strong interest in health and safety issues. They can protect individuals against unfair dismissal, as well as protecting members from employers who are intent on keeping costs down rather than considering employee welfare. In some occupations, most employees belong to a single union which therefore has some bargaining power.

In situations where trade unions find a common sense of purpose with management, they can be partners in the process of making the firm more competitive. Where management interests are seen as being different from those of employees, and especially where the top management has secured very large pay rises, relations may be confrontational rather than collaborative. (See also *wage bargaining*.)

Trade union membership in the UK has fallen substantially. From a high of 13 million in 1980, by 2005 trade union membership was 6.5 million and still falling slowly. The reasons are:
- diminishing numbers of employees in *declining industries*, which had been for the most part strongly unionised
- increased *productivity* and falling employment in manufacturing generally
- increasing numbers of skilled and educated people who are able to negotiate for themselves just as effectively as a union might.

Legislation passed in the early 1980s weakened the trade unions substantially. In particular, they were required to hold a secret ballot before taking strike action and it became much more difficult to start unofficial strikes. They were forced into a situation where confrontation with employers could no longer be sustained. Their capacity to help poorly paid people diminished, as did their bargaining power in negotiation. However, some employers began over the same period to see concern for the welfare of employees as an important element in responsible management.

trade war: a situation in which some governments put in place *import controls*, designed to protect domestic industries from foreign competition, and the exporting countries then retaliate with import controls of their own. This will tend to depress demand for exports generally and lead to falling levels of economic activity. The most serious instance of this occurred during the 1930s depression. The lessons learned then underlie continuing efforts at *trade liberalisation*, visible in trade negotiations in recent years.

Trades Union Congress (TUC): the umbrella organisation for UK trade unions. It formulates the overall policy stance of the trade union movement, representing it in discussions with government and the *Confederation of British Industry (CBI)* and parallel organisations in other countries, especially within the EU. The anti-union legislation of the 1980s greatly reduced its influence but in the context of EU employment protection law, it still has an important role.

trading bloc: a group of countries that have agreed to *free trade* with each other.

training means developing knowledge and skills of direct relevance in the workplace. The Learning and Skills Councils organise local provision. The LSCs are run by local business representatives, working in collaboration with neighbouring further education colleges where off-the-job training will take place. The idea is that the LSCs are able to define local needs and ensure that they are met by a combination of on-the-job training and courses.

transaction costs: the actual cost of buying or selling something. One is most aware of these costs when buying a home or foreign currency. House purchase involves estate agents, solicitors and stamp duty. Buying foreign currency involves a fee to the seller. Effectively, transaction costs add to the price of the product.

transfer earnings: the wages which could be earned in the best alternative employment. For example, if a teacher was able to earn £25 000 working in a bank, that would be that person's transfer earnings.

transfer payments occur when government revenue from one part of society, e.g. taxpayers, is paid to another part. The best-known transfer payments are pensions and social security payments such as *income support*.

transfer pricing is used when products do not actually reach the marketplace but are transferred between one department and another of the firm. Pricing the product in this way at each stage of production may be useful in establishing internal costs of production. It is used by some *multinationals* when transferring the product from one country to another. By setting the price high in a low tax country and vice versa, they may be able to reduce the amount of profits tax they have to pay.

transitional economies are those which have previously had *centrally planned economies* and are now allowing *market forces* to operate at least in parts of the economy. Russia, Poland and many other East European countries are currently in transition.

transmission mechanism is the theoretical process which connects changes in the stock of money in the economy to the level of income and output. It shows how increased bank lending leads to increases in both consumption and investment, then in aggregate demand, and finally in the level of production. (See also *monetary policy*.)

transnational corporation: another name for a *multinational*.

transparency means an open and clear approach to all decisions. It can be important in ensuring that government policies are appropriate to the situation. If it is possible to see clearly what the proposed policy intends, how it works and who will implement it, then the consultation process which precedes implementation will probably ensure that the policy works well. Transparency is particularly important where human rights are involved.

Similarly, in business, transparency means providing a clear and accurate record of events in the published accounts, so that investors, regulators and consumers can see what has happened. Lack of transparency may mean that the company has acted illegally. For example, the reluctance of Swiss banks to provide information about their depositors constitutes a lack of transparency that can lead to criminals being able to deposit funds which they do not legally own. Recently Swiss banks have become somewhat more transparent.

transport modes: the different methods of transport which are in use, including rail, road, sea and air, also inland waterways and pipelines.

Treasury: the government department at the heart of the government's policies on *taxation* and *government spending*. The Chancellor of the Exchequer has control of the Treasury and so also of *fiscal policy*. Because it has the power to withhold or spend money, it is the most influential of all departments. The annual spending round, where Ministers have to bid for money for their individual departments, can make or break a Minister's political career.

The Treasury has its own macro-economic forecasting model which can predict some changes fairly accurately, aiding decision making.

Treasury bills are short-term (three months) government securities. They are sold in order to cover any shortfall between government spending and tax revenue. Because they are so short-term, they provide a very flexible way for governments to borrow.

trend: the longer run direction of change which can be seen in *time series data*. A clear trend can be used to predict some future changes.

trend rate of growth: see *long-run trend rate of growth.*

TUC: see *Trades Union Congress (TUC).*

turnover, or sales turnover, is the same as sales revenue.

A–Z Online

Log on to A–Z Online to search the database of terms, print revision lists and much more. Go to **www.philipallan.co.uk/a-zonline** to get started.

uncertainty: the situation of not knowing what will happen in the future. In contrast, risk is easier to deal with because there are known probabilities of a range of possible events actually occurring. Uncertainty is by its nature impossible to quantify. Obviously uncertainty increases the further forward you try to look. The 2007–09 financial crisis has exposed failures in some methods of calculating the probability of risk, increasing both risk and uncertainty for the time being.

underconsumption applies to *merit goods*, for which demand will be lower than is socially most efficient, if people are left to provide them for themselves. It is in the best interests of society for people to be educated and have access to health care, because in this way the population as a whole will be kept healthy and productive. However, both education and health care are expensive and people on low incomes will not be able to pay for them in the optimum quantities. They will therefore be underconsumed unless provided by the government. This is an example of *market failure*. See also *welfare gain*.

underdeveloped country: see *developing economy*.

underemployment occurs where people work but do not have opportunities sufficient to occupy them full-time. It is common in rural areas in developing economies where most people are dependent on agriculture but are not kept busy with it all year. The outcome is usually a low standard of living. (*Microfinance* addresses this problem, providing opportunities for some additional occupations.) It also affects people in depressed areas where only part-time work is available.

underlying rate of inflation: the long-run trend rate of inflation, now usually known as *core inflation*.

underprovision or underproduction is associated with *underconsumption*. It applies to *merit goods* or public goods for which the *marginal social benefit* is higher than the *marginal social cost*. Public parks are a good example of a merit good. They could be provided by the private sector and charged for but access to all who could benefit will only be available if they are publicly provided. However, it is easy to think of neighbourhoods where the social benefits would be enormous but no park is actually provided. This may be because the financial cost exceeds the social benefits; if it does not, then there is underprovision.

undervalued exchange rate: an *exchange rate* which is below its long-term equilibrium value. This means that exports are very competitive and therefore high and imports appear relatively expensive and will be fairly low. The outcome is a current account surplus on the *balance of payments*. An undervalued exchange rate can be very helpful in encouraging the development of industries which export. China has been accused of keeping its exchange rate down and this could account for its success as an exporter.

underwriting is the business of accepting risks which underpin the entire insurance industry. It can also apply to the way a merchant bank will guarantee that all the shares issued by a firm will be sold, by undertaking to buy them itself.

UNDP: see *United Nations Development Programme (UNDP)*

unearned income: income derived from interest, dividends and rents, i.e. from assets which are owned, rather than from employment.

unemployment: the problem encountered when there are people able and willing to work but unable to find jobs. This leads to a loss of income and of potential output. The two main categories of unemployment are *demand deficiency* (sometimes called cyclical) and *structural unemployment*. Structural unemployment includes *technological unemployment*, which refers to situations where the employer has substituted new kinds of capital equipment for labour. Other types of unemployment include:

- real wage employment – where trade unions have used their monopoly power to push pay above its equilibrium level
- frictional unemployment – people who are between jobs, perhaps for some time if their occupation is very specialised
- regional unemployment – where local industries have declined
- seasonal unemployment – which can affect people working in tourism and construction.

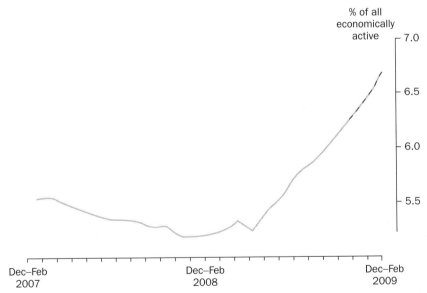

Unemployment rate, % of all economically active, claimant count, seasonally adjusted. (Source: ONS.)

Since the early 1980s unemployment has been consistently higher than previously. This reflects the rapid structural changes which have taken place and the fact that counter-inflation policies have sometimes kept the level of aggregate demand below the level needed to employ more of the working population. Policies to deal with unemployment can be varied:

- When the cause is lack of demand, *expansionary policies* may be appropriate.
- Structural unemployment requires measures which reduce *immobilities*. Training and retraining help. (See also *supply-side policies*.)
- Regional policy can be used to help areas where major industries are declining.

In recent years attention has been focused on whether employment protection laws reduce the rate at which new jobs are created, especially for unskilled jobs. Policies have emphasised the need for *labour* markets to be flexible. Employers hesitate to take on more labour when it is hard to make people redundant later – they want hiring and firing to be easy. In the USA, unemployment has generally been lower than in most of the EU, where unemployment in a number of countries has been above 10% for long periods. In the UK and the Netherlands, unemployment has been higher than in the USA but lower than in the rest of the EU. Commentators have linked this to the more flexible labour markets of these three countries.

Unemployment can be measured in different ways, giving different results. The *claimant count* is the number of people who register as unemployed, which excludes some people who are available for work but do not qualify for unemployment benefit. The figures based on the *Labour Force Survey*, or the ILO definition of unemployment, will include these. The claimant count hovered around 5% throughout the period 2000–07, and then rose sharply as recession set in.

unemployment benefit is the social security payment made to people who have become unemployed. It has recently been renamed the *jobseeker's allowance* and is now paid for a maximum of six months. The intention is to create an enhanced incentive to find work.

unfair competition: the use of methods of competing which in some way break rules which other competitors have to abide by. This can apply in a range of situations:

- some firms may resort to 'dirty tricks', e.g. bus companies have been known to time-table their buses just before the arrival times of other companies' buses, which can drive a smaller competitor out of business
- firms may be in receipt of government subsidies which their competitors cannot get
- firms may be able to cut costs by having lower health and safety standards than their competitors.

Some businesses compete with firms in countries with lower wage rates and mistakenly see this as unfair competition. In reality it simply reflects the relative *comparative advantages* of the competitors.

Uniform Business Rate: a tax paid to the local authority by businesses in its area. It is based on property values, at a rate set by central government. It can be a substantial fixed cost for firms.

union: see *trade union*.

union recognition involves employers in accepting collective bargaining with the union to which members of the workforce belong. Employers must recognise the union if half or more of the workforce are members.

unit cost: the average cost of one unit of the product. Changes in unit costs are a useful measure of competitiveness.

unit elasticity means that *price elasticity of demand* is exactly equal to –1. The percentage change in quantity demanded is exactly the same as the percentage change in price. Price changes will make no difference to the amount of money spent on the product, because an increase in price will be offset by a decrease in quantity demanded. Someone who has a set amount of beer money to spend each week will have unit elasticity of demand.

unit labour cost: the cost of the *labour* needed to make one unit of output. This can be reduced in two ways, without cutting wages:
- by cutting the labour input, adopting a more capital-intensive way of producing
- by using labour more efficiently, e.g. by training in additional skills.

For any *footloose industry* pondering where to locate production facilities, unit labour cost comparisons will be an important element in the decision.

unit trust: a firm which sells its own shares to savers and invests the proceeds in the shares of a wide range of businesses which it hopes will be more profitable than the average. For people who want to buy shares without investing a great deal of cash, this approach reduces the risk of all their shares falling in price. In return, the unit trust will collect the difference between the dividends it receives and those it pays to its shareholders.

United Nations Development Programme (UNDP) funds *soft loans* and technical assistance for developing countries. The latter usually consists of expatriate experts who can work with officials of the country concerned.

universal benefit: a *social security* payment which is given to all who qualify regardless of income. The most important example is the old age pension. In contrast, *means-tested benefits* are given only to those whose incomes are below a certain level, e.g. income support.

unlimited liability: the way in which businesses which do not have the legal status of a company will have to pay all of their debts from their owners' personal funds, if the business cannot cover its costs. Sole traders and partnerships are in this position.

unlimited wants: the endless needs and desires for goods and services which may be felt by consumers. Resources are scarce and all economic goods have a price, so that consumers have to choose which of their unlimited wants will be satisfied.

unofficial economy: see *black economy*.

unsecured loan: a loan which is not covered by any asset which could be used to repay it. A mortgage is secured in the sense that the home can be sold to pay off the debt. Unsecured loans are likely to have higher interest rates.

unsustainable growth: economic growth which is faster than the long-run trend rate of growth, which reflects the actual increase in the productive capacity of the economy. A period of unsustainable growth is likely to be followed by a period of slower than average growth. In 2007, the UK economy grew by 3%. This was almost certainly not sustainable, regardless of what might have happened if the banking system had not collapsed. Inflation was rising towards 5% and the Bank of England raised interest rates. This would have resulted in lower growth in 2008, even if the world economy had behaved normally.

An alternative definition of unsustainable growth would emphasise the environmental considerations. It would be growth at a rate involving the use of depletable resources which cannot be continued in the long run because these will become progressively scarcer and therefore more expensive. Sustainable growth involves the management of resources so that they are replaced as they are used. For example, trees are replanted and reliance on fossil fuels is progressively reduced.

upturn: the point in the *economic cycle*, at the end of a slump, when some firms begin to be optimistic enough to consider new *investment* projects.

urban economy: that part of the economy which is based on developments in city areas. This will contrast with the predominantly agricultural rural economy. There will be a sharp contrast between the two in some developing countries, where the urban economy may be much more modern than the rural economy.

utilities: industries which provide the *infrastructure* for the economy. They include water, energy and communication facilities. They used to be regarded as *natural monopolies*, so were given *regulators* on *privatisation*. Most are now facing some competition (but not water).

utility means satisfaction, to an economist. Some of the underlying theory behind our understanding of demand involves examining the utility which consumers derive from small extra amounts of the goods and services they consume and comparing this to the prices paid.

utility maximisation: economists assume that when consumers choose the goods and services they want to buy, they will maximise their overall *utility*, given current incomes and prices.

Do you need revision help and advice?

Go to pages 326–46 for a range of revision appendices that include plenty of exam advice and tips.

vacancies: job opportunities which are registered with job centres. This is not the number of job vacancies in existence, because many are not registered but are advertised independently in a wide range of publications and agencies. However, the changes in vacancies over time are a very useful indicator of the slackness or tightness of the *labour* market generally. A sharp rise in vacancies indicates that the economy may be running into **supply constraints** across a wide range of occupations. It could be the precursor to a rise in the rate of inflation.

Vacancies running above 650 000 in the UK suggest that there is no demand deficiency unemployment, although there will always be some frictional and structural unemployment. The sharp drop in vacancies in early 2008 is a clear indicator of falling aggregate demand and output as recession bites.

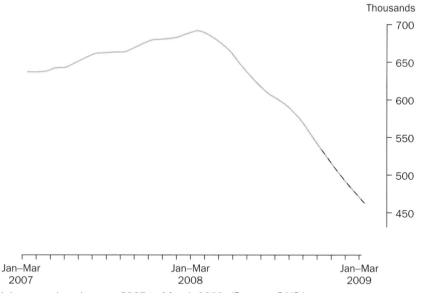

UK job vacancies, January 2007 to March 2009. (Source: ONS.)

value means economic worth. In realistic terms, the value of an asset or a product is what someone is prepared to pay for it, provided that price is at least equal to the price at which someone is willing to supply it. If it is not, the value is low and production will fall.

value added means the value of a firm's output, less the value of all the bought-in inputs. It is the value added by the firm's *factors of production*. It reflects the value of the services of *labour*, land and capital which have been used in creating the product.

value added tax (VAT): the main expenditure tax in the UK, levied at 17.5% on most goods and services. The tax is added by each producer, so that for a car, say, it is paid by the component manufacturer, the final product manufacturer and the car dealer. Each of these can get back the VAT paid on their inputs, so that the tax reflects the value added at each stage of production. Ultimately, of course, the full amount of the tax is paid by the consumer because it is included in the price of the product.

VAT is *regressive* in the sense that it will take a larger proportion of a poor person's income than a rich person's income. In the UK it is less regressive than it appears because some goods and services are either exempt or zero rated. These include food eaten at home, housing, public transport and children's clothes, which are likely together to account for a large proportion of the spending of the less well off.

At the end of 2008 the UK government announced a temporary cut in VAT to 15%, for one year only. This was intended to provide a stimulus to consumer spending and thereby have a positive effect on aggregate demand, at a time when demand was expected to fall quite sharply.

value judgements: conclusions which are based on opinions rather than on verifiable facts. These will vary according to the value systems of the individual. Many value judgements can be traced to the personal position of the individual. For example, opposition to high marginal tax rates is much more common amongst the people who pay them than among non-taxpayers.

variable: a measurement that changes over time and in turn causes other changes to take place. In the macro-economy, changes in variables may be predicted by economic models. For example, the effect on spending of a tax change can be estimated. Changes in independent variables (such as tax rates) can be fed into the model, to give predictions about the effects on dependent variables (such as incomes and expenditure).

variable costs: the costs of production which vary directly with the amount of output. They include raw materials, components and the *labour* and energy which are used in the actual production process.

variable factors of production are those factors which can be varied in quantity in the short run. Raw material or component inputs are an example: the amount used will depend on the level of output and can be varied as necessary. *Labour* may be a variable factor, if the number of people employed or the hours worked can be varied according to the amount of work to be done. This might be the case if overtime was worked in order to increase output. Alternatively, labour may be a fixed factor, if the employees concerned will have to be kept on even if output falls.

VAT: see *value added tax (VAT)*.

Veblen goods: products that carry a high price because the seller believes that the price will help to define the item as a high quality, high status product. Buyers who wish to look wealthy will buy them; it's all about appearances. This can be a profit-maximising strategy though perhaps not for very long if it leads to new entrants into the market. While it lasts, the demand curve slopes upwards. (Not required for most specifications.)

velocity of circulation: the ratio of the value of output to a particular measure of the stock of money in circulation in the economy. Over the years this may change, depending on the extent to which idle bank balances are held. This means that it can be difficult to predict the impact of changes in the money supply on the real economy and on inflation rates.

venture capital is finance for projects which could be very profitable but are also quite risky. It is usually organised by *investment banks* as a source of finance for small and medium-sized firms which are not sufficiently well established to issue shares on the Stock Exchange.

VER: see *voluntary export restraint*.

vertical integration: amalgamation of two firms in the same industry which are specialised in different stages of the production process. The undertaker who set up a florists was becoming vertically integrated. Often, vertical integration involves a merger or takeover.

Backward vertical integration occurs when the firm buys a supplier. A manufacturer of plastic products might buy the firm which supplies the mouldings needed in the production process. Forward vertical integration occurs when a manufacturer takes over a distribution network, i.e. its customer.

vertical merger: see *vertical integration*.

vested interest refers to a situation in which someone is acting in a way which is influenced by their own material interest in the outcome. Farmers have a vested interest in the future of the Common Agricultural Policy. Teachers have a vested interest in the provision of more government funding for education. If they do not declare this interest their enthusiasm for particular outcomes may be misinterpreted.

visible balance: another name for the trade balance, i.e. visible exports minus visible imports.

visible trade is the export and import of goods only, services are not included. The difference between visible exports and visible imports is the *balance of trade*. (See also *balance of payments*.)

volume and value indices: changes in output, exports or imports can be measured using volume or value *index numbers*. A volume index counts changes in the actual quantity of goods and services, using weights for the various categories of product. This can be useful for comparing changes over time when inflation or exchange rates make the value data hard to interpret.

voluntary export restraints (VERs): a quota placed on imports from a particular country, with the agreement of that country's government. (See *quotas* for explanation of the likely impact.) They have mainly been applied to developed countries' imports of manufactures from Asian countries. Their objective is to protect the domestic industry of the importing country. The exporting country may be persuaded to accept them if the alternative is a more damaging trade barrier. They are outside the rules of the *WTO*. They are not much used at the present time.

voluntary unemployment includes anyone who has refused to take a job which is available and anyone who could work but is not actively seeking work. It is extremely difficult to measure voluntary unemployment and some economists even doubt that it exists. Some people will refuse work because they believe they should be able to get a better-paid job or a different type of work. The concept of voluntary unemployment has been associated with some *monetarist* economists; a possible policy to deal with it is to reduce benefits. It may have been somewhat reduced by the *Working Families Tax Credit*, which is designed to provide some incentive to work.

wage bargaining may occur collectively or individually. The outcome depends heavily on the market power of individuals and the organisations concerned. Many people have no choice but simply to accept the going rate of pay, when neither they nor any trade union they might join has any bargaining power. Only a shortage of their particular skill, or of *labour* generally, will then raise their real earnings.

- A highly skilled employee may be able to negotiate pay if it is clear that these particular skills are scarce and badly needed by the employer.
- A *trade union* or a team of unions may negotiate directly with the employers over pay in that particular workplace or firm. National agreements covering all the company factories in the UK are found in the car industry.
- Trade unions may negotiate with employers' organisations to arrive at a national pay bargain which will apply to the whole industry.
- In the public sector, especially the NHS and in education, national pay agreements are the norm. Despite being strongly unionised, however, employees in the public sector tend not to have a great deal of bargaining power.

wage determination in practice reflects some combination of market forces in the occupation concerned and the relative bargaining power of any organisations involved. (See also *wage bargaining*.) For any particular occupation, analysis requires some understanding of both of these.

Assuming markets are competitive, pay will be determined by the interaction of supply and demand in the *labour* market. The important factors affecting demand are:
- the demand for the final product
- the price of capital equipment which could be substituted for labour
- the productivity of labour.

Factors affecting supply are:
- wage rates on offer in other occupations
- the non-monetary attractions of the work
- the amount of training required.

Some very unpleasant work is well paid because few people would accept it otherwise.

A growing industry which can charge relatively high prices will have a high level of demand for labour. Depending on the supply of labour, wage rates are likely to be higher than they would be in a declining industry. This can be seen clearly in the pay of computer software specialists, who are both scarce and very much in demand. This helps to ensure that labour is reallocated when the pattern of demand is changing.

Increasing demand for particular skills takes the demand curve from D_1 to D_2. These skills are relatively scarce so the wage rate rises in order to attract the type of people needed. (See diagram below.) High pay may or may not induce more people to acquire the skills. Rising wage rates may accelerate employers' search for more capital-intensive ways of producing or alternative locations where **unit labour cost** will be lower. Relative wage rates can be a very important determinant of both pay and employment levels.

Changes in the supply of and demand for **labour** will be affected by elasticities. An increase in demand for construction workers during a boom will typically raise pay because the supply of suitably trained people is inelastic in the short run.

If you are studying the labour market option in the OCR specifications, see **marginal revenue product (MRP)**.

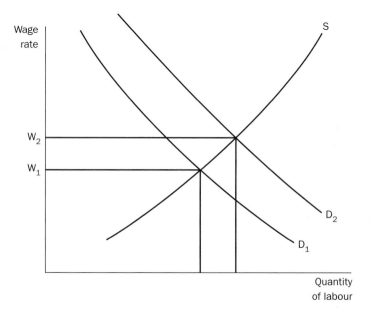

wage differentials: see *differentials*.

wage discrimination: see *discrimination*.

wage–price spiral: if wages are rising, costs of production will also be rising. Also, demand for consumer goods will also rise. Both trends are likely to cause **inflation**. This in turn will cause employees to negotiate higher wages and the cycle starts over again. Inflation becomes built into people's **expectations** and is therefore hard to stop. The only method of stopping people from expecting inflation which has been successful in recent years is to reduce aggregate demand to the point where unemployment rises, so that competition in the **labour** market for scarce jobs causes pay increases to slow down. (See diagram overleaf.)

W

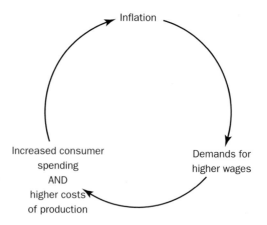

Wage–price spiral

wage rate: the price of *labour*. When wage rates change, the change may be real or it may be just a change in money wages which maintains their existing purchasing power.

wage rigidity: see *sticky wages*.

Wall Street Crash: during the 1920s the US stock market rose dramatically, taking prices beyond anything which reflected likely long-run value. The result was the 1929 crash. The loss of confidence which this caused was a major factor in the 1930s depression. From top to bottom, share prices fell by 89%.

A similar but less dramatic cycle, where a long period of rapid share price increases was followed by a correction which frightened people into selling all at once, has occurred a few times since then. Black Monday in the UK and the US in 1987 marked one such event; some Asian countries experienced the crashes associated with the *Asian financial crisis* in 1997–98. Some share indices fell by about half during late 2008. They rallied later but that may not be the end of the story.

wants: the goods and services for which humankind has unlimited desire. People's capacity to want more creates the *scarcity* that underpins economics as a field of study. There is some evidence coming from recent research into the economics of happiness that what people really want is to have more than their friends and neighbours have. Some people don't feel like this but even they usually want more for people who are living with real poverty, and they may want more leisure too. And maybe a cure for cancer… So wants really are unlimited and scarcity is real.

war: Winston Churchill said 'If the human race wishes to have a prolonged and indefinite period of material prosperity, they have only got to behave in a peaceful and helpful way toward one another, and science will do for them all they wish and more than they can dream.'

wealth: the stock of *assets* held by an individual or organisation. These assets can be used to yield a stream of *income* in the future. They may consist of financial assets, such as bank balances or shares, or real assets, such as property.

wealth distribution: the way in which total *wealth* in the economy is shared out among the population as a whole. In most countries wealth is unevenly distributed, and becoming more so. In the UK, roughly 23% of total wealth is owned by 1% of the population and 52% belongs to the wealthiest 10%. 94% of all wealth belongs to 50% of the population.

wealth effect: the impact of increased *wealth* on consumer demand. When house prices were rising in the USA and the UK, people saw their assets rise in value, and many remortgaged to get more cash for consumption. Falling prices have the reverse effect. This can intensify the swings in the *economic cycle*. The wealth effect can apply when share prices are changing too.

wealth tax: with a view to redistributing income and wealth, it is possible to tax wealth, although valuing some assets can be difficult. There is no direct wealth tax in the UK but *inheritance tax* does reduce large family holdings of wealth. *Capital gains tax (CGT)* reduces the extent to which wealth can be accumulated through rising share and property prices. As with all taxes on the wealthy, there are armies of accountants devising escapes through the loopholes in the law (an occupation which is highly profitable for themselves).

weighted average: an average which takes into account the relative importance of its components. For example, the *retail price index (RPI)* is a weighted average that gives larger weights to the prices of products on which a significant amount of income is spent.

Weights can be regularly revised to ensure that they reflect current spending patterns (for price indices), output patterns or trade patterns – depending on the index concerned.

welfare: a term usually used to refer to people's well-being. It is hard to measure. *National income statistics* are an imperfect guide. Sometimes, other measures are used, which might include life expectancy, child mortality or the ownership of certain *consumer durables*.

welfare economics: aspects of economics which are concerned with *welfare*. It takes in issues of *equity* and *efficiency*, including *Pareto efficiency*; issues associated with *market failure* and all kinds of *externalities*. In defining desirable objectives, welfare economics will include questions about what ought to happen, as well as questions about what does happen. It can therefore be used to explore areas of the subject which involve value judgements and *normative* statements.

welfare gain: the benefit to society of increasing consumption to the point where *marginal social benefits* are equal to *marginal social costs*. For example, when the government spends money on improving public transport, vehicle owners benefit from reduced congestion.

If the government does not subsidise public transport, the amount provided will be the amount that reflects the marginal private benefits, i.e. the fares paid by users. At the equilibrium point, this will be equal to the marginal private cost, determined by market forces. However, improving public transport will reduce congestion and pollution, with benefits for many groups of people. Welfare is optimised at the point where marginal social benefit is equal to marginal social cost. There is a clear welfare gain from the extra benefits obtained, over and above the extra costs, shown by the shaded triangle in the diagram overleaf.

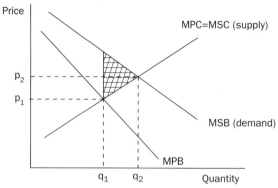

The triangle of welfare gain

The marginal private benefit line is the demand curve resulting from market forces – the amount that people want to pay. This analysis uses the MSB as the new demand curve, which takes into account the value of the improvements paid for with the subsidy. Assuming that the marginal private cost and the marginal social cost are the same (the suppliers will be the same firms or organisations), quantity supplied increases. The higher price is covered by the government subsidy that reflects the social benefits. **Underprovision** ceases.

Other well-known examples include vaccination and ways of beautifying homes and gardens that are visible to passers-by.

welfare loss occurs where there are negative externalities, e.g. air or water pollution. The free market equilibrium price and quantity (p_1 and q_1 in the diagram) reflect the private costs and benefits of the product. These are shown by the marginal private cost curve (which is also the supply curve) and the marginal private benefit curve (which shows demand and is the same as MSB).

But there are additional social costs of production that are incurred by third parties who suffer from the pollution. These additional social costs push the marginal social cost curve upwards and to the left of the MPC. The shaded triangle shows the welfare loss that reflects the adverse effects of the pollution.

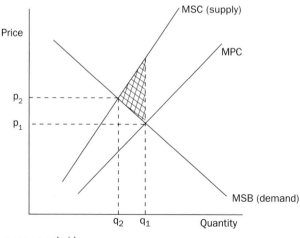

$p_2 = p_1 + \text{subsidy}$

The triangle of welfare loss

If suppliers have to cover the full cost of production, by cleaning up their emissions, private cost rises to the level of the full social cost, MSC; the externality is internalised. The new equilibrium price and quantity are p_2 and q_2. The price now reflects the true costs of production and the fall in quantity means that *overconsumption* ceases. All costs are covered by the users of the product and there is no welfare loss.

A welfare loss can also occur if the social benefits are less than the private benefits.

welfare state: the system of social security benefits and health care which was set up in the UK after 1945. It was designed to help all those in need, but is constantly threatened by efforts to cut costs and avoid raising taxes. The capacity to provide is affected by the ageing population, which increases demands on the welfare state.

White Paper: a government document which describes in detail proposed new policies and laws.

wholesale price index: a measure of changes in wholesale prices. It is useful because it may give an advance warning of impending changes in retail price levels.

wholesaling: buying large quantities of various products and selling them on in smaller quantities to retailers and other firms. Essentially, wholesalers are suppliers to other businesses. Although 'middlemen' are often thought to add to costs, businesses use wholesalers to save them the trouble of having to buy direct from a large number of producers. The fact that they exist shows that they have a role in increasing efficiency.

windfall: an unexpected gain. This could be an inheritance or an exceptional rise in the price of one's home or a much higher profit than usual. The point is that it is exceptional and not something that can be relied upon.

withdrawals occur when money is taken out of the *circular flow of national income*. They are also known as leakages and consist of taxes, imports and savings. In each case, the withdrawal leads to a lower level of aggregate demand for domestic output, i.e. they reduce spending power. A fall in withdrawals will lead to an increase in spending, as with a tax cut.

work in progress (WIP): goods and services which are part way through the production process. In manufacturing, stocks of work in progress may be kept. This may increase efficiency but it may also be costly because the stocks are lying idle rather than being finished and sold.

worker participation: see *employee involvement*.

working capital is the finance needed to pay for production costs until payment is received for the output. For some firms it is financed with an overdraft or it may be financed out of past *retained profit*.

Working Families Tax Credit: a benefit paid to people with families whose pay is low. It helps to ensure that people on low pay do have some incentive to work.

working population: all those who are working or actively seeking work. The UK's working population is currently increasing, from 28.5 million in 1997 to 29.5 million in 2002 and 30.8 million in 2007. Some of this increase comes from immigration; some also from improved incentives to work through the *Working Families Tax Credit*.

working time regulations: a measure resulting from the EU's Social Chapter, which requires that employees work no more than 48 hours per week, averaged over a 17-week period.

W

works council: a body which brings together employees and management for discussion of matters of mutual interest. Likely topics include working conditions and health and safety issues. Works councils are consultative bodies with no capacity to take decisions but they may help to resolve issues before they become a problem. Under the EU's Social Chapter, they are compulsory for firms with interests in more than one EU country and more than 1000 employees in total.

World Bank: see the *International Bank for Reconstruction and Development (IBRD)*.

World Development Report: an annual publication of the World Bank providing extensive data on growth and development issues.

World Trade Organization (WTO): oversees and regulates the international trading environment. It replaced GATT, the *General Agreement on Tariffs and Trade*, early in 1995. Its objectives are to promote freer trade. In practical terms it aims to reduce *trade barriers*. There have been successive rounds of tariff negotiations which have cut tariffs on a wide range of products and sought to eliminate quotas and reduce non-tariff barriers. (The Uruguay Round was implemented from 1995 and had far-reaching effects.)

Most of the world's nations belong to the WTO and participate in its work. In addition to reducing trade barriers, it has mechanisms for resolving international trade disputes. Although the WTO has been highly successful in reducing tariff barriers on trade in manufactures, there are still major restraints on trade in agricultural products which are being reduced only very slowly, if at all.

The *Doha Round* of trade negotiations began in 2001 and finally stalled in 2008. Agriculture and services figured large, having been neglected in previous trade negotiations. It seems unlikely that governments will reactivate the talks while there is a worldwide recession. In the long run, there is still much scope for increasing standards of living through *trade liberalisation*.

The WTO has done much to promote trade. This has improved standards of living for huge numbers of people, including many who were very poor. Free trade does involve structural changes though. These can be painful in the short run, and some people may lose out. This is a criticism of free trade rather than the WTO. However, there are other more direct criticisms of the WTO:

- Sometimes it appears to be defending the interests of the multinationals.
- Small, poor countries have little influence within the WTO.
- High levels of agricultural protection are still permitted in developed countries and these are detrimental to the interests of potential exporters in developing countries.
- In promoting economic growth, the WTO is probably increasing the use of resources in unsustainable ways.
- The WTO has worked to enforce intellectual property rights, which can be costly for developing countries, e.g. in terms of access to pharmaceutical products.

WTO: see *World Trade Organization (WTO)*.

x-inefficiency: the tendency for costs to rise because the organisation has few or no competitors. This is likely to occur if the producer has a degree of monopoly power, whether in the public or the private sector, which allows management to become careless about keeping costs to a minimum.

yield: the annual income derived from a *share* or a *bond*, as a proportion of its current market price.

zero sum game: a situation in which a gain made by one person or organisation can only be made at the expense of a loss to another. It can be important in *game theory*.

Economics revision lists

Using A–Z Online

In addition to the revision lists set out below, you can use the A–Z Online website to access revision lists specific to your exam board and the particular exam you are taking. Log on to **www.philipallan.co.uk/a-zonline** and create an account using the unique code provided on the inside front cover of this book. Once you have logged on, you can print out lists of terms together with their definitions, which will help you to focus your revision.

On the pages that follow, we have listed revision terms for the AS and A-level examinations for the three main awarding bodies:

- AQA, see pages 327–331
- Edexcel, see pages 332–336
- OCR, see pages 337–342

This is to help you use this handbook as effectively as possible. On the website, we have set out revision lists for other examination bodies which may provide the economics exams at your school or college, including:

- Welsh Joint Education Committee (WJEC)
- Cambridge International Examinations (CIE)
- Scottish Higher
- International Baccalaureate (IB)

AQA revision lists

AS Unit 1 Markets and market failure

Allocation of resources

Barriers to entry

Buffer stock

Capital

Choice

Commodity markets

Common Agricultural Policy (CAP)

Competitive markets

Composite demand

Concentration

Conflicting objectives

Consumption

Cross-price elasticity of demand

Demand curve

Demerit good

Derived demand

Diseconomies of scale

Disequilibrium

Distortions

Division of labour

Economic activity

Economic efficiency

Economic models

Economic problem

Economic resources

Economic welfare

Economies of scale

Enterprise

Environment

Equilibrium prices

Excess demand

Excess supply

Exchange

Externalities

Government failure

Government intervention

Immobilities

Imperfect information

Incentives

Income distribution

Income elasticity of demand

Indirect taxes

Inefficiency

Inequality

Inferior good

Interrelationships between markets

Joint demand

Joint supply

Labour

Land

Margin

Marginal social cost

Market economy

Market failure

Market imperfections

Market mechanism

Market power

Merit goods

Misallocation of resources

Monopoly

Natural environment

Needs and wants

Negative externalities

Non-excludability

Non-rivalry

Normal goods

Normative

Opportunity cost

Overproduction

Partial market failure

Pollution permit

Positive externalities

Positive statements

Price controls

Price elasticity of demand

Price elasticity of supply

Price mechanism

Private costs

Product differentiation

Production

Production possibility curve

Productive efficiency

Profit-signalling mechanism

Public goods

Rationing

Regulation

Scarcity

Shift in the demand curve

Shift in the supply curve

Social cost

Specialisation

Subsidy

Supply

Total revenue

Trade-offs

Underprovision

Unit cost

Value judgements

Wealth distribution

AS Unit 2 The national economy

Accelerator

Aggregate demand

Aggregate supply

Balance of payments

Bank of England

Boom

Budget

Claimant count

Consumer price index (CPI)

Consumption

Cost-push inflation

Current account

Cyclical unemployment

Deficit

Deflation

Demand-pull inflation

Economic activity

Economic cycle

Economic growth

Economic performance

Economic policy

Employment

Enterprise

Excess aggregate demand

Exchange rate

Exports

European Union (EU)

Factor mobility

Fiscal policy

Frictional unemployment

Government economic objectives

Government expenditure

Gross domestic product (GDP)

Imports

Incentives

Index numbers

Inflation

Innovation

Interest rates

Investment

Investment income

Labour Force Survey

Long run

Long-run aggregate supply

Long-run trend rate of growth

Macro-economic equilibrium

Macro-economic policy

Mobility

Monetary policy

Monetary Policy Committee

Money supply

Multiplier

Output gap

Per capita income

Policy conflict

Production

Production possibility curve

Productive capacity

Productivity

Real national income

Recession

Retail price index (RPI)

Saving

Seasonal unemployment

Shocks

Short run

Short-run aggregate supply

Structural unemployment

Supply-side policies

Surplus

Surplus on current account

Taxation

Technical or technological change

AQA A2 Unit 3 Business economics and the distribution of income

Absolute poverty

Advertising

Allocative efficiency

Barriers to entry

Cartel

Collusive oligopoly

Competition policy

Competitive tendering

Concentration

Conduct

Consumer surplus

Contestable markets

Cost–benefit analysis

Cost of production

Cost structure

Deadweight loss

Demand

Demand for labour

Derived demand

Discrimination

Distribution of income

Efficiency

Employment protection

Equality

Equity

External growth

Factor inputs

Fixed costs

Fixed factors of production

Free entry

Free movement of people

Game theory

Globalisation

Government failure

Hit-and-run competition

Horizontal and vertical equity

Human capital

Interdependence between firms

Integration

Internal growth

Internal market

Invention

Job satisfaction

Kinked demand curve

Labour market imperfections

Law of diminishing returns

Long run

Marginal cost

Marginal productivity theory

Marginal returns

Marginal revenue

Market failure

Market power

Market structure

Merger

Minimum efficient scale (MES)

Minimum wage

Monopoly

Monopsonistic labour markets

Multinational

Non-collusive oligopoly

Non-price competition

Normal profit

Oligopoly

Perfect competition

Price agreements

Price discrimination

Price leader

Price maker

Price taker

Price war

Privatisation

Producer surplus

Product differentiation

Productive efficiency

Productivity

Profit maximisation

Property rights

Public ownership

Public private partnerships (PPPs)

Quasi-public goods

Redistribution of income

Regulation

Regulatory capture

Relative poverty

Relative wage rates

Research and development (R & D)

Returns to scale

Revenue

Satisficing

Separation of ownership from control

Short run

Sunk costs

Supernormal profit

Supply of labour

Tacit collusion

Takeover

Technical or technological change

Trade union

Variable factors of production

Variable costs

AQA A2 Unit 4 The national and international economy

Balance of payments

Bank of England

Budget deficit

Budget surplus

Capital account

The City

Comparative advantage

Current account

Customs union

Cyclical instability

Developing economies

Economic and Monetary Union (EMU)

EU enlargement

European Central Bank (ECB)

European Commission

Exchange rate

Export subsidy

Family Expenditure Survey

Fiscal policy

Fisher equation

Fixed exchange rate

Floating exchange rate

Free trade

Global imbalances

Globalisation

Human Development Index (HDI)

Incentives

Index numbers

Inflation targeting

Interest rates

International capital flows

International trade

Inward investment

Liquidity

Long run

Long-run Phillips curve

Long-run trend rate of growth

Managed exchange rate

Monetarist model

Monetary policy

Monetary Policy Committee

Money supply

National income statistics

Natural rate of unemployment

Pattern of trade

Policy conflict

Policy instrument

Price stability

Progressive tax

Protectionism

Public expenditure

Quantity theory of money

Quotas (import)

Shocks

Short run

Short-run Phillips curve

Single currency

Single European Market

Stabilisation policy

Stability and Growth Pact

Supply-side policies

Supply-side shocks

Sustainable growth

Tariff

Taxation principles

Unemployment

World Trade Organization (WTO)

Edexcel revision lists

Edexcel Unit 1 Competitive markets – how they work and why they fail

Ad valorem tax

Agricultural stabilisation policies

Allocation of resources

Asymmetric information

Buffer stock

Cartel

Commodity

Complementary goods

Consumer preferences

Consumer surplus

Consumption

Cost of production

Cross-price elasticity of demand

Demand

Demand curve

Demerit good

Derived demand

Division of labour

Economic growth

Economic problem

Efficiency

Equilibrium

External benefits

External costs

Externalities

Free market economy

Free rider problem

Government intervention

Green taxes

Immobilities

Incentives

Incidence of taxation

Income elasticity of demand

Indirect taxes

Inequality

Inferior good

Labour market

Long run

Marginal analysis

Marginal cost

Marginal social benefit

Marginal social cost

Market failure

Market forces

Merit goods

Migration

Minimum guaranteed prices

Minimum wage

Misallocation of resources

Mixed economy

Movement along the demand curve

Movement along the supply curve

Normative

Opportunity cost

Positive externalities

Price elasticity of demand

Price mechanism

Private costs

Private marginal cost

Producer surplus

Production possibility frontier

Productive efficiency

Property rights

Public goods

Regulation

Renewable resources

Shift in the demand curve

Shift in the supply curve

Short run

Social cost

Specialisation

Specific tax

Stock market

Structural unemployment

Subsidy

Substitutes

Supply

Supply curve

Supply elasticity

Technical or technological change

Total revenue

Tradable permits

Trade union

Unlimited wants

Welfare gain

Welfare loss

Edexcel Unit 2 Managing the economy

Aggregate demand

Aggregate supply

Balance of payments

Bank of England

Capacity utilisation

Circular flow of national income

Claimant count

Competitiveness

Consumption

Current account imbalances

Deficit

Deflation

Developed economies

Developing economies

Development indicators

Disequilibrium

Distribution of income

Economic growth

Euro

Exchange rate

Export-led growth

Exports

Fiscal policy

Flexibility

Full employment

Global imbalances

Government expenditure

Gross domestic product (GDP)

Human Development Index (HDI)

Imports

Incentives

Index numbers

Inflation

Injections

Interest rates

Investment

Labour Force Survey

Long run

Long-run trend rate of growth

Macro-economic equilibrium

Marginal propensity to consume (MPC)

Migration

Monetary policy

Monetary Policy Committee

Multiplier

National income

Nominal GDP

Opportunity cost

Output gap

Per capita income

Productive capacity

Productivity

Public private partnerships (PPPs)

Purchasing power parity (PPP)

Real incomes

Regulation

Retail price index (RPI)

Risk

Shift in aggregate demand

Shift in aggregate supply

Short run

Short-run Phillips curve

Skills

Standard of living

Supply-side policies

Sustainable growth

Tax revenue

Technical or technological change

Trade-offs

Unemployment

Volume and value indices

Wealth

Withdrawals

Working Families Tax Credit

Edexcel Unit 3 Business economics and economic efficiency

Allocative efficiency

Average cost

Average revenue

Barriers to entry

Cartel

Collusion

Competition

Competition policy

Competitive tendering

Concentration ratio

Conglomerate

Contestable markets

Corporate objectives

Demerger

Diminishing marginal returns

Diseconomies of scale

Economic efficiency

Entry

Exit

External economies of scale

First-mover advantage

Fixed costs

Forward integration

Game theory

Homogeneous products

Horizontal merger

Imperfect competition

Integration

Interdependence

Internal economies of scale

Limit pricing

Marginal cost

Marginal revenue

Market share

Market structure

Merger

Monopoly power

Monopsony

Multinational

New entrants

Normal profit

Oligopoly

Patent

Perfect competition

Predatory pricing

Price discrimination

Price elasticity of demand

Price leader

Price taker

Prisoners' dilemma

Privatisation

Product differentiation

Productive efficiency

Profit maximisation

Public private partnerships (PPPs)

Regulation

Revenue maximisation

Sales maximisation

Sales promotion

Satisficing

Shutdown point

Sunk costs

Supernormal profit

Tacit collusion

Takeover bid

Total revenue

Variable costs

Vertical integration

X-inefficiency

Edexcel Unit 4 The global economy

Absolute poverty

Automatic stabilisers

Balance of payments

Capital flight

Capital inflows

Capitalism

Capital mobility

Comparative advantage

Competitiveness

Corruption

Current account

Customs union

Debt

Debt relief

Deregulation

Direct taxes

Discretionary policy

Economic and Monetary Union (EMU)

Economic growth

Euro

Exchange rate policy

External shocks

Fair trade

Fiscal policy

Foreign direct investment (FDI)

Free market

Gini coefficient

Global imbalances

Globalisation

Good governance

Government intervention

Human capital

Incentives

Indirect taxes

Industrialisation

Inequality

Inflation targeting

Interdependence

International Monetary Fund (IMF)

Inward investment

Inward-looking trade strategies

Long-run Phillips curve

Lorenz curve

Market orientation

Microfinance

Monetary policy

Non-governmental organisations (NGOs)

Non-tariff barriers (NTBs)

Outward-looking trade strategies

Primary product dependency

Progressive tax

Protectionism

Public expenditure

Public sector borrowing

Quotas (import)

Regressive tax

Regulation

Relative export prices

Relative inflation rates

Relative interest rvates

Relative poverty

Savings gap

Short-run Philips Curve

Short-term capital flows

Skills

Speculation

Structural change

Supply-side policies

Tariff

Terms of trade

Time lag

Trade barriers

Trade liberalisation

Trading bloc

Transnational corporation

Uncertainty

Unemployment

Unit cost

World Bank

World Trade Organization (WTO)

OCR revision lists

OCR Unit F581 Markets in action

Production possibility frontier

Productive efficiency

Productivity

Profit

Public goods

Quasi-public goods

Scarcity

Services

Shift in the demand curve

Social benefits

Social cost

Specialisation

Subsidy

Substitutes

Supply

Supply elasticity

Third parties

Total cost

Total revenue

Tradable permits

Trade-offs

OCR Unit F582 The national and international economy

Aggregate demand

Aggregate supply

Automatic stabilisers

Balance of payments

Balance of payments deficit

Budget deficit

Capacity utilisation

Capital

Circular flow of national income

Claimant count

Consumer price index (CPI)

Consumption

Corporation tax

Cost-push inflation

Cyclical unemployment

Deflationary policies

Demand management

Demand-pull inflation

Developed economies

Developing economies

Direct taxes

Discretionary policy

Disposable income

Distribution of income

Economically active/inactive

Economic cycle

Economic growth

Exchange rate

Exports

Fiscal drag

Fiscal policy

Frictional unemployment

Full employment

Government debt

Government expenditure

Gross domestic product (GDP)

Household

Human capital

Imports

Index numbers

Indirect taxes

Inflation

Informal economy

Injections

Interest rates

Investment

Labour Force Survey

Labour productivity

Land

Leakages

Long-term unemployed

Macro-economic equilibrium

Monetary policy

Monetary Policy Committee

Multiplier

National income

Nominal value

Non-tariff barriers (NTBs)

Occupational immobility

Output gap

Overheating

Privatisation

Progressive tax

Protectionism

Quotas (import)

Real values

Recession

Reflation

Regressive tax

Retail price index (RPI)

Retained profit

Saving

Short run

Structural unemployment

Supply-side policies

Sustainable growth

Tariff

Technical or technological change

Trade deficit

Trade surplus

Unit cost

Wealth

World Trade Organization (WTO)

OCR A2 Unit F583 Economics of work and leisure

Average cost

Average revenue

Backward sloping supply curve of labour

Barriers to entry

Bilateral monopoly

Cartel

Competition

Contestable markets

Demand for labour

Dependency ratio

Derived demand

Discrimination

Diseconomies of scale

Disequilibrium

Earnings

Economically active/inactive

Economic rent

Economies of scale

Elasticity of supply of labour

Employment

Fixed costs

Flexible labour markets

Geographical immobility

Gini coefficient

Human capital

Imperfect information

Income redistribution

Kinked demand curve

Labour intensive

Labour market failure

Labour market flexibility

Lorenz curve

Marginal cost

Marginal revenue

Marginal revenue product (MRP)

Market structure

Minimum wage

Model

Monopolistic competition

Monopoly

Monopsony

Non-price competition

Normal profit

Occupational immobility

Oligopoly

Perfect competition

Performance-related pay (PRP)

Productive efficiency

Profit maximisation

Regulation

Sales maximisation

Satisficing

Segmented labour markets

Supernormal profit

Supply of labour

Total cost

Total revenue

Trade union

Transfer earnings

Unit labour cost

Variable costs

Wage bargaining

Wage determination

OCR A2 F584 Transport economics

Average cost

Average revenue

Barriers to entry

Capital-intensive production

Cartel

Collusion

Competition

Concentration ratio

Congestion charges

Contestability

Contestable markets

Cost-benefit analysis

Deadweight loss

Deregulation

Derived demand

Direct controls

Diseconomies of scale

Earnings

Economies of scale

Efficiency

Excess capacity

Fixed costs

Franchise

Franchise monopoly

Freight transport

Game theory

Imperfect information

Integrated transport policy

Interdependence

Investment

Kinked demand curve

Marginal cost

Marginal revenue

Market structure

Monopolistic competition

Monopoly

Monopsony

Natural monopolies

Negative externalities

Non-price competition

Normal profit

Oligopoly

Perfect competition

Pollution

Price maker

Price taker

Private sector

Privatisation

Productive efficiency

Profit margin

Profit maximisation

Regulation

Resource allocation

Road pricing

Sales maximisation

Satisficing

Segmented labour markets

Social benefits

Social cost

Sunk costs

Supernormal profit

Total cost

Total revenue

Variable costs

OCR A2 Unit F585 The global economy

Absolute advantage

Absolute poverty

Accelerator

Allocative efficiency

Automatic stabilisers

Balance of payments

Capital output ratio

Comparative advantage

Competitiveness

Constraint

Convergence

Current account

Disequilibrium unemployment

Doha Round

Economic and Monetary Union (EMU)

Economic cycle

Economic development

Economic growth

Economic integration

Economic union

Effective exchange rate

EU enlargement

Euro

Expenditure-reducing policies

Expenditure-switching policies

Factor endowment

Fiscal policy

Fiscal rules

Floating exchange rate

Foreign direct investment (FDI)

Foreign exchange reserves

Free trade area

Global imbalances

Globalisation

Government expenditure

Harmonisation

Heckscher–Ohlin theory of international trade

Human Development Index (HDI)

Import controls

Infant industries

Inflation targeting

Interest rates

International Monetary Fund (IMF)

J-curve

Keynesian

Liberalisation

Long-run aggregate supply

Long-term capital flows

Marginal propensity to consume (MPC)

Marshall-Lerner condition

Monetary transmission mechanism

Multinational

Multiplier

Non-accelerating inflation rate of unemployment (NAIRU)

Non-tariff barriers (NTBs)

Optimum currency area

Output gap

Outsourcing

Patterns of trade

Policy conflict

Price stability

Protectionism

Public sector net cash requirement (PSNCR)

Purchasing power parity (PPP)

Quantity theory of money

Quotas (import)

Real GDP

Regional trading blocs

Relative poverty

Savings ratio

Short-run aggregate supply

Single European Market

Stabilisation policy

Structural change

Supply-side policies

Sustainable growth

Technology transfer

Terms of trade

Trade creation

Trade diversion

Trade liberalisation

Transitional economies

Transnational corporation

Unemployment

World Bank

World Trade Organization (WTO)

Grade A revision list

Top 20 terms

Aggregate supply

Allocative efficiency

Competition

Distortions

Economic cycle

Elasticities

Exchange rate

Externalities

Fiscal rules

Globalisation

Market failure

Market forces

Market structure

Monetary policy

Open economy

Productivity

Structural change

Sustainable growth

Welfare gain

Welfare loss

Examiners' terms

The following entries should help explain what examiners mean by the words they use in exam questions. It is important to remember, though, that the words are only half the story. The other key factor is the mark allocation. This not only gives an indication of the length of answer required, but also the depth. The higher the mark allocation, the more likely it is that the examiner is looking for the skills of analysis and, especially, evaluation.

Account for: provide reasons for, exploring the causes.

Analyse: to break a topic down into its component parts. This should help to identify the causes and effects of the issue and to explain the process whereby the causes bring about the effects. This encourages more depth of study. It implies a writing style that uses continuous prose in fully developed paragraphs. Bear in mind the word 'why?' when analysing. Do not ignore opportunities to use diagrams which help to explain what happens.

Assess: weigh up and thereby *evaluate* two or more options or arguments.

Assumptions: see *state your assumptions*.

Comment: draw conclusions from the evidence, possibly in the form of a stated opinion. For example, in the first part of a question you might be required to *analyse* the causes of a specific instance of market failure; part (b) might ask you to comment on the likely consequences. You might reach a conclusion about the likelihood of underconsumption, then state your opinion about the probable loss of welfare involved. It may be helpful to comment upon any further information needed.

Compare: explore the similarities and the differences in two situations.

Consider: another term inviting you to weigh up options or arguments in the form of continuous paragraphs of writing.

Critically analyse means to look in depth at an issue (*analyse*) from the perspective of a critic. In other words the examiner is encouraging you not to take the issue at face value; instead you should be questioning the assumptions or evidence involved. However, it is important to remember that film 'critics' may write a favourable review. You, too, should look at the strengths as well as the weaknesses involved.

Debate: put both sides of the case as forcefully as you can, then criticise each side from the perspective of the other. Take, for example, the essay title 'Debate the issue of whether the UK should raise the standard rate of income tax.' You should put forward the views both for and against, then tackle the arguments of those in favour from the point of view of opponents (and vice versa). You may decide, in the end, to 'vote' or abstain, as in a real debate.

Decide which: make a choice between the options, supported by your reasoning.

Define: explain the meaning of the term as precisely as you can; giving an example can help, but is not a substitute for explanation.

Discuss: put forward both sides of a case before coming to a conclusion. Discussion would require continuous writing and would be likely to be marked on a levels of response basis, with a high proportion of marks awarded for evaluation.

Discuss critically: a little different from '*discuss*', though the examiner appears to be hinting that there may be a reason to be sceptical of the theory or question under discussion. Therefore you should look carefully for weaknesses in the logic.

Distinguish between: (as in 'distinguish between revenue and profit'). Here, you should explain each of the two terms and then look for the point of difference between them: 'the difference is that costs have been deducted from revenue to find profit'.

Evaluate: this vital term means weighing up evidence in order to reach a judgement. In the context of an essay, you will have to present that evidence (explaining the significance of each part of it) before reaching a conclusion. As the term invites your judgement, do be willing to state your opinion within the conclusion, e.g. 'In my view…' It can be helpful to keep in mind the phrase 'to what extent…?'

Examine means to look in detail at the argument, evidence or theory presented. It requires continuous writing and should be rounded off with a conclusion.

Explain: expand upon in order to show your understanding of the term or theory being tested. The depth of explanation required will be indicated by the mark allocation. Giving a well-chosen example will often gain a mark.

Give: this means list, as in 'Give two possible reasons for reducing interest rates.' There is no requirement to explain the points you make.

How might: this phrase suggests a need to explain a process, as in 'How might a firm choose between two investment options?' You must explain the process with care, then consider the mark allocation before deciding whether a conclusion is required. If 5 marks are available, no conclusion would be necessary; with 25 marks, however, you would be wise to evaluate your answer.

Identify: to name one or more examples of the topic being examined. Usually this would require no more than a list, with 1 mark awarded per point made.

Justify your answer: present an argument in favour of the views you are expressing, for example: 'Should the Post Office be privatised? Justify your answer.' Although the question appears to be expecting a yes or no at the outset, it is better to wait until the end to state your opinion, because you will have given the matter enough thought to be able to justify your decision.

Levels of response: a way of marking answers based upon different academic skills rather than the quantity of knowledge shown. This is the way in which most high-mark questions are examined. If 10 marks are available for 'Explain the impact of higher interest rates upon firms', a levels of response marking scheme would put a ceiling on the number of marks available for listing points. Therefore you are better off writing a full explanation of two or three points.

List: briefly state (same as *give*).

Mark allocation: the number of marks on offer for each part of a question.

Outline: provide a description of an event, theory or method. The length and the level of detail will be governed by the mark allocation.

Show your workings: this phrase is used often with numerical questions, but should never be ignored. In the pressure of the exam room, almost every candidate will slip up somewhere in a complex calculation. If there are 10 marks on offer for the answer '£24 800', the candidate who gives the answer '£248 000' with no workings will get 0 marks, while a candidate with the same answer will get 9 marks if the workings show where the single slip was made. The secret with numerical questions is not to get 10 out of 10 one time and 0 the next. It is better to get 8 or 9 marks every time.

Sketch a diagram: this suggests a quick drawing on the ordinary exam writing paper. To convey any meaning, the sketch will need properly labelled axes and lines and a clear title. Where possible the diagram should be drawn in a way which matches precisely the points being made. For example, if in the situation being described, demand is inelastic, the line should have a steep slope.

State: means the same as *give*.

State and explain: this should be tackled exactly in this way, i.e. *give* a reason (in perhaps 4–8 words) then explain it (in perhaps 4–8 lines).

State your assumptions: distinguish clearly between the changes you are analysing and other possible changes which might affect the situation. For example, if you are explaining the effect on exports of the use of new technologies and you are assuming that exchange rates will stay the same, say so.

Suggest means to put forward an idea. If few marks are allocated, this might require no more than a list of points. The word is used more commonly, though, in the context of higher-mark case study or essay questions. In this case it would require a full explanation and justification for the suggestions made.

To what extent: this commonly used examining phrase requires you to reach a judgement about the degree to which a statement, theory or evidence is true. It is likely that the levels of response marking scheme will reward evaluation especially heavily. So focus on relatively few themes, deal with each in depth and then make a judgement about 'to what extent…'

What do you understand by? (or **What is meant by?**): explain the meaning of the term or phrase given. An example may be helpful, but is not a substitute for explanation.

Why might: this phrase invites you to suggest possible explanations for why a firm or individual may have chosen a course of action. Any answer will be accepted as long as it is not too far-fetched; but remember that examiners want to reward your economics understanding, so try to draw from relevant theories.